ENDANGERED CITY

GLOBAL INSECURITIES

A series edited by Catherine Besteman and Daniel M. Goldstein

AUSTIN ZEIDERMAN

ENDANGERED CITY

The Politics of Security
and Risk in Bogotá

DUKE UNIVERSITY PRESS
Durham and London 2016

Printed in the United States of America on acid-free
paper ∞
Typeset in Minion Pro by Westchester Publishing Services
Library of Congress Cataloging-in-Publication Data
Names: Zeiderman, Austin, [date] author.
Title: Endangered city : the politics of security and risk in
Bogotá / Austin Zeiderman
Other titles: Global insecurities.
Description: Durham : Duke University Press, 2016. |
Series: Global insecurities |
Includes bibliographical references and index.
Identifiers: LCCN 2015045616
ISBN 9780822361435 (hardcover : alk. paper)
ISBN 9780822361626 (pbk. : alk. paper)
ISBN 9780822374183 (e-book)
Subjects: LCSH: Emergency management—Government policy—
Colombia—Bogotá. | Natural disasters—Colombia—Bogotá—
Planning. | Risk management—Colombia—Bogotá. | Urban
policy—Colombia—Bogotá.
Classification: LCC HV551.5.C7 Z453 2016 |
DDC 363.34/80986148—dc23
LC record available at http://lccn.loc.gov/2015045616
Cover Art: Diego Delgadillo / Stockimo / Alamy

CONTENTS

PREFACE

It is no exaggeration to say that when I arrived in 2006, Bogotá was safer than it had been for half a century. Compared to the turbulent 1980s and 1990s, crime and violence had dramatically decreased and security had improved. Yet there was something paradoxical about this change. Although the atmosphere was more relaxed—outdoor cafes and restaurants were flourishing, public parks bustled with carefree activity—many of the old anxieties remained. It was as if Bogotá was still in the grip of a violent and dangerous past. During my twenty-month stay, friends and strangers alike urged me to see the city as a threat-ridden place and proposed strategies for negotiating it. This began from the moment of my arrival at my hotel, close to midnight, when the friendly night watchman, Manuel, sat me down with a map to orient me within the city. First he explained how the street names worked, with the *calles* running east to west and the *carreras* north to south. He then shifted to where I should and should not go. He drew a boundary around the "safe zone," a narrow corridor that excluded most of the city, running north from the central Plaza de Bolívar and hugging the mountains. "What happens," I asked, "if one lives or works in the areas that are unsafe?" "Don't worry," he responded reassuringly, "you won't ever have to go there."

Manuel was the first of many to offer me the same lesson. "I grew up in Philadelphia," I would joke, "I know how to take care of myself." But I soon realized these warnings were prompted less by my status as outsider than by a pervasive sense of the city as a space of danger. In Bogotá, it was not just a matter of distinguishing safe areas from unsafe ones, a skill vital in any city. From obvious precautions, like shutting car windows in traffic to discourage street thieves, to more eccentric ones, like wrapping mouth and nose with a scarf to ward off *el sereno*, a mysterious vapor that descends at dusk, *bogotanos* warned of dangers lurking, and offered instructions for their mitigation.

When I started fieldwork in the hillside barrios of Bogotá's southern periphery—where Manuel had assured me I would never have to venture—warnings became all the more pronounced. Acquaintances from the north said I was crazy, and that whatever I had learned about navigating the city would be useless south of the center where insecurity was magnified by poverty, marginality, and exclusion. I nevertheless proceeded, with caution.

Once I got to Ciudad Bolívar, I discovered still more techniques for protecting oneself from the dangers of urban life. The private security guards and *porteros* (doormen) ubiquitous in other parts of the city were few and far between. But along these dusty unpaved streets, guarding nearly every doorstep was a snarling dog, if not two or three. Their manginess suggested they belonged to no one, yet they were fiercely territorial. "Not a bad idea to keep rocks in your pocket," I was told by one resident. "Many of us don't have real locks on our doors and we depend on these dogs to protect our property when we're not around. They recognize our neighbors, but anyone unfamiliar (like you!) puts them on edge." People often alluded to the presence of vigilante or self-defense groups, many with links to paramilitary forces. Speaking in whispers and through euphemisms, like *la vacuna* (the "vaccination" fee charged for protection), I was told that while these groups provided security, you had to watch out for them. "They'll eventually stop and question you," warned the coordinator of a soup kitchen; "if they don't, it's because they've already asked around and found out who you are." Not once during my time in these parts of Bogotá was I harassed, mugged, or assaulted. All the same, duly advised, I continued to adopt more and more tactics for securing myself against potential threats.

Once upon a time, an anthropologist might have equated such measures with the superstitions of some exotic tribe or with a symbolic order that separated good from bad, clean from dirty, insiders from outsiders. I preferred to understand them as historically informed practices adapted to everyday life in a city generally understood to be fraught with danger. Not so long ago, Bogotá's homicide rate was one of the highest in the world and assassinations, kidnappings, and bombings were almost routine. It stands to reason that those who lived through *this* Bogotá—a Bogotá I can never know—would orient their lives, in both the short- and long-term, in relation to threats of many kinds, some more plausible than others. But why at a time when urbanists and security experts from around the world were heralding the dawn of a new age, indeed celebrating the "rebirth" of Bogotá, would this preoccupation with danger remain?

This paradox eventually prompted me to begin thinking less about *danger*, and more about *endangerment*.[1] Though the two terms are cognates, there is a subtle difference between them. While both suggest the possibility of imminent harm, rather than its reality, danger often indicates a specific threat, whereas endangerment refers to the more general condition of being threatened. As a result, the two states might be said to exist in different temporalities. Endangerment is durative and open-ended, while danger is immediate and short-term. The latter often indexes a specific threat that may dissipate when time passes or conditions change. The temporality of endangerment, in contrast, is lasting: the possibility of injury is endured indefinitely, requiring subjects to recalibrate their perception of the city and their place within it.

Endangerment can be thought of more as a condition than an experience; indeed, it is what gives shape to experience. *Endangered City*, therefore, is not about the *direct* experience of danger so much as it is about how endangerment often *indirectly* conditions experiences of the city. This distinction is important for understanding cultural, social, and political life in places like Bogotá, where endangerment has outlasted immediate danger. The fact that trauma persists in the bodies and memories and attitudes of people who have experienced it is well known. So, too, is the fact that histories of violence often produce enduring cultures of fear that are difficult to dispel. This book seeks to extend such analyses to the domain of urban politics and government, to the relationship between the state and the citizen, to the city as a political community. It explores the degree to which endangerment has conditioned politics in Colombia in the past and continues to do so in the present. Endangerment allows us to understand how the state establishes and maintains its authority and legitimacy, how the government intervenes in the lives of its citizens, how citizens inhabit the city as political subjects, and how subjects position themselves when addressing the state. It offers a way of apprehending the politics of security and the government of risk, and their implications for contemporary cities and urban life.

This inevitably raises questions of scale and generality. Is this phenomenon—the *endangered city*—unique to a place like Bogotá, the capital of a country with an intractable history of conflict, crime, violence, and insecurity? Is it specific to Latin America, where military dictatorships, guerrilla insurgencies, and political instability have been troublesome features of the region's modernity? Does it represent a particularly salient example of mounting worldwide anxiety about terrorist attacks, climate change, disease outbreaks, and other potential threats to hubs of the global economy? In sum, is Colombia a particularly convenient, or an inconveniently particular, place to analyze emerging techniques for governing the uncertain future of cities and urban life? Each of these questions highlights an important dimension of my analysis of the endangered city, and together they point to this book's comparative and conceptual reach: certain parts are specific to Bogotá, while others speak to cities of the global South or even to contemporary urbanism at large. As such, this book is intended for readers at any level with an interest in some combination of cities, the environment, citizenship, security, risk, and violence in Latin America and beyond. Ultimately, however, examining the government of risk and the politics of security in contemporary cities—and the specific, and sometimes unpredictable, forms they can take—requires recognizing the historical conditions, cultural sensibilities, and political contingencies from which they emerge.

My focus on endangerment relates not only to the particular moment in which I conducted fieldwork; to some degree, it is also a reflection of (and on) my own personal history. Knowledge is situated not only by historical context, but also by biographical particulars, and my interest in how urban life is organized around the anticipation of potential threats dates back at least to 1990. From the time I began high school in an unfamiliar area of North Philadelphia, my daily commute of over two hours involved crossing neighborhood borders, transportation systems, and social boundaries. I was often apprehensive as I waited for the subway in the graffitied tunnels of the Broad Street Line, and groups of kids from tougher parts of town frequently reminded me I had good reason to be. Philadelphia in the 1990s saw its share of conflict and violence, though not at the level of Bogotá. Yet like the bogotanos I would begin to meet in 2006, I grew up seeing my city as a place of menacing uncertainty and trained myself to analyze its dangers, all the while devising tactics to avoid them. In the ambiguous space underground, I identified certain subway stations as predictably safe, others as off-limits;

seats near the exit doors, I observed, were prime targets, while those in the center of the car were more protected.

When I eventually got to Colombia, I was still prone to visualizing cities as dangerous, though I had long ago left Philadelphia for calmer places. On discovering that long-time residents shared my inclination despite the signs of improvement surrounding them, I felt the makings of a research project. Italo Calvino expressed this feeling quite well. In his rich collection of fables, *Invisible Cities*, he wrote: "Arriving at each new city, the traveler finds again a past of his that he did not know he had: the foreignness of what you no longer are or no longer possess lies in wait for you in foreign, unpossessed places."[2] *Endangered City* is mostly a book about Bogotá, but it is also a book about Philadelphia and all those other cities where daily life is guided by fear of—rather than openness toward—the unknown.

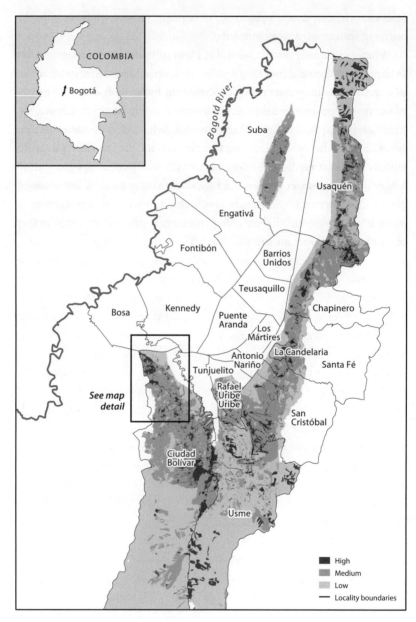

MAP 1 Bogotá's zones of high risk for landslide. Source: Dirección de Atención y Prevención de Emergencias, 2007.

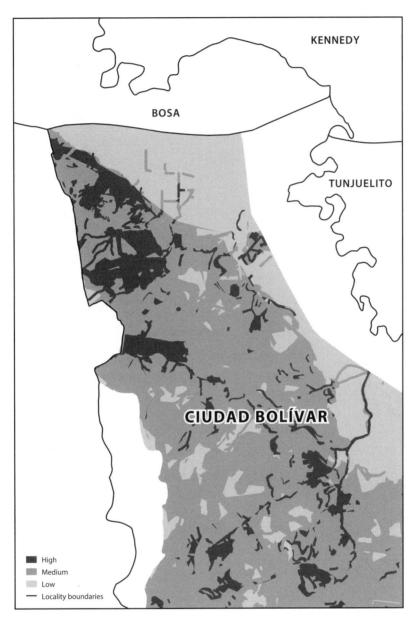

KENNEDY

BOSA

TUNJUELITO

CIUDAD BOLÍVAR

■ High
■ Medium
Low
— Locality boundaries

MAP 2 The northern part of the locality Ciudad Bolívar, where the majority of Bogotá's high-risk zones are located. Source: Dirección de Atención y Prevención de Emergencias, 2007.

ACKNOWLEDGMENTS

As Jorge Luis Borges once wrote, referring to the two sides of himself, one who writes and the other who goes about the routines of daily life: "I do not know which of us has written this page." The same may be said of this text, except that a much higher number than two is needed to acknowledge the many who have made it possible. I am happy for the occasion to thank those who have been especially integral to my research and writing.

My list must begin with a stellar group of mentors in the Department of Anthropology at Stanford University. James Ferguson has been a perpetual inspiration for this project as well as a steady voice of encouragement. I profited repeatedly from his uncanny ability to distill even the most clouded thoughts. For his unique combination of clarity and creativity and his commitment to precise thought and language, Jim remains a model of intellectual engagement. Sylvia Yanagisako has been an invaluable source of guidance and advice, and of astute critique. Her direct and refreshing honesty has helped resolve many conundrums along the way. First at Yale and then at Stanford, I've been lucky to work with Thomas Blom Hansen, always a generous interlocutor and now a trusted friend. Paulla Ebron offered crucial support as I struggled to understand what an updated urban anthropology might look like.

Teresa Caldeira's masterpiece, *City of Walls*, was an early inspiration, and I'm especially grateful for her help, both conceptual and professional, at many critical junctures. Ananya Roy welcomed me as an interloper within the Department of City and Regional Planning at uc Berkeley, where I observed firsthand her heterodox approach to urban theory as well as her exemplary roles as both teacher and public intellectual. At Yale, I was fortunate to collaborate with James Scott, while experiencing his boundless energy and inexhaustible curiosity. Michael Dove shaped my outlook on nature and culture, and I hold him personally responsible for my decision to study anthropology. In the classrooms of New Haven and on the streets of Baltimore, William Burch demonstrated passionately that urban ecology was far from an oxymoron.

The years of work represented here were enriched by an exceptionally talented group of Stanford anthropologists whom I feel honored to call both friends and colleagues. Nikhil Anand, Hannah Appel, Elif Babül, Maura Finkelstein, Ramah McKay, and Robert Samet have been fellow travelers from the beginning, and I would have been lost without them. But the intellectual acuity of others at various stages has also been key, and my thanks go in particular to Javier Arbona, Gautam Bhan, Hiba Bou-Akar, Ashley Carse, Rachel Ama Asaa Engmann, Dolly Kikon, Sylvia Nam, Bruce O'Neill, Carmen Rojas, Adam Rosenblatt, Peter Samuels, and Rania Sweis. Dependable allies Kevin O'Neill and Anne Rademacher deserve special recognition. And thanks to friends outside the field who listened all the same: Page Bertelsen, Brad Carrick, Apsara DiQuinzio, Geoff Perusse, Ross Robertson, Andrew Shapiro, and Abby Weinberg.

My life as a researcher in Colombia relied on a kindhearted group of friends and colleagues. Juan Orrantia and Felipe Gaitan-Ammann, the only people I knew when I first touched down in Bogotá, gave me a warm welcome and set me on the right course. It is difficult to imagine what this book might have looked like if it were not for Zoad Humar, who initially invited me to Ciudad Bolívar, or Paola Fernandez, who cheerfully withstood my diatribes against "culture" as she tutored me in Spanish. Alejandro Guarín shared his network of personal and professional contacts, and in doing so opened more doors for me than he probably realizes. One of them was to the home of Heidi Maldonado and Francisco Ruiz, which remained open to me for nearly two years. Through Andrés Salcedo I found not only an affiliation with the Centro de Estudios Sociales at the Universidad Nacional de Colombia but also a collaborator and friend. In Bogotá, I often sought solace in the company of other researchers, especially Teo Ballvé, Emily Cohen, Meghan Morris, Jean Paul Vélez, and Maria Vidart-Delgado, and I benefited greatly from their companionship. Tianna Paschel's inexhaustible vitality, warmth, and intelligence greatly enriched my time in the field and many moments since.

This book would certainly not have been possible without the patience and generosity of the staff of the Caja de la Vivienda Popular (Caja) and the Dirección de Prevención y Atención de Emergencias (DPAE), particularly Jaime Gonzalez and Angela Gayón. Countless families living on the urban periphery of Bogotá invited me into their homes, and I am immensely grateful for their willingness to trust someone from an unfamiliar background with priorities different from their own. Our wide-ranging conversations repeatedly challenged my assumptions about what it means to live in precarious conditions. Carolina Romero transcribed recorded interviews, and Laura Ramírez assisted with that and with archival research. Although Laura's contributions as a research assistant were invaluable, she quickly revealed her potential as a scholar in her own right.

My network expanded on relocating to London and joining the London School of Economics (LSE), and this book is all the better for it. LSE Cities allowed me the time and space to conduct additional research and complete the manuscript, all the while surrounded by a creative, committed group of urbanists. I am grateful to Ricky Burdett and Philipp Rode for believing in what I was doing and encouraging me to write for a broader audience. For support and sustenance of various kinds, my thanks go to Suzi Hall, Richard Sennett, Sobia Ahmad Kaker, Jonathan Silver, Kavita Ramakrishnan, Mona Sloane, Adam Kaasa, Adam Greenfield, Gunter Gassner, David Madden, Fran Tonkiss, Emma Rees, and Andrew Sherwood, and to Francis Moss for his help with the Bogotá maps. On joining LSE's Department of Geography and Environment, I have found myself in a collegial and inclusive atmosphere. Gareth Jones and Sylvia Chant have been supportive mentors, and I am thankful to my other terrific colleagues in the Cities and Development cluster for welcoming me into the fold. London has been a happy intellectual home thanks also to Laura Bear, Matthew Engelke, Deborah James, Gisa Weszkalnys, Carlo Caduff, Matthew Gandy, and Jennifer Robinson. Although I overlapped only briefly with Asher Ghertner, I have thoroughly enjoyed our subsequent conversations and collaborations. Thanks to Michelle Warbis for the push to amplify my central claims.

My debt of gratitude also extends to institutions that have supported the research and writing of this book. A Travel and Language Study Grant and a Diversity Dissertation Research Grant, both at Stanford, allowed me to spend two summers conducting exploratory research in Colombia. The U.S. Fulbright Program provided funding for my first year of fieldwork and included me in an extraordinary network of students, teachers, and researchers. Thanks to Juana Camacho and the Instituto Colombiano de Antropología e Historia for taking me in as a visiting researcher and for giving me the opportunity to receive feedback from an exceptional group of scholars. I was able to conduct an additional year of fieldwork thanks to a Dissertation Fieldwork Grant from the Wenner-Gren Foundation, while a Doctoral Dissertation Improvement Grant from the National Science Foundation contributed to the cost of travel, materials, and transcription. I was also extremely fortunate to receive the Stanford Interdisciplinary Graduate Fellowship and a Mellon Dissertation Fellowship, which allowed me the luxury of an additional year of writing.

At Duke University Press, it has been a delight to work with Gisela Fosado, who gave the project her enthusiastic support and guided it carefully to fruition. I owe a major debt of gratitude to two anonymous reviewers for their thorough engagement with the full manuscript, not once but twice, and for providing countless helpful comments. I would also like to thank Daniel Goldstein for offering invaluable advice at key moments and the rest of the editorial, production, and marketing teams for their critical contributions.

Underlying every aspect of whatever I have accomplished here is my supportive and caring family. Howard Zeiderman is unique in his ability to unite a deep relationship with big ideas and a profound engagement with the real world. I like to think that this book carries his rare commitment forward in new directions. Stefanie Takacs has been a constant source of light, serenity, and contentment. Colin Thubron introduced me to Latin America, and in doing so sparked my desire to engage with worlds different from my own. There is neither time nor space to account for the ways Margreta de Grazia has contributed to this text. She has read every page within it, sometimes twice or three times, while demonstrating through her own work that clear thinking and clear writing go hand in hand.

And finally, I am infinitely thankful to be able to share a life with Paula Durán. She has maintained her calm and receptive disposition to my work even when I have fully embodied the figure she affectionately calls *el antropóloco*. This book is peppered with traces of her agile mind, ethnographic intuition, and perceptive eye. Moreover, her steady confidence and bountiful optimism have shown me that the future need not be a matter of risk and security. With unconditional love, she has convinced me that uncertainty is to be wholeheartedly embraced. These are contributions as much to the conceptual foundation of this book as to the emotional grounding of our partnership, and are gifts I will treasure for the years to come.

―――――

Elements of chapter 2 appeared in "On Shaky Ground: The Making of Risk in Bogotá," *Environment and Planning A* 44, no. 7 (2012): 1570–88, and in my contribution to *Modes of Uncertainty: Anthropological Cases*, an essay collection edited by Limor Samimian-Darash and Paul Rabinow. An earlier version of chapter 4 was published as "Living Dangerously: Biopolitics and Urban Citizenship in Bogotá, Colombia," *American Ethnologist* 40, no. 1 (2013): 71–87. Bits of chapter 5 went into "Prognosis Past: The Temporal Politics of Disaster in Colombia," forthcoming in the *Journal of the Royal Anthropological Institute*, while some general ideas elaborated in the conclusion were sketched preliminarily in "Cities of the Future? Megacities and the Space/Time of Urban Modernity," *Critical Planning* 15 (2008): 23–39.

―――

THE POLITICS OF SECURITY AND RISK

Neither floods nor plagues, famines nor cataclysms, nor even
the eternal wars of century upon century, have been able to
subdue the persistent advantage of life over death.
—GABRIEL GARCÍA MÁRQUEZ, "THE SOLITUDE OF LATIN
AMERICA" (NOBEL LECTURE), DECEMBER 1982

Hurricane Katrina, 9/11, the Indian Ocean tsunami, another off the coast of
Japan and the subsequent Fukushima nuclear disaster, earthquakes in China
and Chile and Nepal, Superstorm Sandy, Ebola: such catastrophic events,
varying in cause, scale, and duration, have contributed to a mounting sense
that we now live in a world-historical era of uncertainty and insecurity. Political leaders, media pundits, urban planners, environmental activists, security officials, and health experts all seem to agree that catastrophes and
crises are globally on the rise.[1] Social theorists have often seen these developments as signs of a momentous shift within (or even beyond) modernity: the
increase in magnitude and frequency of threats has outrun economic and
technological progress and our collective capacity to manage risk. Whether
or not they are right in heralding an epochal break on a worldwide scale,
their accounts reflect what has become a pervasive view of global transformation. Attending the belief that we have entered a time of singular precar-
ity comes a new political imperative: to govern the present in anticipation

of future harm. *Endangered City* is about that imperative, particularly its consequences for cities and for those who live in them.

To address this concern, key paradigms of social and urban thought will need revisiting. A rich conversation about the rise of risk within modernity already exists within the humanities and social sciences, and it frames a general problematic that remains relevant. It also provides a conceptual lexicon that allows for critical connections between risk, security, liberal governance, and the modern city. The following analysis would not be possible without these contributions, but, as we shall see, they have proven inadequate to the contemporary moment, in two respects. The first is temporal: history is too often understood as a progressive, linear movement of time through discrete periods toward a predictably better future. The second is geographical: for the most part, the accounts we have of risk, governance, and the city reflect how modernity has been understood in and by the West. This book looks to avoid these intertwined biases in offering an alternative approach to the politics of security and risk in contemporary cities. It turns to cities of the global South: once seen to be trailing after models derived from elsewhere, they recently have advanced to the vanguard of urban theory and practice. The turbulent history of Latin American cities positions them at the forefront of discussions about urban insecurity.[2] Drawing on ethnographic and archival research in Bogotá, *Endangered City* aims to shed new light on a world of cities whose future is fundamentally uncertain.

Among twentieth-century theorists, the concept of "risk" has often been seen as a determinant of world-historical change. Ulrich Beck argues that industrial (or first) modernity was the period in which risk became an object of scientific assessment and technological control, and reflexive (or second) modernity followed when risks emerged that could no longer be known or managed.[3] Separating the two historical periods are mechanisms, such as insurance, that enable rational, calculated assessments about the likelihood of future harm; their eventual inadequacy marks the transition to what Beck calls "risk society." In a similar vein, Anthony Giddens claims that the notion of risk is what distinguishes European industrial modernity from medieval feudalism and "modern" from "traditional" societies.[4] Classical anthropological accounts support this view by studying "danger" within the symbolic order of "primitive" groups, associating the rise of risk with the unraveling of cosmologies based on nature, religion, fate, chance, and tradition.[5] Risk marks the threshold dividing past from present, before from after, the modern era from what came before.

Michel Foucault, too, locates the emergence of what he calls the "absolutely crucial notion of risk" at the brink of a major epochal transformation.[6] Around 1800, he claims, sovereignty and discipline were superseded by security, a political rationality that governs according to predictive calculations of the likelihood of future harm. Foucault's schema also associates risk with the rise of "modern" society by locating it at the center of the "new art of government" that emerges in the late eighteenth century—liberalism.[7] Since freedom was the crux of the problem confronted by liberal political and economic thought, security became the "principle of calculation" used to determine the limits of state intervention.[8] For autonomous, responsible individuals to be empowered to make choices unencumbered by the constraints of family, belief, superstition, and convention, they had to envision their future as containing dangers that could be potentially avoided. In Foucault's account, risk was the calculative rationality on which these decisions were based, and its simultaneous emergence in a number of different domains (e.g., town planning, food supply, public health) signaled the rise of liberalism as the predominant form of "modern governmental reason."[9]

These perspectives frame a general problematic that understands modernity in relation to risk, security, and liberal governance. However, the temporal and geographical assumptions embedded within them inhibit our ability to comprehend the politics of security and the government of risk in contemporary cities. These assumptions about time and space are hard to separate, mutually implicated as they are, and their repercussions are many. Positioning risk as an epochal marker of the transition to liberal modernity obscures the fact that it often interacts with, rather than supersedes, supposedly "premodern" and "illiberal" ways of governing threats and understanding danger. Other technologies for managing individual and collective insecurity do not simply "belong" to the past, only to be consumed eventually by the inexorable force of history.[10] In Stephen Collier's estimation, we ought to learn from Foucault's later thinking, which rejects the "kind of account that is epochal in both its temporal structure and its diagnostic reach."[11] Instead of the historical progression of successive epochs or societies, he emphasizes coexistent modalities of power that enter into relations of combination, transformation, and correlation. This approach better prepares us to identify emergent political rationalities without presuming their overtaking what preceded them.[12] Nevertheless, a key question remains: how to conduct a genealogy of risk and security in parts of the world with histories significantly different from those of the West?

Much of the literature on risk has tracked its rise as a technology of government in "advanced" liberal democracies or its worldwide spread through processes of globalization, securitization, and neoliberalization. We may indeed find ourselves in the midst of a global proliferation of security mechanisms, but the experience of liberal modernity in Europe and North America is not necessarily the best guide for understanding what these mechanisms mean and do in other parts of the world. Anthropologists have long been interested in the intersection of "modern" legal and political institutions with "traditional" or "customary" forms in colonial and postcolonial settings.[13] They have shown that the rise of liberalism outside the West, but also in Europe and North America, coexisted with and even depended on relations of power that were often far from liberal.[14] Moreover, they have found that many cultural and political formations considered quintessentially modern were developed initially in the colonies.[15] These insights unsettle genealogies of political thought and practice that are confined to or centered in the West. Pausing to consider the relationship between risk, security, and the modern city will allow me to propose an alternative—a view from the global South but with broader relevance.

A defining characteristic of modernity has been the belief in the progression of time toward an all-around better future; in turn, this promise hinged on the growth and development of cities. The "modern city" was considered the most advanced stage of social evolution and cultural development. Geographical distance was equated with temporal difference, such that the destiny of cities outside Europe and North America was presumed to be a perpetual game of catch-up with the likes of London, Paris, and New York.[16] The history of urbanization in the West functioned as a chronotope—a representational device for ordering time and space—and the "modern city" was the end point on a time line that stretched indefinitely into the future.[17] The teleological certainty of this narrative was both an impetus for and an effect of the power to colonize.[18] Modernity and coloniality, as Walter Mignolo and his collaborators have taught us, were mutually constitutive—one could not exist without the other.[19] The prosperity gained through unequal and exploitative relations of power and exchange enabled modern cities both to manage risk and to project a definitive vision of the global urban future.

In recent years, this arrangement has come undone as even archetypical modern cities have begun to anticipate more uncertain and insecure futures. A global trend toward forecasting futures of catastrophe and crisis has enabled security to take hold as a dominant rationality for governing cities from North to South.[20] Conventional assumptions about progress have been thrown into doubt, and we now face what Daniel Rosenberg and Susan Harding call the "crisis of modern futurity," here in a specifically urban form.[21] One of the implications of this crisis is the imperative to govern the present in anticipation of future harm. This imperative is actively reconfiguring the politics of cities, rich and poor alike. But the conceptual paradigms we have inherited from twentieth-century social theory and urban studies, forged in the global North and predicated on progressive temporalities of growth and development, are unprepared to respond to the twenty-first-century urban condition. In an unexpected twist of fate, cities of the global South have much more to say about a world in which the unlimited improvement of urban life, even its sustained reproduction, are no longer taken for granted.

Latin America is particularly instructive in this regard. Given its position in the world since colonization—always in an awkward relationship to modernity and its future expectations—preoccupations with risk and security run deep. Referring to a current of anxiety running through the genealogy of urbanism in the West, Marshall Berman once wrote: "Myths of urban ruin grow at our culture's root."[22] His comment is even more applicable to Latin America, where cities have long been plagued by security concerns and future uncertainty, as García Márquez's remark in the epigraph attests. In the colonial period, urban settlements in the Americas were haunted by the specter of destruction. From hurricanes and earthquakes to pirate attacks and slave revolts to famines and epidemics, the list of potential threats was extensive. This mattered significantly since, for the Spanish colonizers, the city was the symbolic and material foundation of empire.[23] Yet its stability and longevity—and therefore that of the colonial enterprise itself—were fundamentally uncertain.[24] This continued after independence, as Latin American cities were caught in a continual struggle between "civilization" and "barbarism," aspiring to become "modern" yet facing the impossibility of that dream.[25] From military dictatorships, populist movements, and democratic reforms to experiments with socialism, neoliberalism, and multiculturalism:

visions of the ideal society were hotly contested throughout the twentieth century, and the city was often the stage on which these contests played out.

To fast-forward to the present: Latin America's future remains in question, as Fernando Coronil aptly put it.[26] Security tops the agenda from Caracas to Ciudad Juárez and La Paz to Guatemala City, making these strategic sites for examining how uncertain futures shape cities and urban life. The entanglement of extraordinarily high levels of crime and violence with extreme poverty and inequality has contributed to the production of widespread feelings of fear and insecurity. These sentiments reverberate through everyday experiences of the city, but they also saturate public space and the built environment, politics and government, aesthetics and popular culture, religion and ethics, and law and justice.[27] The centrality of security across each of these domains enables scholars of contemporary Latin America to provide insight into a predicament of global importance. Recognizing this fact, *Endangered City* asks what the region's cities can tell us about the urban condition at large. Given Colombia's long-running struggle with conflict and violence, Bogotá is an especially good place from which to consider how the politics of security and the government of risk is changing what it means to be a twenty-first-century city and urban citizen.

The Pursuit of Security in Colombia

On a January afternoon in 2010, a massive earthquake hit the Haitian capital of Port-au-Prince, leveling the city, killing over three hundred thousand people, and leaving more than a million homeless. This catastrophe was one among many to have received global attention in the early twenty-first century. It struck while I was doing fieldwork in Colombia on how the city of Bogotá was preparing itself for similar threats. My focus was the municipal government's management of disaster risk and its housing relocation program for vulnerable populations living in areas recently designated *zonas de alto riesgo*, or "zones of high risk," for landslide, flood, and earthquake.[28] It came as no surprise that both government officials and the media in Bogotá responded to Haiti's disaster, either to publicize their city's readiness or to call for still greater preparedness.[29] Less predictable was the news that came three weeks after the earthquake: Haiti's interior minister, Paul Antoine Bien-Aimé, flew to Colombia with the express purpose of visiting Armenia, a city of three hundred thousand people in the country's mountainous coffee-growing region that had itself been struck by a massive earthquake in 1999.[30]

Bien-Aimé was accompanied by his Colombian counterpart, Fabio Valencia Cossio, on a visit to El Refugio (The Refuge), a seismic-resistant housing development constructed for survivors, which had been subsequently praised by the United Nations for integrating reconstruction and risk reduction efforts.[31] Sparking comparisons and exchanges in both directions, the Haitian earthquake reflected the global interconnectedness both of catastrophic events and of techniques for mitigating their potential effects.

When I heard about this diplomatic mission, I was initially surprised that Bien-Aimé had not looked to other countries in the global South, for example, Indonesia, Pakistan, or China, where recent earthquakes had resulted in comparable scales of devastation and destruction. Or why not visit San Francisco or Tokyo, two of the most earthquake-savvy cities in the world? But the Colombians I spoke with had a different response: better to be associated with the management of disaster risk, they proudly quipped, than with the masked guerrilla and the murderous *narcotraficante*. They recognized that as a result of its self-promotion as a leader in the field and the praise it had received as a model for the rest of Latin America and the developing world, Colombia's global image had taken on a new cast.[32] As Bien-Aimé's visit to the city of Armenia confirmed, Colombia had become the place to go to learn how to understand, manage, and live with high levels of risk.[33]

Colombia's association with security and risk extends beyond the field of disaster preparedness. Consider, for example, an advertisement circulating on CNN while I was doing fieldwork in Bogotá. Sponsored by Colombia's Ministry of Commerce, Industry, and Tourism, this promotional video was the centerpiece of an elaborate media campaign. Its images were predictably seductive: tropical beaches, snow-capped mountains, verdant countryside, friendly locals. The voice-over evoked a timeless paradise of harmony and beauty—"a place where the past lives harmoniously with the future, and the word 'infinity' is written in color on the beach, the mountains, the jungle, and the sky"—and it showcased a host of enraptured gringos expressing their newly discovered love for the country's countless wonders. The ad's crowning touch was its final sentence: "Colombia, el riesgo es que te quieras quedar" (Colombia, the risk is that you would want to stay).

This slogan had become the unifying concept of a tourism campaign that depicted Colombia as an exotic, bountiful, and flirtatious temptress (as figure I.1 so clearly demonstrates), one who uses her sensuous beauty and

FIG I.1 "Colombia, the risk is that you would want to stay."
Source: Ministerio de Comercio, Industria y Turismo de Colombia.

Latin charm to entice helpless visitors into staying forever. There is a hint of danger to the siren call: you might never return home, not because you've been kidnapped or shot, but because you've fallen in love with the place and its people. The campaign exploited the fact that, for as long as one can remember, travel to Colombia had been seen, above all else, as a risk. It sought not simply to forget Colombia's turbulent, traumatic past and occlude its persistently violent present, but also to acknowledge and capitalize on the power of "risk" as a brand. Risk was thereby converted from threat to allure and Colombia from danger zone to tourist haven.

This campaign cleverly played on the grim reality that has plagued Colombia throughout the twentieth century. Hollywood films and the international news media have sensationalized this reality, to be sure, but there is no denying it. An ongoing history of violence, armed conflict, and political instability continues to orient the popular and political imagination toward the ultimate pursuit of security. This can be traced at least as far back as the late 1980s and early 1990s—a period, in terms of violent crime, comparable to the worst years of *la Violencia*, the bloody midcentury political conflict between the Liberal and Conservative parties that claimed the lives of an estimated two hundred thousand people. However, the soaring rates of crime and violence in this more recent period were tied to the rapid growth of drug trafficking. Many assaults, murders, and kidnappings took place among rival cartels, but drug lords also responded to government crackdowns by carrying out indiscriminate attacks on major cities and assassinating political figures.[34] Although the cartels were eventually dismantled, the production and distribution of narcotics survived the crackdown and continue to fuel armed conflict in the present. Throughout this period, political authority, national unity, and social order were commonly framed in terms of security.

Alongside the spread of drug trafficking, Colombia has also seen a continuation of the battle between the state and leftist guerrilla movements under way since the 1960s. Various attempts at reconciliation have been made, such as a ceasefire negotiated by President Belisario Betancur with the Revolutionary Armed Forces of Colombia (FARC) in 1984, which led to the formation of a new political party, the Patriotic Union (UP). This peace process was short-lived, however, as UP members, leaders, and elected officials were routinely murdered. Attempts to end the conflict gave way to waves of violence, which occasionally struck at the heart of the capital city. The 1985 siege of the Palace of Justice in Bogotá by the M-19 guerrilla group would become a watershed event in the politics of risk and security. Coinciding with a volcanic eruption that took the lives of over twenty-five thousand people, it sparked a crisis of authority and expertise. Future-oriented modes of government were the proposed solution, as they appeared to offer a suitably technical rationality for governing human and nonhuman threats.

As the leftist guerrillas funded their protracted insurgency by kidnapping government officials and wealthy landowners, private militias were formed for the purpose of protection and retaliation. These paramilitary armies would eventually grow in number and strength to the point of controlling major economic interests and exerting broad political influence. They took hold of large territories beyond the reach of the national army and police, and delivered their own version of security by organizing death squads and conducting social-cleansing missions to rid towns and cities of suspected insurgents and *desechables* (disposables), whom they eliminated with impunity. The lines eventually blurred between the paramilitaries and other illegal armed groups as the narcotics trade offered profits irresistible to all sides of the conflict. But paramilitarism was also embraced by right-wing politicians as a quasi-official strategy for governing challenges to political authority and economic stability. *Parapolítica*, as it is called, would eventually be countered by the moderate Left's efforts to promote an alternative, progressive version of security and, thus, to prevent the Right from monopolizing this key political terrain.

In the 1990s, Colombia underwent a process of major political and economic reform initiated by the administration of President Virgilio Barco and subsequently led by his successor César Gaviria. Amid a wave of democratization throughout Latin America, the adoption of a new Constitution in 1991 expanded civil and political rights, decentralized government, strengthened the judiciary, and officially recognized multiculturalism. While liberal democratic ideals and institutions expanded, they were often fused with or subordinated to security imperatives. The impact was strongest on poor and vulnerable populations, whose status as citizens was often predicated on their need for protection. Meanwhile, President Gaviria ushered in a period of neoliberal restructuring, which opened Colombian markets to foreign direct investment, reduced trade barriers, privatized state assets and services, and reformed fiscal policy. This restructuring shaped the pursuit of security thereafter, which has tended to privilege economic interests over social concerns and to favor individualized solutions to structural problems.

Yet center-left mayoral administrations have deployed security logics to such ends as providing social housing, pursuing environmental justice, and building a political base among the urban poor.

The economic liberalization of the 1990s was paired with increased militarization as the defense budget and the size of the army steadily rose, thanks to the flow of military technology and training from the United States. Likewise, the paramilitary movement led by the United Self-Defense Forces of Colombia increased its operations against the guerrillas in order to gain control of strategic territories and the drug trade. With either tacit approval or explicit cooperation from the army, paramilitaries unleashed terror campaigns and civilian massacres targeting peasants suspected of siding with insurgent groups. Violence in the countryside combined with economic shifts forced millions to flee their lands for the city in what has become one of the world's largest crises of internal displacement. This led to the continued growth of self-built settlements on the urban periphery, where the majority of zones of high risk are now located. Internal displacement created a highly vulnerable population of Colombian citizens who, for the most part, reside in precarious living conditions now targeted by the municipal government's relocation program. Adding to the hardship of the armed conflict, Colombia along with other Latin American countries entered a major recession in the late 1990s. As the economy shrank and unemployment shot up, Colombia accepted loans from the International Monetary Fund along with accompanying structural adjustment measures aimed at promoting fiscal austerity and budgetary discipline. In 2000, the U.S. government approved Plan Colombia, which would send hundreds of millions of dollars in military aid to Colombia each year (US$8 billion overall) for drug eradication programs and counterinsurgency operations.

After the breakdown of former president Andrés Pastrana's attempts at reconciliation with the FARC and the National Liberation Army (ELN), hopes of finding a peaceful solution to the armed conflict were all but abandoned. In 2002, Álvaro Uribe was elected president after running a hardline campaign that promised to defeat the guerrillas with military force. Tapping into prevailing "War on Terror" rhetoric, Uribe's policy of *seguridad democrática* (democratic security) sought to rid Colombia of "narcoterrorism" by demonstrating military superiority and establishing the presence of armed forces throughout the country. Democracy and security were fused such that the rights to life and to protection overshadowed certain entitlements, such as the freedom of speech, and reconfigured others, such as the right to housing. During Uribe's two terms in office, the FARC was significantly weakened, Colombia's urban areas and main roads were secured, and the economy grew. However, internal displacement continued, violence became concentrated in rural regions, human rights violations were widespread, poverty and inequality deepened, and drug trafficking adapted yet again. Uribe's successor, former defense minister Juan Manuel Santos, distanced himself from the hardline policies of his predecessor, paying attention to the social underpinnings of the conflict and reopening peace negotiations with the FARC. And a succession of centrist mayors—most notably Antanas Mockus and Enrique Peñalosa in Bogotá and Sergio Fajardo in Medellín—succeeded in reducing urban crime and violence by expanding public space, investing in infrastructure, promoting social inclusion, and fostering civic responsibility. Yet popular sentiments and political campaigns remain oriented toward security as the overarching goal.

Critics argue that "security" in Colombia has been too narrowly focused on combating drug cartels and illegal armed groups in order to ensure political stability and economic growth. Influenced by the geopolitical frictions of the Cold War, the War on Drugs, and the War on Terror, they claim, security has been understood predominantly in military terms, far outweighing mechanisms of social protection.[35] Security, they insist, should focus more broadly on livelihoods and on protecting the life of the population against a range of threats. These demands have found expression within the Polo Democrático Alternativo—a coalition of leftist political parties that has attempted to counter the hegemony of the Right on the national level by focusing on city politics, and in doing so has articulated alternative versions of security focusing more on social and economic factors than on combating the internal enemy.[36] But so, too, centrist mayoral administrations, such as those of Mockus and Peñalosa, have had to position themselves within the national security landscape. As a result, a political consensus—a governing pact, if you will—has formed around the imperative to protect vulnerable populations from threats, both of environmental and human origin. Risk management has been accepted across the political spectrum, in part for its ability to encompass a range of objectives while insulating its proponents from the conservative establishment's efforts to criminalize, persecute, or annihilate anything resembling radical ideology. In this form of government, a series of mayoral administrations with varying political commitments and different visions for the future of Bogotá found an ostensibly neutral, "postpolitical" way to address the social and environmental problems of the urban periphery and to build a political constituency among the urban poor. The politics of security in late-twentieth-century Colombia have set the parameters by which urban life can be governed and lived.

Governing Risk in Bogotá

Enrique Peñalosa was elected mayor of Bogotá in 1998 and immediately established a lofty set of goals for his two-year term. High among them was the recovery of public space, a necessary component of his plan to create a more inclusive, accessible, and secure city.[37] At the time, the mayor's vision for the city must have seemed something of a pipe dream: the infamous barrio of El Cartucho was only a stone's throw from his new office in Plaza de Bolívar, the historic center and political heart. Few dared to set foot in an area that over the past fifty years had become "a sinister urban myth of the capital."[38]

After the *Bogotazo* riots of April 1948 sparked by the assassination of populist presidential candidate Jorge Eliécer Gaitán, the downtown area was left in shambles.[39] Residents started to flee the center in the 1950s, abandoning its stately buildings and elegant streets to a half century of precipitous decline. As a result of the mass exodus of *gente decente* to the north and west, spacious, respectable homes were converted into working-class tenements or simply fell into disrepair. By the 1980s, El Cartucho was the unsafest corner of the inner city, the epicenter of insecurity in one of the most violent and dangerous cities in the world (figure I.2).[40] When Peñalosa took office in the late 1990s, it housed a combination of homeless people, drug addicts, and criminals involved in a range of illegal activities—from drug trafficking and arms dealing to prostitution, theft, and street crime.[41] Cocaine, crack, and their cheap by-product, *bazuco*, were ubiquitous. The streets were lined with rubbish, and petty crime was rampant. So close to the city center and the seats of both national and municipal government, this neighborhood epitomized the dereliction and insecurity of Bogotá's public space.

For Peñalosa's vision to become reality, all this would have to change. As long as El Cartucho remained a blight, he later recalled, "it was impossible to envision the center of Bogotá as dynamic, lively, and attractive to locals and visitors alike."[42] To that end, Peñalosa created the Urban Renewal Program. In the hands of his successor, Antanas Mockus, the program would

FIG I.2 From a series of photographs taken in El Cartucho by a French photographer. Source: Stanislas Guigui, El Fiero, Calle del Cartucho, Colombia.

eventually acquire and demolish 615 properties and relocate thousands of their former occupants, destroying the heart of the barrio. This transformation complemented Mockus's drive to instill a "culture of citizenship" (*una cultura ciudadana*) among those seen to be lacking civility and civic responsibility. To symbolize Bogotá's commitment to a different future, El Cartucho would be replaced by the twenty-hectare Parque Tercer Milenio, or Third Millennium Park.

As the clearance of El Cartucho was under way, a sudden event intensified the need to secure the city center. During President Uribe's inauguration ceremony on August 8, 2002, mortar shells exploded a few hundred feet from where the newly elected leader was being sworn in. Uribe had won on a pledge to crack down on leftist guerrillas, and his *mano dura* stance had been countered by the FARC in the weeks leading up to the election with an escalation of bombings in both rural and urban areas.[43] The shells detonated on Inauguration Day matched those used previously by the FARC, supporting the theory that this group was responsible. Although one of the missiles hit the facade of the presidential palace, at least two others went astray and landed in the midst of the still occupied El Cartucho. Once the damage was fully assessed, twenty-one people were found dead.

Although the strike's origin remained unverified, the government responded as if the bombs had been launched from El Cartucho. Immediately after the explosions, tanks and troops dispatched to patrol the city quickly sealed off its perimeter, attempting to regulate who and what flowed in and out. El Cartucho, in this case, was more victim than perpetrator of violence; nevertheless, it continued to be identified as a security threat. If there had been any doubt before the bombing that the neighborhood would be razed, this event sealed its fate. What began as an *urban* problem had now been raised to the level of counterterrorism and national security.

The inauguration-day bombing fueled latent fears that guerrillas, known for perpetrating violence in the countryside, were coming to terrorize Colombia's cities. President Uribe saw the explosions as an early justification of his intent to govern with a firm hand and to increase military operations targeting rebel groups. He believed that FARC militias were forming in peripheral urban settlements throughout the country and were "time bombs" waiting to go off.[44] While the city center required heightened protection, it was these impoverished, densely populated, and loosely governed neighborhoods—and the possibility that they could become fertile ground for guerrilla recruitment—that were identified as the greatest threat.

This shift from center to periphery was encouraged by the progress of the Urban Renewal Program in El Cartucho. In December 2003, the media celebrated the fall of the last house, drawing a close to what the news magazine *Semana* called "forty years of embarrassment."[45] The creation of Third Millennium Park brought twenty hectares of public space and recreational facilities to the city center to symbolize the dawn of a new era—what urban planners, politicians, and the media now celebrate as its "rebirth."[46] As Ángela Rivas remarks: "It is hard to believe that Bogotá, a city that just a few years ago was known, with good reason, to be an urban area as chaotic as it was violent and insecure, could now be considered a model of urban governance and an exemplary case of the reduction of violence and crime for Latin America."[47] But while crime and homicide rates fell, fear abated, and the physical space of the city was transformed, the problem of urban insecurity did not disappear. There were still hundreds of thousands, if not millions, living in the city's shadowy peripheries. In response, new policies emerged that would redefine security and reconfigure the techniques through which it could be pursued.

As the demolition of El Cartucho was drawing to a close, the municipal government of Bogotá initiated a disaster risk management program aimed at protecting the lives of poor and vulnerable populations from environmental hazards, such as floods, landslides, and earthquakes. The Caja de la Vivienda Popular (or Caja, for short) was put in charge of the program, which began with an inventory of zones of high risk in the two lowest socioeconomic strata. Studies found the peripheral settlements of Ciudad Bolívar—the largest and poorest of Bogotá's twenty localities—to be the most vulnerable (see map 1). Though it became illegal to settle in these areas, qualified existing residents would be granted housing subsidies conditional on their willingness to abandon their homes and relocate to housing developments on the extreme southwestern edge of the city or in the adjacent municipality of Soacha. The sprawling, self-built settlements of the urban periphery—formerly seen as potential breeding grounds for urban insurgency, as threats to political stability and social order, as risks *to* the city—turned out to have the greatest concentration of families living *at* risk.

We have, then, two forms of urban security, each with different ways of defining problems and acting on them.[48] Like the Urban Renewal Program, the Caja was charged with relocating poor and working-class bogotanos. But rather than securing the city as a whole, its primary objective was to protect the lives of vulnerable populations living on the urban periphery. Rather than evicting residents and demolishing buildings, the municipal government began encouraging households to relocate. And rather than relying on the strength of the military and the police to force evacuation, the Caja turned to the technical expertise of engineers, architects, and social workers, who were to play no more than a facilitating role in what was to be a self-directed process of resettlement. While living in these zones had previously been prohibited by law, a hallmark of the program now was that it was voluntary. And whereas security logics motivated both slum clearance in the city center and disaster risk management on the urban periphery, the definition of threat had shifted from disorder, criminality, and insurgency to floods, landslides, and earthquakes. Uniting these two forms of government was the problematization of the city as a security concern and, in response, the relocation of either "risky" or "at risk" populations. This latter approach to governing risk in Bogotá is the empirical focus of the chapters that follow. To understand the processes of displacement central to it, key paradigms of urban theory need rethinking.

Displacement in (and of) Urban Theory

Since the late nineteenth century, studies of the modern city have been concerned with the problematic of displacement. The seminal works of Émile Durkheim and Georg Simmel were motivated by the unprecedented dislocation of peasants and their mass migration to the rapidly industrializing cities of western Europe.[49] Both struggled to explain the social and psychological ramifications of uprooting predominantly rural populations and relocating them in urban environments. A similar concern drove the Chicago school of urban sociology to search for patterns of urban form and function by studying the influx of immigrant populations to the American city.[50] Henri Lefebvre's writings reflected his preoccupation with the ever-expanding reach of urbanization as a process of spatial commodification and its disruptive effects on nature, the countryside, and the rhythms of everyday life.[51] Urbanists today remain attuned to related social and spatial processes: from gentrification and resettlement to dispossession and expropriation, from migration and mobility to evacuation and eviction. This list points to a general problematic that is a central feature of contemporary urban studies—the uncoupling of people and place.

Two influential paradigms structure our understanding of displacement in contemporary cities: urban political economy and neoliberal governmentality. The field of urban studies is too heterogeneous to be sorted quite so neatly. But referring to these two paradigms is a way to highlight key assumptions underlying much writing on social and spatial transformations in today's cities and to identify what those paradigms reveal and occlude.

The geographer David Harvey, a tenacious and insightful critic of urbanization, has played a key role in advancing the first as a powerful analytic. At the heart of capitalism, argues Harvey, are interrelated spatial processes he calls "creative destruction" and "accumulation by dispossession."[52] Creative destruction refers to the cycles of violence required "to build the new urban world on the wreckage of the old" as existing social and spatial orders are destroyed to resolve political and economic crises and create future opportunities for profitable investment. While Karl Marx referred to the "original sin" of "primitive accumulation," which hastened the transformation from feudalism to capitalism, accumulation by dispossession is the ongoing process by which land belonging to poor, marginalized, or otherwise powerless groups is captured by circuits of capital accumulation and converted into a source of surplus value.[53] These interrelated dynamics of displacement, Harvey argues, "lie at the core of urbanization under capitalism."[54] Although modes of accumulation and forms of power vary in scale and scope, according to this paradigm their fundamental logic remains the same from Paris and Manchester in the nineteenth century to New York and Chicago in the twentieth to Mumbai and Rio de Janeiro in the twenty-first.[55]

Like many proponents of urban political economy, Harvey analyzes cities within the overarching structures of global capitalism, for the urbanization process itself, as noted by Henri Lefebvre, "has now become genuinely global."[56] To demonstrate the generality of this framework, Harvey often turns to specific geographies and histories. Having dedicated previous books to North American and European cities, notably Baltimore and Paris, he occasionally references cities outside the West—for example, Mumbai.[57] There he highlights financial interests backed by state power that, in their quest to turn the city into a global financial hub, ratchet up pressure on 6 million slum dwellers without legal title to surrender territories they have occupied for decades. This dispossession is permitted, in Harvey's view, by the state's failure to uphold its constitutional obligation to protect the life and well-being of the population and to guarantee rights to housing.[58] Harvey then shifts to urban transformations in other parts of the world, where he identifies the same dynamic.[59] All processes of urban transformation, it seems, fit within this conceptual framework.

The armed conflict in Colombia is a classic case of displacement: there are now at least 5 million *desplazados*, or internally displaced persons, residing mostly in the self-built settlements of the urban periphery. So, too, is the relocation of "at risk" populations living in these very same areas in Bogotá. To investigate the changes under way, then, we might ask: Who is being dispossessed, and of what? Who is doing the dispossessing? And how, exactly, are they accumulating?

Dispossession was famously analyzed by Marx as the "freeing" of peasants from their attachment to land and access to the means of production.[60] But unlike the dispossession of agricultural producers, whose labor provided them with subsistence, inhabitants of zones of high risk were casual laborers already alienated from the means of production, working primarily outside the formal economy in jobs such as recycling, construction, street peddling, or domestic service. The high-risk designation and the resettlement program that accompanied it have not stripped these settlers of their property; indeed, this program legally entitled them to houses of equal or better value. They became like the enfranchised liberal citizen who, as Marx pointed out, "was not liberated from property; he received the liberty to own property."[61] Their newly acquired rights made them eligible for a government subsidy that equaled the price of a new home, and thus enabled them to become legal property owners—a status that had long eluded them.

If it is not entirely clear who was being dispossessed by the resettlement program, it is even less clear who would have been profiting from their dispossession. Familiar forms of capital accumulation were present, but peripheral. The resettlement program created a population of potential homeowners, thereby increasing demand within the formal property market that private developers could step in to meet. But given the high cost of real estate in Bogotá and the rather strict regulations on developments that qualify as *vivienda de interés social* (social housing), resettling the urban poor is not a lucrative emerging market. Moreover, the requirement that resettlement beneficiaries take out loans to supplement their government subsidy generated income for lending institutions, but not after 2006, when the subsidy was increased to equal the cost of a new home.[62] Nor did the utility companies profit significantly from the formalization of these populations, for most settlers were already account holders paying flat rates for water and electricity, despite lacking official connections to municipal infrastructural systems.

Other possible motives for the resettlement program are even less plausible. Rumors spread among some settlers that their relocation was spurred by the discovery of uranium and other valuable resources. The rich were decried for hoping to build country homes on these hillsides once the poor were resettled. More plausibly, it was thought that as the risk designation caused property values to fall, speculation and gentrification would set in by capturing the land for more profitable forms of extraction and development. But even this seemed highly unlikely, and not just because of the area's stigma as the most dangerous in Bogotá. For no sooner were these zones evacuated by the resettlement program than another round of settlers would move in. Legal eviction orders could not be enforced because of the sheer density of people inhabiting these spaces, and there was no political will to remove them. After more than a decade, despite the failure to turn the situation to profit, the resettlement program remained in effect.

Perhaps in recognition of the difficulty of commodifying the urban periphery, official plans for the future of these high-risk zones now envision their reforestation, their use for recreation, their protection from development, and their function as "lungs of the city." The goal of making Bogotá a "global" or "world-class" city may stimulate these ecologically minded projects; by attracting foreign investment, corporate offices, tourist dollars, and financial markets, they would predictably benefit the elite. But this logic fails to capture the entire process of urban transformation occurring on the edges of Bogotá. While there is no doubt that urban political economy is key to diagnosing displacement and dispossession in cities of the global South, this analytic does not fully explain why, how, and to what end the state has committed itself in Bogotá to protecting the lives of the urban poor from environmental hazards.

An alternative is the paradigm of neoliberal governmentality.[63] Popular throughout the social sciences, this paradigm associates "neoliberalism" with the rise of modern governmental rationality and seeks to identify its dislocating effects. In contrast to proponents of urban political economy, who tend to privilege global, structural, and macropolitical explanations, adherents to this paradigm focus more narrowly on specific governmental techniques and the kinds of subjects created by them.[64] Their analyses draw on Foucault's oft-cited lecture on "governmentality," as well as the many related studies that have followed in its wake, extending their conclusions to rationalities of urban planning, government, and development.[65] In diverse contexts, scholars have examined the deployment of market-based logics, the valorization of private enterprise, the spread of entrepreneurialism, the reform of governmental institutions, the retrenchment of the public sector, and the formation of responsible, self-governing subjects. While many of the influential early works emphasize contingency, diversity, and variability in the specific forms that neoliberal government can take, their analyses have often been transposed uncritically to processes of urban transformation throughout the global South.

Critiques of neoliberalism regularly treat power as something to denounce and resist. They frequently imply the disintegration of earlier, progressive models of governance, which were committed to providing benefits and services to the majority of the population, and the rise of new, regressive ones indifferent to the living conditions of the poor. The foil for these critiques, however, is usually the social democratic welfare state of postwar

Europe and North America and its urban forms, neither of which have been fully established in most other parts of the world.[66] Neoliberalism in Latin America, for example, has been more about imposing loan conditionalities and enforcing structural adjustment measures than rolling back social welfare mechanisms and forming self-governing subjects. In Colombia, it has been so tightly entangled with militarization and armed conflict that the violent terminology used to characterize neoliberalization in the North Atlantic (e.g., "attacks" on the public sector, "war" on the working poor, "infiltration" of market logics) is more than metaphorical.[67] While most critiques in this vein are sensitive to the circulation of neoliberal techniques of government beyond their "sites of origin," they often ignore the fact that these techniques now intermingle with political projects that, in Latin America at least, are set on challenging neoliberalism's hegemony.[68]

Without discounting the theoretical sophistication and political utility of these two paradigms, some urbanists have begun to question the degree to which they adequately explain contemporary transformations in cities of the global South. There is a growing gap, they argue, between the lived reality of these cities and the canon of urban theory, which has by and large been produced in and about the "great" cities of Europe and North America, including London, Chicago, New York, Paris, and Los Angeles. Urban political economy and neoliberal governmentality are based on historical developments in these cities and then "applied" elsewhere. Ananya Roy is critical of the way cities of the global South are treated as "interesting, anomalous, different, and esoteric empirical cases" that either highlight blind spots in existing theories—thereby reinforcing the fiction of universal applicability—or require a different set of theories altogether, creating artificial divides between First and Third World, global cities and megacities, modernity and development.[69] Roy insists that it is time to "articulate a new geography of urban theory" by decentering the Euro-American locus of theoretical production.[70] Urban theory, this suggests, requires displacement of a conceptual sort.

The task of comprehending contemporary cities demands that we interrogate theories of urban transformation—not simply validate them—and query the concrete processes under way.[71] How does urbanization under capitalism function according to specific histories and geographies? Are creative destruction and accumulation by dispossession the logics underpinning every instance of displacement, or are there other dynamics at work?

When does neoliberal governmentality enhance and when does it constrain our ability to understand emerging rationalities of rule? What conceptual tools are necessary for comprehending cities distant from the traditional centers of theoretical production? In considering the adequacy of existing theories, however, we must not forget that processes of urban transformation "always outpace the capacity of analysts to name them," as Achille Mbembe and Sarah Nuttall remind us.[72] Nevertheless, these questions will lead us toward a fuller understanding of cities both in and beyond the West. And they may help us better chart the terrain on which the majority of the world's population struggles to live in cities and to make their cities livable.

This book takes up such challenges in relation to the politics of security and the government of risk in Bogotá. Its burden is to describe urban phenomena that cannot be fully understood by the paradigms of urban political economy and neoliberal governmentality. For example, the displacement of settlers on the urban periphery is based neither on the state's failure to protect the lives of vulnerable populations nor on the negation of urban citizenship, but rather on the fulfillment of these very same rights and responsibilities. Moreover, there is no simple antagonism between acts of dispossession and the popular political responses assumed to oppose them. While our theories predispose us to expect those subject to the municipal government's resettlement program to fight tooth and nail to remain in place, there are many more people who demand relocation than those who reject it. For it is within this program, not outside of or in opposition to it, that thousands of settlers on the urban periphery engage in struggles for political recognition, incorporation, and entitlement. It might be tempting to understand the clamor for resettlement as reflecting a new variety of accumulation by dispossession or neoliberal governmentality that works through the very logics that might otherwise challenge it. But rather than treating cities of the global South as either continuations of or deviations from familiar scripts of urban transformation in Europe and North America, we must attend to dynamics that do not fit neatly within them.

The Politics of Risk

When I began fieldwork in Bogotá, these two theoretical paradigms together had prepared me to investigate "neoliberal urbanism" at work.[73] After all, the resettlement program was run by a public agency (the Caja) founded in 1942 to build housing for the working class according to a social welfare rationality. In its recent adaptation, the Caja was adhering more strictly to neoliberal ideals: valorization of markets and their efficiency, skepticism about the role of the state, devolution of responsibility onto the community and the individual, privatization of public goods and services, and so on. The target of governmental intervention was no longer a social class, such as workers, or society as a whole, but individual households belonging to a narrowly delimited "at risk" population. But since resettlement was ostensibly voluntary, the Caja had to educate members of this population to become rational, responsible, and prudent—that is, to desire and actualize their own relocation. As a result, thousands of settlers on the urban periphery, previously marginal to formal economic and legal institutions, were being thrust onto privatized markets for housing, credit, and utilities. In the process, relocation enabled them to become consumers, taxpayers, and debt holders. But rather than improving lives and livelihoods, the Caja seemed to be shredding the social, economic, and cultural fabric of these communities and pushing them farther to the extreme periphery of the city or even outside its municipal boundaries. Not surprisingly, it was the World Bank that loaned the city of Bogotá substantial sums of money and subsequently praised the municipal government as a model of "good governance."

While Bogotá's recent effort to govern risk did at first look like a typical case of neoliberal urbanism, my first formal interview with two leaders of the Caja's resettlement program challenged this initial assumption. Teresa was the director of the team responsible for relocating households in zones of high risk, while Yolanda was the manager of the Caja's field office in the peripheral locality of Ciudad Bolívar, the hub of the program's day-to-day operations. After the usual pleasantries, I asked Teresa and Yolanda to tell me about their backgrounds. "We're both government functionaries, public servants," Teresa began, gesturing to the bureaucratic officialdom of our surroundings. "But this was not always the case," she said; "I had the good fortune, the opportunity, to have participated in organizing 100 families to lay claim to land in Ciudad Bolívar—*tomárnoslo* [to take it for ourselves]," she paused to exclaim, and then continued:

> I organized the community to arrive at night, and we worked all night long to make sure that we could establish shacks and lay down pathways. The next day, we were ready for a fight when the police tried to remove the *invasión* ["invasion" has become the common name for the

occupation of land by popular classes]. We weren't going to let them kick us out; that was our barrio and we were the ones who built it. Yep, this was back in 1984. We won and the families stayed on the land, in part because the state didn't really care about those hillsides. The authorities must have thought, well, how nice that the poor settled up there and left the flat part of the city to us.

Teresa then fast-forwarded to the present: "Twenty-five years later," she said, "this same area has been declared a zone of high risk. So now I have to show up not as the person who organized the invasion, but as the government agency that is coming to say to them: *Señores, tumbamos y nos vamos* [Let's knock it all down and get out of here]."

Teresa did not specify with whom she had been working as a community organizer. Since many activists who helped during this period to build, defend, and eventually legalize peripheral urban settlements were allied with leftist movements—some that have since been criminalized and persecuted—I thought it best not to press. Her political commitments were implied as she explained how the struggles between different factions in Colombia's decades-old armed conflict played out among the settlements of the urban periphery: "those guys from the M-19 who helped settle a few people over here, *los elenos* [members of the ELN] who staged the invasion of that parcel, the paramilitaries who came along and disoccupied it, the FARC who set up their militias there." "The root of the problem," she told me, "is the same as always: the distribution of wealth under savage capitalism and the absence of both agrarian and urban reform." Yolanda chimed in with a sigh: "Yes, the land reforms that we've never had." Then, laughing, she pointed to Teresa: "Es que ella es medio comunista, y yo, comunista y medio" (She's half communist, whereas I'm a communist and a half).

I was puzzled. Was it possible that the person who once organized the building of settlements for the popular classes was now orchestrating their dispossession? Had Teresa gone through some kind of "neoliberal conversion"? Or did she see a connection between her political activism in the 1980s and what she was doing now? Teresa's account and the questions it raised would continue to stick with me. Perhaps what had changed from the 1980s to the present was not her commitment to improving the lives of the urban poor, but rather the available and legitimate means of doing so.

While there is reason to see this form of urbanism as recognizably "neoliberal," clearly something else was at stake.

To understand Teresa's story and the many like it I would later hear, we have to situate them in relation to the politics of security and risk in Colombia from the late twentieth century to the present. This history has shaped the terrain on which progressives like her search for ostensibly technical, "postpolitical" approaches to addressing the social and environmental conditions of the urban periphery without exposing their proponents to outright political persecution. It is through such programs that political parties and mayoral administrations from left to center have sought to build a political constituency and an electoral majority among the urban poor. To comprehend attempts by Teresa and her colleagues to mobilize risk as a technique of urban government, we must also rethink some of our most ingrained critical tendencies.

What James Ferguson calls the "progressive arts of government" can be extended to cities.[74] In the face of repetitive denunciations, Ferguson asks: "Are the neoliberal 'arts of government' that have transformed the way that states work in so many places around the world inherently and necessarily conservative, or can they be put to different uses?"[75] By attending to the "uses of neoliberalism," Ferguson reminds us that "social technologies need not have any essential or eternal loyalty to the political formations within which they were first developed," and he draws our attention to the possibility that they can be used for potentially progressive purposes.[76] This approach enables a kind of thinking presently unavailable to dominant paradigms of urban theory, which lack a suitable approach to political rationalities that are pro-poor and come from the Left. Neoliberal governmentality and urban political economy constrain our ability to, as Ferguson puts it, "turn a thoughtfully critical and skeptical eye" toward the progressive arts of government and the dangers *and* opportunities they present.[77]

With this in mind, Teresa's story begins to make sense. During our conversation, she made a claim that would be reiterated throughout my fieldwork: that risk management was progressive and pro-poor. Like many of their colleagues, these activists-cum-functionaries joined the Caja during the mayoral administration of Samuel Moreno or his predecessor, Luis Eduardo ("Lucho") Garzón, both of whom represented the political party opposing the conservative political establishment and often espoused (though less frequently delivered) progressive social change. Although the resettlement program was established earlier, these mayors increased both its budget and the number of households eligible for subsidies, and praised it for attending to the problems of the city's most underserved. While some officials were suspicious about the degree to which only the poor were seen to be vulnerable—in the concise words of one, "The mountains of the north [of Bogotá] are high class, but the mountains of the south are high risk!"— my informants regularly stressed that protecting the lives of the urban poor from environmental hazards was a priority of the Left, and one that offered an alternative to the doctrine of "democratic security" that had been a hallmark of the Right for nearly a decade. Most situated the Caja's resettlement program within a spectrum of approaches to security, and they were keen to point out the differences between them. It became clear that security and risk were domains of political struggle over the authority to define terms such as "life," "threat," and "protection," and to govern the city accordingly. These domains shift over time, and people like Teresa position themselves knowingly and strategically within them.

Accounting for the politics of security and risk, therefore, requires that we not only consider how to expose and denounce forms of power but also think about governmental strategies that pursue progressive ends. While it is important to evaluate their impact on lives and livelihoods at the margins of society, must we uniformly oppose the exercise of power or assume that the state invariably works against the interests of those it claims to serve?[78] While I am far from suggesting that risk management in Bogotá is a model to be celebrated and replicated, it attains a new clarity once we consider its political context: from 2002 to 2010, "security" was an overarching imperative across the political spectrum, yet the scope of possibility for pursuing it was radically circumscribed by the conservative establishment in power at the national level. This provokes us to consider what progressive arts of urbanism might look like and, although we may not be satisfied by what we see here, to wonder where else we might find them.

An Ethnography of Endangerment

The politics of security and risk in Bogotá, and the broader implications for contemporary cities and urban life, require an appropriate method: an ethnography of endangerment.[79] Since such a politics is inextricably bound to particular places and histories, understanding how it emerges, and what it subsequently comes to mean and do, demands empirical specificity.[80] We already have ways of apprehending the experiential dimensions of everyday life in places where endangerment has outlasted immediate danger. An extensive literature in the anthropology, sociology, history, and psychology of violence has drawn our attention to the trauma that persists in the subjectivities of people who have experienced it and to the enduring cultures of fear that long outlast violent events themselves. What we lack is a way to extend these analyses to the domain of urban politics and government, to the relationship between the state and the urban citizen, to the city as a political community. An ethnography of endangerment allows us to explore how concerns about insecurity influence urban politics in Colombia even as its cities have gotten remarkably safer.

I conducted ethnographic fieldwork and archival research in Bogotá over a twenty-month period from August 2008 to April 2010, with several follow-up visits thereafter. My first objective was to understand why and how the endangered city had emerged in Colombia when it did, and along with it the imperative to govern the present in anticipation of future harm. I analyzed policy documents, newspaper articles, political speeches, technical studies, historical accounts, and cultural artifacts among other materials, and I conducted extensive interviews with those considered expert on the topic in government ministries, universities, nongovernmental organizations, and development agencies.[81] As I constructed genealogies of "security" and "risk" in Colombia, I also strove to locate them within overlapping geographical scales. To account for the intersection of local, national, and transnational forces, I identified the network of actors, sites, and institutions that had been instrumental in bringing risk onto the political landscape.[82] What had happened in Bogotá, in Colombia, and in the world at large so that security could become the reasoned way of governing best?

I then set out to account for how risk had been defined, measured, and managed ever since it became the municipal government's responsibility to do so. On one level, I sought to understand how specific threats to collective life had been brought into the realm of technical and political intervention, and I did so by analyzing the plans, studies, laws, and maps that guided official security and risk management policy.[83] On another level, I wanted to examine the ongoing process of designating certain areas of the city zones of high risk. Approaching these zones not as static and self-evident spatial units but as techno-political objects, I intended to track how they were being made and remade on a daily basis.[84] I established a relationship with the Directorate for Emergency Prevention and Response (DPAE), the technical agency responsible for managing risk, interviewed members of its staff, and followed its technicians on their daily rounds.[85] My goal was to observe the routine practices and patterned interactions through which the technical expertise of *gestión del riesgo* (risk management) was being assembled and deployed.[86]

I then set out to learn how the municipal government was going about relocating families from zones of high risk. Here my focus was Bogotá's municipal housing agency—the Caja de la Vivienda Popular, or Caja for short—and its approach to governing the spaces and populations of the urban periphery. In addition to interviewing staff members, I situated myself as a participant observer in the Ciudad Bolívar field office and followed Caja officials throughout their workday. I spent the majority of my time there talking with social workers and observing their interactions with the public, but I also frequently accompanied them on excursions to *el terreno* (the field): visits to households in high-risk zones, meetings with community leaders, tours of new housing developments, and other activities. In each context, I paid attention to how these actors carried out and reflected on the resettlement program, and I observed their regular encounters with members of the population subject to it. Doing so allowed me to identify how and to what degree this agency was reconfiguring the relationship between urban citizens and the state.

My study would not be complete, I felt, until I also understood what it meant to be endangered—that is, to be "at risk" in contemporary Bogotá. This led me to focus closely on how people navigated the terrain of political engagement created by official efforts to protect the lives of poor and vulnerable populations. How were they negotiating the rights and responsibilities accompanying the political imperative to govern (and govern through) security and risk? Did this new dynamic of inclusion intersect with older forms of exclusion along lines of class, gender, and race? To complement the insights gained from my ethnography of the Caja field office, I undertook case studies of resettlement beneficiaries. I made contact with a group of families undergoing resettlement, interviewed them, visited their homes, and followed them through the relocation process. Beyond the Caja, I made regular visits to a *comedor comunitario* ("community cafeteria," or soup kitchen) also in Ciudad Bolívar. These combined efforts helped me see whether the

Caja's mission to protect vulnerable lives was producing new forms of citizenship and political subjectivity throughout the self-built settlements of the urban periphery.

Historical specificity is necessary for understanding the emergence of the endangered city in Colombia. However, a common historiographical procedure among ethnographers is to search the archival record for precursors to existing forms of power; when a plausible antecedent is found, the present is understood as its "legacy," "echo," "trace," or "afterlife." While this procedure highlights the complex temporality of what historians may treat as inert artifacts belonging to an earlier period, it often does a poor job of tracing the proximate causes of contemporary political formations. In such cases, the temporality of the present and recent past is flattened as colonial histories, for example, are privileged over the events of the preceding fifty years.[87] Attempts to give ethnographic accounts historical depth often inadvertently strip the present of its own temporality, treating it as an isolated, static "moment." By contrast, this book undertakes a different kind of inquiry into the contemporary politics of security and risk—one that accounts for both how these politics emerge and, when they do, how and what they seek to govern.

During my fieldwork in Bogotá, I was often told that my methodology lacked the one thing expected from it: a direct focus on violence. In one extreme example, a graduate student (referring to a presentation I had just given) demanded to know: "¿Donde está la sangre?" (Where's the blood?). As a topic of research, violence is often isolated and given primacy. This is especially true in studies of Colombia—a place long synonymous with violence, perhaps as much in the social-scientific literature as in the popular imagination; a place where in the 1980s and 1990s *violentología* effectively gained the status of a discipline in its own right. On a rhetorical level, sensational topics like violence demand our attention by signaling urgency and promising relevance. By returning to them compulsively, we endow them with discursive power and authority that overwhelm critical thinking. The overall effect is the elevation of violence to the status of master-signifier and the obfuscation of other, equally important social phenomena.[88]

Much to the displeasure of many I spoke to in Bogotá, I chose to approach violence not head-on, but obliquely. After all, its peripheral position was something I wished to emphasize, for the governmental imperative to protect lives "at risk" opposed itself to violence and often removed violence from its field of vision by temporally locating it either in the past or in the future. The phenomenon of endangerment I sought to document explicitly marks the tension between the presence and absence of violence—it refers not to direct experiences of violence, but to how violence indirectly conditions urban politics, governance, and everyday life. However, I will bring violence directly into view throughout the book in acknowledgment of its centrality to the politics of security and risk in Colombia. Histories of violence are clearly integral to the political formations I analyze, yet the former do not lead in any direct way to the latter. The relationships between violence and security that interest me are contingent and reciprocal rather than causal and linear. This will become clear as I highlight how different forms of endangerment as well as efforts to govern them frequently intersect in time and space, at times reinforcing and at others opposing one another.

Organization of the Book

In the broadest sense, *Endangered City* is an anthropological study of how and to what effect twenty-first-century cities are being imagined, governed, and inhabited in anticipation of future threats. It seeks to provide critical insight into the increasing influence of security and risk on contemporary urban life that defines the endangered city. To understand this wide, even global phenomenon, we must recognize the particular, and sometimes unpredictable, ways that techniques for securing cities are assembled and deployed in specific locations. Both ethnographic and historical in nature, the chapters of this book focus on Bogotá, where, after a long history of insecurity, risk has emerged as a techno-political framework for governing the city's uncertain future. Ultimately, this study reveals how the politics of security and the government of risk are changing what it means to be a city and an urban citizen in the twenty-first century.

Endangered City begins by attending to the cultural sensibilities and political contingencies specific to Colombia's modern history. Chapter 1, "Apocalypse Foretold," centers on the convergence of two catastrophes in 1985. This chapter traces the way these occurrences were constituted as "events" in the ensuing twenty-five years and, in turn, came to underpin the state's responsibility to protect life from potential harm. The focus shifts in chapter 2, "On Shaky Ground," to the invention of the zone of high risk in the capital city and to the everyday work required to render the uncertain future the basis for governmental intervention. It shows that risk management, far from a closed technical domain, is a contingent social field shaped by the politics of security in contemporary Colombia.

The task of chapter 3, "Genealogies of Endangerment," is to investigate how the mandate to protect the lives of vulnerable populations in Bogotá's high-risk zones affects state-subject relations. Focusing on the daily workings of the municipal government's housing resettlement program, it highlights how this emergent political technology combines modern, liberal ideals of rights, citizenship, and freedom with other enduring forms of relationality, such as kinship, patronage, and religion. This chapter argues that the imperative to protect poor and vulnerable populations from environmental hazards reconfigures but does not replace well-established forms of social collectivity, political authority, and ethical responsibility. Chapter 4, "Living Dangerously," then examines how security mechanisms produce novel formations of citizenship and subjectivity and thereby shape the terrain of political engagement for settlers of the urban periphery. It is through the gendered and racialized categories of vitality, vulnerability, and victimhood that those with little other recourse to state benefits negotiate the official imperative to protect them from threat. This chapter reveals how security and risk impact urban politics by highlighting situations in which the rights of urban citizens are mediated by and predicated on the degree to which their lives are in danger.

The book then returns to its concern with futurity. The forms of temporality integral to the endangered city are the subject of chapter 5, "Securing the Future." By examining temporal framings, practices, and sensibilities among municipal authorities and their subjects, this chapter shows how the future becomes the common ground of both urban politics and government. Both the state and the urban poor engage in projects to make and remake the city within an anticipatory domain. However, as counterintuitive as it may sound, security and its predictive calculations of harm are not incompatible with modernist future visions and progressive temporalities of development. The conclusion, "Millennial Cities," broadens the book's scope to examine the implications of seeing the future of cities, and the cities of the future, as problems of risk. Linking recent developments in Bogotá to wider shifts in paradigms of urbanism, it concludes by posing a question of both conceptual and practical importance: what future projections other than apocalyptic and dystopian ones are available or imaginable?

The coda offers a provisional response by reflecting on the surge of urban climate change politics in Bogotá in the time since this research was conducted. This recent development represents an expansion of established approaches to governing risk and security, only now under a different name, suggesting that the phenomenon of the endangered city may continue to condition urban politics, governance, and everyday life for the foreseeable future. However, if the world has indeed entered a new historical age, as scientists, philosophers, and social theorists are claiming, in which the ecological impact of humans is now felt on a planetary scale and the global future is fundamentally uncertain, then Bogotá may be an important source of inspiration for new urban visions emerging from within the politics of the Anthropocene.

1

APOCALYPSE FORETOLD

Omayra's Grave

In 2010, Colombia was inundated by the worst rains in recorded history. The resulting floods and landslides displaced hundreds of thousands of people, took several hundred lives, and affected over 4 million people. Amid the deluge, President Juan Manuel Santos presided over the twenty-fifth anniversary of another catastrophic event: a volcanic eruption in 1985 that set off massive mudslides and buried the town of Armero, killing over twenty-five thousand people. In his commemorative address, he urged Colombians to apply lessons learned from the earlier disaster to the current one in order to avoid falling into "victim syndrome" (*síndrome del damnificado*).[1] Santos encouraged those affected by the recent storms to adopt "an attitude of mutual collaboration and solidarity" and to follow the example of the thirteen-year-old girl whose struggle for survival, though ultimately unsuccessful, had come to symbolize the calamity: "Omayra Sánchez, daughter of this town, who gave us a lesson in strength, in temperance, in courage" while "fighting against death ... with complete dignity." Moreover, he signaled that "among the lessons this great tragedy left behind is the importance of being provident [*la importancia de ser previsivos*] and of doing everything possible to prevent tragedies." In the case of Armero, he recalled, "it may have been possible to prevent many of the deaths. ... This is an important lesson . . . if only the warnings had been heard." Santos then reminded his audience that this event had given birth to Colombia's national institutions of disaster prevention, which have since saved thousands from a similar fate. To this day, the Armero tragedy continues to shape the politics of security and risk in Colombia.

This chapter is an ethnographic and historical account of the constitutive relationship between authority, responsibility, and foresight in the realm of the political. It begins with the Armero tragedy and the tragic fate of Omayra Sánchez. Omayra (as she is commonly called) perished in 1985, but twenty-five years later her story has not faded from national memory. In the aftermath of the catastrophe, her name came to symbolize both the state's responsibility to protect vulnerable lives from threat and the citizen's duty to endure hardship with grace. People often asked me whether I had visited her grave when I mentioned my interest in the catastrophe that took her life. The question always made me feel as though I would not truly understand the significance of this event until I had made a pilgrimage, as many Colombians do, to the site where Omayra was buried. And so I eventually boarded the crowded bus that descends from the high altitude of Bogotá to the dry, sweltering plains that once surrounded Armero. I arrived in Guayabal, the adjacent town that due to a geographical accident was spared the horrible fate of its neighbor. From there, I hired a taxi to take me a few miles down the road to the site of the disaster.

As I approached Armero, signs of the event came into view. Land that once supported cotton plantations lay fallow. The road was elevated above its surroundings as though rebuilt atop the previous one. In the town itself, ruined shells of buildings peered out from sunken pits. Only the top floor of the hospital was visible; the lower ones remained interred. The devastation was still palpable.

We turned off the main road toward the center of town, entering what is now called the Parque a la Vida (Memorial to Life). The only life visible there, aside from the odd Popsicle seller, some rough vegetation, a few stray cows, and the occasional visitor, was a microscopic mosquito called *el jején*. They swarmed and bit incessantly as I wandered paths signed to indicate, for example, where Eleventh Street used to be. The mud was removed to make it possible to discern the remains of the Church of San Lorenzo. Its original tile floor and brick altar beckoned, while a simple Christ figure hung from a makeshift cross. I strolled silently through the memorial, visiting graves scattered about the young forest. Before long, I returned to the taxi and asked to be taken to my real destination, the memorial's centerpiece, which my driver had saved for last: Omayra's grave.

The tomb itself was simple: a slab of white marble, propped upright, topped with a wooden cross bearing her name and the date of her death. White plaster walls surrounded a devotional shrine adorned with white candles, plastic flowers, and religious figurines. Unlike the rest of the memorial, which was solemn and desolate, a steady stream of people came and went. Some gazed silently on the grave, paying tribute to the girl known far and wide as the human face of the tragedy. But others performed a more active ritual. Next to Omayra's tomb was a rudimentary structure of wooden posts connected by metal wires from which visitors to the shrine hang all manner of personal objects: necklaces, ribbons, baby shoes, bracelets, even sunglasses (figure 1.1). Beneath the offerings stood a white metal box with a hole in the top inviting one to leave *peticiones* (or requests) (figure 1.2). "Make a donation and ask for something in return," a woman standing nearby advised. On a small corner of my notebook I wrote: "I ask that there always be health and well-being in my family." I then tore it off, folded it up, and dropped it in the box.

Stepping back from the shrine, I began to understand the significance of the walls that surrounded it. They were covered by small engraved plaques— close to a thousand, I would guess. The plaques were *acciones de gracias*, or "thanks givings," commemorating *favores recibidos* (favors received) or *milagros concebidos* (miracles granted). Most bore the name of individuals or families (Jaime Palacio or la Familia Gomez), although some were donated by towns or even private companies, such as the Bolivariano bus line. The concrete pavement had begun to accommodate the overflow. Omayra's religious significance was clear.

I have since read newspaper articles about those petitioning the Vatican to recognize her as a saint. The pastor of the small congregation remaining in Armero opposed the canonization campaign, recommending that people refrain from praying to Omayra or asking her to perform miracles. "He who performs miracles is God," he told *El Tiempo*.[2] But there are many who disagree. Among them is the Colombian ambassador to Portugal, Germán Santamaría, a journalist who witnessed Omayra's death while covering the Armero tragedy. He declared: "Although I'm not much of a believer, I do believe that Omayra is a saint. There is no Colombian who has shown such

FIG 1.1 Offerings to Omayra. Source: photograph by author, 2009.

FIG 1.2 *Peticiones* or requests. Source: photograph by author, 2009.

spiritual valor in confronting pain and sacrifice. What would be better than for Omayra, in her magnanimity, to become the first Colombian saint?"[3]

Exhausted from the heat, devoured by bugs, and overwhelmed by the solemnity of the place, I told my driver I was ready to leave. The Memorial to Life faded into the distance as we turned back onto the highway. I gazed out the window at the few billboards that dotted this dusty stretch of country road. One belonged to the Ministry of Defense, and it depicted a humble family articulating a simple demand: "We want a Tolima without guerrillas." (Tolima, the surrounding region, was still *rojo*, "red," or *caliente*, "hot": an area, that is, where the FARC retains a strong presence.) Since it was the national security apparatus and not the *tolimenses* who erected the billboard, its rhetorical effect came from the way it structured an imaginary conversation between the state and its subjects—the state hails the subject to turn around and, in return, to hail the state in a particular way. As such, it reflected the political imperative to protect life against a range of threats. The family depicted did not demand progress, development, justice, equality, or prosperity. They did not ask for schools, jobs, hospitals, rights, or roads. When the state is seen (and sees itself) as protector rather than provider, the only conceivable and recognizable demand is simply: more security.

The significance of the Armero tragedy in contemporary Colombia was not immediately clear to me in 2008 when I began fieldwork on disaster risk management in Bogotá. Although I sought to historicize how risk became a technique for governing the city, at first it was difficult to engage my informants in this pursuit. There was an obviousness surrounding the set of assumptions I wanted to examine: that life was sacred, that the future was uncertain, that the city was a space of danger, and that protection was the state's ultimate responsibility. All of this lent disaster risk management an aura of inevitability: it seemed natural to expect the state to govern in anticipation of future threats. When I asked people to consider what may have motivated such initiatives, they often returned to the year 1985. For my informants, this conjured up two of the most unforgettable events in recent memory: both the volcanic eruption that claimed so many lives in Armero and the siege of the Palace of Justice in Bogotá by M-19 guerrilla insurgents, which occurred the very same week. To comprehend the emergence of risk as a technique for governing the city, many suggested, I would first have to understand how these catastrophic events came to define the state's responsibility to protect life from potential harm.[4]

This chapter follows repeated suggestions to that effect by exploring the constitutive relationship among political authority, responsibility, and foresight in Colombia. This domain is specific to places where security is the dominant logic structuring the relationship between state, territory, and population, such that concerns for how to anticipate and govern dangers looming on the horizon are shared across the political spectrum. These concerns became central to the politics of security in Colombia after the converging catastrophes of November 1985.[5] Framed as "apocalypse foretold" (*apocalipsis anunciado*), as the journalist Daniel Samper Pizano succinctly put it, these coinciding tragedies gave shape to political rationalities organized around the imperative to foresee future dangers. Examining the pivotal role of these events over the past three decades lays the groundwork for this book's central concern—the emergence of risk as a technique for governing cities and urban life.[6] Pace Reinhart Koselleck, who argues that rational *prognosis* displaced religious *prophecy* as the paradigmatic conception of futurity in the modern period along with the secularization of political authority, here we find no clear separation of the two.[7] The "year of the tragedies," as it is sometimes called, did not precipitate such an epochal shift from one governmental paradigm to another, but it did shape shared sentiments of how life should be governed and lived in the endangered city. The converging catastrophes of 1985, and their actualization thereafter as "events," created the conditions of possibility for the politics of security and the government of risk in contemporary Bogotá.[8]

"Yesterday, Men . . . Today, Nature . . ."

On November 6, 1985, thirty-five members of the M-19 guerrilla group attacked the Palace of Justice in central Bogotá and took hundreds of hostages, including twenty-four Supreme Court judges. President Belisario Betancur rejected their demand that he come and stand trial for accusations that he had betrayed a previously negotiated peace accord, and instead ordered the army to storm the building. In the ensuing battle between the Colombian armed forces and the rebel gunmen, more than seventy-five hostages were killed, including eleven of the federal justices trapped inside. Exactly one week later, a volcano eighty miles west of Bogotá, the Nevado del Ruiz, erupted suddenly. Warning signs of imminent danger had been ignored, and over twenty-five thousand people died as a massive mudslide buried the nearby town of Armero. The coincidence of these two tragic events marked a turning point in Colombian political rationality. Governmental problems and their proposed solutions began to be increasingly understood within a security framework oriented toward the protection of life from a range of future threats.[9]

These two events were inevitably conjoined in public and political discourse. Speaking a few days after the Armero tragedy, President Betancur referred to the two "difficult tests" that Colombia had just faced:

> One emanating from the violent and irrational action of men, whose objective was to undermine our legal institutions and to destroy the rule of law, was overcome thanks to the self-sacrificing members of our armed forces in charge of defending order and to the courage of the citizenry, but not without leaving an irreparable trail of death and destruction in our justice system and in our community. The other, a terrible blow from nature, we are overcoming with the solidarity of our people and with the support of the entire world, a gesture for which we will be eternally grateful.[10]

A similar framing appeared in an editorial published in the newspaper *El Espectador*, titled "Yesterday, Men . . . Today, Nature . . . ," while political cartoons also juxtaposed the two events (figures 1.3 and 1.4).[11] But not only were these tragedies routinely discussed together, as would be expected; they were also seen as requiring a similar response. To address the two catastrophes, President Betancur convened an emergency summit of both Liberal and Conservative ex-presidents to discuss a range of concerns, such as public order, the peace process, and the legal system.[12] While the siege of the Palace of Justice and the Armero tragedy were disasters of different types, they were both seen as threats to human life, national security, and institutional stability and could be dealt with accordingly.

Meanwhile, media voices began to assign blame for the casualties in both cases to governmental negligence and a lack of foresight. A week after the Armero tragedy, *El Tiempo* published a cartoon simultaneously asking and prescribing: "When will we learn that it is better to prevent than lament?!" (figure 1.5).[13] Two days later, an influential columnist for the same newspaper, Daniel Samper Pizano, authored a scathing reproach under the heading "Apocalypse Foretold."[14] One of Colombia's most renowned journalists, Samper reminded readers of the range of tragedies that had recently struck the country: "massacres of judges and hostages, assassinations

DON ROQUE   Por AL DONADO

FIG 1.3 AND FIG. 1.4 Political cartoons juxtaposing the events of November 1985. Sources: Fig. 1.3, *El Espectador*, November 17, 1985; Fig. 1.4, *El Tiempo*, November 18, 1985.

FIG 1.5 "When will we learn that it is better to prevent than lament?!" Source: *El Tiempo*, November 16, 1985.

of government ministers, floods, earthquakes, and to top it all off, volcanic eruptions." His point was not to mourn these calamities, however, but to cite evidence demonstrating that they should have been foreseen: "We have become the land of tragedies forewarned, of prophecies that come true, of prognoses that materialize."

Samper cited evidence that the M-19 plot to attack the Palace of Justice was discovered in October of the same year and that special security measures were installed and then prematurely lifted. He linked government negligence in this case to the 1980 siege of the Embassy of the Dominican Republic in Bogotá by the same rebel group, which also materialized despite advance warning. Samper then demonstrated the amount of information that had forecasted the eruption of the Nevado del Ruiz—what he called the "most recent catastrophe announced, predicted, foretold, warned, and notified." He cited prior warning by the U.S. Geological Survey, a thorough investigation by a Colombian journalist, a public plea made by a local congressman, and even a civic demonstration planned by the residents of Armero to draw attention to the imminent danger. And he concluded with a call to action: "Once the emergency has passed, it will be unavoidable to prosecute calmly but severely the authorities who had it in their power to avoid the largest tragedy in the country's history, and instead allowed the most apocalyptic of prophecies to come true."[15] Referencing both scientific and religious modes of foreseeing the future, Samper demanded the state be held accountable for what could have been anticipated and, therefore, prevented.

In the wake of the events, accusations of political negligence were accompanied by technical reports on disaster risk in Colombia. *El Tiempo* published a piece on November 14 entitled "Colombia, a Region of High Seismic Risk," which quoted scientific experts warning that Colombia was extremely vulnerable to earthquakes, and that the potential for a large-scale event had been growing over the past few months.[16] Recent earthquakes in Santiago de Chile and Mexico City in March and September of the same year, both causing serious damage to the capitals, added to the sense that Colombia, with nearly all its major cities resting on geological fault lines, had to become better able to predict and prepare for large-scale catastrophe.[17] In addition to these considerations of future disaster risk, an accompanying article looked to similar events in the past. The same newspaper ran a story about an event that occurred 140 years earlier, in February 1845, when thawing ice on the same volcano, the Nevado del Ruiz, led to a mudslide that caused massive destruction and took nearly a thousand lives in the vicinity of the present tragedy.[18] The notion that Colombia was at high risk of disaster—based on both predictive calculations and the historical record—contributed a scientific dimension to the urgent political imperative of foresight.

The catastrophic events of 1985 remain historical referents for contemporary understandings of government authority and responsibility. My interviews with government officials were filled with references to the siege of the Palace of Justice and the Armero disaster as contributing to political rationalities aimed at governing potential threats to collective life. The significance of these tragedies reflects how they were made to constitute a crisis of authority and expertise, in which the government's inability to anticipate and avert them was seen as a monumental failure, and techniques such as prediction, prevention, and preparedness were the solutions proposed.[19] Although prior to November 1985 Colombians were familiar with both political instability and natural disaster, these events altered how similar ones would be understood and managed thereafter. This becomes all the more evident if we examine the government's response to, and the media's representation of, another large-scale disaster that struck just two years earlier.

"Popayán Will Rise from Its Ashes"

In March 1983, the southern Colombian city of Popayán was struck by an earthquake that destroyed much of its historic center, causing 250 deaths and over 3,000 injuries. The city began to tremble just after eight o'clock on the morning of Holy Thursday, or Jueves Santo, an important day of celebration for Catholics during the week leading up to Easter. As news began to spread the following day, the religious symbolism of both the timing and location of the disaster was heavily emphasized.

The front page of *El Tiempo* on April 1 displayed a photograph of the ruins of Popayán's cathedral, the Catedral Basílica de Nuestra Señora de la Asunción, whose cupola had collapsed during morning mass, trapping and killing a number of the faithful (figure 1.6). The cathedral became thereafter known as the "epicenter of the death and destruction" wrought by the earthquake.[20] And Popayán, "the most Catholic city with the greatest religious tradition and symbolism in Colombia," was dubbed by a correspondent sent to cover the crisis "the Colombian Jerusalem" due to the "biblical exodus" it experienced in the aftermath of the disaster.[21] The *payaneses* who had escaped after the collapse of their homes and their sacred churches on that holy day were compared to the "Jews who fled Jerusalem . . . when their temple and city were destroyed by the conquerors."[22]

President Betancur arrived on the scene immediately to head the coordination of the local Emergency Committee. During their initial meeting, according to the press, Betancur not only laid out a plan for emergency aid, but also announced the reconstruction of the city by proclaiming that it would return just as Christ had been resurrected from the dead after the Crucifixion: "Like the Phoenix, Popayán will once again rise from its ashes."[23] After the meeting, Betancur gave a speech on national radio in which he continued to draw upon the religious symbolism that was circulating in the wake of the catastrophe (figure 1.7). He lamented: "This is an immense and moving catastrophe that shook all of Colombia, since Popayán is . . . temple of the homeland [*templo de la Patria*]. And as temple of the homeland and birthplace of the history of Colombia it has now been put to the test."[24]

Betancur went on to assure the public that the Colombian government was in full solidarity with the crippled city, and requested that people remain

FIG 1.6 Catedral Basílica de Nuestra Señora de la Asunción, the "epicenter of the death and destruction." Source: *El Tiempo*, April 1, 1983.

FIG 1.7 Religious imagery circulating in the media. Source: *El Tiempo,* April 1983.

calm and vigilant until the armed forces could "assume total control." This show of force was directed at "antisocial elements" who might "seize upon society and take advantage of the disorder and confusion." After all, guerrilla insurgency was a constant threat in Colombia throughout the 1980s. But Betancur's primary message was less to promise security than foretell a Christ-like resurrection of the heart of Colombia's religious tradition: "We will reconstruct this city, as its temples are temples of the homeland, the stage of history; and we will make sure that public and private buildings rise up like a Phoenix from out of its ashes; from those ashes Popayán will reemerge."[25]

In the aftermath of the earthquake, the bodies of the victims were buried and mourned, emergency aid was brought to the survivors, and the city began the slow process of reconstruction. The Corporation for the Reconstruction and Development of the Department of Cauca was created to promote the rebuilding of Popayán.[26] A law was passed by the Colombian Congress directing the president to organize and put into effect the National Disaster Fund (Fondo Nacional de Calamidades), which was charged with attending to the response and recovery needs of similar catastrophes in the future.[27] The same law also established antiseismic regulations for the reconstruction of Popayán, which was the first time earthquake-resistant construction codes were made mandatory in Colombia.

However, unlike the public outrage that followed the siege of the Palace of Justice and the Armero tragedy, blame was never leveled at the government for failing to foresee the catastrophe. Media coverage of the Popayán earthquake focused not on questions of foresight, but instead on the technical procedures of measuring its magnitude.[28] Of course, earthquakes are notoriously more difficult to predict than other events. Nevertheless, debates that follow in their wake often hold authorities accountable for their lack of preparedness or for failing to assess or communicate risk. In the case of Popayán, though, the rescue and recovery effort was commended for its coordination and swiftness, and the president was praised for his immediate show of solidarity.[29] Rather than highlighting that Popayán was in a highly active seismic zone and that earthquakes had occurred regularly throughout its 450-year history, the task of recovering the city's "lost historic patrimony" and "raising a new Popayán" from the rubble took precedence.[30] After all, the fate of Popayán had been in the hands of God, and his will could not be known in advance. Thus no debate was held over whether the disaster could have been anticipated or whether some casualties could have been averted, as would be the case in November 1985. Although biblical references and religious symbolism circulated freely in both moments of crisis, the backward-looking promise of resurrection that followed the Popayán earthquake would be inaudible two years later next to future-oriented expectations of salvation. The belief that divine providence protected people from (or exposed them to) disaster would eventually be extended to the domain of the state, and political authority and responsibility would be predicated on a combination of prophetic and prognostic foresight.

The Life and Death of Omayra Sánchez

If the coincidental events of November 1985 precipitated a political rationality dedicated to protecting life against foreseeable threats, what would constitute "life," and to which bodies and subjects would it refer? While the eruption of the Nevado del Ruiz and the ensuing mudslide claimed nearly twenty-five thousand victims, it was the life and death of just one of them—the thirteen-year-old Omayra Sánchez—that came to symbolize the disaster for both Colombians and international observers alike. When the avalanche hit Armero late that night, Omayra was one of the few who escaped being buried alive. Instead, she was trapped up to her neck in water, debris, and mud, her legs pinned immovably between a wall and her aunt's corpse lying below. For three full days, Omayra's story was broadcast on television and circulated in magazines and newspapers across Colombia and around the world. Rescue workers tried to free her from captivity with the basic equipment available to them, but they found no way to dislodge her body without causing severe (if not mortal) injuries. As one attempt after another failed, viewers watched in horror as Omayra slowly faded and, after sixty hours of suffering, eventually succumbed to the mud.

While the Armero catastrophe itself, the deadliest tragedy in Colombian history, was lodged in the collective memory of the country, it was through the mass-mediated spectacle of Omayra's heart-wrenching story that the enormous loss of life was personified. The images of Omayra that circulated to the world could not easily be forgotten. Television coverage showed her submerged up to her chin in a pit of mud talking calmly to journalists and rescue workers, sending love to her family members, and asking them to pray for her rescue (figure 1.8). Newspaper articles described to the public the patient and heroic manner in which she awaited the successful rescue attempt that never arrived. But it was perhaps one single photograph, shot by the French photojournalist Frank Fournier, that made the biggest impact.[31] An arresting close-up of Omayra's pallid face just before she died, it was reproduced throughout the national and international news media and would win the World Press Photo of the Year Award for capturing the event of greatest journalistic importance. It also caused an ethical controversy over the photographer's decision to document, rather than help to alleviate, Omayra's suffering—a controversy that further heightened the widespread significance of Omayra Sánchez.[32]

In July 1986, less than a year after the catastrophe in Armero, Pope John Paul II visited the site leveled by the avalanche and mudslide. Although the pope's mission was to commemorate the tragedy and to declare the area a holy cemetery, again the media focused on the life and death of Omayra Sánchez:

FIG 1.8 Television coverage of Omayra Sánchez. The caption says: "In the throes of death for 60 hours in front of television cameras." Source: Televisión Española.

> The prayer of the Holy Father in Armero will be followed by a funeral dirge played by a trumpet that will revive in the mind of Colombians the immensity of the tragedy: the hundreds of men, women, and children covered in boiling mud and the innocent face of the girl Omayra Sánchez, saying goodbye for all eternity, as the symbol of what for Colombia has been the catastrophe [*hecatombe*] of the century.[33]

> It will never be known whether there were 20, 23, or 25,000 deaths. The figure doesn't matter, it says nothing. Perhaps only the remains of Omayra Sánchez give real significance to this loss of life.[34]

Pope John Paul II did not single out Omayra in his benediction that day, but as far as some were concerned, it was her sacred life that the Holy Father was celebrating and commemorating. He delivered his prayer from a papal dais that, as news reports pointed out, was placed five hundred meters away from where Omayra was trapped and died.

In the aftermath of Omayra's death, her story also inspired poets, journalists, musicians, and writers. The overwhelmingly consistent way she has been represented in these works is encapsulated in *Adiós, Omayra*, a book by Colombian author Eduardo Santa that commemorates the catastrophe through a fictionalized but realistic account of the final days of the young girl's life. Santa introduces the story by stating his intentions: "This book is not biography. I have simply tried to recreate an atmosphere, to track the unfolding of the tragedy, to leave a testimony to it, and to pay a warm tribute to Omayra Sánchez, the twelve-year-old [*sic*] girl who . . . has become the symbol of the deadly catastrophe."[35] *Adiós, Omayra* testifies to the well-recognized fact that her life came to symbolize the Armero tragedy, that her image gained a prominent place in the cultural imaginary, and that the story of her death was indelibly marked in the country's collective memory. As Santa's book concludes, the image of Omayra "remains forever implanted in our hearts and minds as the most beautiful and noble symbol of the great catastrophe of Armero."[36]

Less obvious, however, is how Omayra also came to be seen as a tragic victim of the Colombian state's inability to protect the lives of its most vulnerable citizens—again seen as a failure of foresight. In a column that appeared in *El Tiempo* ten days after the tragedy, Germán Santamaría wrote the following accusatory lament under the heading "The Tragedy Foretold" (*la tragedia anunciada*):

> Colombia and half of the world remained with the bitter sensation that Omayra Sánchez could have been able to continue living after remaining for almost 60 hours trapped from head to toe amidst the rubble of Armero. Her face, her words, and her courage, which streamed throughout the world on television and were a heartbreaking image in the largest newspapers and magazines of the United States and Europe, remained a testimony of accusation against those who could have at the very least made the tragedy less serious.[37]

The photographer who took the famous shot of Omayra expressed similar sentiments when he later reflected on the impact he had hoped this image would have: "I believe the photo helped raise money from around the world in aid and helped highlight the irresponsibility and lack of courage of the country's leaders. There was an obvious lack of leadership. There were no evacuation plans, yet scientists had foreseen the catastrophic extent of the volcano's eruption."[38] And nearly twenty-five years after the fact, her name still evokes moral and political indignation, even elsewhere in

Latin America. A Chilean hardcore punk band that formed in 2008 took the name Omayra Sánchez "with the goal of demonstrating the discontent that [they] feel with the negligence on the part of the people who now run the world." For them, Omayra's story continues to represent the ineptitude of the state: "The Colombian government did nothing to save her life during those three days in which the press recorded her agony and her last words were televised." Even today, Omayra Sánchez remains a powerful figure that structures moral and political imaginaries around the state's responsibility to anticipate and govern potential threats.[39]

In addition to symbolizing the negligence of political authorities, Omayra inspired a more introspective focus on what, in Foucault's terms, we could call the "government of the self."[40] Against the foil of a callous state appeared depictions of Omayra's subjective disposition in the face of catastrophe. The Omayra that television viewers and newspaper readers came to know in the three days following the mudslide was a beacon of moral virtue and fortitude who faced her tragic fate with tranquility, patience, and strength. For example, the photographer Fournier, who was close to Omayra in her final days, remembered her this way: "When I took the pictures I felt totally powerless in front of this little girl, who was facing death with courage and dignity."[41] Similar language appears throughout the written record: "She was conscious of her situation and, with the tranquility and integrity that always characterized her, handled things with a disconcerting courage that allowed her to share with the rescue workers, journalists, and others who surrounded her, to whom she expressed urgency that they rescue her so that she would not fail her school exams. In this manner, she succeeded at touching those who in one way or another were aware of her situation."[42] The supreme virtues Omayra was seen to have possessed, and which could be taken as an ethical guide for the personal experience of suffering and endurance, were thereafter cherished and celebrated in almost every representation of her life and death.

Perhaps the best illustration of this is found in *Adiós, Omayra*'s re-creation of the scene of the disaster. According to the author, the book was written "as an homage to the memory of Omayra Sánchez and, by virtue of the serenity of her soul and all that she represents, to the memory of the innocent victims of the violence of nature and the negligence of the authorities."[43] Santa describes the "courageous sacrifice" and "moral fortitude" that characterized her "simple and pure life."[44] His fictionalized rendition of the sixty hours she spent trapped in a pool of mud and debris emphasizes these qualities:

> At no time did she complain. Not even a tear had appeared in her captive face. She didn't even have harsh words about life. Nor did she bitterly lament finding herself in that situation. She spoke with the journalists with a disconcerting serenity. She told them stories of her life. She spoke to them about her school, her parents, her aunt Yaneth. She told them that she hoped they would follow God's will. She sang various children's songs. And when night had already begun to fall, she said finally: "Go and rest for a bit and then come and rescue me."[45]

At one point the Omayra of Santa's account even expresses concern for her schoolwork in the midst of her suffering: "She might have asked those accompanying her what day it was and when told it was Saturday, immediately responded: 'Damn! Yesterday was my math exam and I didn't go to school. I'm going to fail this grade!'"[46]

These renditions of Omayra offered an ethical model for facing the diverse forms of violence and victimhood all too present in Colombia—one that curiously emphasizes acceptance and trust in place of indignation and critique. She shows no sign of emotions like panic, anger, blame, fear, or despair while expressing selfless concern for the well-being of her family and the rescue workers, conscientiousness about her studies, and faith in the righteousness of God's will. As such, Omayra came to represent a distinct form of personhood that continues to serve as a referent in Colombia for the kind of life that deserves to be saved—that is, the ideal citizen of the endangered city. The attribution of responsibility to the state for the life and well-being of its subjects requires the construction of proper and improper objects of care and protection. As Santiago Villaveces Izquierdo puts it, dominant notions of security in Colombia "continue to be based on the simple antagonism of 'the good' against 'the bad.'"[47] The figure of Omayra creates a boundary that differentiates those whose lives matter from those whose lives do not—the outlaws, insurgents, subversives, or terrorists who are dealt with as enemies of the state. On one side, there are bodies and populations subject to programs that aim to preserve, prolong, or protect life. On the other side are those exposed to state-sanctioned violence justified by the sovereign power to kill with impunity.[48] We will now see how the catastrophe of the previous week played an equally pivotal role in shaping the politics of security in contemporary Colombia.

From "Battle Forewarned" to "Silenced Holocaust"

On the morning of November 6, 1985, four M-19 combatants disguised as civilians entered Bogotá's Palace of Justice on foot. Minutes later, two trucks carrying weapons and reinforcements stormed the building. Within an hour, the attackers had taken control of all four floors and were holding close to 350 hostages, including the Supreme Court justices, legal counselors, and service staff. The Colombian armed forces arrived quickly with heavy artillery, and sent blasts of machine-gun fire toward the Palace. Armored vehicles then broke through the building's main entrance, forcing the guerrilla fighters to the top floor, where they had captured the president of the Supreme Court and other high-profile hostages. From there, the command of the M-19 demanded that Betancur order a ceasefire and stand before the Supreme Court, but Betancur rejected their demands and refused to negotiate. Fighting continued the next morning as the armed forces began Operación Rastrillo (Operation Cleanup). When the gunfire finally ceased, all but two of the M-19 rebels had been killed, the Palace of Justice lay in ruins, and over seventy-five hostages were dead, including the president of the Supreme Court, ten other magistrates, and dozens more innocent civilians.[49]

In response to widespread uncertainty about what had transpired, President Betancur created a Special Investigative Tribunal (Tribunal Especial de Instrucción Criminal) a few days after the tragedy. The tribunal was outside the judicial system, however, and had no legal authority to sanction those responsible for the atrocities. Its charge was simply to conduct an inquiry and to issue a public report. Demands for transparency and justice were soon derailed, however: the largest natural disaster in Colombia's history struck just seven days later. The Armero tragedy quickly diverted attention away from the Palace of Justice massacre as the country was mesmerized by images from the disaster zone, especially the footage of Omayra Sánchez. But the two catastrophes of November 1985 were conjoined in public and political discourse, and despite their many obvious differences, critics claimed that in both cases the government had advance warning and had failed to prevent known threats from materializing. For years to come, the joint enframing of these events would serve to authorize the governmental imperative to protect life against a range of potential threats and make prophecy and prognosis foundational to political authority and responsibility. Because both events were constituted as failures of foresight, the Colombian state's complicity in the massacre itself was not at issue.

To this day, many details of the siege of the Palace of Justice remain shrouded. It was "as if a pact had been made to cover up parts of the truth of what happened there," maintains renowned journalist Germán Castro Caycedo.[50] It was not until 2005, twenty years later, that a Truth Commission was established and the attorney general's office began its own investigations. These official inquiries have been supplemented by the work of journalists, artists, and activists committed to memorializing the events and to demanding justice for the victims. While many facts of the case remain unknown, efforts to shed new light on the Palace of Justice massacre continue and together work to reconstitute the occurrence as a different kind of event—one that is less about foresight than about justice.

Among the competing versions of the story, the official one that circulated in the wake of the catastrophe claimed that the M-19 plot was financed by Pablo Escobar, the Medellín drug kingpin, who sought to disrupt ongoing extradition debates and to destroy potentially incriminating documents in the Palace of Justice. Referencing President Betancur's efforts to establish a peace accord with the guerrillas, the M-19 attack was blamed for breaking the truce and making further dialogue impossible. According to this account, a counterattack was the only feasible response and the Colombian armed forces were justified in their use of heavy force. The resulting physical destruction and civilian casualties were attributed to the guerrillas, who supposedly set fire to the building and executed the hostages on realizing a ceasefire was unlikely, their demands would not be met, and their chances of survival were slim.

However, the primary critique of the government's handling of the siege of the Palace of Justice was that it was an event that should have been foreseen. This interpretation has held up consistently throughout the official inquiries made over the past twenty-five years. Based on its investigations, the attorney general's office concludes: "It was and is clear that the armed forces and the state institutions should have established mechanisms to avoid and contain the activities of the M-19 subversive group. Since 1984 and in particular since April 1985 . . . the group's plan to take over the Palace of Justice was a well-known fact, as was the approximate date, and that the goal of the planned attack was the kidnapping of the 24 magistrates of the Supreme Court."[51] Echoing the criticisms leveled at the government for failing to prevent the eruption of the Nevado del Ruiz from becoming a major catastrophe, journalist Germán Castro Caycedo has called the confrontation between the M-19 and the Colombian armed forces a *batalla avisada*, or a "battle forewarned." That said, recent interpretations have worked to give the catastrophe political significance that extends beyond the critique leveled at the government's failure to anticipate it. Journalists have drawn upon the testimony of those closely involved along with other evidence to cast new light on the battle of November 6 and 7. As a result, it has become common to refer to the violence of those fateful days as a "massacre" or, as in the title of one journalistic account, a "silenced holocaust."

One of the key questions pertains to whether the president was in control of the armed forces or whether there had been a power vacuum that was filled by a de facto military coup. At nine o'clock on the night the battle subsided, Betancur gave a televised address to the nation, in which he claimed (referring to himself in the third person) to be fully accountable for the horrific scenes they had just witnessed: "That immense responsibility was assumed by the President of the Republic who, for better or for worse, was making all decisions, giving respective orders, taking absolute control of the situation, and the manner in which he did so was all his own and not influenced by factors that can and should be under his control."[52] But journalists and official inquiries have mobilized evidence in support of the claim that President Betancur had ceded control to the military and was himself unreachable. They have emphasized his refusal to speak with the president of the Supreme Court, Alfonso Reyes Echandía, who was trying desperately to convince him to declare a ceasefire. Although Reyes's plea received no response from the president, it eventually found an audience in the press and was broadcast on radio: "You have to help us. You have to get the government to call a ceasefire. Please beg the army and the police to stand down . . . I have tried to talk with all of the authorities. I have tried to communicate with the president of the Republic, but he's not available. I have been unable to speak with him."[53] In July 2000, Betancur's closest adviser and minister of state, Bernardo Ramírez, told Televisión Española (Spain's public television service) that the president had not been calling the shots:

In the disgrace of Palace of the Justice, in its development, there was a military coup. . . . Look: the bottom line is that the military disobeyed the president's order: get to the Palace of Justice, it's necessary to regain authority, but above all, please respect the lives of the hostages and of the guerrillas too, since they are human beings as well. . . . But the military was thirsty for vengeance, and the command in those days was sinister, their hands were dripping with blood, and they went after what they wanted.[54]

Decades later, investigations attempt to call attention to Betancur's bestowal of power on the military to use any means necessary to reestablish authority.

The Truth Commission has, in turn, blamed the military for using excessive force in their counterattack and with blatantly disregarding their obligation to rescue the hostages and protect innocent civilians.[55] While the commission has condemned the M-19's actions as "barbarous terrorism," it has also declared that the armed forces "overstepped the authority conferred upon them by the Constitution and the law" and that their conduct was "illegitimate, disproportionate, and complicit [coparticipe] in the massacre."[56] Its findings have allowed for the possibility that the guerrillas may not have been responsible for all the casualties: "In the end, no one knows how the hostages and the guerrillas on the fourth floor died. It is unknown which of them died before the flames confounded everything, since there was not one survivor from the group. What is certain is that the large majority of bodies were found dismembered, mutilated, and burned, and at least three of the magistrates . . . showed in their mortal remains projectiles of weapons that were not used by the guerrilla."[57] Journalists have lighted on evidence suggesting that the bullet that killed the president of the Supreme Court came from a gun that the M-19 did not have in their arsenal.[58] Furthermore, they have publicized video footage in which another magistrate found dead in the ruins of the Palace of Justice is seen leaving the building alive in the midst of the battle.[59]

Attempts to question the official version of what occurred have also focused on the relative invisibility of the victims of those two bloody days of fighting. While Omayra Sánchez became an emblematic figure of the Armero disaster, not one of the hostages killed in the Palace of Justice massacre has been remembered in the same way. Although the voice of the president of the Supreme Court, according to journalists Echeverry and Hanssen, "would resonate forever in the memory of those who heard it and would become evidence of the questionable effort the government made to avoid the catastrophe," not even he attained Omayra's emblematic status as a heroic and tragic victim.[60] According to some journalists, the invisibility of the victims of the siege of Palace of Justice was the result of state censorship. The press, which had made Omayra an international celebrity by televising her ultimately unsuccessful struggle to survive, is said to have been prohibited by the minister of communications, Noemí Sanín, from covering the events as they transpired. Based on further investigations, however, the invisibility of these victims has also been seen as evidence of a greater crime.

All attempts to investigate what transpired have puzzled over the fate of eleven of the civilian hostages, mostly service workers from the cafeteria, whose bodies were never found. The same is true for a guerrilla combatant who was evacuated from the building alive, according to a videotape discovered later, and was never seen or heard from again. While their whereabouts remain a mystery, investigators now believe that the army ordered the torture and eventual disappearance of the cafeteria workers they suspected of being complicit in the M-19 plot.[61] According to testimony received by the attorney general's office from former state intelligence agent Ricardo Gámez Mazuera, the army disposed of the corpses of those killed during or after interrogation in mass graves.[62] Efforts to draw attention to the invisibility of the victims of this catastrophe have sought to bring these disappearances to the center of contemporary debates on the politics of security in Colombia.

A number of artists and activists have also made the siege of the Palace of Justice the focus of their work. Perhaps the most famous is Doris Salcedo, an internationally celebrated sculptor whose work has been shown by major galleries in New York, San Francisco, and London. The entirety of Salcedo's oeuvre is concerned with the history of political violence in Colombia, especially with its ethical and aesthetic dimensions. But it was the siege of the Palace of Justice that initially gave urgency to her artistic projects and would later become the specific focus of one of her public installations.[63] Salcedo recalls the importance of this event for her on arriving in Bogotá from art school in New York:

A few months after I returned to Colombia in 1985, having spent a year in Europe and two years in New York, the Palace of Justice in Bogotá was occupied by guerrilla forces. The violence that ensued ended in a horrific tragedy. It was something I witnessed for myself. It is not just a visual memory, but a terrible recollection of the smell of the torched building with human beings inside. . . . It left its mark on me.[64]

For Salcedo, the influence of the event on her art is tied to its significance as a turning point in Colombian history: "November 6 and 7, 1985, were days that changed Colombia forever, the days in which impunity became entrenched in the official facade of democratic institutions and memory erased."[65] Throughout her career, Salcedo would consistently explore how acts of violence can go unpunished by the justice system and be forgotten by society. Although the works of art she produced during the 1990s used the domestic belongings of victims of Colombia's armed conflict to evoke the personal experience of violence, she would eventually return to the Palace of Justice massacre itself as an explicit referent.

In November 2002, on the seventeenth anniversary of the siege, Salcedo created a site-specific installation entitled *Noviembre 6 y 7* (figure 1.9).[66] The piece was designed for and executed on the facade of the new Palace of Justice, which had been rebuilt on the same site in Bogotá's Plaza de Bolívar. Initiating the work at 11:35 a.m., the exact moment when the first person died in the battle, Salcedo gradually suspended a wooden chair over the building's eastern face. Another 280 chairs were then lowered from various points on the roof at different speeds and intervals for the precise duration of the original battle.[67]

Salcedo's reflections on the project emphasize her intent to challenge the invisibility of the victims of the massacre and the official denial that had persistently rebuffed calls for justice from their families, friends, and the general public. Her initial proposal stated that the objective would be to "generate an image that will jolt the memory of passers-by, so that they can confront their own memory of this terrible event."[68] In an essay she wrote soon after the installation, Salcedo recalled in sharper language what prompted the idea behind it: "For 17 years now, I had wanted to remember, to transform this violent event into remembrance through art. As an artist who works with memory, I confront past events whose memory has purposefully been effaced, in which the objects that bear the traces of violence have been destroyed in order to impose oblivion. In this case, I wanted to try to turn this intentional oblivion, this 'no longer present' into 'a still here,' into a presence."[69] By drawing widespread attention to the event, Salcedo's *Noviembre*

FIG 1.9 Doris Salcedo, *Noviembre 6 y 7*, 2002. Source: White Cube, London.

6 y 7 joined the efforts of other artists, journalists, activists, and investigators in attempting to reactualize it as a matter of public concern whose political meaning had not yet been settled.

Despite their quite different causes, the initial coupling of the catastrophes of November 1985 had meant that the political significance of both could be reduced to the need to strengthen the state's ability to anticipate threats of all kinds. Salcedo's intervention, however, made no connection between the two events. In fact, throughout her artistic career, Salcedo has never once referenced the Armero tragedy. Despite her sustained political and aesthetic engagement with violence, the loss of life, and the condition of victimhood, the approximately twenty-five thousand people killed a week after the Palace of Justice massacre remain unmentioned. In another, more recent act of public commemoration, *Acción de Duelo*, a group of artists led by Salcedo assembled twenty-five thousand lighted candles in Bogotá's Plaza de Bolívar in July 2007. That the number of candles approximated the number of victims of the Armero tragedy appears to be a mere coincidence. According to the artists, the lives commemorated were eleven political officials from the department of Valle del Cauca who had recently disappeared.

Rather than an omission, this silence about the victims of the Armero tragedy reflects a separation of "political" catastrophes from those of a different sort. Salcedo, for one, has been explicit about her interest in the former: "I have focused on extreme forms of political violence, forceful displacement, disappearance, massacres, persecution."[70] Perhaps because the toll of death and destruction left by the eruption of the Nevado del Ruiz had drawn initial attention away from the Palace of Justice massacre, effectively diffusing its transformative political potential, efforts to reactualize the latter event have treated it in isolation. And while the tragedies of November 1985 were initially conjoined as failures of foresight, artists, activists, investigators, and journalists have separated the "political catastrophe" from the "natural disaster." In framing the former as a matter of justice, they have inadvertently naturalized the death and destruction caused by the latter. Although in doing so they have challenged the state's authority to unilaterally determine one event's historical significance, what remains unquestioned is that the imperative to protect life by managing threats is the ultimate end of government.[71]

Anticipating Threats, Securing Lives

The relationship between authority, responsibility, and foresight in contemporary Colombia is related intimately to past events, notably the coinciding catastrophes of November 1985. Their generative power is due not to qualities inherent to them, although their scale was momentous and their timing uncanny, but rather to the way in which they have since been actualized—that is, how they have become constituted as "events." This has occurred on technical, political, and cultural registers: from artistic production to political debate; from scientific calculation to military command; from media representation to governmental policy. When taken together, the two catastrophes have been framed as occasions in which potential threats to life were not foreseen and the state failed to prevent them from becoming disasters. As a result, they have jointly lent legitimacy to the constitutive relationship between authority, responsibility, and foresight, which ranges from efforts to prevent household accidents, earthquake preparedness campaigns, and resettlement programs in zones of high risk to efforts to forestall terrorist attacks, reduce rates of crime and violence, and control strategic territories. The imperative to anticipate and govern threats to life is what unites these projects, yet the violence potentially inflicted by armed political actors is now commonly treated as distinct from that attributed to the physical world. The latter is understood primarily as a techno-scientific problem to be controlled through rational forms of governmental management with a clear moral purpose. The former, however, allows neither technical solutions nor moral certitude, despite the state's attempt to equip its national security apparatus with both.

As political authority and responsibility in Colombia are shaped by security logics, other well-established political rationalities, such as development, democracy, and welfare, have been displaced. When we consider the interrelatedness of multiple regimes of rule, however, we see that the politics of security and risk reconfigure, but do not replace, the politics of rights and citizenship in the endangered city. By examining how the ideals of democracy and security have been fused over the past decade in Colombia, we can begin to understand why poor settlers on the urban periphery must be visible as lives at risk in order to be recognized as citizens with rights. Yet we must also see how democracy and security work with and through other deeply embedded conceptions of authority and responsibility that are often treated as separate from "politics" as conventionally understood. For example, when comparing the discussions surrounding the Popayán earthquake in 1983 with the debates following the dual catastrophes of 1985, we see that the temporal shift from reconstruction to prognosis was simultaneously a theological shift from resurrection to prophecy. To understand the politics of security in contemporary Bogotá, we must approach it not as a singular domain of secular rationality but, rather, as a problem space shaped by multiple genealogies of rule.

The domain of security politics in Colombia also hinges on precisely how "life" enters the realm of the political: not as a valuable resource to be cultivated, improved, or promoted, but as a vulnerable possession at risk of being harmed or taken away. In the period analyzed here, however, this imperative was forged alongside a parallel disregard for life and the fact that, all too often, it can be extinguished with impunity. This book focuses primarily on the objective of anticipating threat and securing life through techniques of risk management rather than the imperative to protect some while endangering others. But it should not be forgotten that, in Colombia, the same state that professes a deep concern for the sanctity of human life has also been complicit in horrific acts of violence. The distinctions that become important, then, are political distinctions—actors across the political spectrum promote different versions of "security," engaging in frequent debate over how it is defined and pursued and attempting thereby to build a political constituency and majority, even while they share an overarching commitment to "security" in the abstract. The coinciding catastrophes of November 1985—how in each case the category of victimhood and the event itself was constituted—have been instrumental in shaping the terms and condition of these debates. Precisely how certain threats are foreseen and certain lives secured in Bogotá is the question to which the next chapter turns.

To whom, then, does one turn for the hope of a better life? Returning briefly to Armero and the Memorial to Life that commemorates the 1985 tragedy, consider the demand for "a Tolima without guerrillas" on a roadside billboard in contrast to the *peticiones* left at Omayra's grave: for my son to get a well-paying job, for my daughter to have a good education, for our family to be happy and healthy. Or take the thousands of *acciones de gracias* thanking Omayra for favors received or miracles granted. In the aftermath of November 1985, the figure of Omayra was mobilized for a powerful critique of a state that failed to protect the lives of its most vulnerable, and most deserving, subjects. But my visit to her grave made it clear that she has now lost that critical edge, that worldly relevance, that ability to be used for political purpose. She has ascended to the otherworldly realm, and it is Omayra the saint, Omayra the martyr, that people now look to as benefactor. One might also turn to God, to the Church, perhaps to fate or luck—but not to the state, unless to demand protection from future threats. How to govern these matters of security is the question shared across the political spectrum. In the endangered city, one pleads to higher powers for the good life, or awaits it in life after death.

2

ON SHAKY GROUND

The Map of Risk

It is a slow afternoon in the office of the Caja de la Vivienda Popular. Everyone has just returned from lunch and is passing time until the steady stream of visitors starts up again. The Caja, as it is commonly called, is the branch of Bogotá's municipal government that, since 2003, has managed a housing resettlement program for families living in zones of high risk. Its official duty is to protect the lives of populations deemed vulnerable to environmental hazards, such as landslide and flood, by relocating them. I'm chatting with the social workers, architects, and lawyers who manage the day-to-day operations of the Caja's field office here in Ciudad Bolívar—the poor area in the mountainous southern periphery of Bogotá where the majority of these zones are located. Although the Caja's headquarters are in the city center, this office serves as the hub of the resettlement program for the many households undergoing relocation. Yet it is not merely a place where policies developed elsewhere are put into effect—that is, where the political imperative to protect life from future harm materializes in the daily work of governing the endangered city. It is a key site in which techniques of risk management are made and managed on an everyday basis.

We're discussing a recent political scandal when two women, both resettlement program "beneficiaries," arrive holding a newspaper clipping advertising houses for sale. Although the Caja is responsible for relocating "at risk" households, it relies on the initiative of beneficiaries to manage their own resettlement. These women have been searching for housing to purchase with the subsidy guaranteed to the population living in high-risk zones, and they believe they have finally found ones that suit their criteria. Before they can proceed, however, their selections have to be approved by the *equipo técnico*, or "technical team," according to a strict set of norms, of which the new property's risk designation is the most elemental.

One of the Caja's architects, Ana María, takes the paper and looks at the address: "Unfortunately," she says, "these properties are in a zona de alto riesgo." In a pedagogical tone, Ana María offers to explain. Rising from her chair, she shifts attention toward a map hanging on the wall, which shows the streets of Ciudad Bolívar shaded over in green, yellow, and red to indicate low, medium, and high risk. Ana María first points to the two properties, which are in a yellow zone (medium risk). But her finger then slides up the map an inch higher, stopping at two red lines just north of the street on which these two houses are located. "These red lines," she explains, "are seismic faults where earthquake damage can be severe." Ana María, regardless of the map, pronounces these properties "high risk" and thus disqualifies them.

Initial calculations of disaster risk in Bogotá—that is, which neighborhoods are designated high risk and therefore subject to relocation—were made in the late 1990s. And the more general process of establishing policies of risk management on a national level began the previous decade. Yet as Ana María demonstrated by her simultaneous reference to and adjustment of the map, the boundaries of zones of high risk are not always fixed—neither out there in the field nor here in the office. In the practice of implementation, they are repeatedly formed and re-formed. Risk management is a way of rendering the uncertain future actionable in the present, and it is continually reconfigured on a daily basis. Its history is inseparable from the urbanization of Bogotá's peripheral hillsides, yet it would be a mistake to see the government of risk as simply an obvious response to hazardous living conditions.

Between 1950 and 2010, the population of Bogotá exploded from just over 700,000 to about 8 million. Much of this population increase took place in the southern half of the city and led to the growth of sprawling self-built settlements on the mountainous urban periphery. When the municipal government began conducting technical studies of environmental hazards in the late 1990s, the highest concentration of families in zones of high risk was in this area.[1] In fact, over 50 percent of the 10,715 properties located in risk zones in 2008 were in Ciudad Bolívar—the largest and poorest of Bogotá's twenty localities.[2] The imperative to relocate families from zones of high risk has focused on this area; from 2004 to 2006, for example, 90 percent (1,239) of the households resettled by the government were from this locality alone.[3] Ciudad Bolívar has remained the central focus of risk management programs, which is reflected by the siting of the Caja's field office there.

The question of how the poor in Bogotá came to inhabit landscapes of risk can be answered in at least two ways. The first is what I would call the received narrative.[4] Since the mid-twentieth century, hundreds of thousands of peasants from the Colombian countryside have migrated to the capital city, either seeking economic opportunity or having been displaced from their land by paramilitaries, guerrillas, or the army. While peasants had once been embedded in the social institutions of rural areas, such as the Catholic Church and the hacienda, they were increasingly uprooted in the past half century as economic restructuring and political violence radically transformed the country. On arriving in large numbers in Bogotá, they first settled in rented rooms in centrally located tenement housing (*inquilinatos*). But as the existing housing supply quickly ran out, they began to gravitate to the hillsides of the city's southern periphery.

As early as the nineteenth century, the hillsides were exploited for construction materials. Tunnels and quarries were dug into the deforested slopes in order to extract the gravel, rock, and sand that would be used to build the physical infrastructure of central Bogotá. Once these resources diminished, however, *urbanizadores piratas* (pirate urbanizers) began to appropriate territories, subdividing them into small plots and selling them without legal title. Heavily mined, and therefore unsuitable for most other uses, these lands were of low economic value. Meanwhile, the demand for affordable property in the city was growing rapidly, and the state had neither the interest nor the ability to regulate it; in fact, politicians often permitted ad hoc urbanization in exchange for popular support. Settlers then built their own dwellings using rudimentary construction materials and techniques on what was already precarious terrain. As the story goes, these settlements were fated from the outset to be exposed to risk.

This narrative is useful for understanding the dynamics of twentieth-century urban development in Bogotá. Highlighting economic, demographic, and geographic factors, it critically examines the production of urban social and environmental inequality. Accurate as it may be, however, this explanation unwittingly projects onto the past a way of conceptualizing the city that is a more recent invention; it historicizes everything but the key category of concern: the "zone of high risk." Risk thus appears a physical characteristic of the urban landscape that precedes the policies, studies, maps, and programs that initially brought it into being as a technique of government. We are therefore left with the impression that Bogotá's unequal landscape of risk was inevitable—as Mike Davis puts it, "very poor people have little choice but to live with disaster."[5] According to this line of thinking, risk becomes, as Davis says, "poverty's niche in the ecology of the city."[6]

The tenet of critical urban theory that supports this account is irrefutable: the social production of space is, indeed, a deeply uneven process.[7] There is no doubt that the poor in Bogotá are disproportionately exposed to the devastating effects of environmental disasters, such as landslides and floods. Throughout the informal settlements of Ciudad Bolívar, evidence of erosion, subsidence, and contamination are material signs of the structural inequality that constitutes the urban periphery. But while treating risk as an unfair burden suffered by the disadvantaged may be necessary, it is insufficient. For in Bogotá, the very factors that once enabled slums to exist are now the reason for their removal. Risk is no longer the "Faustian bargain," as Davis calls it, that the poor must accept in order to secure housing; as the municipal government relocates vulnerable populations to protect them from environmental hazard, risk is now the logic underlying their displacement.

To understand how and why the state does more than first produce and then neglect the problem of urban environmental risk, I find it necessary to invert the argument formulated above. Rather than investigating how the poor came to inhabit landscapes of risk, I will ask: How did zones of high risk come to inhabit the territories of the poor? By placing these zones in question, we see that before the 1990s risk did not exist in Bogotá, at least not as a technique for governing urban spaces and populations. By approaching "risk" genealogically and ethnographically, we can analyze the processes through which it is made into an object of governmental intervention in the endangered city. This enables us to think critically not only about the production of unequal geographies of vulnerability, but also about emerging attempts to ameliorate them. Such an ability is necessary for attending to recent paradigms of urbanism, which assert that urban spaces, populations, and environments should be managed according to rationalities of security. In both the global North and South, it is common for cities to be governed through probabilistic calculations of potential events, from financial crises and terrorist attacks to disease outbreaks and natural disasters.[8] But with no consensus on how to calculate such probabilities, risk belongs to a range of security mechanisms used to render the uncertain future an object of official decision-making in the present.[9] These mechanisms become central to political rationalities at specific historical junctures and are operationalized in the everyday work of governing the city. How, I ask, and to what effect?

The Governmentalization of Risk

Despite popular conceptions of "state failure," in the past two decades Colombia has come to be seen as an exemplary site of innovation in approaches to governing future uncertainty in the domain of crime, violence, and insecurity. On the one hand, the state has advanced a militaristic approach to controlling territory, establishing sovereignty, and defeating "narcoterrorism." On the other hand, Colombia has witnessed an elaboration of governmental programs employing techniques of risk management whose aim is to protect the life of the population against a broad range of threats—from violent crime to natural disaster. The emergence of a broad range of security mechanisms reflects a shift in how the state seeks to govern uncertain and potentially threatening futures.

For most of the twentieth century, however, the dominant logic governing the Colombian state's approach to disasters was emergency response.[10] As in other Latin American countries, the role of the state in managing disasters was complemented by the Red Cross, which provided additional humanitarian aid to victims in the aftermath of catastrophic events. Most disaster management took place on the local level, however, since municipal fire brigades were ultimately responsible for attending to calamities. It was not until 1949 that Colombia established a national policy for handling large-scale public emergencies. Following the assassination on April 9, 1948, of populist political leader and presidential candidate Jorge Eliécer Gaitán, and the ensuing popular revolt, which wreaked havoc and left much of Bogotá in ruins, the Colombian government signed an agreement with the Red Cross to create a semi-public parastatal organization, the Socorro Nacional de la Cruz Roja, which would thereafter be responsible for managing emergency response on a national scale.[11]

The burden shifted from the Socorro Nacional de la Cruz Roja in the 1960s, when Latin American countries influenced by the U.S. Agency for International Development (USAID) began creating agencies of civil defense. Adhering to national security policy, these offshoots of the military were given the mission of establishing ties with the civilian population in the interest of combating the "internal enemy." The threat of political subversion posed by local communist movements motivated these agencies to respond to disasters of accidental or nonhuman origin in order to prevent social and political instability.[12] These were the entities that came to the aid of the Colombian city of Popayán following the 1983 earthquake there—a disaster understood primarily as a problem of rescue, recovery, and reconstruction. By contrast, two catastrophes that converged in November 1985—the eruption of the Nevado del Ruiz volcano, which killed over twenty-five thousand people, and the guerrilla siege of the Palace of Justice in Bogotá—precipitated a shift toward future-oriented policies of risk management. The 1985 events were seen not solely as emergencies requiring response, but as catastrophes that could have been foreseen and either prepared for or prevented.

The National Plan for Disaster Prevention and Response from 1998 affirms that a transition occurred at this moment: "The general policy of the Colombian state has been, since 1986, to consolidate and incorporate the mitigation of risks and the prevention of disasters in the socioeconomic development process of the country."[13] Disaster risk management has gone in and out of political favor since the mid-1980s, and it would be a mistake to see its emergence as a linear process. But it is clear that, from this moment onward, the Colombian state would be obligated—legally, politically, and morally—to both respond to emergencies after they occurred *and* plan and govern the national territory according to calculative predictions of threat and danger. The 1985 volcanic eruption and guerrilla attack were quite different catastrophes, yet together they were instrumental in the establishment of risk management as a technique of government in Colombia.

The linkage between diverse security threats was not new in 1985, though. As mentioned, the responsibility of civil defense agencies to protect the nation against foreign and internal enemies implied the imperative to respond to natural disasters. President Belisario Betancur exemplified this approach to disaster management in 1983 when he assured survivors of the Popayán earthquake that the army would soon arrive to ensure that subversive elements did not create disorder and social instability. However, the events of November 1985 brought about a new connection between human and non-human dangers. It was believed that the likelihood of the "political" threat of armed insurgency and the "physical" threat of natural disaster were both known to be high, yet no action was taken. Whatever the source of catastrophe in the future, response alone would no longer be sufficient.

Nevertheless, a boundary separating political-military threats from those of a technical-civilian nature would soon be drawn. When Colombian disaster policy had been limited to emergency response, the same entities aided in rescue, recovery, and reconstruction whether the event was a bomb explosion or a seasonal flood. But once risk management policy was established, the job of collecting, analyzing, and acting on prognostic information about threats was divided between national security agencies, on the one hand (e.g., the Ministry of Defense, the army, the Administrative Department of Security), and technical organizations, on the other (e.g., the National Directorate for Disaster Prevention and Response, the Red Cross, the National Institute of Geological Study and Mining). The institutional disarticulation of disaster risk management and national security meant the creation of separate techniques for predicting threat and calculating risk—that is, for governing future uncertainty.

President Betancur, who was heavily criticized for his handling of the events of November 1985, was succeeded in 1986 by Virgilio Barco. In seeking to rectify the crisis of political authority and technical expertise that plagued his predecessor, and recognizing that doing so demanded a future-oriented approach to disaster management, President Barco summoned a select group of experts. As one of these experts later recalled, Barco told them: "Look, I don't want a Ruiz to happen to me. I don't want what happened to Betancur to happen to me. I don't know anything about this stuff. You guys, watch what you're doing."[14] Following Barco's plea, the National Office of Emergency Response (ONAE) was created in late 1986 with support from the United Nations Development Programme (UNDP).[15] The municipal government of Bogotá followed suit in 1987 after the city council passed an accord creating a Fund for Emergency Prevention and Response. The fund's primary objective would be to "finance the creation of a program of extensive coverage to prevent disasters based on studies and inventories of risk."[16] Its priority would be communities located in "zones of risk" (zonas de riesgo), and these would be identified on "a map of risk" that would cover the entire city.

In 1988, the Colombian government created a National System for Disaster Prevention and Response (SNPAD), which sought to integrate risk management policy on a national scale, as well as with local-level institutions of government.[17] A sense of urgency was evident in Representative Darío Martínez Betancourt's plea for Congress to approve its creation: "There are numerous events that could lead to death and that threaten the life and tranquility of Colombians. Colombia is a country of extremely high risks [*un país de altísimos riesgos*]."[18] Once the SNPAD was adopted, the Colombian state thereafter was obligated to maintain an information system that would locate risks throughout the country, develop the techniques necessary to detect and measure them, and communicate this information.[19] Scientific authority for studying and mapping risks was then distributed among a handful of government agencies according to their particular areas of expertise (geology, hydrology, meteorology, etc.).[20]

The objective of creating a national system for risk management took on greater urgency as another series of events transpired during its initial planning phases. In March 1988, the Ruiz volcano was again threatening; another volcano, Galeras, began to show signs of activity; and in August of the same year, a period of intense rainfall caused death and destruction in nearly four hundred municipalities, mostly along Colombia's Atlantic coast. In the immediate aftermath of these events, legislation was passed giving ONAE the added responsibility of ensuring that disaster prevention regulations for zones of risk would be part of all future development plans.[21] In addition, the same office would be obligated to establish regional and local committees of disaster prevention and response and to administer the execution of studies to identify areas in which "neither human settlements nor buildings should be located."[22]

Risk then became a technique for governing Colombia's cities in 1989, when Congress reformed urban policy and obligated every municipality with more than one hundred thousand inhabitants to formulate development plans.[23] Although it was a move in the direction of decentralization, this law nevertheless determined the basic criteria for how cities throughout Colombia would be legally bound to govern themselves. Contained within these regulations was the imperative that urban governments establish an inventory of vulnerable human settlements by calculating their exposure to flooding, landslide, or other unhealthy living conditions. And if localized mitigation projects were not possible, municipal authorities would then be required to move forward with the relocation of the inhabitants of what would thereafter be designated zones of high risk.

By this point, the classification of possible events had been codified in the legal and policy frameworks governing emergency response. On its initial creation in 1984, the National Disaster Fund could be applied to "catastrophes" caused by "artificial or natural phenomena of great intensity or violence; unique or repetitive unfortunate events; diseases or medical conditions of an epidemic nature; and acts of hostility or armed conflict of a national or international scope that affect the population."[24] However, the 1989 law that brought the fund into operation replaced the term "catastrophes" with "situations of disaster, calamity, or those of a similar nature" and limited its application to "floods, droughts, frosts, hurricane winds, earthquakes, tidal waves, fire, volcanic eruptions, avalanches, landslides and technological risks in declared disaster zones."[25] Likewise, the 1988 law creating the SNPAD also defined "disaster" in such a way as to limit its scope: it became "the grave damage or alteration of the national conditions of life in a determinate geographic area, caused by natural phenomena or by catastrophic effects of the accidental actions of man."[26] With the shift of emphasis from response to risk, the legal and policy framework underpinning disaster management in Colombia divided the problem of future uncertainty according to its human and nonhuman dimensions.

This would be the first time that risk, as an object of scientific study and governmental concern, would enter the juridico-political apparatus in Colombia. Prior to the late 1980s, "risk" had been equivalent to "danger" or "hazard" according to Colombian legal statutes and political directives. Risk might be associated with specific occupations, but it was not until later that it would become a technique for governing potential threats to the population at large. For example, in 1975, a "risk bonus" (*prima de riesgo*) was added to the salary of Bogotá's firemen with five or more years of service in a notoriously dangerous occupation.[27] In 1976, the mayor of Bogotá declared general safety regulations for the capital city, which included a color-coding system for identifying "risks" in businesses and factories and stipulated the type of fire extinguishing device required.[28] Likewise, in 1979, the Colombian Congress established occupational health measures, including those requiring employers to reduce the "risks . . . that could affect individual or collective health in the workplace."[29] Although this law contained the first disaster management regulations in Colombia, mention of preventative measures was scarce. It was not until the law was thoroughly overhauled a decade later that risk would begin to motivate governmental programs aimed at disaster prevention.[30]

The establishment of techniques of risk management in Colombia was not the result of national events alone. The UNDP had sent recovery aid to Colombia after the 1985 Armero disaster and was actively involved in the initial creation of the ONAE in 1986 and 1987. The influence of the international community intensified when the General Assembly of the United Nations proclaimed in 1989 that the 1990s would be the "International Decade for Natural Disaster Reduction." With this declaration, the UN directed development agencies "to pay special attention to fostering international co-operation in the field of natural disaster reduction" and, in particular, to assist developing countries in their effort to implement risk management programs and policies.[31] Asserting that "fatalism about natural disasters is no longer justified," this UN declaration motivated donor countries and multilateral organizations to direct resources and expertise toward disaster risk management in countries of the global South.

The globalization of risk management policy would continue throughout the "International Decade for Natural Disaster Reduction." In the late 1990s, the UN created an interagency collaboration called the International Strategy for Disaster Reduction (ISDR), which would pursue the initiatives that had begun in the previous decade. The ISDR partnered with the World Bank in 2006 to form the Global Facility for Disaster Reduction and Recovery (GFDRR), which would provide technical and financial assistance to "high risk low and middle income countries" in order to focus their national development plans on disaster reduction. By 2009, the World Bank was providing Colombia with over US$340 million in funding for disaster management projects and Colombia had become recognized internationally as a leader in this field.[32] While the coinciding catastrophes of 1985 created an initial opening, the establishment of techniques of risk management in Colombia reflects a more general shift toward endangerment as a central problem for urban planning, government, and development on a global scale.

The Zone of High Risk

Zooming in from the previous section to focus on the zone of high risk in Bogotá requires going back to 1987, when the Bogotá city council created the Fund for Emergency Prevention and Response. This fund was dedicated to financing a comprehensive disaster prevention program based on studies of *zonas de riesgo*, or "zones of risk," as they were initially called.[33] Shortly thereafter, in 1989, the Colombian legislature enacted a broad reform of urban government, which obligated every municipality with a population of over one hundred thousand to maintain an inventory of zonas de alto riesgo and to begin mitigation work or relocation programs in these areas.[34] Although this law applied to all cities, the municipal government of Bogotá became one of the first to implement it. This move was enabled by the decentralization process under way at the time, such as the popular election of Colombian mayors, who until 1988 had been appointed by the president. In 1994, Bogotá's mayor, Jaime Castro, directed what was then the Office of Emergency Prevention and Response to begin analyzing the distribution of environmental risk across the city.[35] A consulting firm, Ingeocim, was hired to conduct these studies and to devise a methodology for calculating risks of a geophysical nature.[36]

The imperative to govern the city as a space of risk extended beyond the domain of environmental hazards in 1995 when an unconventional mathematics professor and university administrator, Antanas Mockus, became mayor of Bogotá in the wake of a barrage of homicides, political assassinations, crime waves, and bomb attacks. Searching for innovative strategies with which to confront problems of insecurity, Mockus found inspiration in Cali, Colombia's third largest city, and its novel Program for Development, Security, and Peace.[37] This program was an initiative of Cali's mayor, Rodrigo Guerrero, a medical doctor whose graduate studies in public health had led him to approach insecurity from an epidemiological perspective.[38] The Mockus administration subsequently adopted a similar strategy in the creation of a Unified Information System of Violence and Delinquency (SUIVD) in Bogotá. Like its predecessor in Cali, this system was based on the idea that outbreaks of crime and violence could be treated like diseases of unknown origin. By collecting and analyzing existing crime data, the SUIVD sought to identify risk factors that could be used to predict when and where violence would be likely to occur in the future. Once the spatial distribution of risk factors was determined, the system could guide a coordinated strategy of governmental intervention targeting high-risk activities, populations, and neighborhoods.

The violence prevention strategy that emerged in the mid-1990s in Bogotá paralleled attempts to map the city's vulnerability to environmental hazards.

Shared between these efforts was the idea that Bogotá was a space of dangers that could be calculated probabilistically and then governed through interventions concentrated in specific zones. While it is difficult to assess how one model influenced the other, it is clear that at this moment a range of problems and their proposed solutions could be conceived in similar ways; both governmental strategies were based on the imperative to protect the life of the population against a range of threats. Although this imperative had coalesced in the aftermath of the two catastrophes that coincided in November 1985, it was a decade later that Mayor Mockus brought it to the forefront of urban policy in Bogotá.[39] Even as social-political threats were separated from technical-environmental ones, protecting life by intervening in high-risk zones would be as common to debates surrounding crime and violence as to concerns about natural disasters.

In 1998, studies of environmental risk in Bogotá were completed. The consulting firm, Ingeocim, had evaluated threats (*amenazas*) of various kinds—earthquakes, landslides, floods, fires, and industrial accidents—and mapped their spatial distribution. "Threat" referred to the probability of occurrence of a given physical phenomenon over a specific period of time. To calculate the threat of landslide, for example, they had used GIS mapping techniques, photographic interpretation, field surveys, and historical data. They broke landslide threat down into three levels—low, medium, and high—and mapped them accordingly.[40] Ingeocim then overlaid levels of landslide threat with measures of social and physical vulnerability (e.g., housing type, tenure, access to services, literacy, occupation), which when combined resulted in a "total loss index" (*índice de pérdida global*).[41] Zones of high risk were those in which the expected average loss of life, property, and infrastructure in the event of landslide was estimated at over 62.5 percent of the total existing in the defined area.[42] Based on these studies, the municipal government then issued maps on the scale of the entire city.[43] Priorities were established for more detailed calculations of risk on the scale of the neighborhood and the individual property.[44] In 2000, these priorities, based on the intersection of high risk levels and low socioeconomic status, were incorporated into Bogotá's master plan (Plan de Ordenamiento Territorial, or POT). While further analysis of the data behind the risk calculations may be warranted, what I wish to emphasize is the field of governmental intervention they enabled.[45]

Under the leadership of Mayor Enrique Peñalosa, the master plan for Bogotá sought to recuperate public space, improve the distribution of services, construct a mass-transit system, and regulate urban land use.[46] In terms of housing, it was also an attempt to address Bogotá's massive problems of informality and illegality fueled by the mass displacement of rural populations to the peripheral barrios of the capital city. To upgrade self-built settlements lacking basic necessities and legal titles, the POT planned to give them access to a comprehensive neighborhood improvement program. However, since preliminary studies had shown that a large percentage of the developed territory of Bogotá was vulnerable to environmental hazards or otherwise unfit for habitation, this implied the need to resettle thousands of households.[47] As a result, the plan adopted Ingeocim's identification of areas in which landslides and floods were likely to cause major damage and loss of life. Bogotá's Directorate for Emergency Prevention and Response (DPAE) was then given the technical responsibility for the ongoing evaluation and monitoring of zones of high risk, and the Fund for Social Housing (Caja) was granted the authority to manage the relocation of populations inhabiting them.

At this moment, the zone of high risk enabled Bogotá's municipal government to confront the dual problems of insecurity and informality. While risk management had been a public and political concern since the 1980s, its migration to the city in the late 1990s and early 2000s depended on its unique ability to unite the two governmental imperatives dominant at that time. According to the objective of protecting life against potential threats, central to the Mockus administration, risk zones were a necessary component of the government's overall effort to govern crime, violence, and accidents. For regulating urban development and upgrading settlements lacking basic necessities, key concerns during Peñalosa's stint at City Hall, they offered a solution to areas that resisted legalization and formalization. Capable of adhering to both imperatives, the zone of high risk became a versatile technique for governing the spaces and populations of the urban periphery in Bogotá. Risk management could address problems ranging from crime and violence to landslide and flood, but it could also encompass different political objectives and ends—such as building a political constituency among the urban poor—without confronting the state and paramilitary forces known for persecuting activists or leaders with even vaguely radical agendas. The depoliticized, technical character of "risk" made it especially attractive as a framework within which to address the social and environmental problems of the urban periphery.

The Technical Diagnosis

Thus far we have seen how the calculative predictions leading to the designation of zones of high risk were subsequently incorporated into urban policy, planning, and government. This may give the impression that risk management, once established on a national and urban scale, has been relatively static. The problem, however, is that the topography of the city is not. The municipal government always recognized that this was the case; a caveat accompanying DPAE maps states: "The map of landslide threat is of a temporal nature, and therefore subject to conditions present at any given moment. Since these are changeable through time, the threat levels could be variable."[48] Because of the city's unstable ground, calculative predictions of risk had to be regularly monitored. Thus DPAE created an instrument called the *diagnóstico técnico* (technical diagnosis)—an on-site evaluation conducted by staff engineers and architects. During these visits, DPAE technicians perform visual inspections and qualitative assessments of both the inhabitability of the property and the infrastructure of the neighborhood. The technicians then recommend immediate action, if necessary, and decide whether the property should be included in the Caja's resettlement program.[49] As we will see, this draws DPAE technicians into a series of interactions both with inhabitants of these zones and with the nonhuman world.

The routine work of conducting a technical diagnosis reveals that the zone of high risk is not a static technique of government, but rather an ongoing effort to render the uncertain future an object of official decision-making in the present. As highlighted by the map of risk described above, these techniques are not the exclusive domain of government technicians; rather, they are constituted by encounters between these technicians and the spaces and populations subject to their authority and expertise. And although that encounter took place in 2006—before the governmental agencies responsible for risk management began to differentiate strictly between the "technical" expertise of DPAE and the "social" expertise of the Caja—the entangled relationality of these calculations persists. The following ethnographic account demonstrates that high-risk zones continue to be made and remade in situations involving government officials, beneficiaries of their programs, and the urban environment. Hybrid assemblages of human and nonhuman agents come together to produce risk management as a technique of government in Bogotá.

On the ride to the barrio of San Rafael, the two government technicians I'm accompanying, Tatiana and Miguel, explain the purpose of our trip. We're setting out to monitor risk in a neighborhood that borders the site of a 1999 landslide, which destroyed hundreds of houses and took several lives. This case of *remoción en masa* (a geological process combining subterranean and surface movement) is the largest of any Latin American city, they say, covering 110 hectares. We pass the Escarpment of San Rafael, which the DPAE regards as the phenomenon causing this mountain to rise in some places, fall in others, and occasionally open up to swallow houses into gaping crevices. Over 150 homes were affected by a second landslide in 2000; 85 more were toppled in 2001; and then, in 2002, a major movement of earth damaged over 800 dwellings in the same vicinity.[50] Although technical studies began in 1999 immediately after the initial disaster—and rescue, reconstruction, and resettlement efforts have been under way ever since—the area was not officially declared a zone of high risk until over a thousand properties had been damaged or destroyed.[51] Its official boundary was demarcated in 2004, and from that moment on it determined who would be entitled to the Caja's resettlement program.[52] However, the boundary of the risk zone—and therefore who has the right to housing subsidies and who does not, who is destined for relocation and who will remain—must remain flexible in order to keep up with the shifting ground beneath it.

The truck bumps and grinds up the steep, rutted dirt roads typical of the hillside settlements that make up the southern periphery of Bogotá. Tatiana points to a vast stretch of empty land once inhabited by over three thousand families (figure 2.1). She then indicates where mitigation works will soon begin to protect the neighborhoods surrounding the now evacuated zone of high risk from further damage. Drains will be installed to channel water, and retaining walls will be built to stabilize collapsing hillsides. Before starting work, however, DPAE must conduct house-by-house inspections to determine whether the phenomenon causing landslides in the adjacent area is also threatening this neighborhood. Far from inert, the zone's boundaries must be monitored regularly to keep up with a city in motion.

We're dropped off at the border separating the evacuated zone from a dense settlement of self-built houses that vary in size, material, and

FIG 2.1 Evacuated zone of high risk. Source: Photograph by author, 2009.

construction. Though some are two or three stories tall with concrete or brick facades, most are rudimentary one-floor dwellings made of cinder block, wood, and tin. As we begin our survey, a middle-age woman with a small child passes by and asks: "Are you here to evict us from our houses?" Responding to her perception of the work government does here in Ciudad Bolívar, Miguel reassures her: "No, we're from the Directorate of Emergency Prevention and Response and we're just monitoring the area."

Tatiana raps on a window of the first house on our list. A woman answers from behind a locked door, "Who is it?" Tatiana responds, "Good day. How is everything?" "Very well, thanks," answers the woman cautiously. Looking down at his map, Miguel asks her, "Is this lot number 10, Señora?" Somewhat tentatively, she responds, "Yes, it's lot 10."

"OK, good," Tatiana says as she begins to explain the purpose of our visit: "We're with the Directorate of Emergency Prevention and Response, and we are doing inspections of the houses on this block. Due to the landslide phenomenon we have behind us," she says gesturing toward the zone of high risk in the distance, "we need to verify whether you've recently noticed any cracks in the walls, floors, or roof of your house."

"No, I haven't noticed anything like that," the woman answers. Miguel follows with a further request: "Would you allow us to come in and look around and maybe take some photographs of the walls and the floor? Are you sure that your house has not been affected recently by any sort of cracking?" The woman hesitates for a moment before consenting. "I haven't noticed any cracks or anything like that. But sure, you can come in if you'd like."

The three of us enter, glance quickly at the walls, floors, and ceiling, take a few photographs, and then leave, thanking her for her time. Tatiana then scrolls down to "Block 2, Lot 10" on her list and next to it enters: "No apparent effects."

The rest of our monitoring day goes about like this. We move from house to house, introduce the purpose of our visit, ask whether the resident has noticed any recent cracking, and then conduct a brief inspection (figure 2.2). Though occasionally we have to skip properties where no one is home, many encounters are identical to the one described above. Sometimes, however, the head of the household is not so trusting and cooperative. On a number of occasions, we are told bluntly: "No, there's no cracking here." And when Tatiana or Miguel asks permission to conduct a brief inspection, the request is met with abrupt rejection: "No, at the moment, no." Perhaps it is simply an inconvenient time—a young mother feeding her newborn baby, for example. But in many cases there is noticeable hostility. Experience might lead people to assume that if government officials are knocking on doors today, they will be delivering eviction notices tomorrow. As far as the monitoring goes, however, these rejections do not pose a problem. Tatiana simply responds, "OK, fine, many thanks," and marks down on her list: "Entry not permitted. Resident reports no apparent effects."

I start to get bored, and find myself actually hoping that we'll stumble upon something exciting—a collapsing wall, a falling roof, perhaps a cracking floor. And eventually we do. On entering one house, we find fissures that to me look serious in both the walls of the bedroom and the living room floor. Looking concerned, Miguel snaps a number of photographs and then goes outside to examine the cinder blocks behind the cracking walls. He returns, informing the residents that their house is in danger of collapsing but that the problem is due to *deficiencia constructiva* (faulty construction) and not to *un fenómeno natural* (a natural phenomenon). As Tatiana makes note of this evaluation on her list and we return to the street, I begin to wonder

FIG 2.2 *Diagnóstico técnico* in action. Source: Photograph by author, 2010.

how one differentiates between these two types of damage. I ask, somewhat self-consciously: "How do you distinguish cracks caused by faulty construction from those caused by movement of the earth?"

Miguel patiently explains: "When there are problems with the way concrete is mixed, you see small cracks between the cinder blocks, telling you the builder did not use enough cement." I then look to Tatiana to get her view: "You just know when it's *mala construcción* [bad construction] and when it's *algo natural* [something natural]."[53]

We continue with our technical diagnosis, moving to an adjacent street bordering the evacuated area. Turning the corner, we stumble upon a mud-filled ditch where a water supply tube is actively leaking. Though originally installed by the utility company, it was later tapped into by households not formally served by it. Water gushes out of a thin rubber hose, which is most likely the work of the local *fontanero*, a self-employed water manager who installs informal connections, regulates flows, and fixes leaks. Miguel and Tatiana examine the ditch with great concern. In addition to the water escaping from the hose, the ditch collects and channels rainwater during the wet season, both of which further destabilize ground already dangerously unstable. Miguel and I follow the seepage to the point at which it eventually disappears beneath the foundation of a nearby house, while Tatiana marks down our exact location. "I'm going to have to alert Rosa," the *gestora local* (local manager) who represents DPAE at the neighborhood level. "She'll contact the water utility company and have them come remove the connection and repair the leak." Thinking we have finally discovered reason to declare this area a zone of high risk, I ask: "Will this affect the boundary and therefore who will be relocated?" "No, no, no," she responds; "we're looking for structural damage caused by *remoción en masa*. Anything beyond that is a different kind of problem. In fact," she goes on to explain, "it's good that we saw this; it means that any subsidence in the houses downhill from here is probably attributable to this." The recognition that landslides are a more-than-natural phenomenon officially justifies inaction.

The day is finally winding down and only one more property remains. Miguel knocks on the door and the woman who opens it looks at his yellow DPAE jacket and asks with a smile, "Are you coming to kick me out?" "No," Tatiana responds, "we're just monitoring the block to see if there are signs of movement and we haven't found any." "Too bad," the woman says, "*Ya me quiero ir!* [I want to get out of here!] I've been here for two years and I don't like this neighborhood. I don't like living up here on this hillside."

Still hoping that we will find evidence that the ground beneath her house is unstable, she invites us to come in and inspect. She guides us from room to room, showing us where the roof leaks when it rains and where the floor is not level—signs, she hopes, that will convince us that she should be eligible for resettlement. "Unfortunately," Tatiana informs her, "these problems have nothing to do with *remoción en masa*," or the geophysical movement occurring nearby. With this final inspection our technical diagnosis comes to an end, and the boundary remains as before.

This is the work that goes into making zones of high risk. It shows that these zones are far from inert boundaries conclusively designating the space of intervention for an established governmental technique. In their efforts to calculate the likelihood of landslide, government technicians are drawn into repeated interactions with inhabitants of these areas. In these interactions, expert assessments cannot be disentangled from those being made independently by nonexperts. Ultimately, such assessments depend on how both groups engage in the sometimes collaborative, sometimes contentious process of codifying the world in terms of risk. The boundaries of the zone might have been expanded to include these households had Tatiana and Miguel seen things differently, had people reported more recent damage, had their walls and floors cracked in another way. There is no infallible method of determining whether a fissure is the result of a poorly built house or the unstable ground beneath it—or perhaps both. Substandard materials and building techniques are widespread in the self-built settlements of the urban periphery, but faulty construction does not negate the probability of a landslide. And the decision to allow inspection or reveal damages clearly depends on such factors as mistrust of government or desire to relocate; it was often necessary to rely on the word of the residents. What we encountered during our inspections—collapsing houses, bursting water tubes, willing evacuees, their recalcitrant neighbors—did not collectively translate into a definitive change in the risk level of the area. According to the interactions that took place, data were collected and a decision was made. The neighborhood may collapse tomorrow, but it remains, at least for the time being, outside the zone of high risk.

Hybrid Threats

The institutionalization of risk management in Colombia relies on the construction of a boundary between threats of human and nonhuman origin. This split divides the field of governmental intervention by separating the world of people from the world of things and demarcating the domains of social and technical expertise. However, these divisions all too often break down in zones of high risk, where crime and violence are as common as sliding hillsides and cracking foundations. It is the entanglement of diverse dangers that ultimately matters to "at risk" populations. And it is the ability of "risk" to encapsulate multiple forms of threat that ultimately explains its versatility as a technique for governing the endangered city.

Before joining the government's resettlement program, Joaquín and Helena lived in a neighborhood called Nueva Esperanza on the southern periphery of Bogotá, sandwiched between dense urbanization on the flatlands and a forest reserve in the hills. In 1997, desplazados, rural migrants, and members of the urban poor began occupying this unpopulated area on the urban fringe. In what is known in Bogotá as an *invasión* (invasion), they cleared vegetation, excavated rocks, cut footpaths, and built rudimentary houses on the steep slopes without governmental consent. In 2003, Joaquín and Helena agreed to purchase an empty six-by-twelve meter plot of land there for 1.6 million pesos (US$800). They agreed to pay the man who owned it—or claimed to own it—monthly installments of 50,000 pesos (US$25) over the course of a few years. This allowed them to begin construction right away. They cut back on buying food to save money for building materials and cobbled together a small shack out of wood and tin. When we met in 2009, it was not here but rather in the living room of their new home in Alta Vista de Sidel, a low-income housing development where a number of former residents of Nueva Esperanza now reside. After studies conducted in 2003 and 2004, the area had been declared a zone of high risk and its inhabitants relocated elsewhere. Joaquín and Helena explained to me why they were so relieved to have been resettled: from the moment they arrived in Nueva Esperanza until the day they left, they were subjected to relentless threats. While the municipal government of Bogotá ultimately intervened to protect them from landslides, the dangers they had long faced did not conform to any neat separation of the human from the nonhuman world.

As Joaquín explained to me, they were from a part of Nueva Esperanza called El Valle—the most dangerous part of the settlement—where there were *autodefensas* (paramilitary groups), rampant street crime, and a concentration of *ollas de droga* (open-air drug markets). "One couldn't go outside after 8 p.m.," he said; "there were always shootouts and that sort of thing. It was a scary place to be." The paramilitaries took advantage of the insecurity by charging residents a *vacuna* ("vaccination," or protection fee). Joaquín and Helena's home was visited regularly by men with masks and guns who would come to collect weekly payments of 3,000 pesos (US$1.50). That was a meaningful sum to a couple who often made just a bit more than that for a day's work. But it was the fear of what would happen if they did not pay that weighed on them. They had been robbed multiple times, they told me. On one occasion, the burglars poisoned both of their dogs. One died, but they were able to resuscitate the other. "That's how one lived in Nueva Esperanza," Joaquín stressed, "always fighting to survive."

When the couple had initially settled in the area, public services were unavailable. Helena recalled, "*Todo pirateado* [Everything was pirated]." Water was distributed through narrow tubes, which illegally siphoned water from a storage tank on a nearby hilltop. These tubes always leaked, and that caused problems because it softened the earth and caused it to slide. Disposing of wastewater compounded the problem, since the only option was to dump it into the stream running down the hillside. "People were always getting sick," Helena said; "there were mosquitoes and rats everywhere." Right next to the stream were some sixty or seventy houses, and when it rained, the people living in them had to evacuate temporarily until the water level dropped. "If it rained all night," Joaquín recounted, "we'd make a bonfire, drink coffee, and stay up talking until morning." Staying elsewhere was not an option, since their belongings might be gone by the time they returned. So they would wait until the rains died down, and then move back in. The situation they described was one where everyday life was imperiled by a combination of hazards and there was no conceivable means of escape.

In Helena's telling, things got worse before they got better. Since the settlement's early days, a certain don Panadero had run the neighborhood. Everyone called him "don," a term of respect, since he was "the most fearsome criminal around," and "Panadero" because he owned a bakery. He controlled the sale of marijuana and *bazuco* (a cheap cocaine by-product) but also kept the area safe. "Do you see?" Helena asked rhetorically. "He was like the president of the neighborhood who was also a drug dealer." But then "those guys in masks started to come—*paramilitares*; they wanted to take over don Panadero's territory." They pursued that objective using techniques tried and tested over years of paramilitary activity throughout Colombia: surveillance, intimidation, extortion, and violence.

Helena described a day she was spending at home with Joaquín's elderly mother. Hearing a knock at the door and thinking Joaquín had arrived, she leaned out the window to welcome him. Instead she saw two bulky figures outfitted in green army jackets. Trying to remain calm, she asked whether she could help them in any way. "We're with the *grupos armados*," the men retorted. "You need to pay la vacuna." Having recently been robbed of the few valuable items they had, Helena told them that her household no longer had anything worth protecting. When they said it was a basic fee for security and that everyone had to pay, Helena tried to bargain. The men then pulled out weapons from under their jackets and pointed them at Helena, threatening to kill her unless she paid up. Helena felt she had no choice but to give them all the money she had in the house, and once she did the men walked away. Helen then looked out the window to see where they were going. Although the men had disappeared, one of Joaquín and Helena's neighbors appeared, asking what was going on.

At this point in the story, Joaquín interjected to make sure the implication was clear: "He was the one who brought them—our own neighbor!" He then left it to Helena to pick up where she left off.

She complained to the neighbor that she had just been threatened into paying a vacuna. "No, that's a good thing," he responded, "since they're going to get rid of all the drug addicts." Helena confirmed that this was indeed what they were doing. "That month they killed three kids," she remembered. "Cinco tiros en la cabeza le dieron a un muchacho" (They gave one of the guys five shots in the head). The *paras* would search for drug users, occasionally murdering them to send don Panadero a message. They were also intent on sending a message to the whole neighborhood.

> They'd go house to house of all the clean folks [*gente sana*], telling everyone, "Look, we're the ones doing the cleansing [*limpieza*]." People were scared and so they said, "Well, perhaps it's better that they finish off with those drug addicts because they are the ones who are robbing us. They are the ones who are breaking into our houses when we're not home." Of course, those people didn't realize that the paras were the ones organizing the robberies and that ultimately they wanted to take over the drug trade for themselves.

Eventually a violent turf war ensued, with groups of armed men with revolvers fighting it out in the streets. The police and the military turned a blind eye until, as Joaquín saw it, the paras paid them off. Don Panadero was captured and jailed, and "the paras eventually took over and ran things in the same way don Panadero had . . . only with more authority, with more fear."

Beginning to understand the intense pressure Helena and Joaquín were under in Nueva Esperanza, I asked what they could possibly do to protect themselves. "Say hi to everyone and be friendly," Joaquín responded. "Make friends with them," Helena added. "If you become their enemy, you won't even make it safely home. They watch for *sapos* [informants], and when they think you are informing, they wait until you are walking alone and then attack you. 'Ahhh, *a ese cucho péguele un susto* [Give that old man a scare]!'" Unable to complain to the police, they kept their mouths shut and tried to carry on with their lives. And fleeing was not a viable option, either. "If someone is hiding, they say, 'Uyyy, they're hiding for a reason.' If someone leaves the neighborhood, they say, 'Uyyy, those guys, why did they leave? They left because they're sapos.' And then they start trying to track you down. So, you see, one has to just stay put and keep quiet. What else can one do?"

Before long, things got worse. Joaquín described that it had been raining nonstop for a week and that the hoses supplying the settlement with water were not being maintained. Small streams were developing along the steep slopes, and loose earth dislodged by people clearing new lots began sliding into existing homes. Joaquín also noted that people were not replacing the wooden posts supporting their roofs and that many of them had begun to rot. Eventually, Joaquín concluded, "the earth couldn't hold up any longer and started to slide. It took out homes . . . *bam, bam, bam* . . . they all fell to bits. The stream turned into a flow of mud and buried the houses. Roofs, walls, gas tanks, tables, pots, televisions . . . Everything was swept away." The rains continued for three more days. Fearing for their own lives, Joaquín and Helena lay awake at night. They heard the sounds of other shacks collapsing and of their inhabitants shouting for help. Although there were no deaths or serious injuries, when the weather dried out a total of 129 homes were damaged and approximately 60 families left without homes. An emergency situation was then declared by the Bogotá municipal government, and the process of evacuating the neighborhood began.

The Caja and DPAE both arrived to respond to the disaster in Nueva Esperanza and to facilitate the relocation of the remaining households. The police went house to house, Helena recalled, forcing people to abandon their homes. "They kicked us out by force [*Nos sacaron a las malas*]. They said they were protecting our lives, the lives of everyone. . . . So they were knocking down doors and dragging people out. Those who couldn't walk, they would carry them. People would say, 'No, why? I don't want to leave. Where am I supposed to go?' They would respond, 'Our orders are to evacuate you to save your lives. You are in a high-risk site and the rest of the mountain could, at any moment, come down on top of you and you'd be trapped.'" Joaquín and Helena refused to go far, camping out close enough to their house to prevent looting. Despite DPAE's prohibition on reentering the area, they returned to their shack at night to sleep. "But we were afraid," Joaquín remembered. "We would fall asleep and something would startle us and wake us up. I mean, we were thinking that . . ." His voice trailed off, accentuating the anticipation and fear they were feeling.

Helena chimed in: "We thought that the mountain was going to come crashing down on top of us. I mean, we were just a block away from the houses that were destroyed. We were so scared. We were saying, 'No, what if we're sleeping and it starts to rain and that mountain starts to fall?' Well, we were so worried since people were saying, 'The way that it collapsed last night, it could rain more today and collapse again!'"

By day, DPAE carried on with their evaluation of the likelihood of another disaster. After taking extensive photographs, measurements, and GPS coordinates, they declared the entire area a zone of high risk and ordered the relocation of everyone still living there. "We told them we'd go," Joaquín said, "but in the middle of the night we just went right back." When the Caja then followed up with household surveys, they were met with suspicion from residents. According to Joaquín, "We didn't believe them. We were all saying, 'No, those people have their studies and all that, and they're going to try to confuse us and get us to sign something, and then kick us out.' So we decided to be stubborn about turning in any papers, giving them our identification." The general perception was that the Caja was trying to lure people to leave their homes so they could demolish the area and then cut off support. Many were afraid that they would be left homeless.

Helena and Joaquín stayed in place for an additional six months. They remained skeptical about the relocation plans and were determined to keep their house. "We had gone through so much to build this little shack. We carried each piece of wood up here, one at a time," Helena said. But before long their house started showing signs that it, too, was on the verge of collapse. It had started to creak, and the wooden posts had begun to crack. This was not the only fear that was on their mind. "After the emergency, things had gotten much more dangerous," Joaquín added. "Most people had left." Helena chimed in:

Yeah, it really emptied out, and practically the only people who had stayed behind were the dangerous ones. One night we were coming back late from selling plastic bags and incense on the street, around 10 or 11 p.m. On the way, some people grabbed Joaquín and told him to give up his money. They knocked him down, broke his foot. And so he ran limping back to the house. And so we said, "No, if that's what is going to happen, hopefully God will protect us. But around here they stab people. It's not good. What if they stab us and leave us to die?" So we said, "No, it's better that we go."

Meanwhile, they started hearing stories about former neighbors whose rental accommodation had been paid for by the Caja for five months and who were being taken to see more permanent housing alternatives. "I make 18,000 pesos (US$9) a day," Joaquín reported. "I could not take the risk." But when they finally saw with their own eyes that the first group of families had been relocated in new homes, he and Helena decided to leave once and for all.

This is how things look from the perspective of those living in a zone of high risk. Survival in the neighborhood was not just a struggle against threats of *human* origin, since fears of crime and violence intermingle with threats of landslide and flood. The experience of everyday life on the urban periphery is often shaped by multiple forms of endangerment. And this is, of course, a reality that DPAE's risk calculations do not and cannot pretend to capture. It was after being repeatedly robbed and threatened, in addition to fearing their house would collapse, that Joaquín and Helena sought to escape Nueva Esperanza. They saw the governmental resettlement program based on the imperative to protect their lives from *environmental* risk to be the only way to escape from a mix of dangers—a mix that never conformed to the separate realms of social and physical problems, human and nonhuman causes, political and technical solutions. Although these distinctions matter regarding how risk functions as a technique of urban government, it is the polysemic character of risk on an experiential level that gives it credibility and persuasiveness in the eyes of those governed by it. Like the mayoral administrations who created and supported the relocation program for households in zones of high risk, those subject to the program also take advantage of their ostensibly technical, apolitical character.

An Enlivened Field of Intervention

The risk maps adorning the walls of government offices in Bogotá, such as the one that appeared at the beginning of this chapter, often made their way out into the field. They were a tool for governing not only at a distance, but also face to face. On one occasion, I accompanied two Caja social workers to visit the homes of a few holdouts who were refusing relocation. They brought with them a risk map in support of their case. However, when they arrived at their destination—a one-room wooden hut at the edge of a large swath of evacuated land—its occupant, don Luis, greeted them with a map collection of his own (figure 2.3). An elderly man with a head of gray hair

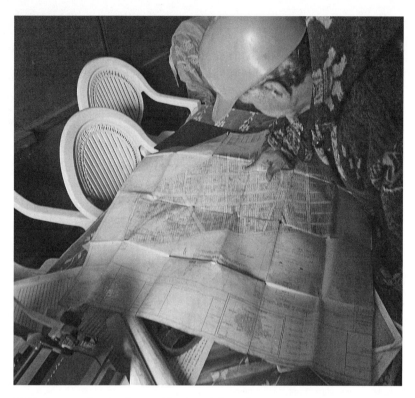

FIG 2.3 A map collection. Source: Photograph by author, 2010.

topped by a bright orange safety helmet, don Luis had once been a neighborhood leader. Among his few possessions was a typewriter he would often use when drawing up letters or filling out forms for his illiterate neighbors. His map collection was another resource he relied on when advocating on their behalf. But since he was now one of the few left, it was enrolled this time in defense of his own claims. His collection contained decades-old planning documents since the moment his settlement was legalized by the municipal government. Unrolling one after another, don Luis narrated a local history of progressive formalization to counter the state's arguments urging relocation. The Caja social workers who made the trip were surprised to have encountered an enlivened field of intervention that demanded more than the single risk map they had brought with them. Don Luis was later incensed to discover that the risk designation of his parcel trumped its legal status, but his map collection had managed to buy him some extra time.

The rise of risk management in Bogotá not only tells us something about the political climate in Colombia over the past two decades. It offers insight into a general pattern in which the informal settlements that predominate in cities of Asia, Africa, and Latin America, along with the populations inhabiting them, are brought into novel governmental frameworks. It also reflects another broad phenomenon, wherein risk management along with other security mechanisms are emerging across a range of apparently disparate domains in both the global North and South as essential elements of "good governance."[54] These widespread transformations can be understood by examining how and why risk becomes a way of governing the uncertain future of cities and urban life in a place like Bogotá, and by focusing critical attention not only on the production of unequal geographies of vulnerability but also on actually existing attempts to ameliorate them by municipal governments and other urban political actors. The fundamentally mutable object of risk reveals the continuous work required for rendering the uncertain future the basis for governmental intervention. This has both methodological and conceptual consequences, as it raises questions about the degree to which "risk" denotes a stable field of meaning, a coherent set of techniques, or a common phenomenon. While an affirmative response may be possible on an abstract level, we must recognize the heterogeneous practices that constitute the everyday work of governing risk.

Much of this is acknowledged by scholars of risk, yet their analyses tend to objectify the world being governed, as if that world were inert and stationary. Yet the people and things subject to techniques of risk management often play an active role in their own governing, at times complicating, at others facilitating, and sometimes even inciting governmental thought and action. Although technical experts attempt to separate themselves from the humans and nonhumans they seek to define, measure, and manage, they rarely succeed at doing so; they almost always remain entangled with them. As a result, risk designations encompass concerns that far exceed statistical calculations of geophysical threat. And since zones of high risk contain a range of problems—from poverty, crime, and violence to landslides, floods, and earthquakes—assessments made by government officials are often incongruent with those of governed populations. At least culturally speaking, the relativity of risk is a truism. My reason for highlighting it is neither to emphasize that risk is socially constructed nor to fault governments for simplifying more complex realities. It is to demonstrate that the discrepancy between "official" and "popular" forms of reasoning about risk does not interfere with the work of government. This mutability is precisely what makes risk productive both as a technique for governing cities and as a domain within which "at risk" citizens make claims upon the state.

These insights lead to a more nuanced view of the politics of security, the government of risk, and the overarching imperative to protect poor and vulnerable urban populations from environmental hazards. Moreover, they enable us to consider whether explicitly acknowledging the hybridity of technical and social expertise, the fluid boundaries separating expert and nonexpert knowledge, and the entangled relationality between governors and the governed could lead to more effective, egalitarian, and equitable approaches to securing the urban milieu. As this becomes an ever more pressing pursuit—not just in Bogotá, but in other endangered cities throughout the world—we must grapple with the undeniable fact that urban environments and their populations do not stand by while techniques of risk management are applied to them. Governments, as well as those who analyze them, might do well to acknowledge that risk always rests on shaky ground.

3

GENEALOGIES OF ENDANGERMENT

Signs of Danger

How was the imperative to govern risk in Bogotá made meaningful, and what sorts of relations between the state and its subjects were expected to follow? We can begin to answer this question by examining the different ways in which endangerment was represented in public spaces throughout the city on billboards, at bus stops, and in print. Offering information, warnings, and advice to the casual passerby, these representations reflected official expectations for how society, the state, and the individual were expected to behave in relation to potential dangers, from the exceptional to the routine. A prime example was emblazoned on a temporary wall surrounding a construction site in a gritty area just a few blocks west of city hall (figure 3.1). The billboard contained the image of a fireman rescuing a young girl accompanied by the text: "Every day in Bogotá we conduct thirty-eight operations to protect the life of our residents." The fireman is outfitted in full protective clothing, helmet, and respiratory apparatus, while the girl is in shorts, T-shirt, and tennis shoes. Female, young, helpless, scared, perhaps poor—she is a figure of extreme vulnerability. Her shirt and shoes are soiled, suggesting exposure to hardship or danger. The fireman, on the other hand, is male, confident, heroic, and strong. In contrast to the young girl held in his arms, his body is erect and in motion. And stamped on his helmet is the official seal of the

Cada día
en Bogotá

Realizamos 38 operativos para
proteger la vida de nuestros
habitantes.

Bogotá sin indiferencia   Porque es tu derecho!

FIG 3.1 "Every day in Bogotá . . ." Source: Photograph by author, 2008.

city government, identifying him as the personification of a patriarchal state committed to protecting the lives of its feminized and infantilized subjects.

As such, this billboard shared common ground with the municipal government's relocation program for households living in zones of high risk. In both cases, the stated objective of protecting vulnerable populations from harm was the same, as was its moral and political justification: "Porque es tu derecho!" (Because it's your right!) No one is asking, yet the billboard preemptively responds to the implicit question "What authorizes the state to exercise its powers of protection?" If the fireman were rescuing this young girl from a burning building, as might be inferred, she and her family would certainly be grateful; it is unlikely they would demand justification. But there are other situations in which such intervention might not be welcome. The girl may be living in unsanitary conditions because her family is poor, and the government may be taking her into custody. Perhaps her home is in an area declared unsafe for habitation and her family is being forcefully relocated. In these situations, one could imagine the demand to know what legitimates such interventions. Hence the need to affirm that the state is working not, for example, to protect private property or to maintain social order, but to uphold her right to life.

What exactly is the threat from which the fireman is rescuing this young girl? We do not know whether she is being saved from a blazing inferno, from a family unfit to care for her, from the destruction wrought by an earthquake, or perhaps even from a terrorist attack. The danger is imminent and demands action, yet it remains invisible and unidentified. Its identity is perhaps known only to those with the authority and expertise to define who or what is dangerous. The solid yellow background out of which the fireman emerges is a tabula rasa. Attributable to anyone or anything, the threat serves as a blank screen onto which viewers' fears may be projected. It is assumed that Bogotá is a city of dangers—explosions, landslides, robberies, murders, kidnappings—and that its inhabitants are perpetually under threat. Unlike the rights of the individual that legitimate the protective power of the state, the threat to which this power responds need not be explicitly affirmed.

Throughout Bogotá, a variety of images conveyed to the city's inhabitants the message that they were in danger. Occasionally the threats were visible, and they ranged from everyday household hazards to large-scale catastrophes. A sign on a newspaper kiosk in the city center depicted a young girl in front of a stove (figure 3.2, right). She is tilting a frying pan full of scalding hot oil toward her face. The warning, put out by the city government, informs us: "159 children suffered burns in the home last year." Adjacent to it was another one of a boy reaching for a pair of scissors and a knife lying at eye level on the kitchen counter (figure 3.2, left). This sign also reports precise statistics of injury: "285 children suffered wounds from sharp objects in the home last year." And the message beneath both images indicates to whom these warnings are addressed: "Preventing household accidents is everyone's responsibility."

Like the billboard of the fireman rescuing the little girl, these signs referenced a fundamentally patriarchal relationship between the state and its subjects—the latter were depicted as small children exposed to danger and in need of protective care. However, a number of features set them apart from the first image. First of all, the threat is made apparent. Rather than an invisible danger that can refer to anyone or anything, encountered here are the everyday household hazards of hot oil in a frying pan and an unprotected pair of scissors. These are not catastrophic events like fires or explosions; rather, they are regularly occurring accidents. Thus the threat is domesticated and

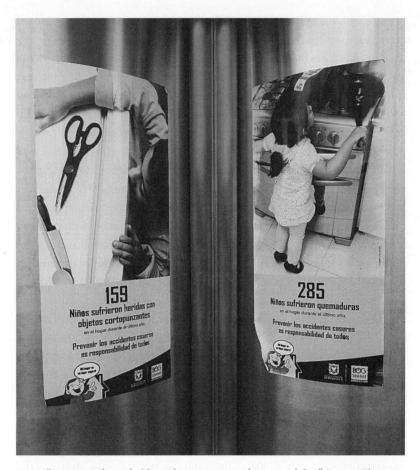

FIG 3.2 "Preventing household accidents is everyone's responsibility." Source: Photograph by author, 2008.

the home is identified as the space of danger. And this move to the private realm of the household also brings with it a shift in emphasis from protection to prevention, as well as a redirection of accountability. Rather than depicting a state saving the lives of its subjects, these signs maintain that preventing accidents in the home is "everyone's responsibility."

Bus stops around town displayed a series of posters with the warning "An earthquake could occur at any moment." The portentous prognosis was followed by a list of "six smart moves [*jugadas maestras*] that could save your life" (figure 3.3). These techniques for "mastering" danger ranged from securing furniture that might cause injury, defining evacuation routes, and

FIG 3.3 "Six smart moves." Source: Photograph by author, 2008.

preparing emergency supplies to reinforcing the home against seismic activity, locating safety zones, and carrying out damage inventories after the event. A handsome young man wearing the yellow vest typical of the DPAE, the governmental agency sponsoring this campaign, points his finger directly outward from the sign toward the viewer. And beneath the list of "smart moves" the public is expected to learn is the simultaneously reassuring and disconcerting motto: "In Bogotá, we are preparing ourselves."

Responsibility was again directed to each and every individual, and the home was identified as the space of potential safety and danger. The state was personified not as a heroic protector or cautious caretaker, but as a technical adviser telling people how to protect their own lives. Rather than depicting the governmental response to a catastrophic event that has already happened or reporting on the number of domestic accidents that have occurred in the previous year, the poster directed attention forward in time toward an unpredictable natural disaster—an earthquake that "could occur at any moment." Furthermore, this warning did not assert that lives would be protected by the state; instead it affirmed that all bogotanos are, or at least ought to be, immersed in the ongoing and incomplete process of preparing themselves for an event which cannot be prevented and from which one must not expect protection.

Occasionally threats were depicted in animated form, such as in the advertisement for an emergency hotline used to report suspicious activity (figure 3.4). The heading read: "I take the safe road. If you see something strange or dangerous, immediately dial 123." In the image, a tortoise, whose gender is unspecified, encounters a male figure while walking a dog on a city street. The latter is dressed respectably in a business suit and is carrying a briefcase. But in reality he is a malicious, dark-faced wolf in sheep's clothing, hiding behind a white mask, and his briefcase contains an explosive device about to detonate. Recognizing the figure's true identity and intentions, the tortoise acts with the prudence and caution for which it is known proverbially and calls the emergency hotline. In its vigilance, the tortoise is doing a job that pertains to all responsible urban citizens. A message below the wolf tells us: "Security is a shared goal!"

This type of threat may be encountered anywhere in the public space of the city. One must therefore be on guard at all times. But the threat is disguised—anyone could be a wolf. And thus preventing such an attack depends on inculcating the public with suspicion, and it presumes the average

FIG 3.4 "I take the safe road." Source: Secretaría de Gobierno.

citizen's ability to know how to detect and decipher signs of danger. The threat is not an unpredictable future event, like an earthquake, for which one can only hope to be sufficiently prepared. Nor is it the sort of danger whose probability can be calculated across the population, as with domestic accidents. It follows no discernable logic, but can be prevented if people are alert and act quickly and vigilantly. No heroic savior is swooping in to protect the vulnerable, nor are expert advisers working to ensure everyone's safety. Although the imperative to dial "123" invokes the ultimate power of the state to intervene, the job of providing security depends on each and every individual. A population of citizen watchdogs (or watch-tortoises, as the case may be) leads to collective safety.

All the signs mentioned thus far appeared in public places in and around the city center. A final one, however, was set into the steep hillside of a self-built settlement on the southern periphery of Bogotá (figure 3.5). In contrast to the others, this sign had only the solid orange background that conventionally accompanies warning messages overlaid with bold, block lettering. The text communicated both a firm directive ("Protect your family") and a stern admonition ("For your safety, do not purchase lots in zones of high risk"). The sign identified itself with the insignia of the municipal government of Bogotá as well as with the name of the local governing body. The expertise required to determine risk was clearly in the hands of the state, as was the authority to issue the prohibitive injunction against settling in a high-risk zone. The threat, however, remained unspecified.

Among government officials, zona de alto riesgo referred to a technical designation denoting an area vulnerable to landslides, floods, and other environmental hazards. Its meaning, however, was more ambiguous for local viewers: it referenced the responsibility to protect one's family from danger and, since this area was unsafe, to look elsewhere for housing. The state asserted its knowledge of what must be done to ensure everyone's safety, and by informing the public it performed a protective function. But aside from providing a phone number to call for additional information, the sign instructed viewers that the ultimate responsibility for protecting life was theirs. Notably absent when compared to the previous examples are gestures toward prevention; though it directed potential settlers away from this area, nothing was being done to reduce the probability of landslide. Preparedness was also sidelined, since there was no indication of how to get ready for an

FIG 3.5 "Protect your family." Source: Photograph by author, 2009.

event that will likely, or perhaps inevitably, occur. Rather, the state accepted that a disaster may happen and enjoined people to do what was prudent to protect themselves from it.

The sign's intended audience was not the average bogotano, as in the previous examples, but the poor and working-class settlers who either lived in, or were likely to move to, the rough edges of the city. It implied that where the viewer was standing (or perhaps living) was unsafe. For those who knew the area, the sign's location meant something more. The ground on which it stood had been occupied by dwellings similar to those remaining adjacent to it. The families once living in them were relocated by the municipal government, and their shacks subsequently demolished. Since 2003, the Caja has been in charge of resettling populations living in zones of high risk. Areas cleared of habitation were frequently "invaded," as they say, by others in need of a place to settle, hence the sign's prohibition against buying lots here. While the Caja subsidized the relocation of those inhabiting the area when it was designated a high-risk zone, it did not allocate the same benefits to those who arrived after the fact. Simultaneously prohibiting some while entitling others, the resettlement program employed a combination of techniques in the name of safeguarding the lives of its subjects.

Taken together, these signs reflect how the condition of endangerment shapes the terrain of political engagement between the state and its subjects in contemporary Bogotá—a phenomenon designated here as the *endangered city*. Each conveyed the message that the city is a space of threat and implied that the pursuit of security ought to extend from the scale of the city down to that of the home. Common to them was also the assumption that life is not a resource to be prolonged, cultivated, or improved, but a precarious possession perpetually in danger of being harmed or taken away. However, their projections of potential threat differed, as did their ascriptions of authority and responsibility and their targets and techniques of intervention. Alongside references to the state's duty to actively protect lives and allusions to the imperative that people must be disciplined to avoid dangers were indications that free, autonomous individuals are responsible for preparing themselves for events likely to occur. Confounding the epochal claims of social theories of risk, liberal governance, and modernity, there is no overarching logic of power that replaces what came before; rather, there is an assemblage of overlapping technical, ethical, and political guidelines for how society, the state, and the individual are expected to behave. In highlighting the coexistence of what "before and after" approaches commonly relegate to different periods of history, these signs suggest that the field of government intervention organized around endangerment is a problem space in which heterogeneous imperatives coexist and intersect.

The remainder of this chapter draws upon ethnographic research conducted alongside the social workers who managed the municipal government's resettlement program for families living in recently designated zones of high risk. Based on daily interactions between government officials and this program's beneficiaries, as well as interviews with both groups, it highlights the state-subject relations embedded within techniques of risk management and the imperative to protect vulnerable lives. This imperative institutes a new regime for governing urban spaces and populations, but in doing so it draws upon and is constituted by multiple genealogies of power. In addition to its recognizably "liberal" and "neoliberal" characteristics, risk management in Bogotá is saturated with other rationalities of rule, particularly kinship, patronage, and religion. The relations of government encapsulated in the endangered city contain a mix of elements that resist easy categorization.

Making Sense

The warning signs analyzed above attest to the fact that the municipal government of Bogotá uses educational campaigns to raise awareness among the general public about danger. Instilling a collective ethos of risk management is a specific objective of the Caja's resettlement program. Caja staff refer to this as a process of *sensibilización*. Although no direct translation exists, the adjective from which it derives, *sensible*, equates to "sensitive," or conscious of and responsive to one's surroundings. The closely related verb *sensibilizar* means "to make aware" or "to raise awareness." When the process of sensibilización is directed at an individual, it implies the need to educate someone to see, feel, or comprehend what is going on around them. When it involves a group of people or the general public, sensibilización aims to increase awareness of and responsibility for an issue, such as domestic violence or racial discrimination. The sensibility implied in both cases is perceptual, such as the ability to sense something in the external environment, as well as moral, as in expressing adequate concern for an existing problem. In the context of risk management in Bogotá, sensibilización sets the terms according to which the poor in Bogotá should behave in relation to future threats.[1]

The social workers staffing the Caja's field office in Ciudad Bolívar were charged with facilitating this sensibility among those subject to the resettlement program. As an informal policy guiding their work, sensibilización implied the formation of new values, behaviors, and concerns among the "at risk" population. A young social worker, Carmela, explained further. A subjective transformation must take place, she said, "so that the families accept and participate in their own resettlement." This meant that Carmela and her colleagues felt the responsibility to foster an awareness that their lives may be in danger: "We work with quite a difficult population. Therefore, what one does as a social worker is make them conscious, that is, enable them to be conscious that the situation in which they are in risks their lives and the lives of their children, and that every time they go to work they don't know whether their children will arrive safely, whether their children are all right, whether there will be some natural disaster, or whether their house will collapse." Although members of this population were routinely exposed to a wide range of threats—robbery, kidnapping, violence, landslide, extortion, sickness, and unemployment, among others—the Caja assumed the pedagogical role of educating them how to be conscious of and concerned about these threats.

On the one hand, sensibilización carried the implicit assumption that those subject to the resettlement program did not have the capacity to protect and care for themselves and that the municipal government must intervene on their behalf.[2] On the other hand, Caja staff often stressed the concept of *co-responsabilidad*, or the responsibility shared between resettlement beneficiaries and the state. Yolanda, the coordinator of the Caja's field office in the peripheral locality of Ciudad Bolívar, explained this to me in the following terms:

> Let's say that there is a responsibility that applies as much to the state as to the families living in the high-risk area. The state did not put them there, nor will we solve their housing problems as a constitutional right. From the moment at which the zone of high risk is designated, carrying out the [resettlement] process should be the *co-responsabilidad* of the two parties. What does this entail? It entails that the families recognize that they are equally responsible: they have to submit the documentation required of them, show they were living there when the risk designation took place, prove that they possess titles corresponding to the property, search for alternative solutions, attend meetings, etc. In addition, it is their responsibility to be supportive [*solidario*] of the entire process.

In targeting a population assumed unable to recognize and respond to the dangers they face, and in training them to carry out their own relocation, the Caja distributed the responsibility for risk among individual households. In this sense, sensibilización resembles the technique of "responsibilization," which has been a cornerstone of neoliberal reforms of the welfare state and the relations of government associated with it.[3] The poor and the vulnerable should no longer expect the state to provide them with security; they must learn to accept responsibility for their own protection by prudentially governing themselves.

That said, sensibilización does not only aim to create rational, responsible, and self-governing "neoliberal subjects." Caja staff also frequently emphasized the importance of educating members of the urban poor in the appropriate legal and political grammar in which to claim their rights. As Carlos put it on one occasion: "It's about teaching them the rules of the game and how to play it." For example, Caja social workers often joked about their beneficiaries' misuse of bureaucratic terminology: saying *suicidio* (suicide) when they meant *subsidio* (subsidy), demanding *vivienda indigna* (wretched housing) instead of *vivienda digna* (decent housing), referring to their *previos* (an adjective meaning "previous") rather than their *predios* (lands), and mistaking Davivienda (a local bank) for the Caja de la Vivienda Popular (the governmental housing agency) or de Páez (a mountain in southern Colombia) for DPAE (Bogotá's risk management agency). Ridiculing resettlement beneficiaries for their lack of bureaucratic fluency reinforces hierarchies between governors and the governed. But as Carlos implied, his job was to train the latter to become competent in governmental discourse in order to be recognized as deserving of certain entitlements.

Other aspects of sensibilización aimed to increase the state's presence in the lives of its subjects. According to Yolanda, the coordinator of the Ciudad Bolívar field office:

> The sensibilización that I think is the most important in Ciudad Bolívar is that the people feel we are on their side . . . as friends and not as enemies. . . . I've noticed that in every meeting with the community, they expect to fight with the state because they believe state institutions are to be fought with. Therefore, I believe the most difficult work is to make them understand otherwise, that we have moved over to their side, which in other words is to "sensibilize them" [*sensibilizarlos*] to a different model of government.

Yolanda, like many Caja managers and staff, was a member of the Polo Democratico Alternativo, the left-of-center political party that occupied the mayor's office in Bogotá from 2004 to 2011. Teresa, director of the Caja's social team, told me that the resettlement program had been central to both Lucho Garzón's (2004–7) and Samuel Moreno's (2008–11) commitment to governing the city in the interest of the people and to building a political constituency among the urban poor. She reminded me of their campaign slogans—*Bogotá sin indiferencia* (Bogotá without indifference) and *Bogotá positiva* (Positive Bogotá)—and emphasized that they were not empty rhetoric. "Truly," she said, "they represent the demands [*reivindicaciones*] of the communities." When independent Enrique Peñalosa was mayor (1998–2002), Teresa told me, resettlement was not conceived in the same way. It required families to match their government subsidy with an equal amount of credit, and if they could not acquire the latter, they would not qualify for the former. Many families were forced to relocate with only the value of their existing property (usually around 1 million pesos, or US$500). As Teresa put it, "All you can do with a million pesos is move back to a zone of high risk. Garzón understood this," she underlined, "and pushed the city council to double the subsidy. Since 2007, the program has taken off." Risk management provided a technical language in which to address the social and environmental problems of the urban periphery and achieve an electoral majority—all this in a political climate dominated by a conservative national government known for cracking down on anything resembling radical ideology. Connecting the resettlement program and the process of sensibilización to the overall goal of increasing ties between the state and its subjects in the peripheral settlements of Bogotá, Teresa concluded: "This is the *modelo de gobierno distinto* [different model of government] I'm talking about." How, then, to think about these emerging ways of governing in relation to what came before?

Regimes of Housing

During my fieldwork, the Caja's resettlement program was organized by a division of labor separating "technical" from "social" expertise. The former was possessed primarily by the technicians of the DPAE and by the architects and engineers of the Caja's *equipo técnico* (technical team). Those who staffed the Caja's field office in Ciudad Bolívar were members of the *equipo social* (social team) and were trained mostly in social psychology, sociology, or social work. This office was the resettlement program's hub, where its beneficiaries interacted on a daily basis with those whose job it was to facilitate the process of relocation. It was also my primary field site, and I spent the majority of my days sitting beside Caja social workers as they attended to members of the "at risk" population.

I was often curious how these professionals understood the technical designations of risk that determined who was eligible for resettlement benefits. On one occasion, I took advantage of a lull in activity to strike up a conversation with Daniel, a young sociologist with a ponytail and glasses who had worked for the Caja for six months. I asked him with a hint of skepticism: "Do *you* believe that the areas being evacuated are zones of high risk?" My question was intended to elicit critical reflection on these designations; instead, it was met with disbelief. Daniel responded: "You've been with us on a number of visits [to the high-risk zones]. Haven't you noticed the conditions people are living in, that they are extremely poor?" Startled by the implication, I tried a slightly different tack: "I mean, why is it that there are no zones of high risk in the wealthier parts of the city?" Again, Daniel looked at me bewildered.

After this conversation and others like it, I became frustrated by my inability to elicit critical reflection on Bogotá's zones of high risk. It was not until a friend was visiting from Venezuela that I began to realize what was going on. He asked: "What do people in Bogotá call 'slums' (or what, in Caracas, we refer to as barrios)?" I hesitated: was it possible that I didn't know the local term for the settlements in which I had been conducting fieldwork? "In Bogotá," I said, "barrio is a generic term for 'neighborhood.' I live in the barrio of Chapinero Alto and it is far from a slum." I then scrolled through what I knew from other cities in the region: in Lima, they are called *pueblos jovenes*; in Buenos Aires, *villas miseria*; in Rio de Janeiro, *favelas*. Even in Medellín, Colombia's second city, I knew they had a name—*comunas*. I had read historical accounts of Bogotá's *tugurios*, but I had never heard the term used. And while people refer to *invasiones* (invasions), this denotes illegal occupations, whereas many settlers purchased their lots and have since seen them legally recognized. I then realized that the problem was due less to my ethnographic incompetence than to the disappearance of ways of explicitly naming spaces of poverty in the city. "Well," I concluded somewhat ironically, "I think they're called zonas de alto riesgo."

Recognizing that "slums" no longer had a popular name in Bogotá—that the technical category "zone of high risk" is the only one that came close—helped me understand Daniel's response to my questions.[4] For Daniel and other Caja social workers, "risk" referred not just to a technical calculation of the likelihood of future harm, but to a broad range of social problems, such as poverty, inequality, and marginality. Accordingly, my question about the validity of the state's designation of high-risk zones was equivalent to having doubted the existence of the poor in Bogotá. To imply that zones of high risk were not physical realities but rather governmental inventions was like suggesting that poverty was merely a social construct. And as for my question of whether there were also high-risk zones in wealthy parts of the city, it was tantamount to asking whether there were poor people who lived in rich neighborhoods. Although social problems, such as poverty, had by no means disappeared in Bogotá, they had been displaced within what Foucault called the "art of governing" or "the reasoned way of governing best."[5] In the endangered city, social problems are frequently denoted indirectly through other idioms, such as "risk."

This is reminiscent of what Nikolas Rose famously named "the death of the social," or the broad transformation of political rationalities that occurred in many parts of the world during the second half of the twentieth century as social security mechanisms central to welfare state policy were discredited and dismantled.[6] Since adopting a new constitution in 1991, Colombia has implemented a number of political and economic reforms that have sought to transfer responsibility from the state to the community or the individual and to prescribe technical, market-based solutions for what, in other times and places, have been understood as social or political problems.[7] On the scale of the city, reforms in the name of competitiveness, efficiency, and accountability have decentralized state power, privileged technical expertise, deregulated land and housing markets, and devolved the provision of some basic services to the private sector. In an ideological climate in which governmental expenditure on social programs is labeled pejoratively *asistencialismo* (a neologism akin to "welfarism"), the living conditions of the poor, while not rendered invisible, are now understood and addressed in other terms.

The municipal agency Daniel worked for went through parallel shifts throughout the twentieth century (see table 3.1). Public housing in Bogotá dates back to the epidemic of Spanish influenza in 1918–19, which infected approximately one hundred thousand people in the capital city and took fifteen hundred lives.[8] Medical experts and city councilmen argued that the disease had been spread by working-class neighborhoods with poor housing conditions, and legislation was passed requiring all municipal governments to dedicate a percentage of their overall budget to the provision of "hygienic housing for the proletariat" (*habitaciones higiénicas para la clase proletaria*).[9] By the 1930s, public concern for hygiene was overshadowed by a state-led drive for economic modernization and the related imperative to house the growing population of urban industrial laborers. When the Caja de la Vivienda Popular—literally, the Fund for Popular Housing—was created by an agreement between the national and municipal governments in 1942, its mandate was to build *barrios populares modelos*, or model neighborhoods for the popular classes.[10] This lasted until 1959, when the Caja ceased constructing housing and instead began using public funds to acquire lands on

TABLE 3.1 Schematic Comparison of Governmental Housing Regimes in Bogotá, 1918–present

	Target of intervention	Technical approach	Political rationality	Projected future
1918–42	Unhealthy	Public health standards, public housing construction	Hygiene	Healthy, disease-free city
1942–60	Workers	Public housing construction, model popular neighborhoods	Modernization, industrialization	Progress, development
1960s–70s	The poor	Acquisition and selling of lots, social housing	Poverty alleviation	Equality, betterment
1980s–90s	Marginal and illegal	Slum eradication and upgrading, formalization	Urban renewal	Formality, legality
1996–present	At risk, vulnerable	Resettlement of populations living in zones of high risk	Risk management	Threat, security

Although it is tempting to view these regimes as a succession, we must remain attentive to the coexistence of modes of governing associated with distinct periods.

the urban periphery where families with scarce resources could build their own homes. The category of *vivienda de interés social* (social interest housing) emerged in the 1960s amid a concern for the living conditions not of laborers but of low-income populations. Poverty alleviation overtook modernization as the municipal housing agency's orienting telos, and the "poor" displaced the "worker" as the target of government intervention.

In the 1980s, the Caja's mission shifted again, this time in the direction of slum eradication and upgrading. Municipal housing policy no longer centered explicitly on workers or the needy; rather, it now focused on marginal spaces and populations in the rapidly urbanizing periphery of the city. The rationality of urban renewal current at that time saw the proliferation of slums (*tugurios*) and illegal occupations (*invasiones*) as problems of physical deterioration to be impeded. The Caja was charged with providing infrastructural improvements and legal recognition to some neighborhoods while facilitating the removal of others. Although the ratification of a new constitution in 1991 granted all Colombian citizens the right to *vivienda digna* (decent housing), the Supreme Court subsequently ruled that the state could not be expected to guarantee this right to everyone living in substandard conditions.

Since the late 1990s, the Caja has had an altogether different mission: to protect the lives of populations living in Bogotá's zones of high risk by facilitating their relocation. Although the Caja's resettlement program coexists alongside other initiatives, such as neighborhood improvement and land titling, 70 percent of the agency's 2009 budget of US$28 million was allocated to the resettlement of households located in areas vulnerable to landslides, floods, and other environmental hazards. As the director of the resettlement program's social team put it: "The Caja's objective is now to safeguard [*salvaguardar*] life; that is the priority, and in order to safeguard life it is necessary to guarantee that people do not inhabit properties in high risk." Clarifying this recent transformation, she insisted that the Caja was no longer in the business of building houses for the poor: "Many families come to the Caja de la Vivienda saying: 'Listen, I don't have housing, I want a house, and you guys are the ones who give houses!' No, our principal objective with the resettlement program is now to protect lives in danger. This should lead us to compensate them for the housing they had, of course! But this does not correspond to a policy of public housing for the homeless [*la gente sin techo*]." As the political rationality shifted to risk management, so did the target of governmental intervention. Rather than organizing housing policy in terms of social class, political membership, or economic necessity, vulnerability became the primary criterion that determined one's eligibility to receive state benefits. "Life at risk" displaced "worker," "citizen," and "poor" as a new category of political recognition and entitlement. At a moment when class-based demands for social transformation were perpetually in danger of being targeted as subversive—even to the point of being equated with the guerrilla insurgents who had themselves been relabeled "terrorist organizations"—risk management offered a seemingly neutral political rationality.

That said, the above conversation with Daniel shows that the application of risk management principles to housing regimes in Bogotá did not effect a wholesale transformation. For example, it is significant that the imperative to protect the life of the population in zones of high risk only applied to members of strata 1 or 2 (Bogotá is zoned into six socioeconomic *estratos*; 1 and 2 are the lowest). So while governmental intervention no longer targeted "poverty" and the housing conditions of the "poor," these priorities remained important in terms of how Caja social workers understood and performed their jobs. Another Caja social worker, Carlos, once remarked to me that, in adopting risk management principles, his agency had found a way to give housing subsidies to disadvantaged families while remaining in compliance with the priorities of international development agencies and financial institutions, which were resolutely opposed to welfare state policies, while also avoiding accusations from the conservative political establishment. He did not go as far as to celebrate the Caja's resettlement program as a heroic act of local resistance to the hegemony of externally imposed models of development and to the authoritarian national state. But "risk" functioned as a metonym for other social and political problems, and Caja officials stretched it beyond its usage as a technique for guiding action in the present according to predictive calculations of future harm.

In the government of risk in Bogotá, recognizably "neoliberal" principles (responsibilization, calculability, risk-taking, etc.) were mobilized in the service of state-based projects of social welfare that directed public expenditure to the housing conditions of the poor. For example, Carlos and I discussed the frequent practice of informally expediting the resettlement of families he deemed more needy or deserving, rather than those prioritized by technical risk calculations. When Caja social workers combined the imperatives of risk management and social welfare, however, this had a limited effect on the functioning of the resettlement program. The rise of the former in Bogotá narrowed the state's responsibility for other social problems like poverty, inequality, or forced displacement wrought by violence. For there were hundreds of thousands, if not millions, of bogotanos living in substandard or hazardous conditions, yet only those few (approximately 10,000 households in 2008) officially included within the boundaries of zones of high risk, and not even all of them, were eligible for housing subsidies. These regimes of housing neither gave "sustained attention to the welfare of the population," as Andrew Lakoff puts it, nor sought "to intervene in the living conditions of human beings as members of a social collectivity."[11] Risk offered a politically safe way to address the social and environmental problems of the urban periphery, but ultimately worked only to protect the lives of a small number of potential victims from a narrowly defined set of threats.

The Risks of Liberalism

At the heart of the municipal government's resettlement program for households in zones of high risk was the state's responsibility, enshrined in the Colombian constitution, to protect the right to life (*derecho a la vida*) of its citizens.[12] Beyond this broad declaration, of particular relevance is another article, which declares that all Colombians have the right to "decent housing" (*derecho a una vivienda digna*). Risk management emerged from the conjunction of these rights. The imperative to protect life from environmental hazards, and the rights and responsibilities it entails, were furthered by Bogotá's 2008 development plan.[13] Adopting the "right to the city" (*derecho a la ciudad*) as an organizing principle of urban development and a mechanism for combating social exclusion, the government of Bogotá made risk management a critical part of that plan.[14] Notwithstanding the obvious differences between the right to the city and other constitutionally mandated rights, it is fair to say that relations of government in Bogotá's zones of high risk are understood as matters of right, broadly conceived.

Underpinning the Caja's resettlement program is also the right to private property. According to John Locke's political theory, God gave the earth to men in common (only men, of course, and only certain men). Since, according to Locke, "every man has property in his own person" and in "the labor of his body," what he transforms from nature becomes rightfully his.[15] Land cultivated, tilled, or otherwise improved is considered private property. Yet entitlement depends not only on labor, but also rationality: or, for Locke, the "reason to make use of [property] for the best advantage of life."[16] The migrants and workers who built settlements on Bogotá's peripheral slopes transformed lands that had been laid to waste. Yet what Lockean liberalism might see as a divine right to private property conflicted with another gift from God to men—reason. One's right to property, insofar as it is based on the natural right to one's own body and life, is contradicted when the exercise of that property right jeopardizes the right to life on which it rests. That is to say, if people do not relocate from a zone of high risk, irrationally risking their own lives, then their right to property is put into question.

The dialectic of possession and dispossession in Locke's formulation was reflected in Bogotá's resettlement program. Those living in areas prior to their being designated zones of high risk were entitled to resettlement, and the legitimacy of their ownership was not challenged even though most were *poseedores* (landholders) rather than *propietarios* (property owners) and formal titles were uncommon among them. Moreover, settlers in other areas had the right to hold the state accountable for protecting their lives by petitioning that the specific settlements they lived in be included in risk inventories, and thus relocation programs. But urban reform legislation passed in 1989 made clear that these entitlements did not extend to those who preferred to remain in place: "If the inhabitants of buildings located in zones of high risk refuse to abandon the site, it is incumbent upon the mayor . . . to order the evacuation with the help of the police, as well as the demolition of the afflicted buildings. This order is considered, for all intents and purposes, a police matter."[17] The rights of settlers on the urban periphery were mediated by and predicated on what Foucault describes as the biopolitical imperative to protect the life of the population, or to "make live."[18]

Locke's definition of property "justifies, as natural, a class differential in rights and rationality," as C. B. Macpherson points out.[19] Since women, the unemployed, the poor, and the working classes "did not and could not live a fully rational life," Locke understood them as part of the nation but not incorporated into the body politic, fully subject to the state but not full citizens: in Macpherson's terms, "in but not of political society."[20] This differential in rights and rationality, he argues, provided a legal and moral foundation for accumulation by some at the expense of others. Similarly, calling into question the rights and rationality of those who act against their own self-interest—by remaining in areas the state deems high risk—justifies their dispossession.

The right to "decent housing" was shared equally by all citizens, yet the resettlement program applied only to those living in zones of high risk. There were degrees of entitlement based on levels of vulnerability. Teresa explained this apparent contradiction in the following way: "This is what happens in poor states that abide by the rule of law [*los estados de derecho pobres*]. Let's say that in states that have understood that human beings are just human beings, it is sufficient for the constitution to say, 'The right to housing is for everyone!' and this does not require any fine print. In a poor country like ours with a weak state, when the constitution says 'right to housing' this requires lots of fine print." Teresa then went on to explain what happens when someone comes to the Caja asking for housing. "I have to tell them:

'Yes, but the law does not prioritize you. It prioritizes those who live in zonas de alto riesgo. Do you live in one of those zones? Among them, the law prioritizes single women who are heads of households. Is that you?' And if you say no or cannot show me that you are, then I have to say: 'Well, get in line because single mothers come first, after that the disabled, and so on.' Although you are living in the same conditions as they are, you end up being treated differently."

Risk management in Bogotá was based on rights belonging equally to all citizens, yet it was not applied universally. Instead it depended on gradations in entitlement tied to categories of vulnerability. Teresa told me that one of the most difficult parts of her job was to get the community to understand, as she put it, "why doña María is different from don José when they appear to be in the same predicament. If you visit their homes," she reported, "you will find that the conditions in which they are living are the same. But by law, we have to treat them differently. So when we say no, don José responds: 'Doña María and I are both citizens and we deserve equal attention. You think I am any less poor than she is? No! I am just as poor.'" Teresa had to impart to don José and other settlers in Bogotá's urban periphery that their claims to rights and urban citizenship were predicated on and mediated by the degree to which their lives were in danger. As vulnerability structured the terrain of political engagement between the state and its subjects, the urban poor demanded recognition, entitlement, and protection as lives at risk.

As far as the Caja's resettlement program was concerned, citizenship was neither a good people possessed nor an entitlement they could claim. In part, this reflects the historical development of citizenship throughout much of Latin America. Far from political communities organized around principles of universal membership and civic participation, the Spanish colonies were stratified by categories of race, gender, status, and belonging that applied to Spaniards themselves as well as to native indigenous and enslaved African populations. In both early modern Spain and Spanish America, the categories of *vecindad* and *naturaleza*, which predated the formal definition of political citizenship, determined who possessed the rights and responsibilities of membership.[21] In the overseas colonies, *vecindad* was equated with the white, Spanish settlers and excluded all nonwhites and non-Spaniards.[22] In the early nineteenth century, new republics won their autonomy through revolutions that initially had little to do with integrating the disenfranchised into political life.[23] But as the collapse of the Spanish colonial system and the birth of democratic republics ushered in a new kind of politics, it became necessary to create citizens who would ultimately constitute the collective social formations of "the people" and "the public."[24]

In the republican period, the definition of political citizenship and the creation of a national citizenry became central to nation-building projects. As historian Hilda Sabato describes, the "figure of the modern citizen proposed by the liberals—the abstract and universal individual, free and equal to the rest—started to circulate early in the century, when it overlapped with more traditional notions of the body politic that evoked the institutions of colonial and even pre-colonial times: the *pueblos*, the *comunidades*, the subject, the *vecino* (neighbor or resident)."[25] The influence of these earlier forms of political identity and belonging led enlightened elites to believe that the majority of the population was unprepared for participatory democracy. According to Sabato, the "long-term answer to the challenges of modern representation was the 'invention' of the citizen."[26] This particular configuration of citizenship has ongoing significance.

Since Antanas Mockus occupied the mayor's office in Bogotá from 1995 to 1996 and again from 2001 to 2003, urban citizenship has been understood as a set of practices and sensibilities that people living in the city are expected to adopt. One of the most enduring aspects of Mockus's legacy was his emphasis on "the culture of citizenship" (*la cultura ciudadana*), a pedagogical project pursued by the government on behalf of those seen to be lacking a sense of civic responsibility. Many of the creative initiatives Mockus implemented in Bogotá—from employing mimes to direct traffic at busy intersections to giving drivers red and yellow cards like the ones used by soccer referees to "penalize" one another—were aimed explicitly at transforming bogotanos into *ciudadanos* (citizens). The municipal government's resettlement program with its mission to protect lives "at risk," which emerged around the same time, was also motivated by the imperative to create a "culture of citizenship" among the urban poor. Through the process of sensibilización, Caja managers and staff aimed not simply to raise awareness about risk but also to foster a sense of what it means to belong in and to the city. As the director of the program's social team made clear during an interview, this involves a transformation in both the actions and attitudes of beneficiaries:

> Let's say that *sensibilizar* is about getting the citizen to assimilate what risk means as well as what it means to be a legal citizen . . . that is, a citizen

who does not live in substandard conditions [*subnormalidad*], a citizen who understands that in the twenty-first century water has to come out of a pipe just as it has to be drained by a pipe . . . who understands that he has obligations in the legal city and that one of those obligations is to not live in high-risk areas.

The cost of being legal is the cost of being a citizen. Within the resettlement process we "sensibilize" them [*les hacemos la sensibilización*] to the implications of citizenship, and being a citizen means paying yearly property taxes, paying monthly water and electricity bills, and remaining outside the informal economy. I would say that one should also assimilate these concepts as an attitude.

With references not only to the practices required of citizens, but also to the internalization of ways of being proper to life in the city, these quotations demonstrate how citizenship is a technique with which some govern the conduct of others and through which others are expected to govern themselves.

The resettlement program's imperative was less to create citizens appropriate to modern liberal democracy than to transform rural subjects unaccustomed to urban life into ciudadanos in the most literal sense of "city dwellers." This became clear when resettlement beneficiaries rejected alternative housing options on the grounds that they were too small. Caja social workers would often respond that these houses were ample for a family of five, and emphasized the option to expand. Sometimes directly with the beneficiaries, but more often in private, Caja staff would discuss the "cultural" difference at the root of the problem:

They all want more space, and this has to do with where they come from . . . that is, with their transition from the country to the city. They think they can have their domestic animals, their dogs, their chickens, their ducks, their goats. They are campesinos with rural minds and rural characteristics, and they bring this to their new habitat. Our population comes from the country, where they had a different relationship with their homes and with their surroundings, so when we offer them houses of thirty-three square meters of floor space they exclaim: "Uyyy, no! This is way too small. What is this? How are we supposed to live here? Where can we keep our *gallinas* [hens]? We can't even fit a bed in here!"

Since few beneficiaries fit the image of a campesino—most appeared well-accustomed to the styles and rhythms of urban life—I once asked Carlos to specify where in rural Colombia a particular woman was from. "I don't know for sure," he said. "She might not actually be from the countryside herself, but she inherited it. If you go out into the neighborhoods where we work, you see it all over." Identifying resettlement beneficiaries as rural campesinos, regardless of their actual provenance, rendered their demands unreasonable, ill suited to life in the urban environment. The Caja aimed to convince them not to perform the civic duties expected of the citizen but to assimilate the behavior and mentality appropriate to ciudadanos—those who belong in and to the city.

The relocation of households from Bogotá's zones of high risk also drew upon the ideal of freedom so basic to liberal political and economic thought, reflecting the assumption that autonomy, choice, responsibility, and individuality hinge on the calculative rationality of risk. Resettlement was supposed to be a self-directed process in which the Caja's architects, lawyers, social workers, and engineers played no more than a facilitating role. Although it began when the government delivered notices to those living in zones of high risk, it proceeded according to the initiative of beneficiaries who assumed personal responsibility for their own relocation. It was expected that people in high-risk zones would accept relocation subsidies and then exercise their agency as market-savvy consumers by finding alternative housing elsewhere in the city. In fact, a hallmark of the resettlement program was its insistence that the decision to relocate was voluntary. One of the program's slogans, emblazoned on a poster in the Caja's field office, read, "Libre elección por cada beneficiario" (Free choice for every beneficiary). Even the demolition of properties was the duty of the individual household. But if liberal ideals of freedom, choice, and responsibility were often referenced within the resettlement program, we must consider the conditions in which the "voluntary" decision to relocate was often made.

Once an area was declared a zone of high risk, it became illegal to live there. As a Caja social worker put it before a meeting with a group of recalcitrant householders: "The families are not at liberty to refuse to participate in the [resettlement] program. They cannot say: 'I take responsibility for my life here no matter what happens. If something bad happens, I'll accept it.' That would be a right that the families do not have." Moreover, pressure mounted as the area became increasingly insecure and the expiration date of the relocation subsidies drew near. This contrasts with studies of risk and liberalism, which presume that personal responsibility and individual culpability come with the ability to make informed decisions based on the likelihood of future harm. In contrast, here one had to decide between relocating elsewhere or waiting for the authorities to evacuate the area, as they were legally entitled to do. At no point was one in a position to "take the risk" or not. The Caja mobilized liberal ideals of freedom, citizenship, equality, and rights in order to produce the conditions in which certain predetermined transformations could take place.

Governing Affections

If the politics of security and risk in Bogotá reconfigured state-subject relations, to what degree did it break with the past, and to what extent did it draw upon well-established genealogies of power? The answer to this question lies in the ways Caja social workers were positioned, and positioned themselves, in relation to beneficiaries of the municipal government's resettlement program. On entering the program, each beneficiary was assigned a social worker as their primary contact for the duration of the relocation process. During my fieldwork, each social worker had eighty to one hundred cases on average. While this relationship between social workers and their clients may be typical, the resettlement program relied on other terms of engagement. In addition to technical, bureaucratic designations, such as *profesional social* (social professional) and *beneficiario* (beneficiary), members of Caja's social team adopted the titles of *padrino* (godfather) and *madrina* (godmother) and referred to their cases as *mis familias* (my families) or *nuestros ahijados* (our godchildren). Underlying the government of risk in Bogotá were models of kinship and familial relations of guidance, care, and protection.

Presenting to a group of researchers in Bogotá, the director of the Caja's social team described the ideal relation between her staff and those they served. The audience had asked about the caseload managed by each social professional. In response, Teresa explained:

> The issue is really how to make sure that [social professionals] are able to get to know each family. At the outset, we decided to give every beneficiary a godparent [*decidimos apadrinarlos a todos*]. This year we assigned an average of eighty families to each social professional. If they have more

than that, it is guaranteed that they are going to neglect [*descuidar*] one here and there. What we have noticed is that it is extremely important that the affectionate relations [*relaciones de afecto*] between the social professional and the family become very strong. It's normal to hear them come to the Caja and say: *Hola madrina! Hola padrino!* And then the social professional responds: *Quibo, ahijado! ¿Usted qué?* [What's up, godson! How are you?] To tell you the truth, one really notices the level of empathy we have been able to achieve.

When Caja social workers occasionally neglected to maintain these relations, their superiors reminded them of their familial obligations. During a staff meeting, the coordinator of the field office in Ciudad Bolívar rebuked her staff for not caring enough about their charges. "We have to treat them like they are our families," she said, urging them to involve themselves more deeply in the resettlement of each household. It was as important that Caja social workers felt an affective bond with their subjects as it was that their subjects felt the same toward the state. As I was told by the social worker Adriana: "We have to create new relationships between us and them, and this depends on our ability to break down the separation between the state and the people [*la gente*]. You have to go out and meet them, and if you do they tend to warm up [*acercarse mucho más*] to the resettlement program. You have to show them that you are not above them on a pedestal and that you don't just live in the office. So I go visit them in their homes as though we were family." While inspiring feelings of affection for the state was key to the resettlement program, another Caja staff member, Fernando, showed me that fostering these relations remained a goal even after relocation.

When he arrived at the resettlement housing complex of Arborizadora Alta, he set about convening a meeting with residents by the playground in the common area. After discussing utility bills and door locks, Fernando reminded everyone that they could count on him just as they would a close friend or relative: "You know that you can call me anytime, day or night, right? My cell phone is public for everyone here. It doesn't anger me in the slightest if you call me. I could be jogging in the park over the weekend, and your call would not bother me." He then turned to me and with a smile said: "The people here love me very much!" But as Fernando demonstrated on this visit, all relations of kinship, whether or not based on blood ties, imply unequal positions of power, authority, and obedience. While the condescending nature of Fernando's relationship to "his families" might trouble liberal ideals of equality, it should be noted that the verb *condescender* (to condescend) does not carry the negative connotation in Spanish that it does in English. In Spanish, it indexes the conception of society as fundamentally hierarchical and the belief that those with privilege and power must occasionally "descend" to the level of their inferiors. When representatives of the state treated adults (usually significantly older than them) as children, this did not offend popular notions of propriety and justice; on the contrary, it reinforced them. This was especially evident when padrinos and madrinas took responsibility for the moral upbringing of their "godchildren," the resettlement beneficiaries.

Fernando had told me on the way to Arborizadora Alta that the purpose of his visit was to motivate self-management (*auto-gestión*) and to ensure that the resettled were adapting to their new surroundings. These imperatives reflected the additional responsibility, common to godparents in the Catholic tradition, of guiding those under their supervision in matters of moral conduct. This was evident throughout the meeting, as Fernando framed the discussion as a lesson in coexistence (*convivencia*). He cited reports of loud music being played late at night: "Parties should be for each of us in our homes, and not for our neighbors, isn't that true? The police code dictates this, neither I nor the Caja," he said distancing himself and his employer from the potentially unpopular prohibition. "We all have the right to party. I'm just here to help you all learn to live better and to live in harmony [*aprender a vivir mejor y a convivir*] in this pleasant location. I find it pleasant, which is why I spent Christmas and New Year's Eve here with you." Fernando's lesson in neighborliness then addressed the younger generation: "I've also heard that not everyone knows how to be respectful to their elders. I'm making a cordial call to my buddies from the neighborhood to show respect to your parents and to your neighbors." These lessons in *convivencia* reflected the institutions of familial authority, moral guidance, and affectionate care that animated the Caja's approach to governing the "at risk" population in Bogotá.

Some Caja social workers were self-reflexive about this relationship. During an interview, I asked Carlos to comment on his role as padrino for close to eighty families.

Well, that term, you know they invented it not too long ago, right? Yeah, padrino has a connotation that one should be like a godfather, a patron, as in the person who they depend on, the person who should make things happen, the person who should give generously, right? This puts families in a position of inequality. The padrino is . . . the one who has to provide incentives in order for them to carry through with the [resettlement] process.

Curious to learn more about these familial modes of governing and their recent invention, I asked: "Whose idea was it to use these titles?" Carlos thought for a moment: "You know, I'm not sure what to tell you. I think it originally came from management. I used to think it was just a semantic term, you know like official propaganda, in that it did not have much influence on the philosophy of the program. I now think that this relation of guardianship (*padrinazgo*) has started to catch on." Carlos explained that not only did his fellow social workers describe themselves as "godparents," but their "families" responded by addressing the Caja staff in the same traditional idioms of respect and authority.

Without a doubt, the "godparent/godchild" relation has a Catholic inflection. The significance it carries, however, is more social than religious: padrinos and madrinas in Colombia are responsible for guiding their godchildren in matters such as morality, employment, and love as much as faith, piety, and devotion. Familial modes of political authority have a more recent precedent, as well. Cristina Rojas argues that the "democratic security" regime of President Álvaro Uribe (2002–10) was founded on a paternalistic vision of the state's relationship to its subjects: "Uribe's electoral platform envisioned a communitarian society in which the nation is like a big family living a fraternal coexistence under the care of 'the father rather than the politician.'"[27] While this model resonates with the familial relations of government I have described, the latter are founded on ethics of care, guidance, and protection rather than authoritarian forms of control. The state appears not as a heavy-handed father wielding the powers of violence and discipline, but as an affectionate godparent responsible for governing the conduct of those not (or not yet) capable of governing themselves.

From the Hacienda to the City

Assuming the role of padrino inserted the Caja social worker into another genealogy of power. While the title indexes a Church-sanctioned relation of extended kinship, it also carries the more general connotation of guardian, benefactor, and protector. In this sense, it relates to forms of patronage descended from the hacienda, or the large agrarian estates established during Spanish colonial rule that remained influential throughout the Colombian countryside into the early twentieth century.[28] While the hacienda system no longer dominates the rural economy, Sebastián Cuéllar Sarmiento and Carlo Tognato argue that it continues to serve as a cultural framework in contemporary Colombia.[29] Their argument sheds light on the discourse surrounding the Colombian armed conflict, but it has less to say about how the forms of political authority, moral regulation, and social relation associated with the hacienda are enacted, sustained, and contested. It is through governmental initiatives like the Caja's resettlement program that they are formed and reformed on a daily basis.

The discourse of the hacienda is organized around the figures of *patrón* and *peón*. Elaborating on Tognato and Cuéllar's argument, we can say that the patrón is, at once, a symbol of economic, political, moral, and religious superiority. As the lord of the manor, he rules over his territory and tenants in exchange for their loyalty, labor, and rent. Though he holds no formal political office, the patrón is the ultimate authority in all matters concerning the government of his family, his laborers, and his land. His right is that of the sovereign, and this is reflected in the responsibilities he holds toward his subjects. He is obliged to provide those dependent on him with physical protection, moral guidance, and material support. In contrast, the peón is the perpetual guest who has no defensible claim to territory and is dependent on the patrón in all respects. He may, by convention, expect kindness, charity, or generosity, but these are customary privileges and not constitutional entitlements. His life and livelihood are, thus, contingent on the patrón's goodwill and the degree to which the peón humbly accepts and loyally fulfills traditionally ascribed duties.

The labor relations of Colombian haciendas were far from uniform, and the generic category of peón does not do justice to the complexity of arrangements that bound the laborer to his lord and to the land.[30] Moreover, the analogy can only be taken so far, since the economic structure of the hacienda finds no parallel among the peripheral settlements of Bogotá. Nevertheless, the category usefully indexes enduring rationalities of rule that continue to condition the relationship between the state and its subjects. The most obvious manifestation of this was the administration of former President Uribe, whose control over territory, society, and the state could be seen as the fullest embodiment of the figure of the patrón. But the relations of government associated with the hacienda are evident throughout the informal settlements of Bogotá, as well, and have been for decades.

Many of Bogotá's peripheral neighborhoods were initially settled by groups who pledged allegiance to a particular politician, political party, or social movement. For the most part, they were established not through land invasion or squatting, as in other Latin American cities, but by "pirate" urbanization (*urbanización pirata*)—the illegal parceling of land by the legal owner who then sold it without basic infrastructure to poor settlers to construct their own housing.[31] While this process relied on market mechanisms more than political relations, it was facilitated in many cases by candidates or elected officials who did so in exchange for popular support. "Regularizing" or "formalizing" settlements also required political connections, and this set a populist precedent throughout the urban periphery whereby both the neighborhood's legal status and infrastructural development were contingent on patron-client relationships and promises of loyalty and obedience. The legitimacy of this form of patronage harkens back to the territorial relations of the hacienda, in which the peón was permitted to occupy a plot of land controlled by the patrón but his tenancy was always in question. It depended on the degree to which he fulfilled his obligations by either working the landlord's fields or providing him with a share of the harvest. Even those allowed to clear an undeveloped parcel on the property for their own use had to return it to the lord in an improved state within a period of two or three years. It was always within the patrón's dominion to decide what his tenants were allowed to do on the land and for precisely how long.

Risk management reasserted the territorial control of the patrón as well as the patron-client relations established during the settlement of the urban periphery. While the patrón promised protection from external threats, such as famine, flood, and theft, those living in high-risk zones had come to expect similar kinds of protection from the state. Their tenancy, too, was always uncertain. Whether one was allowed to continue inhabiting the area, forced to look elsewhere for housing, or deemed eligible for a resettlement subsidy, this decision was ultimately based on risk designations, legal statutes, and policy directives. Even if settlers had title to their property, which many of them did, the declaration that an area was high risk entitled them to a relocation subsidy—but not to remain. Tenancy and property were not rights but privileges that the "at risk" population had to work to retain. If they provided loyalty and obedience and successfully demonstrated their competence and responsibility, in return they could expect to receive the protection, kindness, and generosity of the state.

While the forms of power associated with the hacienda were evident in the resettlement program, they were reconfigured by principles of risk management. The subject was not required to perform labor, of course, as the peón did, but there was an implicit expectation of political loyalty. Whereas the promise of protection and generosity in exchange for labor and obedience once hinged on tradition and looked toward the past, the relationship between the state and its subjects instituted by the Caja was oriented toward the future. The latter was justified by technical expertise that foresaw potential threats looming on the horizon rather than on historical precedent or favors received. Moreover, the technical designation of risk and the interventions that followed opened up terrains of political engagement on which the urban poor sought recognition and claimed entitlement based on the degree to which their lives were in danger.

Between God and Government

As with the forms of power based on the hacienda, religious imaginaries also underpinned the politics of security and risk in Bogotá. As I sat with Daniel at his desk in the Caja's field office, we chatted in between visits from resettlement beneficiaries. The next to arrive was Liliana, a single mother who had lived most of her life in the hillside settlements of Ciudad Bolívar. She was only twenty-six years old, but she looked more than twice that. Since 2006, when a landslide destroyed a group of nearby houses and took the lives of four of her neighbors, Liliana had been petitioning the municipal government to recognize her as eligible for relocation. Her property was eventually included within the adjacent zone of high risk, and she became a beneficiary of the Caja's resettlement program. Liliana then settled in a temporary rental apartment while she navigated the complicated bureaucratic channels of various governmental agencies. Daniel had been her trusty guide throughout the protracted relocation process, and today she had come to pay a visit to her padrino.

Liliana arrived with two objectives in mind. The first was to submit papers she had recently obtained from Catastro, the branch of the municipal government in charge of property values and land records. The second purpose of her visit, perhaps of equal importance, was to bring her padrino a gift. From a ragged grocery bag, Liliana produced a carefully wrapped package containing a *nieve*, a baseball-sized ball of popcorn coated with sugary syrup. As she handed it to Daniel, she added words of gratitude: "You have helped me so very much, and I just wanted to show you how much I truly appreciate it." Daniel blushed as he accepted the gift with noticeable reluctance. He thanked Liliana matter-of-factly as he put the sweet in his desk drawer, and jumped back to official business. After they finished their conversation and said goodbye, Daniel confessed to me that the gift from Liliana had made him uncomfortable. "This is the third time she has given me something like this. I know it's just nieve, which you can get on the street for less than 500 pesos (25 cents), but that's a lot for someone of her means."

Although these exchanges often caused dismay among Caja social workers, they were consistent with the affectionate relationships being created. However, Daniel's discomfort suggested that there was something else going on, and I inquired further: "Is it that now you feel like you should give her special treatment?" "Well, that's part of it," he responded. "But Liliana is very religious, and I bet she brings this kind of offering every time she goes to church. I guess it feels a bit odd to be treated in the same way." Given the significance of the title "padrino," however, and the fact that many resettlement beneficiaries were devout Catholics or evangelical Christians, such acts were not so surprising. It was possible that such an offering could have facilitated the resettlement process for Liliana.

For many contemporary social theorists, a theological thread runs through ostensibly secular political configurations. This is true in Colombia, where religion has long played an important role in the consolidation of political authority and the exercise of political power. In the colonial period, there was a close relationship—though not always harmonious—between the Catholic Church and Spanish rule. The same remained true during the formation of the republican nation-state in the nineteenth century, when political identities (both Liberal and Conservative) were defined by one's relation to the clergy.[32] The political influence of the Church was such that the Colombian archbishop vetted candidates for president and other national offices, as did bishops and parish priests in local and regional elections.[33] While the influence of the Catholic Church in Colombian politics decreased throughout the twentieth century, the political significance of Catholicism in the contemporary period involves more than the mixing of formal religious institutions with matters of state.[34] Political power in Colombia, as well as the enactment of political violence with which it has been so strongly associated, are both closely tied to religious themes of sacrifice, suffering, and salvation.[35]

Throughout the resettlement process, too, boundaries blurred between church and state, between sacred and secular, between the power of God and the authority of the bureaucrat. The domain of risk management and its orientation toward potential catastrophes was especially saturated with references to faith, providence, and the divine. Many resettlement beneficiaries saw the future as not only unknown but unknowable, and since it was in God's hands they trusted that whatever happened would happen for a reason. Consider the commentary by doña María, an elderly woman still living in a high-risk zone:

> There are many people down in the ravine very close to the stream, even lower down than where I live. In some of the gullies, their little shacks are on the edge and are about ready to go [ya para irse]. So I pray to God, and not just for myself but for everyone in the same situation, that mi Diosito [a familiar diminutive referring to the Holy Father] will grant us the pleasure someday of being relocated. May God be blessed, praise the Lord. And may God bless everyone who works for the Caja as well. . . . I can tell you for sure that everything that the Caja does is with a good heart, and that they do God's work day in and day out for each one of us. . . . Thanks to their efforts and to the kindness of God, we will go wherever they send us.

In her appeals for guidance and salvation, doña María shuttled back and forth between the state and a higher power, as when she described her plans for the future:

> I'm just going to wait and see what happens. I think I'll come back in two weeks, and when I come, God willing, I'm hoping they will say to me: "Yes, something will be possible. Your case will be approved this year." I pray to mi Diosito that this will happen, but if not that he will give me the strength to carry on. You see, my shack may well collapse. All the poles buried into the ground have been pulled up, and when you open the door, the cardboard [of the walls] shakes. . . . I pray that the doctora [an honorific used for anyone with education or authority, in this case a Caja social worker] will come and inspect my house. It's a dreadful situation.

Seeking intervention both profane and divine, and maintaining faith in her destiny, doña María's pleas and praise were addressed to both God and government. Although the risk of landslide demanded good behavior and diligent prayer, it could also be mitigated by appeals to the Caja's benevolent expertise.

This perspective was not peculiar to those subject to the resettlement program, and was in fact shared by Caja managers and staff. Adriana recounted a similar situation faced by one of her families: "Doña Gladys had selected housing in Torres del Progreso by paying 600,000 pesos for registering the title. This means she was set to receive her new home, except for one small detail. It turned out that it was her husband who was officially registered with the resettlement program as the primary beneficiary, and he had been forced to flee . . . to leave [the neighborhood] and to leave Bogotá as well . . . after a threatening situation." "What sort of threatening situation?" I asked. "A death threat," Adriana responded without hesitating, and then continued:

> So I told doña Gladys what she had to do: "If your husband happens to contact you, ask him to send a notarized letter transferring to you his power of attorney. This will allow you to use your own signature to continue with the resettlement process." But for a while after that, we knew absolutely nothing about doña Gladys, until about two months ago when it was now or never for her case. If she couldn't sign the contract, she would lose her spot. This woman made me so worried that I prayed for her until at long last she appeared. I don't know what strange coincidences [*casualidades extrañas*] were at work, but I believe it was a miracle of God. Yep, that's right, by the grace of God she received the power of attorney. It arrived to her by fax, but we cannot accept faxes here in the Caja. So I told her: "Call your husband, pray, do whatever you have to do to get the original." She did this somehow, and when she arrived she had it in her hands. The lawyer looked it over and approved. And by the grace of God, doña Gladys signed an agreement for her new home. That gave me satisfaction beyond compare and for an entire week I was happy, happy, happy that God listened to our prayers.

The compatibility of risk management with devotional faith was made even clearer during the weeks leading up to Easter Sunday, when Bogotá was hit by the heaviest rainstorm in fifty years. In seven hours, the media reported, the capital city was drenched with as much rain as usually falls in a month. In an editorial that ran the following weekend, the Bogotá-based newspaper *El Tiempo* called it the "Downpour of the Century."[36] The lives and livelihoods of over five thousand bogotanos were adversely affected by subsequent floods and landslides. An entire housing development was inundated by over a meter of water, and houses, cars, and personal belongings were washed away by rivers and streams that overflowed their banks. Expecting another deluge later in the week, the authorities began to assign blame. They traded accusations about the inaccuracy of meteorological monitoring and the inadequacy of emergency response systems. But concern was focused as much on the technical aspects of the event as on the religious symbolism surrounding it.

In anticipation of the worshippers and pilgrims who traditionally flock to the mountaintop sanctuary of Monserrate overlooking Bogotá during Holy Week, the municipal government closed the footpath leading to the site. To avert public outcry or divine retribution, or perhaps both, the Shrine of the Fallen Lord (el Señor Caido), whose mutilated body solemnly backs the altar, was moved to the Capilla del Sagrario in downtown Bogotá. But these spiritual preoccupations neither outweighed nor undercut technical approaches. As the editors of *El Tiempo* put it: "In terms of protecting bogotanos from these increasingly common biblical downpours [*aguaceros bíblicos*], the investments made by Acueducto [the water company] and the creation of emergency response plans are neither sufficient nor completely secure. . . . The deluge of biblical proportions that lashed [*diluvio de bíblicas proporciones que azotó*] the capital reveals that, despite everything that has been done, there remains much more to do in the zones of high risk." The religious significance of the emergency reinforced the imperative of risk management central to the endangered city.

Beyond Great Divides

The calculative rationality of risk is less than helpful as a marker of the divide between liberal modernity and whatever came before. The articulation of emergent governmental forms with familial authority, patronage relations, and religious sensibilities confounds theories that assume the replacement of "traditional" moral or social imperatives with those of a "modern" technical nature. These theories center on risk, for it is supposedly the capacity to make autonomous decisions based on rational calculations of future probability that frees the modern, liberal subject from the constraints of nature, family, tradition, despotism, and religion. Accordingly, it is this ability that is thought to empower individuals to enter into voluntary social contracts, engage in rational economic behavior, and participate in democratic political institutions. However, forms of social collectivity, political authority, and ethical responsibility deemed "premodern" or "illiberal" are not necessarily succeeded by individual autonomy, calculative decision-making, free will, and related ideals of liberal modernity. For resettlement beneficiaries and government workers alike, there was nothing incompatible or contradictory about the fact that risk management in Bogotá drew on and was shaped by liberal democratic notions of freedom, equality, citizenship, and rights as well as nonliberal genealogies of power, such as kinship, patronage, and religion. As we have seen, the risk subject of liberalism and the citizen of modern democracy are accompanied by the dependent child of the patriarchal family, the loyal serf of the colonial hacienda, and the faithful acolyte of the Catholic Church.

This insight may force us to reconsider whether we have witnessed the epochal rise of security as the "general economy of power in our societies," as Foucault asked presciently over three decades ago.[37] While we may indeed find ourselves in the midst of a global proliferation of security mechanisms, evidence from Bogotá suggests that they have not everywhere produced predictable transformations in governmental forms and state-subject relations. Moreover, they do not necessarily follow the progression from one stage of history to the next. The public warnings distributed throughout Bogotá suggest that the endangered city denotes a much more heterogeneous field of governmental intervention. According to certain epochal narratives, however, the imperative to limit the presence of the state in the lives of its subjects and to allow the "natural" functioning of society and the market has effectively displaced the social programs, safety nets, and centralized planning of the welfare state. In Colombia, however, preexisting political institutions differ significantly from those transformed by liberalism and neoliberalism in the North Atlantic world. Risk management here belongs to a history in which economic modernization has been a perpetual promise more than an accomplished reality, the welfare state was never fully established, and liberalism has been an ongoing project with limited reach and success. The experience of liberal modernity in Europe and North America is not necessarily the best guide for understanding the government of risk in other parts of the world.

One possible conclusion is that the Colombian state is not yet fully modern or liberal, since it continually struggles to overcome the vestiges of the past and fails to "rationally" manage risk. Another is that Colombia represents either a "hybrid" modernity or an "impure" liberalism that fuses elements "belonging" to two or more distinct geographies and histories. These conclusions are possible only if we allow certain "advanced" societies to serve as the "pure" or "complete" standard against which "alternative" variations may be judged. But in the West, too, liberal democracy and the modern state have always had to grapple with illiberal dynamics (religious fundamentalism, clientalism, and sectarian strife, among others) at the heart of dominant legal and political orders.[38] Political technologies developed in one context always undergo mutations determined by the contingencies of history and the specificities of place, and those forged by the politics of security in Colombia are no exception. By following what "risk" comes to mean and do at specific conjunctures, we see how it takes on new significance, is put to unintended uses, enables certain ends, and disables others. This recognition will allow us to engage with recent governmental shifts taking place elsewhere, which resonate with those conditioned by the predicament of endangerment in Bogotá.

4

LIVING DANGEROUSLY

A Life at Risk

Endangerment is both a condition of everyday life and a terrain of political engagement in Bogotá. As such, it influences how the city is organized as a political community, how people become political subjects, and how urban citizens engage in political relationships with the state. Take the case of Liliana, a single mother of five who, from the age of thirteen, lived in a house built by relatives in the peripheral locality of Ciudad Bolívar. In May 2006, heavy rains sent an avalanche of mud crashing down onto a group of nearby houses.[1] Four of Liliana's neighbors, two adults and two children, were buried by the landslide. At the time of the tragic event, the municipal government was already in the process of relocating households throughout the city, especially those in the poor, hillside settlements of Ciudad Bolívar, to protect them from just this sort of disaster. However, since Liliana's property lay outside the designated boundaries of the zone of high risk, she had been excluded from the resettlement program. Unlike others in her neighborhood who had been declared "at risk," Liliana was ineligible for a government subsidy based on the constitutional right to *vivienda digna* (decent housing).[2] Recognizing that her entitlement depended on her risk status, she sat down in October of that year to write a letter of appeal.

Dear Sirs:

The intention of this letter is to request a visit to the property I live in, where the floor is cracking. I cannot stay here or inhabit this property with complete tranquility, since I live with my 5 children who are minors; I am worried about the rainy season that we are presently in. God willing we are not going to fall down, that is, have a landslide, and God willing we won't experience what happened to our neighbors in Caracolí, which resulted in 4 deaths. I beg you to do me the favor of visiting me to determine whether I am at high risk, or if I am not to tell me what procedures currently exist, and to subject me to them, as much for relocation as for the legalization of my property, since I am worried that the inevitable will happen, and I am worried about the life of my children. With nothing more to say and in anticipation of an affirmative response, I close this letter.

Sincerely,
Liliana

In her petition, Liliana expressed concern that both she and her children were in danger. She appealed to God for protection from disasters and feared their inevitability. However, Liliana's plea was ultimately addressed to the governmental agencies responsible for risk management: the DPAE, which designates zones of high risk, and the Caja, which relocates families living within them. These agencies possess both the political-scientific authority to declare her "at risk" as well as the legal responsibility to protect her life. Government technicians responded to Liliana's letter and determined that the conditions of her property did, in fact, warrant its inclusion within the zone of high risk. She then became a beneficiary of the Caja's resettlement program. When we met, Liliana was living in a temporary rental apartment in another part of Ciudad Bolívar (the barrio of Sierra Morena) while she waited patiently for the process of purchasing her new home to go through.

For Liliana and others like her, citizenship and the benefits it confers are mediated by and predicated on a governmental rationality that classifies subjects and manages populations according to the degree to which their lives are in danger. Her vulnerability determined whether she would be recognized as the bearer of certain rights. Liliana did not demand that the state recognize her within the political community of the city or the nation or that it fulfill her entitlements on the basis of such claims. Although she appealed to God and begged her superiors for protection, Liliana's petition ultimately implored the municipal government to recognize her as belonging to the population living in zones of high risk. It was in these terms that she could establish herself as a worthy beneficiary of the resettlement program. Although this case deals with struggles over housing and access to urban space, a similar dynamic of political engagement has emerged in other governmental sectors: To become a citizen with rights, Liliana first had to be visible as a life at risk.

Having shown how cities become the stage for the reconfiguration of citizenship, anthropologists are attuned to situations in which residents make demands on state agencies according to their rights as members of an urban community. Situations like these are widespread throughout Latin America. My ethnographic material makes sense, however, only once we acknowledge other frames of social inclusion and political recognition. As Partha Chatterjee argues, urban populations in most of the world "are only tenuously, and even then ambiguously and contextually, rights-bearing citizens in the sense imagined by the constitution."[3] They are not "outside the reach of the state or even excluded from the domain of politics," he clarifies, but as "populations within the territorial jurisdiction of the state, they have to be both looked after and controlled by various governmental agencies."[4] It is often their classification as targets of governmental intervention, Chatterjee shows, that brings the urban poor "into a certain *political* relationship with the state."[5] Thus he directs our attention to "political society," or the "site of negotiation and contestation opened up by the activities of governmental agencies aimed at population groups."[6] Although the dichotomy between "civil" and "political" society may be reductive, it nevertheless forces us to ask why citizens with rights appeal as population groups to a multiplicity of governmental agencies for recognition, inclusion, and protection.[7]

Following a liberal democratic paradigm, we could see Liliana's petition as prefiguring an expansion of rights to the urban poor and a progression toward equal citizenship. We might acknowledge that most settlers on the urban periphery are not rights-bearing citizens in the fullest, most substantive sense but then mistake her case for an example of the process by which members of this population struggle to be recognized as such. However, once we shift our gaze to what Chatterjee calls the "politics of the governed" and examine the political terrain on which claims are made, we recognize that the politics of rights is subordinated to a politics of life. Indeed, the re-settlement program sets out to provide "decent housing" not to everyone but, rather, to those living in zones of high risk. And while this constitutional right is shared formally by all citizens, it is dependent on the degree to which their lives are in danger.[8] The right to housing is thus a privilege bestowed on members of a collectivity whose entitlements are grounded not only in shared membership within a political community but also in their common condition of vulnerability. In the endangered city, this is often how the poor must define and execute their citizenship claims.

In Bogotá, forms of government organized around the imperative to pro-tect the lives of vulnerable populations from future threat shape how people on the urban periphery engage in political relationships with the state. That said, when we consider the coexistence and asymmetrical application of mul-tiple regimes of power, we find that the politics of rights is not separate from, but rather entangled with, the politics of risk. By examining the relationship between liberalism and security in Colombia, and how their objectives and ideals have been fused over the past decade, we begin to understand why some must strive to become visible as lives at risk in order to be recognized as citizens with rights.

Genealogies of Urban Citizenship

While security is globally ascendant as a paradigm for organizing social and political life, Latin America is a particularly good place to analyze its en-tanglement with democracy and neoliberalism.[9] This is especially true in Colombia, nominally Latin America's oldest democracy, where decades of violent conflict combined with (and fueled by) neoliberal reforms have sub-ordinated citizenship to security.[10] While some conflicts between security and rights are distinctly neoliberal, Latin America has witnessed a number of recent challenges to neoliberalism's hegemony; even Colombia has seen shifts in this direction.[11] Experiments with democracy abound in what has been tentatively called the "post-neoliberal" era.[12] Yet, as Coronil observes, "there is a pervasive uncertainty with respect to the specific form of the ideal future."[13] Debates continue across the political spectrum over how best to balance demands for security *and* rights. In the context of global processes of urbanization, and as the locus of security itself continues to urbanize, this issue has had profound consequences for urban politics and citizenship.

In the liberal democratic tradition, the city has been synonymous with political community and the principles of universal membership and civic participation, even as projects of nation-building sought to replace it.[14] Among Marxists, the city has been the space of industrial production and the site of working-class struggles that would ultimately lead to the creation of a society without class, the state, and private property.[15] Most cities in the global South, however, are the product of histories that have not shared the telos implicit in both liberal and Marxist urban theories. In the colonial period, Spanish American cities functioned as both tools of conquest and symbols of imperial power, and they were built to express and enforce ostensibly natural hierarchies. Cities of colony and metropole alike were socially stratified and spatially divided according to race, gender, class, profession, and other classifications. While universal ideals accompanied both North Atlantic political transformations of the late eighteenth century and Latin American national independence movements in the early nineteenth, liberal democracy had limited reach and success in the latter case. In Colombia, for example, the "will to civilization," as Cristina Rojas puts it, rather than the pursuit of equality or freedom, animated republican efforts to lead a divided society away from its colonial past.[16] Ultimately, colonial divisions between cities and their hinterlands, between whites and nonwhites, and between elites and the popular classes—all shaped by the durable opposition between "civilization" and "barbarism"—proved stronger than the ideal of a national citizenry endowed with universal rights.[17]

State-led modernization efforts in the twentieth century sought to remake Latin American cities in the mold of their European counterparts. For urban elites and rural migrants, the city symbolized hopes of modernity more than the promise of democracy. Political struggles emerging from the urban periphery did challenge patterns of entrenched social exclusion, but their central demand was development rather than enfranchisement.[18] The rapid pace of urbanization, however, quickly outpaced states' capacity to extend the benefits of urban life to squatter settlements springing up throughout the region. Cities were divided yet again between the white and mestizo elite, who enjoyed the substantive benefits of citizenship, and the poor and working classes, predominantly nonwhite, who belonged only nominally to the collective identities of liberal democracy. Although these latter groups were occasionally acknowledged to belong to "the citizenry" or "the public," they were more often addressed by the developmental state as populations in need of interventions in domains such as health, housing, and education.[19]

The association of the city with civilization and with related ideals of progress, development, and modernity has figured centrally in Colombia, as elsewhere in Latin America. However, in recent decades these ideals have been increasingly subordinated to the political rationality of security, and it is in this context that risk emerges as a technique of urban government and vulnerability as a frame of political recognition. The displacement of welfare-oriented policies of development by protection-based logics of security followed neoliberal political and economic reforms and a half century of violent conflict. Colombia has the second highest number of internally displaced persons in the world, and the city is now figured as a refuge from the barbaric violence of the countryside. Those who escape to the self-built settlements of the urban periphery see the state more as protector than as provider. This dynamic was given a liberal democratic framing by former president Álvaro Uribe (2002–10), who sought to legitimate his regime by hitching the concepts of "rights" and "citizenship" to those of "security" and "protection."[20] While it may appear that security was included among the package of rights to which citizens were entitled, it would be more accurate to say that liberal democratic institutions were subordinated to security logics. As a result, those claiming their rights as citizens must first be recognizable as lives at risk.

This brief genealogy shows that Latin American cities have long been spaces of hierarchy and division above equality and inclusion, imagined in terms more of civilization, development, and security than of democracy, citizenship, and rights. Without recognizing this, we may risk misunderstanding how the politics of risk in contemporary Bogotá both reconfigures and reinforces older forms of exclusion, such as those that follow lines of race, class, and gender. As I have mentioned, struggles for recognition and entitlement in the urban periphery do sometimes claim rights, and often are about urban space. But in Colombia, urban citizenship is predicated on and subordinated to the political rationality of security. It is embedded within a field of governmental intervention organized around the imperative to protect vulnerable populations from potential threats, and it is within this domain that settlers of the urban periphery engage in political relationships with the state. Urban space may serve as the stage for social movements and oppositional struggles, but the city and the right to it may not always be the ultimate goals of political struggle.

Invasions

Since 1950, Bogotá has grown from about seven hundred thousand inhabitants to over 8 million, according to current estimates, and the city continues to grow. Some migrants come to look for work, join their families, or pursue opportunities not available elsewhere. Many others, however, are desplazados, or victims of the armed conflict who have been forced to leave their homes. As a result, since the mid-1980s, Bogotá has received close to a million internal refugees fleeing violence.[21] According to the municipal government, an average of fifty-two displaced families arrive every day.[22] Some rely on kinship ties for shelter, food, and employment. Those who have no one, or whose families cannot accommodate them, have to fend for themselves. Their first concern, inevitably, is where to spend the night.

Parts of the city are known to be receptive to the displaced—areas where one might set up camp for a few days without being hassled. Few and far between, however, are spaces in which to settle permanently. While finding a foothold in the city has always been a struggle for poor migrants, those arriving a decade ago had a better chance of acquiring a plot of land and building a humble shack. In the past, populist political organizations frequently mobilized recent migrants to the city by helping them lay claim to the urban peripheries, build housing, and eventually equip them with infrastructure. The zones of high risk recently cleared by the municipal government are the few remaining areas in which squatting is still possible or where today's refugees can hope to settle for a small fee.[23] The very same zones evacuated by the government to protect people from one kind of threat have become, for this population, spaces of potential safety from an altogether different danger.

Some desplazados occupy evacuated zones of high risk hoping to access the municipal government's resettlement program. After all, becoming visible to the state as "lives at risk" entitles them to rights, such as decent housing, and to benefits from other governmental programs. Liliana's plea was successful after she demonstrated her exposure to environmental hazards, but most attempts to access housing subsidies by moving into zones of high risk are not. By law, the program applies to those living in these areas before they

FIG 4.1 New constructions, or "invasions," in a previously evacuated high-risk zone. Source: Photograph by author, 2009.

were designated high risk, and a number of techniques (such as examination of census records and aerial photographs) are used to verify this. As I was told by one government official, "We are prepared to deal with people who try to take advantage of the state's goodwill by inserting themselves into the resettlement program." Those attempting to be recognized as lives at risk must be able to navigate this regulatory landscape.

This became especially clear to me as I accompanied Tatiana and Miguel, two government technicians, on a trip to monitor an evacuated zone of high risk. About four months ago, Tatiana explained, a group of over a hundred settlers arrived in this area under cover of darkness with whatever building materials they could round up and by morning had constructed a cluster of makeshift shelters among the ruins of the former settlement (figure 4.1). When local authorities tried to remove the invasión, representatives from the Personería de Bogotá—the municipal agency charged with defending human rights—arrived to support the settlers, saying that they were desplazados and could not be forced to relocate. Being officially recognized as belonging to this vulnerable population confers certain forms of governmental protection.

Toward the end of our long, rough ride, we came upon Mauricio, the head of the local *vigías ambientales*, or "environmental guards." These guards are municipal employees who patrol the steep hillsides of the urban periphery once they have been cleared of settlers. They are armed with pickaxes and shovels rather than badges and guns, but their mission is to secure these zones and prevent their future occupation. The environmental guards monitor daily for "invasions" and immediately alert the police if they find any.

Mauricio looked winded and concerned. There was another invasion last night, he said, and the police have just arrived to tell the *invasores* (invaders) to leave. Catching his breath, Mauricio then conveyed his assessment of the new arrivals: "It appears the desplazados who arrived a few months ago have turned this into a business. They are going around looking for other desplazados who have no place to live and offering to facilitate their settlement in this area in exchange for 40,000 pesos (US$20)." Calling into question the motives behind the occupation, he continued: "They are telling all sorts of lies in order to make a few bucks. They claim the police cannot evict anyone who says they are a desplazado. And they are promising the desplazados that if they move into this area, they will be eligible for relocation subsidies." Conveying both disbelief and admiration, Mauricio stressed the degree to which an informal political formation was taking shape: "There is even a guy who has given himself the title of president of the relocation zone!"

Saying goodbye to Mauricio, we carried on toward the new settlement and, within a few minutes, arrived at a cluster of rudimentary shacks. Two police officers standing next to their motorcycles (figure 4.2) were immersed in a heated conversation with Catalina, a young woman in shorts and flip-flops—the typical attire of *tierra caliente*, or the hot lowlands, but not in Bogotá. Obviously new to the city, she looked frustrated and distraught. Tatiana got out of the truck and began to explain to Catalina that what the officers were saying is true: If she and the other "invaders" do not leave on their own accord, they will soon be evicted.

Catalina said she understood but that she had nowhere else to go. "Tengo la carta de desplazado" (I have documentation showing that I'm one of the displaced), she pleaded while gesturing to a paper she gripped as if it was her most important possession. Tatiana examined the document, which was official proof that Catalina was a victim of the armed conflict, and wrote down her name and place of origin as she inquired further: "When did you

FIG 4.2 A technician working for the municipal government's risk management agency consults a policeman about the status of recently arrived *desplazados*. Source: Photograph by author, 2009.

arrive?" Catalina responded, "I've been in Bogotá for two weeks. I don't have anywhere else to go!"

"How many are there in your family?" "I have two children, so we're three . . . or four," Catalina said tentatively, not sure whether to count her husband. The urgency in her voice began to build:

> What else can we do? The government hasn't given us anything! We were forced from our home. It was a *zona roja* [an area in which active combat is taking place]. They threatened us and said they were going to kill us if we didn't leave, and that's how we ended up here. We want to go back, but we can't. The government says that we have to wait . . . that we should wait for assistance. But when? And what are we supposed to do in the meantime? We need a place to live! They are supposed to give us a new home because this is a relocation zone. It's a zona de alto riesgo. There's water coming out of a broken water pipe and the ground is unstable. This area is not safe to live in.

Tatiana interrupted:

> Look, this was declared a zone of high risk in 2004, after which point no one is allowed to live here. If you do, you are in violation of the law and ineligible for resettlement. Since this occupation occurred in the last seventy-two hours, we have the authority to evict you. It's our responsibility to evacuate this zone. It's as simple as that. That's why I am telling you to look for another place to live, because here . . . sooner or later they are going to kick you out. And if that happens, they're not going to come with two or three policemen, but many. They'll kick you out, and it won't be pretty [*Los van a sacar a las malas*].

Sensing that her bid to access the resettlement program had failed, Catalina reiterated that her status as one of the desplazados entitled her to benefits: "I have this document, and it means I have rights." Tatiana responded,

> Look, you know that unfortunately the internal conflict in this country is very complicated and that we have many desplazados. I am just informing you what's going to happen. I am making a suggestion. Go to another part of the city—I don't know, maybe in Soacha, or I don't know where. There are so many [displaced] people and the state doesn't have the resources to deal with them all. But at any moment, we are going to come with the backing of the police and they're going to kick you out and destroy everything you've got.

As far as I know, the police never did evict these desplazados. I returned two months later, and, although unable to locate Catalina, I found the settlement looking as it had before. The settlers told me that, like the group that arrived four months earlier, they had been able to hold back the threat of eviction because of their officially documented status as members of the internally displaced population. But this did not mean that they successfully fought for their right to the city. For people like Catalina, membership within the political community of the city depends on the need for governmental protection. To be recognized as citizens with rights, they have to engage the state as lives at risk, for citizenship claims are predicated on vulnerability and mediated by exposure to danger. Although Catalina and her fellow settlers were successful at being recognized as desplazados and were spared from eviction, they were unable to persuade the authorities that they were vulnerable to landslides and thus eligible for housing subsidies. Whereas the resettlement program targets those exposed to nonhuman dangers, vulnera-bility to a convergence of threats makes one eligible for and subject to an even broader extension of the state's protective care. However, "vulnerability," as a category of political subjectivity and recognition linked to the political rationality of security, is internally stratified along lines of gender and race.

Landslides and Death Threats

Jairo and I sat on two wooden benches in the front room of the newly built house he had received recently from the Caja. He had come to Bogotá with his family from Valle del Cauca in the 1980s and settled in Altos de Cazucá, a neighborhood on the periphery of Bogotá. He was incredulous, he admitted, when DPAE informed him that he was living in a zone of high risk. "Sup-posedly," he told me, "the house we had been living in for over a decade was in danger of falling down." Having never experienced landslides or floods, and believing that the engineers who made this designation were wrong, Jairo's family faced a complicated choice. They could enroll in the resettlement program and receive a subsidy for a new home or remain in place knowing that the local authorities could evacuate the area at any mo-ment. Jairo's skepticism about the government's risk designation was fa-miliar: I had often heard similar doubts from those refusing to leave their homes. But Jairo had relocated, and so I asked him, "Why, if you were not in agreement with the risk assessment, did you decide to participate in the resettlement program?"

Jairo then leaned in close, his voice softening almost to a whisper: "I ac-cepted it because I was displaced from there. There was *raterismo y delin-cuencia* [thievery and crime] at all hours of the day and night. Leaving the house was dangerous, and if you can't leave the house to go to work," he said, "what can you do?" Paramilitaries took advantage of the insecurity in the area by charging a vacuna, which most people grudgingly paid in exchange for protection. "However," Jairo told me, "I was never in agreement with what the *paracos* [paramilitaries] were doing." And as a well-liked and re-spected leader within the Afro-Colombian community in Altos de Cazucá, his opposition was particularly unwelcome to the paramilitaries. When they tried to get him not just to pay for protection but also to collaborate with them, and he refused, they told him to leave or he would be killed.

Jairo then focused on finding a strategy for self-protection—"The first priority was to preserve my life," he told me—and went for help. His first stop was the Caja's field office, where he was encouraged to go directly to the police. The police then sent him to the Procuraduría, a government agency where citizens can report threats to their life through an official process known as *denuncia*, or "denunciation." After receiving Jairo's denunciation, the Procuraduría declared him a desplazado. Unlike Catalina, whose desplazado status did not qualify her for a housing subsidy because she had "invaded" a high-risk zone, Jairo was already recognized as a legitimate beneficiary of the Caja's resettlement program. Once officially classified as a member of the internally displaced population, he was expedited through the process of selecting and receiving a new home.

In Jairo's version of the story, the Caja enabled him to leave Altos de Cazucá before the paramilitaries followed through on their threats. But according to Carlos, a Caja social worker, Jairo had used and deceived the government (*nos engañó, nos utilizó*) for his own advantage. To ensure and hasten access to a resettlement property, Carlos told me, Jairo invented the story about his life being threatened. The Caja social worker referred to Jairo using a term I discuss further below: "Este tipo es un vivo!" ("This guy is a vivo!") Carlos had no doubt that paramilitaries were active throughout the area and that those who resisted or opposed their territorial control were regularly threatened if not disappeared or murdered. Nevertheless, he was suspicious of Jairo's story.

If Carlos's suspicion was warranted, this scenario would be telling. It would show that threats to one's life can be manipulated to strengthen claims made on the state and that accentuating one's exposure to danger can ensure the distribution of entitled benefits. It would highlight that, among certain populations, the rights conferred by citizenship are mediated by and predicated on the governmental imperative to protect lives at risk. However, it is likely that Jairo was indeed threatened by paramilitaries and saw the resettlement program's mission to protect his life from one kind of threat as an escape from one of an altogether different sort. Landslides and death threats are two forms of officially recognized vulnerability, and in combination they enabled Jairo to be recognized as "at risk" and entitled to governmental assistance. In the end, it was DPAE's calculation of the probability of environmental hazard that offered him a more expeditious route to safety. This parallels the wider political context in which risk management has functioned as an opportune way for the municipal government to address the social conditions of the urban periphery in a political climate dominated by security.

Jairo's room to maneuver, like that of left-of-center government workers or elected officials, was circumscribed by powerful forces both within and beyond the state.

Assumptions about race and space complicate matters, since Afro-Colombians living in the predominantly white and mestizo capital city are inevitably presumed to be "displaced" (in the more general sense of not being where they "belong"—that is, on the Atlantic or Pacific coasts). This compromises their ability to be recognized as members of the political community of the city and therefore to qualify for housing subsidies from the municipal government's resettlement program, whose objective is to protect the lives of *urban* citizens deemed vulnerable to landslides and floods. But while Afro-Colombians in Bogotá are understood as "out of place," this does not mean they are automatically considered deserving beneficiaries of the protections entitled to those officially recognized as forcibly displaced by the armed conflict. Both the resettlement program for "at risk" populations and the protections granted to desplazados privilege those lives considered to matter more. In Colombia, as elsewhere in the Americas, the capacity of certain forms of life to survive, endure, or flourish—while others are abandoned, extinguished, or left to go extinct—is distributed unevenly according to racialized regimes of hierarchy and dispossession. The tendency for black lives to be dehumanized, devalued, and discarded intersects here with the politics of security, internally stratifying the category of "vulnerability" on which it is based.

Carlos's doubt also raises the question of what constitutes credibility within these techniques of government. The imperative to protect life often calls on systems of verification to separate authentic from inauthentic claims and to adjudicate between deserving and undeserving claimants. In such cases, recognition depends less on prior categories of cultural or political membership, such as belonging to a racial or ethnic group, religious community, national citizenry, or political party.[24] While these distinctions sometimes reemerge—Jairo's credibility to municipal government workers may have been influenced by the fact that he is an Afro-Colombian man, for example—the salient categories of individual and collective identification are based primarily on calculations of vulnerability and victimhood. To be recognized as an internally displaced person, one must go through a bureaucratic process that begins with a declaration of the facts of one's case, which must then be corroborated through an investigation.[25] Once the declaration is verified, the individual joins the official registry of victims of the armed conflict eligible for government benefits. A similar process of verification applies to those who seek to be recognized as vulnerable to landslides, floods, or other hazards.

Certain practices and performances, then, are required for recognition as a deserving subject of the state's protective care. Jairo's initial dismissal of his former neighborhood's high-risk designation made him suspect as a beneficiary of the resettlement program. Jairo may not have believed that his house was in danger, but he saw relocation as a desirable option. Of course, if his house had been in danger of collapsing, it would have fallen down regardless of his opinion of the official prognosis. However, suspicion surrounds those who understand that being officially recognizable as "life at risk" ensures access to benefits and entitlements and who then take initiative to make themselves visible as such.

The doubts surrounding claims of vulnerability, and the practices and performances required of subjects "at risk," resemble the politics of recognition accompanying state-led multicultural reforms.[26] In Latin America as elsewhere, new frames of inclusion and exclusion determine how subjects must position themselves to be visible to legal institutions and governmental apparatuses.[27] In Colombia, legal and political rights granted to Afro-Colombians and indigenous populations have generated conflicts over who is eligible for and deserving of such rights.[28] The politics of recognition takes on a different character, however, when security structures the relationship between the state and its subjects. In Colombia, we find collective categories of governmental intervention and political subjectivity based on ethnicity, language, race, territory, and religion, but also on biopolitical criteria, such as vulnerability and victimhood. On some occasions, belonging to categories such as *indígena* (indigenous) or *afrodescendente* (of African descent) may be of less use to those struggling for survival on the urban periphery than being recognized as "at risk." The latter frame of inclusion takes precedence in the endangered city, where the politics of recognition is predicated on the politics of life.

An even more apt parallel can be found in humanitarian situations in which both state and nonstate actors work to deliver aid and assistance to victims of armed conflicts, natural disasters, disease outbreaks, and other emergencies.[29] Victimhood becomes the target of governmental intervention as well as the position from which people make claims on powerful institutions.[30] In targeting lives to be saved, as Didier Fassin and Richard Rechtman demonstrate, humanitarianism demands veritable performances from those seeking protective care.[31] When the state is involved, citizenship returns to center stage. As in the case Adriana Petryna describes, in which victims of the Chernobyl disaster were entitled to compensation only when recognized as irradiated bodies, political status has a biological predicate.[32] In such cases, as Nikolas Rose puts it, "citizenship has been shaped by conceptions of the specific vital characteristics of human beings."[33]

Yet these analogies must not obscure what is unique about the politics of security in Bogotá. In both multicultural reforms and humanitarian emergencies, logics of governmental intervention and forms of political subjectivity are oriented temporally toward the past, and the problem of recognition is consequently historical. Indigeneity is judged according to family genealogy, cultural traditions, or place of origin; victimhood is determined by evidence of a previous encounter with violence; suffering is verified by a test demonstrating infection. In each case, the condition or event is prior to the act of identification. In contrast, to be recognized as a "life at risk," one must demonstrate vulnerability to a potential event that may or may not ever occur.[34] As with refugees seeking asylum outside their home countries, recognition in the endangered city is oriented toward the future and depends on the authentication of one's vulnerability to projected threats.[35] As the next section highlights, opportunities to access much-needed state support are further constrained by another distinction between legitimate and illegitimate subjects of protection.

Vitality and Vulnerability

On the morning of July 31, 2008, two hundred desplazados occupied Bogotá's Parque de la 93 (Ninety-Third Street Park).[36] In a nonviolent action, they protested the government's failure to provide humanitarian assistance guaranteed by law to the displaced population. Their demonstration followed on the heels of the Assistance to Displaced Persons Day, which brought together twenty-four government agencies in a five-thousand-seat sports arena to attend to the needs of victims of the armed conflict. While the event provided aid to over seventy-five hundred people, thousands more were turned away. One of the leaders of the protest, Ricardo Jiménez, announced that the agency responsible for providing assistance to desplazados, Acción Social de la Presidencia, "has failed to distribute subsidies for food, housing, humanitarian aid, and even education for our children" and that "they do not respond to our rightful petitions."[37] Another demonstrator, José Antonio Iserra, affirmed, "We don't want more lies from Acción Social. We will stay here until Mayor Samuel Moreno gets here."[38] Later that night, after Moreno had arrived on the scene and promised to intercede on their behalf, the protestors agreed to evacuate the park.

The park they occupied is one of Bogotá's premier symbols of wealth, exclusivity, and privilege. It is flanked by foreign embassies, corporate headquarters, and luxury condominiums, and the surrounding area boasts some of the city's highest-priced real estate. It is public, so anyone can enter, but it is primarily frequented by the *gente de bien* (lit. "the good people," but referring to the well-to-do). Héctor Giraldo, one of the demonstrators, emphasized the obvious class implications of their action: "Since the wealthy of this country have not paid us any mind, we decided to get their attention by visiting them and making them take notice of the reality of our situation."[39] Blanca Durán, the mayor of the locality governing the park, summed up the opinion of the local residents and business owners who saw the desplazados as somewhere between a threat and an annoyance and wanted them removed: "Any occupation of this sort generates security problems. It creates inconveniences for the citizenry of the surrounding area and for organizations such as embassies and multinationals."[40]

Opposition to the cause of the protestors also came from other quarters and circulated in the media and among public officials. As news of the protest was just getting out, Bogotá's secretary of government, Clara López, told the Bogotá-based newspaper *El Tiempo* that the demonstration taking place was the work of "the same person who orchestrated the 1999 occupation [by desplazados] of the Red Cross office in the Zona Rosa."[41] Secretary López denounced City Councilman Antonio Navia for having been the motivating force behind both rebellious actions—an accusation meant to render the protestors' demands insincere and inauthentic. (She corrected herself in writing two weeks later, admitting that Councilman Navia was neither present at nor involved in the demonstration.)[42] Other voices were equally certain that a predatory, deceitful figure was using the demonstrators for personal gain. A government official I spoke with decried attempts by some to take advantage of the plight of the desplazados and hoped that the authorities would refuse their demands. He said, "There is a leader who is personally benefiting from the situation by manipulating other desplazados and even young children." Echoing the charge against Jairo, who supposedly took advantage of the resettlement program, he said about this anonymous character: "Es un vivo!"

In Colombia, *vivo* is a colloquial term derived from the verb *vivir* (to live). As an adjective, it means "alive" or "living" and can designate someone who is full of vigor, and it need not carry a pejorative sense (*una persona viva* is sharp-witted, clever, and astute). As a noun, however, it denotes a category of person who is opportunistic, manipulative, and selfish; to call someone *un vivo* (and it usually does refer to a man) is to call his motives into question. The term is also frequently applied to *costeños* (a racialized marker of regional identity) or to Colombians of African descent more generally, as in Jairo's case, who according to enduring racist stereotypes are presumed by many whites or mestizos from the interior to be lazy, dishonest, and untrustworthy. Vivo often accompanies the verb *aprovecharse*, which means "to take advantage of" an opportunity or another person. Someone who falls into this category is a hustler and is presumed to have the power to make things happen and to get other people to act, often against their will, through his possession of what Thomas Blom Hansen and Oskar Verkaaik call "urban charisma."[43] The category applies usually to men with guile, gumption, and cunning who are inherently shady, scam artists, or deceitful tricksters. And it invariably sets up a gendered dichotomy between the predator and the victim—if *el vivo* is taking advantage of a situation and benefiting personally, there must be someone powerless, gullible, or vulnerable (mostly women and children) on the losing end. The imagined relationship between *el vivo* and *los vulnerables*, between masculine vitality and feminine vulnerability, places urban politics within a biopolitical frame, and the response to the occupation of this city park is a prime example of its influence.[44]

The official who argued that the protestors were being manipulated and that their demands should not be met had undoubtedly seen images on television and in newspapers depicting children, some only a few weeks old, among those occupying the park. The media had pounced on this right away, and the alleged presence of an exploitative mastermind, as well as accusations that protestors were abusing an especially vulnerable population (their children), served to delegitimize their demands.[45] *El Espectador* ran an article that led with a quote from an eleven-year-old girl: "They used us as shields so [the authorities] wouldn't spray us with water and beat us with their batons."[46] That these children were themselves members of the displaced population—they had no school to go to, no home to be left in, and no maid to take care of them—was noticeably absent from media commentary. It was a cruel irony that the protestors were asking for the very help that the media and public officials used to delegitimize their cause.

Pursuant to a 1997 law, internally displaced persons in Colombia are entitled to food support, a basic subsistence kit, medical and psychological attention, living accommodations, and transportation. Since a 2007 ruling by the Constitutional Court, the government is obligated to provide aid until the displaced person or family is economically self-sufficient. However, an investigation by the news magazine *Semana* concluded that this policy has had unexpected results: "If the Court was in fact seeking to benefit the victims, it served to create a lucrative business for many others."[47] This investigation discovered reports throughout the country of people filing fraudulent petitions on behalf of desplazados, charging them fees to process their claims, taking commissions from their entitlements, and organizing demonstrations to profit from the settlement. Biopolitical economies had apparently sprung up around the desplazados. However, *Semana*'s report did not question the motives behind every instance of collective mobilization among this population: "There is nothing bad about a demonstration when it has good reasons. . . . But there is a big difference between that and taking advantage of the very little assistance that [the desplazados] receive."[48] When the subtlety of this distinction is lost, all forms of collective action among desplazados appear as further instances of the abuse of the vulnerable by the vital.

Protestors occupied the park for a second time on September 8, denouncing the government for not having complied with promises made by Mayor Moreno after the initial demonstration. On this occasion, however, a forty-member riot-police squadron quickly surrounded the park and removed the demonstrators by force. Police chief General Rodolfo Palomino spoke to news cameras amid the ruckus: "Unfortunately, it was necessary to go ahead with the eviction. The attitude of the demonstrators became hostile. . . . There are certain people who were electing themselves as leaders, but more than leaders they were acting as agitators who wanted to be subversive and to take advantage of the unwary [*aprovecharse de las personas incautas*], and they forced those people to bring along their children and use them as screens." The protestors' spokesman, Ricardo Jiménez, was detained by the police along with six others. General Palomino said that Jiménez would be "prosecuted for taking advantage of both the situation and the displaced population in order to extract economic benefits."[49] Fifteen officers of the Policía de Menores (Police for Minors) took charge of the children, nine of whom were taken into custody by the Colombian Institute of Family Welfare (ICBF). It was illegal, they told the press, for minors to participate in protests; to be reunited with their children, mothers would have to convince the welfare agency that they were no longer involved in such activities.[50] The interpretive frame activated during the first demonstration facilitated the immediate intervention that brought a swift end to the second one.

Becoming Biomedical

Seven months later, a group of desplazados occupied another of Bogotá's prominent public parks. In contrast to the earlier demonstrations, this one took place in the historical center just blocks from City Hall and the Presidential Palace. The site of the occupation was the Parque Tercer Milenio (Third Millennium Park), which was created in 2002 by an urban renewal project. The park was a relatively underused expanse of open space and recreational facilities until April 2009, when close to five hundred desplazados descended on it. They pitched tents and constructed makeshift shelters out of scavenged materials, and overnight the park was turned into a veritable refugee camp. While the two previous actions had lasted only a day each, these demonstrators were there to stay.

By early May, the number of desplazados had risen to twelve hundred, and their spokesmen were entering into negotiations with representatives from both the national and municipal governments. The demonstrators, it seemed, had succeeded in investing a governmental category, the displaced population, with a physical presence in the city, a common rhetoric for making claims, and a collective identity with which to engage the state. "Although our situations are different, our needs and demands are the same," said one of the occupants of the park.[51] They demanded their rights to protection, housing, food, and employment, but first they had to be recognized as belonging to the population guaranteed entitlements on account of their vulnerability. This is the politics of the governed in biopolitical form, and urban space is simultaneously its terrain, target, and technique. The desplazados occupied the park to make their voices heard in ways reminiscent of other urban political movements. Yet their demands emphasized security over citizenship, the right to life more than to the city.

The national government was reticent to acquiesce. The Justice Department announced it would pursue legal action against individuals promoting demonstrations by desplazados, and Acción Social warned it would not privilege groups engaging in unlawful occupations of public space. The municipal government of Bogotá was more attentive to the situation, and by the end of May an agreement between city hall and the desplazados was on the horizon. The mayor's office was promising to make eight hundred jobs available to members of the group and was offering them temporary shelter while funds for additional support were sought. On the basis of these terms, three hundred of the demonstrators agreed to relocate, and the municipal government was confident that the rest would soon follow.

With this success, public officials and the media kicked off a brief campaign to convince the remaining squatters to accept the same terms. It began by publicizing the positive aspects of relocation. For example, *El Tiempo* ran an upbeat story about the first night spent away from Third Millennium Park by those who had taken the government's deal. A young girl, the newspaper reported, "was jumping for joy at having arrived at the temporary shelter."[52] It described the miseries of desplazados as a thing of the past: "To be exposed to the inclement weather, the powerful rays of the sun, the frosty daybreak hours; without water, without bathrooms, and without a roof to sleep under; these are no longer problems for this group of desplazados."[53] And the article emphasized that it was they who, "on their own initiative, decided to take advantage of the agreement."[54] The incentives quickly expired, however, as the pressure to bring an end to the occupation mounted.

As deliberations continued, the media spread allegations of a manipulative force behind the protest and reports of demonstrators being held against their will. *El Tiempo* published an account of a woman who "dared to denounce the leaders of the occupation . . . for forcing [the protestors] to remain in place."[55] The newspaper quoted her under the pseudonym "Nancy" to protect her identity: "I am afraid. There could be a massacre here. They could come into my hut at any time and kill me for saying that the leaders of the displaced are obligating us to stay here. I want to get out of here right away." The article told the story of her displacement from the department of Tolima, where she was living until guerrillas forced her to flee. But it emphasized the insecurity she now felt during the occupation of Third Millennium Park on account of the "authoritarianism of her supposed leaders." The predatory dynamic allegedly present among the demonstrators extended to the relation between parents and children: "The children are already victims of displacement because of violence, and now they are being used as a tool for making demands," warned Olga Lucía Velásquez, the state's attorney for matters concerning youth.[56] As in the occupation of Ninety-Third Street Park, the distinction between *el vivo* and *los vulnerables* began to frame this crisis, and it seemed only a matter of time before the remaining occupants of the park would be removed by force.

Then a crisis of global proportion hit Bogotá and changed the fate of the desplazados still struggling to make their demands heard. On July 13, Colombia's National Institute of Health announced the appearance of *gripa porcina* (swine flu), otherwise known as the H1N1 virus. A few days later, health officials reported that 59 of the 185 cases throughout the country were in Bogotá, and that 5 of the 7 deaths attributed to the flu had occurred in the capital city.[57] The media then relayed a message from Bogotá's secretary of health, Héctor Zambrano, in which he "asked the citizenry to increase preventive measures: wash hands with soap and water, use masks if you have flu symptoms, avoid shaking hands and kissing if you have the virus, and go to the hospital if you have a persistent fever over thirty-eight degrees, a cough, and difficulty breathing."[58] Zambrano expressed concern about the concentration of desplazados in Third Millennium Park, which, he feared, could become a "niche for the H1N1 epidemic." Although not a single case of swine flu had been detected among the displaced population, Zambrano said they "are highly vulnerable, both emotionally and physically, and their conditions of health and nutrition are not good. We are all aware that many efforts have been made, but these cases demand more forceful responses."[59] Whereas preventative measures for controlling the spread of the virus were directed at the general citizenry, disciplinary techniques were required for this population.

Two days after the H1N1 scare began, three hundred uniformed policemen installed a cordon sanitaire around the encampment (figure 4.3). The "epidemiological barrier" (*cordón epidemiológico*), as it was called, consisted of an inner ring of metallic fencing covered by an outer ring of heavy-duty plastic. The secretary of government, Clara López, justified the quarantine: "The H1N1 virus is a danger, it's a time bomb, and the mayor has done the responsible thing in ordering the sanitary ring."[60] Face masks were handed out, clean water was brought in, and a medical team of close to two hundred began to administer daily checkups.[61] At two o'clock in the morning, just a few hours after the cordon sanitaire was installed, the team conducted a

FIG 4.3 Cordon sanitaire surrounding the encampment in Third Millennium Park.
Source: Photograph by author, 2009.

thorough census to register each person in the encampment and to identify the most vulnerable among them.

At the single entrance to the encampment, police set up a security check-point (figure 4.4). Protected by a tent, four government officials operated two computers on which they recorded the identity of each protestor and monitored his or her comings and goings. Those passing through were required to show identification cards; those not registered as participants in the occupation were barred from entering. The cordon sanitaire thus blocked additional people from joining the demonstration and ensured that outsiders could not make contact with the desplazados. In addition, those on the inside worried they would not be allowed to return if they left to search for food for their children or supplies for their camp. A woman called out from inside to members of the press: "How do you think we feel?" Seconds later, she answered her own question: "Like prisoners!"[62] The governmental logic being applied to the displaced population was now clear to those on the inside: "We are running a terrible risk, and when we leave to rummage for money or food, we obviously put the rest of the city at risk, too."

FIG 4.4 Security checkpoint. Source: Photograph by author, 2009.

With the containment strategy in place and the census conducted, Mayor Moreno held a press conference to discuss the way forward. He informed the media that the health department had examined the desplazados in the park and had found approximately 130 people with acute respiratory symptoms. As Health Secretary Zambrano put it, there was "a high risk of contagion of serious illness" because of the potential for these cases to become a focal point for the spread of the H1N1 virus.[63] Zambrano said that 80 of the 130 cases were children and recommended their immediate removal.[64] The mayor also warned that those in the encampment risked fire and electrocution because of the burning of wood outside the huts and the electrical connections being used inside them.[65] The convergence of multiple risks, Moreno informed the public, led the District Emergency Committee to declare a health alert in Third Millennium Park. This declaration, he concluded, "permits us to intervene and to take all necessary preventative measures in order to reduce risks to public health."[66]

The mayor then ordered the unwell, as well as all minors, to leave the park. Moreno assured them they would be taken to hospitals, receive medical attention, and undergo constant monitoring. This decision, he reiterated, was a guarantee that the rights of these highly vulnerable persons would be defended, especially those rights pertaining to health and living conditions.[67] Secretary López explained the situation in the same way: "We are implementing the instructions of the mayor, and we are going to evacuate everyone with any kind of flu symptoms or sickness and direct them to the city's network of hospitals, because it is our constitutional obligation to protect the lives and the integrity of these persons."[68] The mayor then appealed to the United Nations Refugee Agency (UNHCR) for mediation, expressing hope that it could lead the national and municipal governments to a solution. UN representatives met with each agency involved and began to pursue an agreement that would put an end to the occupation.

When only twenty-seven protestors responded to his plea, Moreno began to express concern that the demonstration would continue to grow and that the municipal government was powerless to stop it. In an article titled "Time Bomb," *Semana* reported that between forty and fifty displaced families arrived each day in Bogotá and that the "instruction among them now is to join the occupation."[69] In response to these concerns, the mayor conceded that the "situation is getting out of hand" and lamented that "we cannot close off the borders of the city."[70] As the pressure built, the figures of the vital and the vulnerable came back into view. *El Tiempo* cited reports from visitors to the occupation who said that few sick people had responded to the government's call to seek medical attention because "the leaders of the occupation threatened to kill those desplazados who wanted to leave Third Millennium Park."[71] Another article quoted a city councilwoman, Gilma Jiménez, who claimed to have discovered manipulative forces among the encamped: "There are professional opportunists here whose economic motivations have led them to become leaders to the detriment of the desplazados themselves."[72] Councilwoman Jiménez told the newspaper that one of the demonstrators had told her: "Our children are our shields. If the authorities remove them, the ESMAD [riot police] can enter." Although the police department stated its intention to avoid using force, this framing foreshadowed another act of removal.

The UNHCR continued to mediate between leaders of the occupation and delegates from the national and municipal governments. By late July, negotiations were progressing. An agreement was being considered that would cover the estimated two thousand desplazados gathered in the park at that moment and provide them with long-term housing solutions, temporary shelter, employment assistance, food support, transportation subsidies, and security assurances. Just before midnight on July 29, the UNHCR announced that an agreement had been signed that would provide broad humanitarian assistance to the desplazados following their voluntary withdrawal from the park.[73] On the morning of Sunday, August 2, four months after the occupation began, the desplazados called an end to their protest and started to break down their camp. They lined up at city hall to receive subsidies, and by early afternoon many had cash in hand. Some moved to temporary shelters, and others boarded chartered buses and trucks bound for their places of origin. As the remaining few packed up and went to collect their benefits, their leaders promised to occupy the park again if the agreement was not fulfilled within three months.[74]

In the days that followed, government officials reflected on the crisis that had just been resolved. Secretary López clarified that the agreement reached with the desplazados was not the result of their prolonged occupation of Third Millennium Park, which was illegal, but rather the necessary response to a public health crisis. "This agreement," she told the press, "is not a resolution that comes by way of an abuse of discretion [*vías de hecho*],[75] but a health emergency that required the evacuation of the park in order to prevent unhealthy conditions and the extremely high risk [*altísimo riesgo*] of . . . an H1N1 pandemic."[76] On the one hand, Secretary López's comments responded to concerns that the settlement would "open the door to new occupations," as one newspaper put it, by creating incentives for others to pursue extralegal means of making their demands heard.[77] She assured the public that the government would "take measures so that this does not happen again." On the other hand, in insisting that the situation was a health crisis and that it was "in that context that we signed the agreement," López revealed something else. It was by becoming recognizable not simply as victims of violence or members of the urban poor but as lives at risk that the protestors could succeed at having their demands met. They were like Jairo, who was threatened by both paramilitaries and landslides but whose exposure to nonhuman dangers allowed him to receive governmental protection and care. Once the desplazados occupying Third Millennium Park were identified as vulnerable in a biomedical sense, they could finally be recognized as proper citizens of the endangered city.

From Living Dangerously to Living Well

Governing risk in Bogotá is enmeshed in Colombia's protracted security predicament, whereby political incorporation is often predicated on conditions of vulnerability and victimhood. It is within this domain, rather than solely in the realm of citizenship and rights, that settlers of the urban periphery engage in political relationships with the state. In Colombia, life often enters the realm of the political as a precarious possession permanently in danger of being harmed or taken away rather than as a resource to be managed, cultivated, or improved.[78] As liberal democratic institutions have been shaped by the imperative to secure life against threat, "life at risk" becomes a category of entitlement through which the urban poor claim assistance, protection, and care. At stake is Foucault's insight into the relationship between juridical and biopolitical power: "It was life more than the law that became the issue of political struggles, even if the latter were formulated through affirmations concerning rights."[79] This chapter reveals how those with little recourse to state benefits access the opportunities created by the imperative to protect the lives of poor and vulnerable populations from future harm.[80] It also allows us to see how the politics of security and the government of risk shape urban politics. While our analyses must not ignore rights and citizenship, it is time to examine how other frames of recognition, inclusion, and entitlement come to shape the political terrain of cities.[81]

The domain of political engagement organized around security and risk both enables and constrains the urban poor in Colombia. To become rights-bearing citizens belonging to the city, they must first be identifiable as vulnerable lives at risk and in need of protection. Yet when this population too actively engages the state on these grounds, another kind of agency is seen to be at work. The manipulative, opportunistic figure of *el vivo*, the vital, is perceived to be taking advantage of the state's goodwill, gaming the system, and acting deviously or even unlawfully. In such cases, desplazados occupying a city park and demanding their rights, for example, are viewed as helpless, gullible victims in need of protection from the predatory ploys of *los vivos*. This dynamic unfolds along lines of inclusion and exclusion common to the unequal forms of citizenship found throughout Latin American cities. Since the vulnerable (presumably women and children) are expected to be passive, their activity must be attributed to a hypothetical (usually masculine) vital force. When the active subject in question is identified as Afro-Colombian, this association is all the more automatic. The gendered and racialized distinction between vitality and vulnerability upholds an interpretive frame central to the politics of security and the government of risk in Bogotá.

To understand why vulnerability is valorized and vitality suspect, we must recognize Colombia's historically specific combination between liberalism and security, which distinguishes between lives needing protective care and those identified as imminent threats.[82] Citing widespread violence against activists, union leaders, and political dissidents in Colombia, Rojas argues that "the life of those participating in democratic politics continues to be at risk, and thus the space for democratic politics is shrinking."[83] Her analysis supports the argument that risk management gained traction in Bogotá precisely because it offered a technical way of governing social and environmental problems and safely engaging in urban politics. Yet it might be productive to reframe Rojas's argument as such: it is not just that those who participate in democratic politics in Colombia are in danger but that political existence itself depends, for many, on their recognition as "lives at risk." When liberal democratic ideals are subordinated to rationalities of security, categories like vitality, vulnerability, and victimhood structure how people engage in political relationships with the state. Confounding clear-cut distinctions between the political life (*bios*) of democratic citizenship and the bare life (*zoe*) of humanitarian care, they participate both in the politics of rights and the politics of life.[84] This has implications for urban citizenship, but it also demands that we reflect critically on efforts to mobilize vitalist philosophies as a source of radical opposition to power, capital, and empire.[85]

In recent years, "life" has gained prominence as the ground for political struggle because of its assumed irreducible, insubordinate, and uncontrollable nature—as Michael Hardt and Antonio Negri argue, global capitalism "can never capture all of life."[86] Foucault's work on biopower is often attached to the vitalist claim that, in Gilles Deleuze's rendition, life "becomes resistance to power when power takes life as its object."[87] Enrique Dussel has influentially adopted this proposition for Latin America, and Arturo Escobar has done so in Colombia specifically.[88] In their search for a liberatory, "decolonial" politics, these scholars attempt to look beyond the reach of the state-capital nexus and to the experience of the indigenous, the minority, and the oppressed.[89] Their arguments hinge on Dussel's concept of "exteriority," which they claim does not imply a subject position external to the "modern/colonial" world order but, rather, one constituted by hegemonic discourses as other. However, their "otherwise" politics of life—in its devotion to the vulnerable, the dispossessed, and the victim—bears an uncanny resemblance to the governmental rationalities analyzed above.

This correspondence raises doubt about the radical otherness of the politics of life to existing political formations: does this dualism obscure important issues of political praxis? The politics of life is a domain of political engagement, strategy, and struggle that is neither exterior to nor isomorphic with state power; neither in functional equilibrium with the politics of death nor an irrepressible force of resistance against it; neither necessarily complicit in acts of dispossession nor a perpetual source of radical opposition. In Colombia, security shapes the terrain of urban politics, but it does not fully determine how that terrain is traversed. Thus we might engage critically with existing political formations and explore the opportunities and dangers created by them; indeed, this is precisely what the urban poor in Bogotá are doing. Without foreclosing the possibility of a radical politics of life, this chapter has highlighted the many contradictions and constraints that such a politics would have to contend with in seeking to transform regimes of living dangerously into regimes of living well.

5

SECURING THE FUTURE

Anticipatory Urbanism

Of the state agencies serving the self-built settlements of the urban periphery, the Caja is one of the most visible. With a staff of twelve full-time social workers and a handful of legal and technical experts on site, the Caja's field office is known throughout the locality of Ciudad Bolívar as the place to go to make face-to-face contact with the municipal government. In close proximity to the zones of high risk, the field office is also the base from which members of the Caja's staff make visits to the homes of families whose relocation they are responsible for facilitating. How people in the peripheral neighborhoods of Ciudad Bolívar interact with the Caja influences how, on a more general level, they come to see the state and understand themselves as urban citizens with certain rights and responsibilities.[1] It is one of the key sites in which the political community of the endangered city comes into being. Thus it was in this office that I spent the majority of my time getting to know the staff members of the Caja's resettlement program, accompanying them on visits to zones of high risk, observing their daily interactions with program beneficiaries, and reflecting with them on their work. These everyday encounters shape visions of the future and temporal sensibilities among both government officials and governed populations in Bogotá.

After the first few months, I began to notice that conversations among Caja social workers often revolved around a puzzling fact: while many people go to great lengths to participate in the resettlement program, others fight tooth and nail to remain in place. The enthusiasm some express toward official relocation schemes may be surprising to scholars who expect the urban poor to perennially position themselves in opposition to such interventions. And yet Caja social workers familiar with the living conditions of the urban poor in Bogotá clearly understood that the settlers of the urban periphery often saw the municipal government's resettlement program as one of their only opportunities to access the official beneficence of the state. It came as no surprise when people arrived at the office prepared to petition the Caja to recognize them as "at risk" and, therefore, as eligible for housing relocation subsidies. Social workers frequently agonized about how to distinguish the "truly vulnerable" from those attempting to take advantage of the "state's goodwill." This led them to evaluate the hazards faced by each household and to hierarchically rank beneficiaries according to levels of vulnerability. Formal as well as informal calculations of potential threats ultimately determined who would be granted a housing subsidy during a given budget cycle. Entitlements were predicated upon endangerment, which in turn relied on the assessment of possible futures.

Recalcitrance among those eligible for resettlement was also discussed as a temporal problem. Since participation was ostensibly "voluntary"—that is, residents would not be permitted to remain in the area indefinitely, but were free to decline their relocation subsidy—Caja social workers spent a good deal of time discussing what led some people to accept the program and others to reject it. More often than not, they attributed the reluctance to relocate to a lack of precautionary instinct and to foreshortened temporal horizons, blaming the absence of middle-class values, such as planning, prudentialism, and inheritance. For example, Diana reflected on the problem in the following terms: "What we [the social workers] do is raise their awareness [*concientizarlos*] toward the dangers that exist all around them: landslides, floods, robberies, sexual assaults, murders, theft. That is, we tell them that they ought to not just think about the present, but also to look ahead to the future [*que no solamente piense en el ahora sino se proyecte*]. It is the future that matters, since it's what they will leave behind to their children." In her short commentary, Diana brought the future into the present in at least three ways. First, she projected a range of potential dangers that may not ever materialize: from environmental hazards to human menaces. Second, she insisted on a course of action that resettlement subjects ought to follow: to be aware of threats and to do what is prudent for the safety and security of their families. And, finally, she urged them to expand their temporal horizons to take into account not just what is happening today, but also what might happen tomorrow.

Throughout our discussion, Diana revealed the class-based assumptions embedded within the anticipatory form of urban government through which the Caja intervenes in Bogotá's peripheral settlements. Although the official future is one of imminent hazard and potential harm, Caja social workers often articulated an alternative, and more optimistic, expectation—social mobility. Diana continued:

> Many people only think about *el ya* [slang for the "current moment," or the "immediate present"]. Yes, *el ya* is about searching for enough to eat, scraping together tuition for the children, making sure they have shoes and clothes. *El ya* is about living in poverty, and not having a vision for the future. This is not the case for everyone, since some people look ahead [*se visionan*] and say: "No, my son is not going to grow up here. I will take him to a better place." This is what we can offer them.

For those able to project into the future, Diana insisted, the resettlement program offers a path to what the Caja terms "progressive development," or the gradual advance of living conditions that begins with relocation and continues through the habitation of a new home. Wrapped within the vision of a future filled with potential dangers are forward-looking promises of betterment, uplift, and advancement—but only if these dangers are apprehended and dealt with in the proper way. Hopes of progressive development sit in tension with the prognosis of disaster that enables them. Yet the fusion of divergent, even contradictory, futures is characteristic of anticipatory urbanism in Bogotá.

Both inside and outside urban studies, futurity has become a present concern. Most analyses, however, make epochal claims, theoretical generalizations, and political denouncements that often break down under ethnographic scrutiny.[2] While much can be gained by theorizing temporal transformations on a grand scale, or what Rosenberg and Harding refer to as the "big stories of the future," this often leads to reductive denunciations of temporality as a domain of power, hegemony, and domination.[3] In many cases, a tautological truism is at work: temporality is seen as fundamental to the structures of power that produce subjection and inequality, which in turn are found to operate through the structuring of time. The claim that time has a politics is irrefutable. Once we acknowledge, with Reinhart Koselleck, that historical time "is bound up with social and political actions, with concretely acting and suffering human beings and their institutions and organizations," then it logically follows that all forms of temporality are suffused with power relations.[4] But while we ought to critically analyze the politics of temporality and identify its pernicious effects on certain bodies, spaces, and populations, it would be a mistake to resort to simple diagnostics and denunciations of power. For doing so would risk ascribing an almost totalizing quality to the politics of time and leave us devoid of resources for thinking about the heterodox temporalities existing alongside and within hegemonic formations. Without turning away from ethical questions of justice and equality, I argue that these pursuits deserve a way of analyzing temporality both as a domain of social control and as a terrain of political possibility.

This chapter builds on AbdouMaliq Simone's understanding of "anticipatory urban politics" to explore the forms of temporality—especially those oriented toward the future—that are emerging and circulating in specific sites and situations within the city of Bogotá.[5] Focusing on the rise of security and risk over the past decade, it examines temporal framings, practices, and sensibilities among architects and engineers charged with the technical designation of zones of high risk, government social workers who manage the resettlement of "at risk" populations, and inhabitants of the self-built settlements of the urban periphery, where the majority of high-risk zones are located. My objective is to identify the forms of temporality and futurity integral to the endangered city. This, in turn, reveals how terrains of political engagement are shaped by a focus on what has not yet happened and may never actually occur. But what also needs emphasizing is the coexistence of multiple temporalities and figurations of urban futurity. An ethnographic approach sacrifices an emphasis on theoretical generalization and on epochal shifts, but not to retreat to local specificity and uniqueness. Rather, it identifies the diverse ways in which the future comes to inhabit the present of cities and then shapes how they are planned, built, governed, experienced, and inhabited. The politics of security has indeed produced new forms of urban futurity, yet they belie a successional schema that treats anticipatory regimes as newly hegemonic.

To a certain degree, all forms of urbanism display a futuristic orientation. After all, the raison d'être of urbanists—planners, architects, designers, and so on—is to envision and create the city of tomorrow.[6] Urban planner John Friedmann describes his field as "a forward-looking activity that selects from the past those elements that are useful in analyzing existing conditions from a vantage point of the future—the changes that are thought to be desirable and how they might be brought about."[7] This definition has been faulted for presuming that urbanism has an ubiquitous relationship with the future, as David Connell puts it, and that this relationship is "universal, both across cultures and through time."[8] Taking issue with this view, Connell proposes a progressive time line of distinct urban paradigms—traditional, modern, postmodern—each one defined by a different relationship to the future.[9] In the case of Bogotá, this allows us to recognize contemporary forms of urbanism as reflections of broader ideological shifts. And what is worth noting is not just that they are oriented toward an uncertain and indeterminate future—what Connell's schema would define as "postmodern"—but that this configuration of urbanism does not entirely displace and render obsolete "modern" expectations (development, progress, opportunity, growth, and advancement) or even for that matter "traditional" ones (divination, eschatology, prophecy, fate, destiny). Visions of urban futurity in Bogotá are indeed historically and culturally specific, yet they do not conform to a neat, linear progression from futures past to futures present.

The Subjunctive State

Let us now return to situations in which resettlement "beneficiaries" are denied permission to use their subsidies to purchase housing in areas where the risk of landslide is deemed high. I regularly encountered such situations throughout my fieldwork, since most people began their relocation process by searching for properties similar in size, location, and construction to their previous homes. As such properties rarely satisfied the building codes and zoning regulations enforced by the Caja's technical team, attempts to relocate to *vivienda usada* (used housing) were frequently turned down. Prospective buyers were then encouraged to relocate to *vivienda nueva* (new housing) in one of the complexes built by private developers to house those living in Bogotá's zones of high risk who were eligible for government housing subsidies.

Like many of her fellow beneficiaries, Doris was crestfallen on learning that she would not be allowed to use her relocation subsidy to purchase the *casita preciosa* (precious little house) she had discovered just a few blocks from her daughter's school. However, within minutes of receiving the bad news, her disappointment morphed into optimism. Nuria, her madrina (or "godmother," as female social workers are called), unrolled three large color posters revealing a planned housing development with the felicitous name of Ciudadela Porvenir—*ciudadela* means "citadel" or "fortress," though more commonly it refers to self-contained residential or commercial developments, while *porvenir*, literally "that which has yet to come," connotes a future full of promising possibility. The name of the planned development could have only counted for so much. But the promise of both security and progress it signified must have put a smile back on Doris's face.

The first poster Nuria unveiled showed ten housing blocks, each containing approximately fifteen two-story units, clustered together in a group. The second depicted the street plan of the surrounding area, including the proposed location of parks, recreation centers, and bus routes. The third displayed the floor plans and specifications of the individual units. Nuria then explained to Doris that this project was being built by a private developer, and that she would have no problem putting her housing subsidy to use there. Although their discussion was based entirely on images, measurements, and plans—after all, a model house had not yet been built—these future projections stimulated Doris's anticipation, imagination, and excitement. Fittingly, the subjunctive was the discursive register within which this conversation transpired. "Ojalá que tenga la oportunidad de ver esas casitas tan bonitas antes de que se acaben" (Hopefully I would have the opportunity to see these lovely houses before they are all spoken for), wished Doris. "Es probable que las casas construidas vayan a ser iguales que las que aparecen en los planos" (It is probable that the built houses would be the same as the ones that appear in the drawings), Nuria speculated. Although the posters estimated what would eventually be built, they allowed Doris to project her own hopes and dreams onto the future they momentarily brought into view. After listening to Nuria's pitch, she was eager to join the list of potential buyers and to sign up for a visit to the future site of Ciudadela Porvenir.

FIG 5.1 Site of planned development. Source: Photograph by author, 2010.

Three weeks later, Doris was more than ready to tour the planned housing development endorsed by the Caja. On Nuria's invitation, I piled onto
a chartered bus with other potential buyers. We passed through neighborhoods with paved roads, TransMilenio stations, and shopping centers, but
the urbanized landscape began to disappear as we neared the extreme southwestern border of the city. Eventually, the bus came to a stop on a newly cut
roadway surrounded on all sides by empty lots and dirt paths (figure 5.1).
Many of the passengers looked disoriented as they descended upon an unfamiliar location on the periurban edge of Bogotá. Those who thought they
would at least have the opportunity to see a model unit expressed disappointment when all they found were two representatives of the construction company. Nuria welcomed everyone and introduced Germán, the developer's
spokesperson, who was dressed in blue jeans and a crisp button-down shirt
embroidered with the name and logo of his employer. Germán explained
that three housing blocks were planned for the first phase of development
and that 154 units would be reserved for beneficiaries of the Caja's resettlement program. He added: "Sin embargo, la construcción no puede arrancar
hasta que se firmen contratos para cada unidad" (However, construction

cannot begin until contracts can be signed for every single unit). Again, the discussion took the subjunctive form.

Without having seen plans, let alone a model home, some prospective buyers were wary of such an agreement. "This is just an empty field," one exclaimed. Nuria intervened by pleading with the group to wait and listen. The developer's spokesman then introduced José Antonio, the project's lead engineer, who offered a tour of the empty lot. But this exercise quickly seemed ridiculous, and more questions and concerns bubbled up. A few visitors remarked on the remote location and lack of basic infrastructure, such as water, electricity, and sewage, and the engineer assured the group that all this would change in time. "This is a zone of high risk," a prospective buyer said under her breath. "There will be flooding from the two rivers over there," she gestured. "There used to be a flower processing facility there, but it flooded when the heavy rains came. They're trying to move us from one zone of high risk to another. But my house is just fine. Nothing has ever happened to us there, thank God, but they tell us we have to move." Although her faith in providence had kept her safe, she contradicted the future projected by the developers and questioned the municipal government's authority to unilaterally define the limits of habitability, concluding, "En este lugar es donde está el riesgo" (Here is where the risk is). The purpose of our visit to Ciudadela Porvenir, however, was to attract buyers, and the spokesmen quickly focused the conversation by unveiling a cardboard model of two housing units. Everyone gathered around to lay eyes on a miniature rendition of what they were being asked to purchase sight unseen. José Antonio then gave a "tour" of the model house, removing the roof so everyone could see the floor plan (figure 5.2). The visitors huddled in closer, crouching down to get a better look and to touch the model. Meanwhile, the spokesman reminded the group that construction awaited signed contracts. Coupled with the fact that relocation subsidies expire after one year, resettlement beneficiaries were in a bind. They had to act quickly, but were expected to base their decisions on empty lots, colorful plans, and cardboard models. The absence of houses, bus routes, electricity wires, water pipes, garbage trucks, schools, markets, and playgrounds incited beneficiaries to imagine the final product in an ideal form. An existing housing development might have been a harder sell than a blank screen onto which an imagined future could be projected: "La vivienda que siempre ha esperado" (The housing that you've always hoped for), as advertisements for another resettlement option

FIG 5.2 Tour of a model home. Source: Photograph by author, 2010.

promised. Nuria assured the visitors that all this would follow—but first the contracts had to be signed. When it was time to get back on the bus, the developer's spokesman was inundated by requests for contract agreements.

During my fieldwork, I had the chance to join various tours of planned housing developments on the urban periphery. On one occasion, the visit was not nearly so successful. It was just before eight o'clock on Saturday morning when I arrived at the Caja's headquarters in central Bogotá. Dozens of beneficiaries were already assembled outside waiting to board a flotilla of buses that would take us on a tour of Quintas de Santa Ana, a housing development planned for a remote plot of land in Soacha—an administratively autonomous municipality contiguous with Bogotá's southern extremity. Land is cheaper in Soacha because the area lacks much of the urban infrastructure and services of the capital, and developers were finding it profitable to build low-income housing there, such as the kind that could be purchased with a resettlement subsidy. With time to kill before our departure, I started up a conversation with a noticeably animated group.

"So, your houses are in zonas de alto riesgo," I said just to get the conversation going. A few of them responded immediately in unison: "That's what they say!" "In reality," an elderly woman elaborated, "the government is going to give our land to the wealthy so they can build nice country estates [*buenas quintas*]." Another chimed in, expressing her own powerlessness, as well as that of the state, to determine the fate of her neighborhood: "Que pase lo que tenga que pasar" (Whatever would have to happen will happen: if there's going to be a landslide, there's nothing we or they can do to stop it). I expressed my curiosity as to why they had shown up for this morning's tour if they were skeptical about the risk designation and the motives of the resettlement program, or if they felt that destiny would ultimately decide their fate: "Then why are you here? I thought resettlement was *voluntary*." They burst out in laughter. "Voluntary, sure," the elderly woman scoffed. "But we've already moved into temporary rental housing because they told us that our neighborhood was going to be evacuated by the police. And now they are telling us that we have to find alternative living arrangements before the end of October. If we don't, the Caja says that by law they have to close the budget for this year. At that point, unless we've begun the process of resettlement, we'll lose our subsidies. So we need to see what options are out there."

The temporal logics integral to the endangered city were evident. Residents of zones of high risk were meant to act in anticipation of an impending environmental disaster, whereas they were acutely aware of the menacing likelihood of police action and an imminent bureaucratic deadline. And they, too, adopted an anticipatory sensibility in relation to the opportunities accompanying the resettlement program and its offer of "the housing you have always hoped for." This is what Simone calls the "two-edged sword" of anticipatory urban politics, in which anticipation is both a resource and a danger for members of the urban poor.[10] Inhabitants of zones of high risk look ahead to what may happen in their neighborhood, what the government is willing and able to do, what chances they have to either facilitate or forestall certain plans, what threats are lurking on the horizon, and what possibilities for social mobility are available. They wait to see what is being offered and what they can possibly negotiate, knowing that the authorities are legally entitled to remove inhabitants of high-risk zones at any moment.[11] But they must do so before the window of opportunity shuts or the predicted disaster occurs.

In Bogotá, situations like these are characteristic of the governmental rationality I call *the subjunctive state*. In Spanish, the subjunctive is a way of expressing uncertainty, doubt, contingency, and possibility.[12] It belongs to the realm of imagination, anticipation, expectation, and speculation; it pertains to what is hypothetical or not yet realized. In contrast to the conditional tense, which suggests what would happen under certain circumstances, and to the future tense, which confidently predicts what will occur, the subjunctive mood describes a more uncertain and indeterminate future whose probability is unknown. But the subjunctive can also express desire, and therefore often invokes a wishful future that will manifest itself if everything else goes according to plan.[13] In some cases, subjunctive expressions of want and need additionally imply a relation of power, as they can be used to mandate, require, or oblige certain behaviors from others. However, relative to the imperative, with which one authoritatively directs the conduct of another, the subjunctive allows recipients greater freedom and responsibility to decide their own course of action. In each case, the subjunctive frames a contingent domain of reality composed of that which could have been, maybe never was, and may or may not turn out to be.

In the domain of government, the subjunctive *state* usefully denotes a rationality of rule oriented toward future horizons of possibility. It governs through multiple temporal orientations, such as expectation, anticipation, and speculation. Forms of urban government in Bogotá involve future projections that imply a range of anticipatory actions: the imminent threat posed by landslides, floods, and other environmental hazards; the eternal promise of *un mejor futuro* (a better future) attached to housing relocation programs; the pressure to take advantage of such opportunities before time runs out; the push to relocate before the neighborhood becomes more insecure. In combining logics of security, freedom, and possibility, the subjunctive state articulates with the political rationality of liberalism.[14] However, it may be more productive to see it as a distinct if overlapping modality of urban government that fosters its own set of relations between state agents and subject populations. It forms a terrain of political engagement constituted by future projection and anticipatory action on the part of both governors and the governed. The temporal horizons of government officials and "at risk" populations may differ, yet they converge on the domain of potentiality. It is within this domain that settlers on the urban periphery make claims for recognition, inclusion, and entitlement and formulate their critiques of the state for its failure to protect its most vulnerable subjects. But these registers of futurity and anticipation are not fully determined by principles of risk management. Both government workers and "beneficiaries" of Bogotá's resettlement program envision and act on futures that have as much to do with development, progress, and uplift as with risk, security, and danger.

Estela's Future

Let us now focus more closely on the subjects of risk management in Bogotá and the anticipatory horizons that shape their future outlooks. For the most part, members of this population lack the opportunity, skills, and education to gain full-time employment, are chronically excluded from the labor market, and are usually deemed unproductive in an economic sense. They are the unemployed, marginalized, and impoverished populations that commentators like Mike Davis often expect to act out against the structures of power that govern them.[15] When they do not, the question becomes: what are they waiting for? This question is usually posed rhetorically and therefore serves as an injunction directed at the supposed passivity, inertia, and inactivity of the urban poor. In the case of Bogotá, this line of critique would show that anticipatory forms of urban government create opportunities for capital accumulation and reproduce dominant relations of power. It might then blame government initiatives, such as the Caja's resettlement program, for their depoliticizing and demobilizing effects and call for an alternative politics of action. But if anticipation is also common to movements of political struggle and to patterns of everyday life and survival, then we must attempt to understand what those deemed inactive and inert are, in fact, doing.[16] It is often within an anticipatory domain, not outside of or in opposition to it, that poor settlers on the urban periphery engage in political relationships with the state and find opportunities, however limited, to make and remake their cities. Take, for example, the case of Estela, whom I met at the field office of the municipal government agency in charge of the resettlement for the population living in Bogotá's zones of high risk. She then took me to visit the site of her former home.

As we spoke, Estela stood atop a pile of debris. Scattered about were chunks of concrete, shards of glass, piles of bricks, scraps of aluminum. The concrete was once her floor, the bricks her walls, the glass her windows, the aluminum her roof. Surrounding her in all directions were the shacks of her former neighbors, similar in material and construction to the one she lived in for eleven years until just two months before we met. Although Estela's home was recently demolished, most of the others on the street were still standing. Yet in time their destiny would most likely be the same. This area was declared a zone of high risk for landslides in 2004, and ever since, the city government has been working to empty it of human occupation and resettle its inhabitants elsewhere. Estela was just a few steps closer to the future planned for everyone living in the high-risk zone.

Estela posed in the center of the vacant lot as I took her photograph, but I was not the only one awkwardly documenting this situation. Before Estela could claim a housing relocation subsidy as a member of the population living in zones of high risk, she had to show that her former property had been demolished. In her hand was a folder, which contained the documentation required of her as a "beneficiary" of the resettlement program (copies of her identification card, land title, utility bills, tax receipts). She was accompanied by Camilo, an architect who worked for the Caja. His job was to photograph Estela on the site of her former property, thereby verifying that no habitable structure remained. Only then could Estela advance to the next stage of the resettlement process.

Waiting patiently in Estela's former backyard was an unassuming stack of about fifty bricks. This stack was identical to those found throughout Bogotá's informal settlements (figure 5.3). When times are not as tight as usual, it is common to put the little money left over at the end of the month toward a few extra building materials. Cash is immediate, too easy to spend or lose. Buying a small quantity of bricks, on the other hand, is an investment in the future. With these bricks, an additional room or perhaps a second story can be added on and rented out. Like the metal rods, or rebar, that shoot skyward from the rooftops of self-built settlements throughout the world, these bricks hold out the promise of growth, progress, and development. They are material signs of a future-in-waiting. But in Bogotá they signal more than just that. The bustling center and the wealthy northern reaches of the city—their high-rises, their libraries, their shopping malls, and their universities—are made of the same material, and its reddish hue dominates the view from these hillside settlements. For those who live here, a stack of bricks is an aspiration to somehow become part of *that* world, to someday belong to *that* city.

The bricks in Estela's backyard would not go to their originally intended use, however. Most likely she will sell them for a small sum in hopes of recouping some of their initial value. In fact, this is what she and her husband

FIG 5.3 Stacks of bricks are a common sight throughout the settlements of Ciudad Bolívar. Source: Photographs by author, 2009.

had already done with the other salvageable materials from their former home. They might have hired someone else to do the job—handwritten signs offering demolition services hang on houses throughout the settlement—but this would have cut into the small amount they had hoped to recover from the property. So Estela and her husband, like most other families being relocated from Bogotá's zones of high risk, took it upon themselves to dismantle and sell off their former home piece by piece. These bricks were the only material remaining to be sold. Once they were gone, so too would be their ability to signify hopes of betterment, uplift, progress, and mobility—those all-powerful, progressivist myths of modernity.

But Estela had not abandoned hope; she was full of enthusiasm about moving into a newly built housing development appropriately called Towers of Progress. Although the house she would soon call home was on the farthest edge of Bogotá, where the arrival of corner stores, bus routes, schools, and health clinics was still a matter of speculation, she told me she was proud to be moving forward, outward, and upward. She often thanked God for protecting her from harm and trusted in his power to determine her fate. But she admitted to feeling relief at the prospect of leaving behind an area that she had often found difficult and even downright dangerous. There was no nostalgic melancholia for the loss of what was never all that good to begin with. The government resettlement program promotes itself as one of the few paths people are going to find to a better future (another housing development is named New Hope), and those who accept its terms often describe it in the same way. Both Estela and the Caja social workers seemed to agree that this was the best opportunity people in her situation were going to find. "How else," she asked me, "can we improve the conditions in which we live?"

Moreover, Estela's hopes for the future remained pinned to the city. Like many living in the self-built settlements of Bogotá's periphery, she was one of los desplazados, a category of legal personhood bestowed on those forced by the armed conflict to abandon their homes. The extreme insecurity people have endured in the Colombian countryside since the mid-twentieth century has strengthened the pull of the urban as the symbol of modernity. The promising futures associated with the city stand in sharp contrast to the threatening ones that haunt rural peasants caught in the midst of on-going battles between guerrillas, paramilitaries, and the Colombian army. For people like Estela, the city is not imagined as the dark, dangerous counterpart to the peaceful, idyllic countryside.[17] It is a refuge from the bar-baric violence that has terrorized *el campo* for decades. Her eventual return is not just undesirable, but unimaginable.

The critique of historical progress and urban modernity expressed by the ruins of Estela's house recall Walter Benjamin's haunting depiction of a Paul Klee painting, *Angelus Novus*, in which Benjamin describes the Angel of History gazing backward upon the wreckage of the past as he is thrust vio-lently into the future:

> His face is turned toward the past. Where we perceive a chain of events, he sees one single catastrophe which keeps piling wreckage upon wreck-age and hurls it in front of his feet. The angel would like to stay, awaken the dead, and make whole what has been smashed. But a storm is blowing from Paradise; it has got caught in his wings with such violence that the angel can no longer close them. The storm irresistibly propels him into the future to which his back is turned, while the pile of debris before him grows skyward. This storm is what we call progress.[18]

Benjamin's parable is more than a polemic against the destructiveness of capitalist modernity and the violent forces terrorizing Europe at the time of his writing. For him, the accumulating pile of debris at the angel's feet may also represent a resource for the creation of different futures. For those inspired by this passage, ruins have come to express both the wreckage of dominant notions of history and the source of their alternatives.

Ann Stoler also turns to ruins as conceptual resources for a critique of the persistence of imperial pasts in the present. For Stoler, ruins point to the "longevity of structures of dominance, and the uneven pace with which people can extricate themselves from the colonial order of things."[19] While colonialism and empire are not my focus, I am persuaded by her claim that "ruins are also sites that condense alternative senses of history" or, in Svetlana Boym's terms, that "make us think of the past that could have been and the future that never took place."[20] Stoler urges us to resist the tendency to see ruins through a melancholic gaze or to allow the "redemptive satisfaction of chronicling loss," and instead suggests that we "turn to ruins . . . as sites that animate new possibilities, bids for entitlement, and unexpected political projects." It might be fruitful to think about the ruins I describe as imperial, but I am more inclined to see them as what Stoler calls "modernist ruins."[21] As such, they reflect the afterlife of "schemes to improve the human condition," as James Scott has documented, and developmental narratives thrown into question, as Ferguson has shown.[22] But as Boym puts it, ruins also "make us aware of the vagaries of progressive vision" and therefore animate diverse efforts to claim futures other than those promised by myths of urban modernity.[23] Whereas modernism heralded futures of progress, efficiency, and stability, there is a global trend toward envisioning urban futures as futures of potential crisis, catastrophe, and collapse. According to this paradigm, the ruins I have just described in Bogotá represent both the perceived problem and its solution. They are the outcome of efforts to protect life and property from imminent disaster, yet they resemble the effects of the disaster itself.

Thus these ruins draw attention to the temporalities bound up with forms of anticipatory urbanism motivated by the imperative to govern (and govern *through*) risk, and to the contours and limits of futurity for those subject to them. As Claudio Lomnitz observes: "The complex calculus of risk is . . . a geometry that calibrates our intimate decisions. Our most prized feelings— love, hope, compassion—are moored in today's chronic and systemic insecurities."[24] Lomnitz then pertinently asks: "What is the connection between the strategic calculation of risk and the existential commitments of the people?"[25] In this vein, I argue that following risk management outside its official parameters allows us to see how it intersects with and occasionally enables other claims and expectations, which do not necessarily align with or reproduce its visions of the future. This is what ruins can tell us about the material and symbolic registers in which urban futures are made, unmade, and remade. We already have languages of creative destruction, disaster capitalism, and empire, which refer us to the devastations of the past—the ruination of landscapes, lives, and livelihoods that our critical vocabularies so comfortably and fluidly discuss.[26] But they tell us very little about ruins as sites that animate new claims on and expectations of the future.

If we think in terms of the "capacity to aspire," in Arjun Appadurai's terms, then the question is how to strengthen that capacity in order to facilitate efforts to escape from poverty.[27] In the cases I have described, however, aspirations for the future are very much alive even among the extremely poor. What bears noting, then, is not that they lack aspirational capacity, but that their aspirations are increasingly tied to political projects that no longer imagine the city as a space of modernist improvement, developmental time, and poverty reduction; instead, the future is problematized as threat and governed through logics of security. But outside the techno-political domain, the futures governed through risk are entangled with claims, aspirations, and expectations of many kinds.

Urban Futures, Past and Present

Estela came to Bogotá eleven years ago and was able to purchase a plot of land. For desplazados arriving today, however, it is tougher to find a foothold in the urban housing market. Areas recently evacuated by the municipal government are some of the few spaces left in which squatting is still possible or where one can buy a plot of land for a small fee. The new arrivals come by night with whatever building materials they can round up and carry—cardboard, plywood, plastic tarps—and by morning have constructed a makeshift shelter among the ruins of the earlier settlement. As ironic as it sounds, their future was in serious enough jeopardy to warrant settling in one of Bogotá's zone of high risk. As rumors circulate about the possibility of accessing scarce housing subsidies set aside for those exposed to *environmental* hazards, the very same zones evacuated by the government to protect people from one kind of threat become, for this population, spaces of potential safety and security from an altogether different sort of danger.

This dynamic of urban settlement has historical precedent in Bogotá, as in many other Latin American cities. In the 1970s and 1980s, *urbanizadores piratas* (pirate urbanizers) fueled informal urbanization by appropriating, subdividing, and selling land on the urban periphery to migrants and refugees.[28] Today an analogous figure searches for vacant land in recently evacuated zones of high risk, organizes desplazados and others in dire need of housing, facilitates their settlement, and charges them a fee for his services. Both urbanizadores piratas and their contemporary counterparts capitalize on the problems of displacement, poverty, and homelessness by targeting people with meager resources and limited options and then offering them places to live that straddle the border between legality and illegality. But the promises of the new "pirate urbanizers" are altogether different from those of the old, and the difference reveals a great deal about how urban futures are being imagined in and for present-day Bogotá.

Urbanizadores piratas once assured people that the settlement they were buying into would undergo progressive development, formalization, and legalization. Their business model relied on the widespread belief that everyone moving to the city would eventually be recognized by the state as urban citizens and incorporated within civil society. Becoming a participating member of urban modernity might require persistence and political struggle, but one could aspire to a right to the city and its associated benefits, such as water, electricity, paved streets, schools, and transportation (which, in the case in most of these settlements, did eventually come).[29] Today, however, the deal offered to recent arrivals no longer relies on the credibility of that narrative. These new entrepreneurs are less inclined to make lofty promises of progressively better futures for everyone. They are aware that many people now see the state more as protector than as provider. Despite government signs warning against similar scams ("Danger—high risk of landslide—do not buy or sell lots in this zone"), both pirate urbanizers and desplazados understand that recognition and inclusion can now be achieved by inhabiting spaces and subject positions "at risk."

Once Estela and her husband sell off the remains of their property, the *vigías ambientales* will take over (figure 5.4). The vigías ambientales, or "environmental guards," are a team of 120 municipal employees whose job is to roam the evacuated settlements, remove the remains of human

FIG 5.4 Vigías ambientales. Source: Photograph by author, 2009.

occupation, and, by periodically planting trees and shrubs and encouraging vegetation to spread, eventually return these areas to a state of nature. Their green coveralls bear the insignia of their sponsor, the Municipal Department of the Environment (Secretaría Distrital de Ambiente), and their mission reflects the imperatives of urban ecology: promote conservation ethics, preserve the environment, recuperate protected areas, and so on. "What's the future of these risk zones?" I often found myself asking government officials. Their response—parks, recreational spaces, the lungs of the city—invariably imagined Bogotá contributing less to a "planet of slums" than to a "green planet."

Their status as "guards," however, reveals their dual objective. They are armed with pickaxes and shovels rather than badges and guns, but their mission is also to secure these zones and prevent future occupation. The vigías ambientales monitor daily for invasiones, illegal occupations that often occur under the cover of darkness, and immediately alert the police if they find any. By erasing traces of an inhabited past and enforcing the policy that prohibits future settlement, they hope to discourage unplanned and uncontrolled urbanization in areas of potential political instability or even clandestine insurgency. In contrast to the imperatives of development or modernization, the dual objectives of ecology and security are conjoined in the future imagined by official policies and plans for Bogotá's zones of high risk.

For the most part, this team of vigías ambientales is composed of former inhabitants of these settlements who are now employed by the government. But unlike public works projects that create employment by investing public funds in the construction of urban infrastructure, these job opportunities follow a different logic. The vigías ambientales are hired not to build a better future, but to dismantle what remains of a future that now belongs to the past. Those not lucky enough to get these jobs rove through areas the vigías have yet to reach, collecting recyclable material they can sell for a small sum. Just as Estela found resources for social mobility in a risk management program, the futures of many on the peripheries of the city are predicated not on the myth of urban modernity and its promises of growth, prosperity, and development for all, but on predictions of decline and hazard: people dismantling their homes in order to be resettled elsewhere, scavengers sifting through debris to make a living, government workers returning former human settlements to nature, desplazados escaping conflict by settling on top of the rubble. Likewise, the ruins that dot the landscape throughout Bogotá's zones of high risk are not simply the remains of futures lost. They are also the site of claims, aspirations, and expectations. Progressive hopes for the future are bound to governmental logics that imagine the city as a space of potential risk, regress, and ruin.

The Politics of Anticipation

The emergence of risk management in Bogotá is part of a broader shift in how futures are being imagined in and for the city. This shift shapes the terrain of political engagement for settlers of the urban periphery, who negotiate official efforts to protect life from potential disasters by pursuing opportunities created by it and by adopting an anticipatory stance in their critiques of the state. *Denuncias prospectivas*, or "prospective denunciations," harness anticipation to mobilizations of popular discontent and to demands for political accountability. They represent a specific modality of popular political expression that derives its meaning and force from the security logics dominant in Colombia. While denuncia is a discursive formation used throughout Latin America by victims of past violence or injustice, in Bogotá it often references the future horizon of potential victimhood.[30] This form of anticipatory urban politics is evidenced by a recent emergency.

In 2010 and 2011, Colombia was besieged by the worst rains in recorded history.[31] The unusually high levels of precipitation were attributed both to La Niña, or the cyclical cooling of the Pacific Ocean that disrupts typical weather patterns, and to the increased severity of meteorological events associated with climate change. The resulting floods and landslides displaced hundreds of thousands of people, destroyed homes throughout the country, severely impacted the economy, and claimed the lives of several hundred citizens. In response to the torrential *olas invernales*, or winter storms, that deluged the country, in December 2010 President Juan Manuel Santos declared a state of emergency, created a dedicated "crisis room" in the Ministry of the Interior, and allocated US$2.5 million of public funds to recovery and reconstruction efforts. Even at that early date, Santos recognized the severity of the situation: "This crisis . . . is the worst natural disaster [*tragedia natural*] in our history. Never before have the lives, health, property, and futures of so many people been affected."[32] The public-private organization created to distribute humanitarian aid, Colombia Humanitaria, estimated in September 2011 that the rains had severely impacted over one thousand municipalities (nearly 70 percent of the country) and the lives and livelihoods of over 4 million people.[33] A more recent period of rain, which lasted until December 2011, caused the death of an additional 182 people, destroyed more than twelve hundred homes, and resulted in damages estimated to amount to 6 percent of Colombia's GDP.[34] Although rural areas in the north of the country and along the Caribbean coast were the hardest hit, urban areas, such as Manizales, as well as a suburb of Colombia's second largest city, Medellín, also witnessed grave tragedies. In comparison, Bogotá escaped relatively unscathed.

How has the capital city avoided major property damage and loss of life, when many of its 8 million inhabitants live in low-lying areas vulnerable to flooding or on hillsides susceptible to landslides? Not surprisingly, the municipal government's disaster risk management agency took full credit. In a bulletin released in late 2011, the Fund for Emergency Prevention and Response (FOPAE) asserted that "despite the heavy rains of the last six months in Bogotá, the most intense in 70 years, the capital has been able to overcome the winter season without significant damage to the physical integrity of the community. . . . Bogotá can say that it was through actions of *alistamiento* [readiness], *preparación* [preparation], *respuesta* [response], and *recuperación* [recovery] that not a single person has been injured or killed due to the winter weather."[35] As I was told by Alberto, a preparedness expert with FOPAE, the municipal government's "responsible and serious" policy of integrated risk management has greatly reduced the city's vulnerability. He continued: "We have an effective warning system, programs for families living in zones of high risk, preventive measures, evacuations, emergency simulations, and so on. The cases in which the rains did have adverse effects," Alberto assured me, "were caused by the weakness of *control urbanistico* [land-use planning] in Bogotá—this was the problem, not our lack of preparedness." From the standpoint of FOPAE and other government representatives, Bogotá has been spared the devastation felt elsewhere in Colombia thanks to its future-oriented approach to urban government.

The most recent, and perhaps most significant, exception to this narrative comes from the peripheral locality of Bosa. On Monday, December 5, 2011, the country's largest daily newspaper, *El Tiempo*, reported that following a forty-eight-hour deluge, the Bogotá River was nearly overflowing its banks.[36] Andrés González, the governor of the department of Cundinamarca, which surrounds Bogotá, cautioned that water levels had risen rapidly in rural areas and could soon cause flooding downstream in the capital: "We are reaching the highest levels registered in the last seven months," he warned.[37] On the following afternoon, these predictions began to come true. Another rainstorm developed, and the canals draining *aguas negras* (wastewater) from the city were blocked from conveying effluent to the Bogotá River, as they do under normal circumstances, due to the river's abnormally high level. Instead of discharging storm water and sewage, the Cundinamarca Canal began to function as a reservoir, collecting aguas negras and distributing them across the residential neighborhoods of Bosa and Kennedy on Bogotá's southwestern edge. The water not only rushed through the streets, but also percolated up through sewers and drains, and within a few hours had risen to nearly a meter in height. Residents retreated to the second floor of their homes until rescue workers arrived with inflatable boats to transport them to dry land. The municipal government responded with an emergency declaration and interim Mayor Clara López ordered the installation of a unified command post in the flooded areas. She called on her staff to work with regional authorities to identify areas in which to discharge the river's excess flow and pleaded with bogotanos to conserve water.[38] These responses were effective but insufficient, so the water utility company began asking neighboring countries to lend Bogotá a high-capacity pump.[39] Aided by a respite of dry, sunny weather, these measures eventually succeeded in reducing the force of the river and draining the inundated neighborhoods.

On December 9, Mayor López accompanied President Santos to the barrio of El Recreo, one of the most heavily affected areas, to commence the provision of humanitarian aid. López had already agreed to provide tax relief as well as a rental subsidy of 550,000 pesos (US$300) to those forced by the flooding to abandon their homes.[40] In addition, the municipal water utility had guaranteed fifteen days of free delivery.[41] Donning a red Colombia Humanitaria windbreaker, President Santos announced that the national government would provide an additional 1.5 million pesos (US$775) to each family adversely affected by the flooding.[42] Santos estimated that more than ten thousand families would be eligible for aid, but this was contingent on an official census of the victims.[43] The Secretary of Social Integration then began compiling a registry by consulting the administrator of each residential housing complex and other community leaders. FOPAE followed with house-by-house inspections to determine the extent of property damage and the number of people affected. Although preliminary estimates were as low as 5,000 victims, FOPAE soon announced that the flooding had adversely affected 45,196 people in total.[44] Once the official census was complete, FOPAE issued a certificate of damages to each household, and the aid promised by López and Santos could be disbursed.[45]

Long lines formed wherever aid was being handed out, and residents declared that there was not enough for the number of families in need. Reports came back that food rations were being proportioned *a ojo* (by sight) and that there was no systematic process for allocating assistance.[46] Meanwhile, rumors circulated of people with false certificates arriving from other neighborhoods to steal from those in need. Others complained of flaws in the census, claiming they had been wrongfully excluded. For several hours, protestors blocked the Avenida Ciudad de Cali, a main thoroughfare in southwestern Bogotá, citing unreasonable delays in the distribution of aid.[47] Reporters from the news magazine *Semana* visited Bosa and Kennedy in January and found the neighborhoods rife with accusations that the government had not made good on its promise to disburse subsidies by Christmas.[48] In response to the pressure, the secretary of government ordered a review of the census, and FOPAE returned to verify their count. Draining the city after the flooding was proving less of a challenge than providing aid to the victims.

The spotlight soon shifted away from the government's management of the census and the distribution of aid. Residents from the flooded neighborhoods began organizing protests in which they blamed the authorities for ignoring the fact that the Bogotá River had overflowed its banks three times in recent years. They enjoined the state to exercise greater vigilance in preventing developers from constructing housing in high-risk zones and demanded accountability from the construction company that had built the housing complexes.[49] A group of 150 protestors blocked a local transportation hub, Portal de las Américas, drawing attention to the fact that it was social housing that had been inundated. A resident framed the issue as follows: "These houses turned out to be a scam [*el paquete chileno*]: they [the state] promised us development [*valorización y vías*] and we ended up living in a gutter."[50] Shared among these expressions of popular discontent and demands for accountability was the sense that the state had permitted urbanization in areas susceptible to environmental hazards and had failed to take precautions to protect residents from a known threat. That is, the government should have foreseen the disaster and been able to prevent it from taking place.

As the victims of the flooding were making their voices heard, similar perspectives circulated in *El Tiempo*'s editorial pages. Yolanda Reyes cited a history of irresponsible housing policy: "I remember when Mayor Peñalosa invited 'opinion leaders' on a helicopter tour of the urban developments of Metrovivienda [social housing] in Bosa. Journalists admired the bicycle routes, the avenues, and the public spaces on the edge of what is now a sewer of aguas negras. . . . Against logic, [Metrovivienda] developed these urbanizations with the promise that risk mitigation would happen later."[51] Reyes also refuted President Santos's constant references to La Niña by shouldering the government with blame for not having taken preventive measures and for ignoring the past: "They know that what happened in Bogotá is not new, that it is not simply the consequence of global climate change or the fault of '*la maldita niña*,' but rather of *maldita improvisación* [damned improvisation]. If they consulted historical documents they would see that from Mosquera to San Victorino [a large area of western Bogotá], there have been times when those who were sold on the model homes in Bosa had to use the very same inflatable boats that are carrying them away today." Emphasizing the error of uncontrolled growth of the urban periphery, Reyes asked: "Which public agencies approved those licenses and allowed these developers to profit? Was there any fine print that warned about the probability of flooding?" She concluded that protecting the urban poor from potential disasters is a far more important concern than building them homes.

As Reyes's op-ed makes clear, the flooding in Bosa and Kennedy was not discussed publicly as only a problem of housing policy and land-use planning, or *control urbanistico*, as I had been told by the FOPAE official; issues of precaution, prevention, and preparedness were front and center. In an interview with Mayor López, *El Tiempo* asked bluntly whether the emergency in Bosa could have been prevented. "It was foreseen," she admitted, "and this is why we built flood control channels, maintained the drainage systems, and dredged the Bogotá River."[52] Looking ahead to the future, the media also initiated discussions about how to ensure that the same situation would not repeat itself during the next rainy season. In another op-ed, Ernesto Cortés argued that more anticipatory approaches to governing zones of high risk would be necessary: "There are a million and a half souls sitting on the bank of the river in permanent danger, and rather than just asking ourselves what they are doing there, we have to respond to the question, what are we going to do about it?"[53] Many technical solutions were considered, such as removing the sediment and debris that impeded the flow of water through the system and widening the river to increase its conveyance capacity.[54] When asked whether Bogotá was prepared for more rain, Secretary of Government Antonio Navarro assured the public that he would prioritize preventive measures (*acciones preventivas*) so that the same problems would not return in the future.[55]

In January 2012, I went to visit the neighborhoods that had been inundated by storm water and sewage just a month before. I rode the Trans-Milenio from central Bogotá to its southwestern terminus, the Portal de la Américas, which had been brought to a standstill by protestors from Bosa and Kennedy just weeks before. As I transferred to a feeder bus that would take me closer to the Bogotá River and the now infamous Cundinamarca Canal, I noticed the stench of raw sewage still floating in the air. Exiting the terminal, the bus ran alongside one of the canals carrying wastewater to the outskirts of the city. Debris lay stranded along its edges and hung from the bottom branches of the squat trees lining its banks. Sensing that I was getting close to the site of the flooding, I hopped off the bus at a corner bakery.

While ordering a coffee, I struck up a conversation with a waitress, who told me that this was indeed where the flooding had taken place. The water level had risen a couple of feet in this part of the neighborhood, and the bakery had been forced to close for five days. Pointing out the door and down the street, the waitress indicated where to go if I wanted to visit the area that had been badly affected. "It's pretty much all cleaned up by now," she said, "but you'll find people who are still angry. They knew that something like this was going to happen, but nobody would listen."

Following her advice, I made my way in the direction of the Bogotá River. The majority of the buildings I passed were *vivienda de interés social* (social housing) constructed in the last ten to fifteen years. This was no squatter settlement that had sprung up in a flood zone because people had nowhere else to live. Although this was the urban periphery in a geographical sense—I could see where the pavement ended and the grazing pastures began—these housing complexes had been officially planned and built with public funds. I stopped in a small convenience store operating out of the front room of a two-story brick townhouse and began to chat with the woman behind the counter. When I asked about the flooding, she gestured to the point on her leg up to where the water had risen. "You've done a good job getting everything back into shape," I remarked, noting the absence of visible damage. "Yeah, but it hasn't been easy. The government promised us three *ayudas* [forms of assistance], but we have only received one." She then told me that people in the neighborhood were planning legal action against the state and the developer. "If you want to know more," she offered, "you should talk to doña Lucia, the president of the housing complex. She runs a *supermercado* on the next block."

I did as she said, and found doña Lucia in a shop similar to the one I had just visited, except that it stocked fresh fruits and vegetables and had a refrigerator case for meat and dairy. At first doña Lucia seemed hesitant to talk about the flooding: "What exactly do you want to know?" "I'm interested in the government's response to the emergency," I answered, "and how the people living here feel about it." This caught her attention, and she showed me where President Santos addressed the residents of the neighborhood, promising each victim a subsidy of 1.5 million pesos. "Ever since then," she said shaking her head, "there has been major disorganization on the part of the government in complying with its promises. Four days after Santos stood right outside my house, they came to conduct a census.

This was necessary since there were lots of *gente deshonesta* [dishonest people] trying to pass themselves off as victims. But the census was completely disorganized. Some people were listed under the wrong identification number, others were excluded altogether, and this made it difficult for people who needed help to get it." *El desorden del estado*, she called it—"the disorder of the state."

"Is that what the protests have been about?" I asked. Doña Lucia then made an important clarification: "Well, there were some people who tried to falsify their identity in order to get themselves counted by the census. They are not from here. But the others who were protesting in the Portal de la Américas were promised subsidies that never arrived. Many of the *tomas* [protests] have been organized by people whose houses had flooded." I then asked whether these demonstrations had made a difference. "They came back to conduct another census," she noted, "so I suppose we forced them to try to get it right. But there are still many people who deserve assistance and have not gotten any help. However, the main problem, as I see it, is that none of this should ever have happened in the first place."

Surprised by this change of direction, I asked doña Lucia what she meant, and she gave me the following explanation: "I mean, we all knew this was going to happen. A group of us, maybe about forty in total, got together back in September to call attention to the risk of flooding in the area and to denounce the government for not doing anything to prevent it." I had heard similar claims before from individuals, but was taken aback by the idea that these residents had organized collectively to demand that the government respond to an event that had not yet taken place.

Look it up. It was on September 8. City TV, Caracol, RCN, all the networks came to cover the story. We told them they had to clean out all the debris in the canals before the next heavy rain. Acueducto [the water utility] did a bit of cleanup, but in general the government just ignored us. And as a result, they were not prepared in December when the weather got really bad. We knew this was going to happen. They did too, but they didn't do anything. They just waited for it to happen, and then opened the floodgates once it was already too late. They have to be more prepared. The *olas invernales* are just going to get stronger and stronger every year. We're worried! The river is going to fill up again next time there are heavy rains. We're always gazing up at the sky.

After our conversation, I did indeed look it up, as doña Lucia had instructed me to do. I started with the archive of *El Tiempo*, but found nothing indicating that residents from Bosa had made a denuncia back in September about the risk of flooding in their neighborhood. I then looked through past editions of the other major Bogotá newspaper, *El Espectador*, and found nothing there either. I checked a few other media sources, but again came up empty. I was about to give up and conclude that doña Lucia's hindsight was 20/20, as they say, when I came across a page on the RCN Television website posted on December 9 with the heading "Flood in Bosa Had Been Denounced Three Months Ago."[56] Sure enough, what doña Lucia had said was true. And since I could find no record of the denuncia until after the flooding had already occurred, it seemed that their warnings had indeed fallen on deaf ears.

The video clip reveals a group of demonstrators gathered in front of television cameras on the morning of September 8 in the locality of Bosa. Some were dressed formally in suit and tie, while others were bundled up with scarves and hoods to ward off the cold morning air. Men and women of all ages faced the cameras with expressions conveying seriousness and conviction. The newscaster explained that residents were worried that the area's drainage system was inadequate and that they feared that it would be unable to withstand the coming winter rains. With handwritten signs, residents warned of a potential threat that could lead to grave consequences, and they asked the government to take immediate action (figure 5.5). "Exigimos que la Alcaldía Distrital solucione el problema del río. ¡Evitemos una gran tragedia!" (We demand that City Hall solve the problem of the river. Let's avoid a huge tragedy!) "El Consejo de Kasay de los Venados II presente. . . . Ante el inminente riesgo de desbordamiento del río no queremos un gobierno distrital indiferente" (The Administrative Council of Kasay de los Venados II [housing complex] is present. . . . In light of the imminent risk of the river overflowing, we don't want an indifferent city government). The microphone was given to a middle-aged man, who took on the responsibility of speaking for the group: "Our worry is that we are staring in the face of an imminent flood [*ante una inminente inundación*] throughout the neighborhood of El Recreo, and therefore we are making an urgent call to the Empresa Acueducto [water utility] to please dredge this river . . . this drainage canal . . . in an urgent manner. And we call not just on Acueducto but also on the municipal government to help us, because as soon as this area floods all pos-

FIG 5.5 Denuncia prospectiva, September 8, 2011. Source: RCN *Noticias*.

sible solutions are going to be unnecessary. . . . They won't do us any good at all." The video clip then jumps ahead to footage of the December floods, pointing out that the denuncia was not heard and that the residents of Bosa were now facing the consequences.

As the Bosa floods demonstrate, denuncias prospectivas make use of anticipatory logics to mobilize popular discontent and to demand accountability and action from the state. This was true of the denuncias that followed the December emergency, as well as of those made months before. Whether looking forward to potential disasters looming on the horizon or backward to ones that have already occurred, this modality of anticipatory urban politics targets the state's failure to prepare for future events. It mobilizes security logics for the purpose of popular political critique. Although denuncias prospectivas share an orientation toward the future, a closer examination of their temporal dimensions suggests they can take different forms and may have different implications and effects.

In the case of the flooding in Bosa, we find at least two possible variations. In the first, an individual or group criticizes a political figure, government agency, or the state for not being adequately aware of, attentive to, or prepared for an event that has yet to take place. This form of critique looks to the future, identifies a threat, organizes potential victims, demonstrates their vulnerability, and demands anticipatory action. In the case of Bosa, residents unified collectively around their common exposure to flood risk and argued that this entitled them to protection by the municipal government. It is often within a political domain organized around the imperative to protect life from threats that settlers of the urban periphery engage in political relationships with the state. After over a year of chronic landslides and floods, members of the urban poor were even more likely to position themselves as "lives at risk" and to engage the state in these terms. Without calling into question anticipatory techniques of government, denuncias prospectivas operate within them: they mobilize concern for an additional threat or seek to recognize a larger group of potential victims. Thus, while positioning themselves as critical of the state, they ultimately reinforce the security logics dominant in Colombia.

The second form of denuncias prospectivas is more complex. It involves a critique aimed at political authorities for not having been adequately aware of, attentive to, or prepared for an event that eventually did occur. There is an anticipatory dimension to these denuncias in their reference to a future threat. Yet temporally speaking, they are both prospective and retrospective: they position themselves simultaneously in the aftermath of the event in question and at a moment prior to it, when it could (or should) have been possible to foresee what would eventually happen. This is how doña Lucia formulated her argument that the municipal government was aware of the risk of flooding months before the Bogotá River overflowed yet had done nothing to prevent an imminent social and environmental disaster. Media critics made similar denunciations when they accused the state of having allowed urban development to take place in areas known to be at risk of flooding and for having done little to prepare for an eminently predictable outcome. These mobilizations of popular discontent refer to an actual event in the past. As such, they often demand financial reparations, humanitarian aid, or emergency response by making the state accountable for something that has already occurred. Moreover, they have the potential to catalyze wider political change, since the state's authority and legitimacy may be eroded by its failure to secure the future. But like the former variation, these denuncias prospectivas also uphold the political rationality of security even as they challenge specific actions of the state.

Anticipation as Possibility

What does all this tell us about anticipatory urbanism and about urban futures more generally? The rise of risk management over the past decade reflects a broader shift toward future-oriented rationalities of rule in Colombia, and this has led to the increasing problematization of threat, danger, and disaster. According to the modality of urban government I have called *the subjunctive state*, techniques for governing the spaces and populations of the urban periphery now target events that may not ever materialize, and this logic motivates and legitimates projects of urban transformation in the present. However, in examining temporal framings, practices, and sensibilities among government officials in charge of risk management programs, as well as among the vulnerable populations governed by them, we see that forms of anticipatory urbanism and their projection of future threats are not incompatible with "modern" expectations of development, growth, and progress. As emphasized more fully in earlier chapters, government officials and governed populations also draw frequently on "traditional" understandings of fate, destiny, redemption, and providence. In contrast to "big stories of the future," according to which new regimes of temporality displace earlier ones, an ethnographic approach reveals that multiple forms of futurity are emerging and circulating simultaneously in the city of Bogotá—sometimes complementing, at other times contradicting one another. Even as projections of imminent danger become increasingly common to politics, government, and everyday life, heterogeneous temporal configurations continue to coexist alongside and within them.

These observations offer us insight into the terrain of political engagement in the endangered city. They show that the future, while central to urban government, is also the ground on which people both engage with the state and formulate critiques of it. Government planners, engineers, architects, and social workers do not always share the timescales and temporal framings of those they are responsible for governing—the sheer precariousness of life and livelihood on Bogotá's urban periphery ensures it. Yet horizons of possibility allow the state to govern urban spaces and populations and enable people to organize their demands for recognition and entitlement. Anticipation is both a resource and a danger for the urban poor. Although their claims, aspirations, and expectations are tied to nonprogressive temporalities of risk and ruin, anticipation can be mobilized for the purpose of political opposition. It is often deployed in order to draw attention to the state's shortcomings, contradictions, and inadequacies by demonstrating the failure to provide protective care to its most vulnerable subjects in the face of potentially catastrophic outcomes. Since anticipatory urban politics can come from all sides of the political spectrum, the key concern should be to analyze how certain configurations of urban futurity are being harnessed to specific political projects and to what effect.

This is an important recognition, since a great deal of urban and social theory treats temporality as a domain of hegemony and domination and assumes a limited set of possibilities. Regimes of anticipation are typically characterized as mechanisms of social control, whereby the state manipulates temporal framings, practices, and sensibilities to consolidate political authority, facilitate capital accumulation, and produce subjects amenable to both. In the cases I have described, anticipation is neither friend nor enemy, but rather the common ground on which urban government and politics takes place. It is often *within* an anticipatory domain, and not outside or against it, that the urban poor seek opportunities to make and remake their cities. Yet its transformative potential as a domain of urban politics is limited. Rather than calling into question, destabilizing, or taking hold of political authority, the forms of anticipatory urban politics I have analyzed in Bogotá reinforce logics of security rather than challenging them. Ultimately, while prospective denunciations take an oppositional stance vis-à-vis the state, they uphold the established rationalities from which they derive their meaning and force as forms of popular political expression. The alternative is not to resist or refuse anticipatory urbanism altogether, but to assess its creative and strategic potential for those usually resigned to simply wait for something better to come along.

MILLENNIAL CITIES

The endangered city has come into being at a specific historical conjuncture in Bogotá. At a time when violence was on the decline and yet security concerns persisted, risk became an object of governmental concern and began to reconfigure the relationship between the state and its subjects in the self-built settlements of the urban periphery. Emerging out of Colombia's protracted struggle with insecurity in the latter half of the twentieth century, the imperative to protect vulnerable lives from threat underpinned a new way of governing the city and urban life but without fully replacing existing forms of political authority and technical expertise or established social relations and ethical responsibilities. This history is essential not only for understanding Bogotá's recent urban experiments, but also for leveraging them to cast light on the proliferation of security mechanisms in cities throughout the world. So what can the politics of security and risk in Bogotá tell us about the global urban imagination at large?

The case of Bogotá allows us to step back and to examine the implications of seeing the future of cities, and the cities of the future, as problems of threat and danger, problems of security and risk. This trend could be read as signaling a break from the evolutionary models of development central to modernist paradigms of urban thought and practice. Those paradigms and their promises of perpetual progress have been thoroughly challenged, and for good reason, yet some of their problematic assumptions about temporality and geography remain. As such, the critique of epochal accounts of risk, liberal governance, and modernity elaborated here also applies to claims that the world has entered a time of singular uncertainty and insecurity and that cities should no longer be expected to follow in the footsteps of the "modern cities" of Europe and North America. Recent challenges to linear narratives of development and attempts to reimagine the spatiotemporal coordinates of urban modernity—as important as these efforts are—do not render earlier models of urbanism obsolete. The key question, then, is precisely how those models are being reassembled.

The "Bogotá Model"

From the 1980s to the present, Bogotá went through a series of transformations that have since won the city abundant accolades. From the Golden Lion Award for Cities, bestowed on Bogotá in 2006 at the prestigious International Architectural Exhibition of the Venice Biennale, to more modest honors received from the likes of the Stockholm Partnerships for Sustainable Cities, the United Nations, the Institute for Transportation and Development Policy, and the Bill and Melinda Gates Foundation, the city has in the last decade become recognized internationally as a "model city" for its achievements in "good urban governance" across realms as diverse as education, security, transportation, and public space.[1] With troops of international visitors arriving every year to learn from its "success story" and then attempting to replicate it back home, Bogotá has become a prime example of how models of urbanism circulate transnationally.[2] For urban planners, designers, and policymakers around the world, the "Bogotá model" appears to provide lessons in successful urban transformation that can be applied universally. In the words of the 2006 Venice Biennale jury, "Bogotá is, in short, a beacon of hope for other cities, whether rich or poor."[3]

During this same period, both Colombia and its capital city were being praised for another distinction: their advances in governing disaster risk. For example, in a 2009 report, the World Bank acknowledged the country's international reputation: "Colombia is widely considered a leader in instituting a policy and legal framework that enables a comprehensive, multisectoral approach to disaster risk management."[4] As a specialist in this area from the bank told me, the municipal government of Bogotá has been leading the way: "Bogotá is very advanced. It is probably number one in Latin America and in the top five, or maybe even number one, among cities of the developing world in terms of disaster and risk management policy." Dollars and cents are a crude measure of the extent to which risk management has infused governance in the city, yet it is worth noting that by 2009 Colombia had received over US$340 million in funding for disaster risk management projects from the World Bank, US$80 million of which was dedicated to Bogotá.[5] This rarely figures in celebrations of the city's transformation from a chaotic inferno of crime, fear, and violence to a cosmopolitan hub of commerce, culture, and creativity. However, recognizing techniques for governing risk as central to the "Bogotá model" highlights shifts in the global urban imagination following profound challenges to modernist narratives of progress and development.

What does figure prominently in discussions of the "Bogotá model" is TransMilenio, the bus rapid transit (BRT) network, which is now one of the city's most internationally recognized icons. Here, too, we see signs of a shift in visions of the global urban future. Over the past decade, TransMilenio has become famous, thanks in part to the efforts of Enrique Peñalosa, who has actively promoted the capital city's experience with BRT throughout the world.[6] Unveiled to the public in 2000, the bright red buses carrying commuters across Bogotá in record numbers have been credited with greatly improving mobility in a city once hamstrung by its decrepit and inefficient transportation system. Over two thousand visitors from forty-one countries have since visited Bogotá to study TransMilenio, and at least twenty-six cities have built BRT systems inspired by it.[7] Without a doubt, the TransMilenio story conforms to familiar developmental narratives: it claims to have resolved a persistent problem through technological innovation and rational management. Moreover, it upholds certain key modernist ideals: the integration of the city through a single transportation system that frees up mobility and circulation for all. Yet the transnational success of TransMilenio—and, indeed, Bogotá's ascendance to the upper echelons of city stardom—turns parts of the modernist development narrative on their head.

Peñalosa has touted BRT as a mass transit alternative for a world in which cities of the global South must find their own solutions to their problems. The ability of TransMilenio to travel relies on an increase in South-South frames of reference, which have enabled Bogotá to emerge as a model that circulates between cities like Delhi, Jakarta, and Johannesburg.[8] The newly reconfigured circuits of global urbanism through which the "Bogotá model" travels are predicated on a revision of long-standing modernist narratives of development. Cities like Bogotá should no longer hope to replicate the historical experience of Europe and North America, where modernity has long been associated with accomplishments now acknowledged to be impractical or unobtainable elsewhere, such as the construction of a comprehensive subway system like that of London, Paris, or New York. In contrast to the notion that "the future is riding on Metro," as the slogan for the Washington, DC, subway once boasted, Peñalosa would have us believe that, in the cities of the global South, the future is riding on bus rapid transit.[9] As in the field of risk management, Bogotá's fame in transportation circles reflects an unsettling of the teleological assumptions of modernist development paradigms and the progressive urban futures they once promised.

Whether or not Bogotá has been *truly* transformed is not my interest, nor is whether its celebrity status among urbanists is in fact deserved.[10] My objective is not to evaluate the changes that have taken place in Bogotá during the past two decades, or to critique the limitations and failures of the "Bogotá model" and the city's supposed rebirth.[11] What interests me, from the analytical position of "second-order observer," is that Bogotá has become an example other cities seek to emulate, in both the global North and South.[12] Is the city's ability to serve as a globally circulating model predicated on the degree to which its leaders have embraced risk as a technique of urban government? Does Bogotá's rise to stardom depend on it?

These questions, however difficult, enable us to reflect on the visions of the urban future emerging as dominant in the twenty-first century. At stake is what has happened in the world at large to make it possible now for Bogotá to be seen as a "model city." Recent transformations in transnational circuits of urban policy and practice are part of the story, but so too is a global trend toward envisioning the "megacities" of the global South as harbingers of the city yet to come. Although specific historical conjunctures shape how the political technology of risk is assembled and deployed in Bogotá and elsewhere, such shifts in the global urban imagination also set the conditions of possibility for cities.

Global Projections, Local Anxieties

At the end of the millennium, representations of "megacities" began to circulate widely as the burgeoning metropolises of the global South became the focus of intense interest. As we often hear, the urban population of the planet now outnumbers the rural, and cities, it is predicted, will absorb nearly all additional world population growth. Yet it is not the "global" or "world" cities—the command and control nodes of the global economy—that are expected to host this demographic explosion, but the "megacities" of the developing world.[13] The metropolitan centers that once represented for much of the world the imagined future of modernity—London or Paris in the nineteenth century, New York or Chicago in the twentieth—are now widely seen as relics of the past. They continue to be emulated across the world, but in a rather nostalgic way. The model cities of the modern era now appear as anachronistic bygones, while places like São Paulo, Mumbai, or Shanghai seem to presage what is to come. According to some calculations, twenty-seven of the thirty-three urban agglomerations predicted to dominate the global cityscape within ten years will be located in the least developed countries.[14] We are told that more than 1 billion people now live in the urban slums and shantytowns of the global South, and that this is where the majority of world population growth will take place. In the twenty-first century, it is hard to resist the conclusion that these rapidly expanding metropolises have become the new cities of the future.

The idea that the cities of the global South portend the global urban future is compelling. Indeed, it has succeeded in capturing the imagination of a wide range of commentators in Europe and North America who claim to offer their readers, for the most part also located in the global North, a view from which to envision a future urban world in which the cities of the global South loom large.[15] Such a view is reinforced by the proliferation of cultural productions in the global North that take place in or focus on "megacities," which novelist and critic Rana Dasgupta interprets as follows: "The Third-World metropolis is becoming the symbol of the 'new.' . . . If, for the better part of the 20th century, it was New York and its glistening imitations that symbolised the future, it is now the stacked-up, sprawling, impromptu city-countries of the Third World."[16] Referring to the fear and fascination such spectacles arouse, Dasgupta surmises that what Northern eyes see in films like *City of God* (Rio de Janeiro), *The Constant Gardener* (Nairobi), *Tsotsi* (Johannesburg), and *Slumdog Millionaire* (Mumbai) is what they believe will become increasingly familiar to them at home in years to come.

At first glance, envisioning the world in this manner seems to counteract representations central to the durable fiction of Euro-American superiority. Other commentators discussing the portentous nature of "megacities" appear to do the same. For example, Mike Davis, in *Planet of Slums*, argues,

"The cities of the future, rather than being made out of glass and steel as envisioned by earlier generations of urbanists, are instead largely constructed out of crude brick, straw, recycled plastic, cement blocks, and scrap wood."[17] Likewise, journalist Robert Neuwirth, reporting on squatter settlements in the megacities of four continents, sees them as visions of the "new urban world."[18] However, where Neuwirth finds optimism in a future of industrious squatters building lasting communities in the most adverse and precarious conditions, Davis sees a truly horrific global transformation: "Instead of cities of light soaring toward heaven, much of the twenty-first century urban world squats in squalor, surrounded by pollution, excrement, and decay."[19]

These are the two dominant modes of analysis and interpretation: alarmist predictions of urban apocalypse discovered in the misery of the slums and hopeful new models of urbanism found in the ingenuity of informal markets and unplanned settlements.[20] But while the "megacity" is sometimes discussed in a positive, even romantic, light, more often it is seen as the cause for alarm. Cities of the global South are commonly indexed as sites of explosive population growth and massive concentration of poverty, and these conditions are seen to be exacerbated by the peril of environmental deterioration and natural disaster. Jonathan Shapiro Anjaria observes that commentators of diverse political positions share the same view of these cities as failures.[21] In line with Davis's vision, cited above, Robert Kaplan finds, in the cities of West Africa, "the symbol of worldwide demographic, environmental, and societal stress."[22] And Kaplan, like Davis, foresees disaster eventually coming "home." These cities, he argues, are "an appropriate introduction to the issues, often extremely unpleasant to discuss, that *will soon confront our civilization*."[23] Although this dystopian view may pose new challenges to the temporalities and geographies of urban modernity, it has a long legacy. For centuries, North American and European aesthetic sensibilities have been appalled by the non-Western city.

This compounded anxiety—a dystopia that is not just "over there," but one that will soon be "over here"—has become almost routine. Consider, for example, a cover story entitled "Cities of the Future" in a popular environmental magazine. It, too, argued that the North must look to cities like Jakarta, Dhaka, and Lagos as predictors of the living conditions for the majority of the earth's population in the twenty-first century. The article drew attention to the chronic disasters of "megacities," all of which suffer from "a catalog of environmental ills."[24] Other periodicals, when focusing on cities of the global South, have also tended to conjure futures of crisis, chaos, and collapse. An article in *Harper's* concurs: "Metropolitan Manila . . . in its poverty, enormity, utter squalor, and lack of services perfectly represents the catastrophic twenty-first-century vision of the megacity."[25] In a similar vein, the caption beneath a two-page photograph in the *New Yorker* of women living in the Lagos city dump reads: "Lagos has become the archetype of the megacity, perhaps because its growth has been so explosive, perhaps because its cityscape has become so apocalyptic."[26]

Whether these forecasts have utopian or dystopian inflections, what ultimately concerns me is their shared sense of global transformation, in which the "megacity" is the paradigmatic urban space of the twenty-first century. As world-renowned architect Rem Koolhaas says of Africa's largest megacity: "Lagos is not catching up with us. Rather, we may be catching up with Lagos."[27] Given the ubiquity of this view, we need to ask: According to what relationships between history and geography, between time and space, do megacities and their slums perform such proleptic work? What is at stake in claiming that familiar linear developmental narratives have collapsed, such that places once thought to be advancing toward the so-called great modern cities have now come to represent to the North its own future?

The Space/Time of Urban Modernity

Initially, one may be tempted to view this as a radical reordering of the presumed relationship between temporality and geography so central to urban modernity—a shift that would reflect, in cultural terms, the waning political and economic power of European (or, more recently, American) imperialism.[28] It might then constitute a postcolonial critique par excellence by scrambling these imagined spatiotemporal coordinates and displacing the relative positions of the Third and First Worlds. Coincidentally, this kind of thinking about cities has a counterpart in Jean and John Comaroff's provocative suggestion that Euro-American social theory may now be "evolving" toward Africa rather than the other way around.[29] In their self-consciously parodic inversion of evolutionary teleology, places often thought to be "behind the times" are, in fact, where major global developments are now happening first. However, less nuanced versions of this claim that focus on the "megacity" paradoxically reinforce, even as they seem to challenge, the temporal logic and geographical order that have been central to the staging of urban modernity. As modernist promises are rendered obsolete, the manner in which cities of rich and poor countries are expected to converge is inverted.

Seeing "megacities" as the cities of the future expands the boundaries of urban modernity to include places once thought to be either outside of historical time or lagging behind it. Yet in the process, their heterogeneous histories are folded into a "global" history that remains centered in the global North.[30] Though, in the accounts cited above, developmental time is unsettled by what Ferguson calls a "nonprogressive re-temporalization"—that is, history is believed to be moving "backward" in the direction of Lima and Lagos rather than "forward" toward Paris and New York—the singular logic of historical time unfolding from one stage to the next remains intact.[31] Here we can expand Sarah Nuttall and Achille Mbembe's objection to treating the "slum" as the metonymic sign of the African metropolis, as it "reinserts the city [of Johannesburg] into a more recognizable frame."[32] With Nuttall and Mbembe, we can ask of the category of the megacity, "Doesn't [it] serve to confirm a dominant North American research mode for carving up the globe?"[33] The cities of the global North remain the hidden referent as this way of "enframing" the world, in Timothy Mitchell's terms, "recaptures histories happening elsewhere and returns them to the historical home of the West."[34] Simply put, *whose* future is foreseen in the megacity?[35]

Meanwhile, such an enframing allows the current crisis and imminent catastrophe Northern observers see in the cities of the global South to appear as the inevitable culmination of a singular and universally unfolding history. It removes from view the fact that images of "disorder" are actually signs of an uneven geography of wealth and power produced within, not outside of or prior to, histories of global capitalism.[36] The notion of a linear evolution of historical time toward the global South does mystifying work, concealing the extent to which the prosperity of cities of the imperial metropole was often made possible by exploitative political-economic relations with the colonial periphery. We see here a reversal of the geography of historical progress and a rejection of the assumption that time always moves in progressive directions. Yet this enframing ignores histories of capital accumulation and structural underdevelopment by placing cities of the global South at the static end point of a linear, historical narrative centered in Europe and North America.

Imagining these cities to portend an imminent, dystopian global urban future—to no longer see them as struggling to catch up with the West—is a variation on the belief that, at any one moment in time, places occupy different stages of history. World systems theorists and the Latin American *dependentista* school long ago argued against the "Eurocentric denial of coevalness" enacted by ideologies of modernization and development.[37] A paradigm shift was necessary to fully understand the unequal relations between countries, regions, and continents within the global economy, which led to the crucial point that, as Ramón Grosfoguel puts it, "development and underdevelopment coexist simultaneously in historical time."[38] Paradoxically, the same critique pertains to the idea that "megacities" are the cities of the future. Obfuscated by this framing is the fact that many cities of the global South were planned and built under colonial rule not to mirror the "modern" cities of the metropole, but as socially segmented and racially divided spaces of control. The "megacity" is *neither* an early stage *nor* the ultimate end point on a supposedly global time line of urbanization.[39]

If history is "retemporalized" in such a way, cities once thought to be advancing toward modernity are fixed in place within a static global hierarchy.[40] When time is no longer expected to transform poor cities into rich ones, waiting patiently for progress makes little sense. Yet, as Ferguson points out, something is lost when modernist developmental narratives are seen as failures and discarded: "No one talks about African economic convergence with the First World anymore."[41] Likewise, within discussions of megacities, rarely is there talk about Lagos becoming like London; yet, as some begin to foresee London becoming more like Lagos, the notion of convergence still carries weight—just not in the progressive way it once did. If the status of cities of the global South is fixed, and the cities of the global North foresee in them their own future, then hopes of development in the former morph into fears of degeneration in the latter. As evidenced by immigration anxieties in the United States and Europe, as well as by the fortification of national borders, this dystopian vision of the global urban future stimulates technologies of fortressing and exclusion.[42]

A City at Risk

That the category of "megacity" operates on the scale that it does, focusing on the cities of the global South as indicators of a worldwide trend even though it emanates primarily from North America and Europe, demonstrates its simultaneously globalist aspirations and provincial assumptions.[43] Though universal in scope, this seemingly unlocated discourse is always articulated from particular locations. The explosion of interest in these places does not come from the places themselves—as Walter Mignolo might say, its "locus of enunciation" is elsewhere.[44] That said, this way of thinking often becomes grounded in particular places. Thus a discussion of the global order enframed by the "megacity" would be incomplete without raising the question of what the category does in the world—what concrete and localized projects are enabled by it? If we can see the "global city" as a normative ideal that encourages calculated projects of city management or "urban entrepreneurialism" that work to attain such a status, we ought to view the "megacity" as a category that encourages other governmental rationalities, which may have equally important real-world effects.[45] Following Jennifer Robinson's assertion that the "global city" is a "regulating fiction," we must ask: what sorts of projects are inspired and enabled by the "megacity"?[46]

One answer can be found in models of urbanism that operate through rationalities of security and techniques of risk management—the phenomenon designated here as the endangered city. In the late twentieth century, risk was tied to a set of political programs aimed at the liberalization of economies and societies around the world.[47] The state's active concern for the welfare of the population, as well as its commitment to developmental imperatives such as jobs, education, and health care, shifted to operations that rational, self-regulating individuals were expected to perform on their own bodies, thoughts, and conduct.[48] Familiar now are rationalities of rule that promote "prudentialism" and personal responsibility for security from dangers.[49] However, the experience of liberal modernity in Europe and North America fails to explain how security mechanisms emerge and operate in the rest of the world. The spread of neoliberalism, the dismantling of the welfare (or developmental) state, the influence of risk governance: all of these look different when examined from specific locations.

From the beginning, Bogotá's relocation program targeting self-built settlements in zones of high risk has been aided by the World Bank's financial support and technical expertise and has drawn upon a generalized policy for risk reduction and population resettlement in cities of the developing world.[50] This situates it within the familiar history of relations between Northern development agencies and Southern governments, whereby the former have imposed structural adjustment reforms through loan conditionalities and promoted "good governance" among the latter.[51] Though the founding mandate of Bogotá's municipal housing agency in the 1940s was to build housing for poor and working-class citizens and public employees, since 2003 it has had the more limited responsibility of protecting the lives of those living in zones of high risk by facilitating their relocation. This shift is, in part, why Bogotá has become a "model city" in the eyes of the World Bank: it signals a break from policies associated with the welfare state. Yet governmental techniques undergo mutations determined by the contingencies of history and the specificities of place; as with risk management, these techniques are malleable in the hands of those in charge of them, as well as those subject to them. Nevertheless, possibilities for improvisation are limited by wider shifts in the global urban imagination.

The general trend of envisioning urban futures as futures of risk is reflected throughout the field of international development. Although it is impossible to identify the precise moment in which risk management arrived on the development agenda, we might provisionally locate it somewhere around December 1989, when the General Assembly of the United Nations proclaimed the 1990s the "International Decade for Natural Disaster Reduction" and, in doing so, initiated the process by which donor agencies and multilateral organizations would begin to direct financial resources and technical expertise toward disaster risk management in the global South.[52] Risk management has been a priority of every major development agenda put forth since, from the 1992 Earth Summit in Rio de Janeiro to the 2005 World Summit in New York. This shift, however, was neither immediate nor seamless. Rather, it generated debate between "development people" and "disaster people" as to whether investment in risk reduction should complement or even replace traditional development priorities, such as housing, poverty, transportation, health, and education.[53]

Although the two are not mutually exclusive, risk management is clearly vying for dominance.[54] For example, a global assessment published in 2004 by the United Nations Development Programme (UNDP) argued that development and disasters are so closely linked that the two must be integrated into a common framework that would "place disaster risk at the forefront of development planners' minds."[55] This imperative was given greater urgency in a later publication in which the UN urged development agencies to consider disasters as part of "a wider constellation of risks related to food and energy insecurity, financial and economic instability, global climate change, environmental degradation, disease and epidemics, conflict and extreme poverty."[56] That the development community also envisions the future in an apocalyptic light is clear if one examines the World Bank's 2009 annual report, which began: "The title of this year's *Global Monitoring Report* is 'A Development Emergency.' Appropriately so. We are in the midst of a global financial crisis for which there has been no equal in over 70 years. It is a dangerous time. The financial crisis that grew into an economic crisis is now becoming an unemployment crisis. It risks becoming a human and social crisis—with political implications. No region is immune."[57] Intensified by mounting catastrophes with massive human and financial losses, the debate is now more urgent than ever—there is a general sense that development, as we knew it, and the futures it once promised, are themselves "at risk."

The locus of this new paradigm of future thinking is in cities. In recent years there have been many efforts to bring risk management to the forefront of urban policy and practice.[58] The last decade has seen a steady proliferation of technical manuals, progress reports, international conferences, and academic studies discussing how and to what degree cities, their governments, and their populations are preparing themselves for a range of threats.[59] Urban futures in both the global North and South are being increasingly envisioned through the lens of security and risk. Although it used to be that only the future of "megacities" was "conceptualized in terms of crisis," urbanists from London to Mumbai are now focused on the risks of natural disaster, climate change, terrorist attack, financial meltdown, and disease outbreak.[60] A new urban security paradigm demands that all cities deploy protective and precautionary strategies against a range of threats in order to ensure their own reproduction.[61] Within transnational circuits of contemporary urbanism, the endangered city is becoming a prominent way of thinking about and acting on the urban future.

There are concrete consequences on multiple scales once cities become problematized as endangered. We see the rise of popular education campaigns designed to train prudential individuals to prepare themselves and their families for potential misfortunes, ranging from the loss of a job or a fire in the home to a terrorist attack or an earthquake. Such efforts inevitably draw from and promote new sources of knowledge and expertise, from actuarial science to military intelligence. There are similar shifts on an institutional level, such as increased investment in preparedness plans seeking to ensure that governmental agencies can and will respond efficiently to events that threaten to disturb the productive capacity or political stability of the city. The fortunes of national economies are now increasingly predicated on the ability of major cities to attract and maintain foreign investment in tourism, services, infrastructure, manufacturing, real estate, and information technology. Since a significant disturbance in the normal functioning of the city might result in widespread economic downturn and capital flight, not to mention social and political unrest, governments have come to view the entire urban assemblage as a security concern.

Thus the rise of risk and security as political rationalities in Bogotá is not only a response to local circumstances or a narrowly Colombian phenomenon.[62] It also pertains to the way Bogotá is positioned as a "place-in-the-world."[63] After all, it has long been classified among a group of cities with certain dysfunctional characteristics, even as it has been applauded more recently for its attempts to ameliorate them. Once framed in these terms, Bogotá becomes an endangered city, which in turn diagnoses the problem to be addressed by its government. When the modernist teleology of progress is discarded, transnational aid and expertise that may have once been invested in social services, welfare, infrastructure, education, and health care can be replaced by programs designed to promote precaution, preparedness, and prudentialism throughout a population of "responsibilized" citizens left to fend for themselves.[64] The break with the development models central to modernist paradigms of urban thought and practice is never absolute, and governmental techniques like risk management can be hitched to diverse political rationalities and mobilized to achieve a variety of ends. Nevertheless, cities in both the global North and South now find themselves in a de-developmentalized present whose future looks rather ominous.

Future Futures

All around us are signs of an urban imagination that envisions cities as spaces of menacing uncertainty, imminent threat, and potential crisis—in sum, as endangered. The logical response is the imperative to govern them in anticipation of future harm through the rationality of security underpinned by techniques of risk management. *Endangered City* offers a critical perspective on this globally widespread yet historically peculiar trend. Its critique of models of urbanism that focus exclusively on risk and security—and, in doing so, draw resources away from concerns such as poverty, rights, equality, education, housing, health care, or justice—suggests a reorientation of urban theory and practice. But the aim is neither to condemn these models nor to denounce their dissemination and circulation.[65] After all, techniques for governing cities often come to mean and do unexpected things when assembled and deployed in particular locations. This book's critical lens is focused less on transnational circuits of urban expertise than on the assumptions on which the circulation of certain ideas, models, practices, and resources are based. What deserves sustained scrutiny is the notion that risk and security are essential features of a new paradigm for planning, building, governing, and inhabiting cities in an age of uncertainty.

It is perhaps only once we denaturalize the staging of the world according to this script that it becomes possible to imagine other forms of "city-ness."[66] Such a task is especially necessary at the present moment, as influential imaginations of the global urban future fix the cities of the global South in place within a de-developmentalized global hierarchy. The question, then, as Mitchell puts it, "is whether one can find a way to theorize the question of modernity"—or the city—"that relocates it within a global context and, at the same time, enables that context to complicate, rather than simply reverse, the narrative logic of modernization."[67] To move beyond this predicament, we must examine how cities of the global South are made to appear different, peculiar, or dysfunctional. Yet we can also look to these cities, as this book has done, to see what new light they cast on the contemporary urban condition and to consider what displacements of urban theory and practice are necessary. There is a clear need to search for new vocabularies and epistemologies—to "practice ways of seeing and engaging urban spaces," as Simone puts it—that present alternatives to the ones supplied by the rationalities of security and risk.[68] This book has addressed these challenges by dissecting approaches to the city that appear to elude the spatiotemporal coordinates of urban modernity while they, in effect, reinscribe them—but reinscribe them, this time, without their salutary promise of change for the better.

In closing, let us return to the rather unsettling observation that Bogotá has become "a beacon of *hope* for other cities," as the Venice Biennale jury put it, partly because it has been at the forefront of experiments in how to govern (and govern through) security and risk—a "model" endangered city. *Endangered City* has demonstrated the specific conjuncture in which municipal authorities have embraced this political imperative and how it articulates with other logics of urbanism and their future visions. Yet the overall implications of this shift are clear: once cities are viewed as problems of risk and security rather than, say, modernization or development, resources once dedicated to concerns such as housing, poverty, health, and education are reduced and redirected to the basic goal of survival. Critics of modernist narratives, their teleological foundations, and their unfulfilled promises have had good reason to question the notion of progress. But as Walter Benjamin put it long before such narratives came under attack: "Overcoming the concept of 'progress' and overcoming the concept of 'period of decline' are two sides of one and the same thing."[69] Inspired by Benjamin's imperative to push beyond this binary, *Endangered City* has confronted global shifts in ways of thinking about and acting on cities. Its ultimate goal has been to put into question such shifts in the hope of opening space for urban theory and practice that would challenge apocalyptic projections and enable new forms of urbanity to emerge. Future futures beyond the endangered city remain to be invented.

CODA

In May 2013, the mayor of Bogotá, Gustavo Petro, announced his intention to revise the city's master plan. The Plan de Ordenamiento Territorial, or POT, is the set of rules and regulations that determines much of what can and cannot be done within municipal boundaries.[1] Petro's announcement confirmed his status in Colombian politics as a controversial and polarizing figure, much hated by the conservative political establishment. The POT had undergone a number of minor revisions since it was established in 2000, but nothing on the scale of the major overhaul Petro intended. The city council initially refused to discuss his proposal, leading Petro to pass it by decree— illegally, according to his opponents. While various aspects of the revision were met with disapproval, one dimension proved especially incendiary: Petro's desire to reorganize the master plan around climate change. In the words of a critic, though his supporters would not disagree, Petro's goal was to make this "the core principle guiding the planning of the city."[2]

Before Petro became mayor in 2012, he was known as a former member of the M-19 leftist guerrillas who had spent two years in prison before contributing to the militant group's demobilization. Once elected to the House of Representatives and eventually the Senate, Petro became one of the key leaders of the opposition to the Uribe administration. He made a name for himself as a fiery critic of corruption, persistently condemning the intimate relationship between elected politicians, drug traffickers, paramilitary forces, and other private interests. Once elected mayor of Bogotá, Petro expanded his political horizons: in his first year in office, he became an outspoken advocate of the imperative to respond to the changing climate. He addressed the Bogotá Summit on Cities and Climate Change in November 2012 with a remarkably blunt statement: "Global warming is irreversible. The damage is done, and we can't undo it. It may be possible to slow it down. But if we don't do something now, we're all dead." Petro's focus on climate change adaptation and mitigation angered many powerful interests, and his revised master plan became a lightning rod for criticism. Though he would not achieve all of his goals, he had clearly raised climate change to the top of the political agenda.[3]

I returned to Bogotá in 2013 to find out what this surge in climate change politics had meant for the field of risk management. A number of people I spoke with discussed Petro's concern for the risks associated with extreme weather events and his support for the relocation of families living in zones of high risk. Around the same time, he issued a decree ordering twelve thousand additional households to be resettled over the next three years. This was a dramatic increase both in the scale of the relocation program and in the housing subsidy the municipal government would provide to each family (up to 45 million pesos, or about US$25,000). Petro explained to *El Tiempo* that this decision was long overdue. Thanks to inaction on the part of previous administrations, he was quoted as saying, "thousands of families have settled in immitigable high-risk zones. Living in a zona de alto riesgo means an increased probability of death due to environmental risks. . . . 45 million [pesos] is the amount required to speed up the process of relocation and completely undo a decade of delay in the city of Bogotá."[4] Petro was clearly committed to expanding the Caja's resettlement program in the self-built settlements of the urban periphery—to using techniques of risk management to respond to the precarious living conditions of those on the margins of Colombian society. But I wanted to hear directly how those managing this program understood city hall's new enthusiasm for their work.

The program director confirmed what I had read in the papers: "The budget for relocation has quintupled under Petro! Initially we were in charge of relocating about three thousand households annually, but this number has now increased to fifteen thousand." I then asked him why he thought Petro found this program so important. He told me: "As you know, the guiding concern behind our work is to save lives. This hasn't changed. Everything else follows that principle. Petro knows that every four months or so we're hit hard by heavy rains and landslides. He's got that clear. He says time and time again that he doesn't want to lose a single life in the zonas de alto riesgo." Until this point we were on familiar ground, and I told him that each of his predecessors had told me the same thing. "But," he retorted, "Petro understands what no previous mayor of Bogotá has understood: that climate change is absolutely real and serious, and that what we're doing here with the resettlement program could become the foundation for a citywide strategy of adaptation."

Petro's agenda can be understood as an expansion of established approaches to governing risk in Bogotá. During his mayoral administration, what began as a relatively limited experiment was on its way to becoming a generalized strategy for governing the city. But the escalation of interventions in high-risk areas also signaled a shift in the way these interventions were framed. What was once a way to protect poor and vulnerable populations from regularly occurring disasters had morphed into a citywide response to the potentially dire consequences of climate change. The problem was no longer the relatively constant periodicity of the rainy season in Colombia and its rather predictable effects in the city's steep hillside settlements. Petro recognized that global warming would increase the severity and frequency of extreme weather events, thereby intensifying pressure on urban infrastructure and housing. The compounded uncertainty inherent to climate change meant that existing techniques for governing risk in Bogotá were necessary but insufficient. This required not only expanding the Caja's resettlement program throughout the self-built settlements of the urban periphery but also using this program as a guide to planning, building, and governing the city as a whole. With climate change looming on the horizon, the phenomenon designated here as the endangered city appears set to play an increasingly pivotal role in urban government, politics, and everyday life.

What will this surge in climate politics ultimately mean for Bogotá? In recent years, philosophers and social theorists have declared the arrival of two new eras: the postpolitical and the Anthropocene. The former is characterized by the removal of radical critique and ideological conflict from the space of public debate, the reduction of politics to consensus-building and policymaking, and the triumph of technocratic, managerial liberalism as the hegemonic form of "global governance."[5] The latter is defined as a new historical age in which humans have come to exist as a geological force in their own right whose ecological impact is felt on a planetary scale.[6] Some have argued that these dynamics are interconnected and that climate change is one of the key domains in which the postpolitical condition is produced and sustained.[7] The geographer Erik Swyngedouw summarizes "postpolitical" climate politics as one in which disagreements are allowed, but only over technical matters.[8] He urges that another climate politics is possible—one that fully politicizes nature by "foregrounding and naming different socio-environmental futures and recognizing conflict, difference and struggle over the naming and trajectories of these futures."[9] Finding an alternative requires strategies for radically reconfiguring the unequal social and economic relations underpinning the ecological crisis defining the present.

In Bogotá, urban climate politics is caught between these two possibilities. The key distinction has to do with the futures they envision. Postpolitical climate politics mobilizes apocalyptic scenarios of human extinction and ecological annihilation. It foresees threat and danger on the horizon and projects futures of crisis, chaos, and collapse. In this sense, it has a strong affinity with the rationalities of security and techniques of risk management that have developed in Bogotá over the past few decades. It favors dystopian visions of disaster over progressive hopes of change. However, the politics of climate change in Bogotá has the potential to enable alternative visions for the future of the city. There are currents of thought that seek to respond to the potentially dire consequences of global environmental change with ambitious strategies of social transformation, for example: reducing marginality and inequality; strengthening social infrastructure and collective resilience among vulnerable communities; opening spaces of political debate and participation for previously excluded sectors of society; making vital infrastructures work in the interest of people rather than profit; and promoting democratic values of transparency, justice, and accountability. While there are those in Bogotá who seek to preserve technocratic, managerial approaches to governing security and risk, recent developments suggest the potential for other visions of the urban future to emerge from within the politics of the Anthropocene.

NOTES

Preface

1. The concept of "endangerment" has been most fully engaged in anthropology by Tim Choy in the context of environmental politics in Hong Kong. See Choy, *Ecologies of Comparison*. I use the concept in a rather different way to frame a terrain of political engagement between the state and urban citizens that is organized around threat and danger. Recent work by Joseph Masco on national security affect in the United States has also been a source of inspiration. See Masco, *The Theater of Operations*.

2. Calvino, *Invisible Cities*, 28–29.

Introduction. The Politics of Security and Risk

1. Earthquakes may seem an exception, since until recently they were understood as geological events outside the realm of human agency. Yet as Dipesh Chakrabarty argues, the "scientific consensus around the proposition that the present crisis of climate change is man-made" has collapsed the distinction between natural and human history: "Now it is being claimed that humans are a force of nature in the geological sense." See "The Climate of History," 201, 207. Slavoj Žižek points out that even earthquakes can now be understood as "included in the scope of phenomena influenced by human activity." See *Living in the End Times*, 331 n. 13. Recent controversies surrounding hydraulic fracturing, or "fracking," have centered on this very possibility.

2. Jones and Rodgers, "Gangs, Guns, and the City." What Jones and Rodgers call "security governance" is one way to name the problem analyzed here.

3. Beck, *Risk Society* and *World at Risk*. For a sympathetic critique of Beck's work, see Collier, "Enacting Catastrophe."

4. Giddens, "Risk and Responsibility," 3; see also *The Consequences of Modernity*. For Niklas Luhmann, modern society is distinctive in that it "experiences its future in the form of the risk of deciding." See *Observations on Modernity*, 70–71. See also Bauman, *Liquid Times*.

5. See Douglas, *Purity and Danger* and *Risk and Blame*; Douglas and Wildavsky, *Risk and Culture*.

6. This argument appears primarily in Foucault's 1977–78 lectures, *Security, Territory, Population*. This particular formulation appears on page 61.

7. Foucault's analysis of liberalism is in *The Birth of Biopolitics*.

8. Ibid., 65.

9. Foucault, *Security, Territory, Population* and *The Birth of Biopolitics*, 10. Foucault's analysis laid the foundation for a series of studies tracking the genealogy of risk and security in the liberal democracies of the West. Key studies in this tradition are Barry, Osborne, and Rose, *Foucault and Political Reason*; Burchell, Gordon, and Miller, *The Foucault Effect*; Rose, *Powers of Freedom*; O'Malley, *Risk, Uncertainty and Government*; Dean, *Governmentality*; Ewald, *L'État providence*.

10. Mariana Valverde urges us to examine "the complex connections and disjunctions between liberal governance (as a set of typical rationalities and technologies) and the concrete combinations of liberal and non-liberal practices of government" that persist alongside but also within them. See "'Despotism' and Ethical Liberal Governance," 358–59.

11. Collier, "Topologies of Power," 89. For Foucault's own attempts to discourage epochal, successionary analytics of power, see *Security, Territory, Population*. In the "Governmentality" lecture, he states that "in reality one has a triangle, sovereignty-discipline-government, which has as its primary target the population and as its essential mechanism the apparatuses of security." See *Security, Territory, Population*, 102.

12. Debates within the Marxist tradition have centered on how capitalism not only coexists with, but also depends on, other modes of production. See Althusser and Balibar, *Reading Capital*; Balibar, "On the Basic Concepts of Historical Materialism." Balibar broke from teleological readings of Marx by rejecting "succession" and "supersession" in favor of "articulation," or the synchronic combination of forces and relations of production ostensibly belonging to different temporalities. Raymond Williams sought to understand the overlap and interdependence of "dominant," "residual," and "emergent" forms of cultural production. See *Marxism and Literature*, 121–27. The articulation of modes of production has also been a key concern for economic anthropology. See Meillassoux, "From Reproduction to Production."

13. See Geertz, *The Interpretation of Cultures*; Sally Falk Moore, *Social Facts and Fabrications*; Geschiere, *The Modernity of Witchcraft*; Mamdani, *Citizen and Subject*; Rabinow, *French Modern*.

14. See Stoler, *Race and the Education of Desire*; Chatterjee, *The Politics of the Governed*; von Schnitzler, "Citizenship Prepaid"; Valverde, "'Despotism' and

Ethical Liberal Governance." Other alternatives to "supersessional" models can also be drawn from theorists who have examined the supposed divide between the religious/theological and the secular/political, such as Schmitt, *Political Theology*; Benjamin, "Critique of Violence"; Derrida, "Force of Law"; Agamben, *Homo Sacer*. Their work examines the mutually constitutive relationship between religious authority and political sovereignty in liberal democracy, thereby questioning narratives of modernity in which the latter replaces the former.

15. See Rofel, *Other Modernities*; Donald S. Moore, *Suffering for Territory*; Timothy Mitchell, *Colonising Egypt*.

16. See Fabian, *Time and the Other*.

17. For elaborations on Bakhtin's concept of "chronotope," see Bear, "Doubt, Conflict, Mediation."

18. In this sense, the "modern city" belonged to the global transformation that Timothy Mitchell identifies as the "age of the exhibition." Mitchell describes this age, which is also "the colonial age, the age of world economy and of global power in which we live," as follows: "Everything collected and arranged to stand for something, to represent progress and history, human industry and empire; everything set up, and the whole set-up always evoking somehow some larger truth." See *Colonising Egypt*, 6, 13.

19. See Mignolo, *Local Histories/Global Designs* and "Introduction: Coloniality of Power and De-colonial Thinking"; Maldonado-Torres, *Against War*. World systems theorists tackle this issue by arguing that "development" is not a historical progression, but that "development and underdevelopment coexist simultaneously in historical time." For a summary, see Grosfoguel, "Developmentalism, Modernity, and Dependency Theory in Latin America," 360. For key texts, see Wallerstein, *The Modern World-System*; Frank, *Capitalism and Underdevelopment in Latin America*; Cardoso and Faletto, *Dependency and Development in Latin America*.

20. The work of urban security scholars, such as Stephen Graham, is one inspiration for this project. My interest is in how the militarized policies and practices deployed to combat crime and violence intersect with diverse attempts to govern a wide range of threats to the city and urban life. See Graham, *Cities under Siege*.

21. Rosenberg and Harding, introduction to *Histories of the Future*, 4.

22. Berman, "Falling Towers," cited in Graham, *Cities under Siege*, 10.

23. This point has been elaborated by a number of historians of colonial Latin America. See Joseph and Szuchman, *I Saw a City Invincible*; Socolow, introduction to *Cities and Society in Colonial Latin America*; Schwartz, "Cities of Empire"; Kagan and Marías, *Urban Images of the Hispanic World, 1493–1793*.

24. See Walker, *Shaky Colonialism*.

25. The classic expression of the mythical battle between "civilization" and "barbarism" is attributed to the influential Argentine politician and intellectual of the mid-nineteenth century, Sarmiento, *Life in the Argentine Republic*. Teresa A. Meade argues that Sarmiento's concerns about the balance of power between the barbaric country and the civilized city pertained to all the South American republics. See

"Civilizing" Rio, 28. For a study of the politics of disaster in twentieth-century Argentina, and subsequent reconstruction attempts by modernist architects and urbanists, see Healey, *The Ruins of the New Argentina*.

26. Coronil, "The Future in Question."

27. There are many more studies of security and the city in Latin America than can possibly be mentioned here. Of particular interest to my argument are Caldeira, *City of Walls*; Caldeira and Holston, "Democracy and Violence in Brazil"; Goldstein, "Toward a Critical Anthropology of Security" and *Outlawed*; Arias and Goldstein, *Violent Democracies in Latin America*; Samet, "The Photographer's Body"; Auyero, "The Hyper-Shantytown"; O'Neill and Thomas, *Securing the City*; Taussig, *Shamanism, Colonialism, and the Wild Man* and *The Devil and Commodity Fetishism in South America*; O'Neill, "Left Behind"; Denyer Willis, *The Killing Consensus*; Jones and Rodgers, "Gangs, Guns, and the City" and *Youth Violence in Latin America*; Rodgers, "'Disembedding' the City."

28. The "zone of high risk" is a techno-political category used by the municipal government of Bogotá to demarcate areas in which the probability of landslides, floods, or other disasters is believed to be strong. Although it is one of the book's primary objects of analysis, I have resisted the urge to put quotation marks around the phrase throughout the text. However, it should be assumed that all references to *zonas de alto riesgo*, "zones of high risk," and "high-risk zones" denote areas officially designated as such.

29. Framed as an event that might well strike Bogotá, it demanded still greater preparedness. When the mayor's office sent a team to assist with recovery in Port-au-Prince, for example, the Bogotá-based newspaper *El Tiempo* saw it as a learning opportunity: "Thanks to the dispatch of this support group, the emergency response agencies of Bogotá are going to see with their own eyes what our city could face and how they can improve their ability to respond to this eventuality." Yet it was also an opportunity for the government to publicize its readiness. The media quoted the fire chief reassuring the public that Bogotá's "emergency system is prepared to respond to this type of disaster." "Bogotá prestará ayuda humanitaria a Haití," *El Tiempo*, January 13, 2010.

30. "Haiti Studies Colombian Town for Quake Rebuilding," *Reuters*, February 8, 2010. In 1999, Armenia was struck by a massive earthquake that killed over twelve hundred people and destroyed more than half the city's buildings. In 2000, the United Nations awarded a prize to the public agency responsible for Armenia's reconstruction, and its efforts were quickly recognized as an example of how to integrate risk reduction into disaster recovery efforts. The UN Sasakawa Award for Disaster Reduction is given to individuals or institutions for their efforts to reduce disaster risk in their communities.

31. "Ministro del Interior de Haití recorrió Armenia para conocer su reconstrucción tras sismo de 1999," *El Tiempo*, February 8, 2010.

32. According to a recent UN publication on best practices: "The high level of advance and sustainability achieved by Bogotá in the application of risk manage-

ment policies has become a model for the region." See Ramírez, Ghesquiere, and Costa, *Un modelo para la planificación de la gestión del riesgo de desastres en grandes ciudades*, 112. President Uribe boasted to the Union of South American Nations as he promoted his aid plan for Haiti: "Ever since 1999, we have had many, many delicate problems: volcanic eruptions, seismic shifts that have affected rural and urban communities, floods. That is, we have permanently been dedicated to this task." "Texto de la intervención del presidente Álvaro Uribe ante el pleno de Unasur," *El Tiempo*, February 9, 2010.

33. A related phenomenon is the recent demand for former members of the Colombian state's security apparatus to serve as consultants in other parts of the world. See Tomaselli, "Colombia's New Export."

34. Justice Minister Rodrigo Lara Bonilla was killed in 1984 and the presidential candidate Luis Carlos Galán gunned down in 1989 by assassins allegedly working for the head of the Medellín cartel, Pablo Escobar.

35. See, for example, Villaveces Izquierdo, "Seguridad," 375.

36. For example, the mayor of Bogotá during most of my fieldwork, Samuel Moreno, referred to "comprehensive security" (*seguridad integral*), which he defined "not only in terms of public security and the reduction of violence . . . but from a comprehensive and holistic perspective that integrates different components of an economic, social, environmental, cultural, and political nature, with the objective of guaranteeing a safe and secure city for its inhabitants." See Moreno Rojas, "Seguridad integral en la Bogotá Positiva."

37. See Montezuma, "The Transformation of Bogotá, Colombia, 1995–2000."

38. Silva Téllez, *Bogotá imaginada*; Niño Murcia, *Territorios del miedo en Santafé de Bogotá*. See also "Milagro en riesgo," *Semana*, February 19, 2002.

39. Llano, "Plaza de Bolívar"; Donovan, "Informal Cities and the Contestation of Public Space."

40. See Rivas Gamboa, *Gorgeous Monster*, 33–34; Llorente and Rivas, "La caída del crimen en Bogotá"; Silva Téllez, *Bogotá imaginada*. On the quadrupling of homicides in Bogotá over a ten-year period, which increased from 1,237 in 1983 to 4,470 in 1992, see Donovan, "Informal Cities and the Contestation of Public Space," 34. The downtown locality of Santa Fé, Donovan reports, contributed a disproportionate share of violent incidents to these statistics and had a homicide rate "comparable with countries undergoing high-intensity civil war" (497 deaths per 100,000 people).

41. As recently as 1997, the World Health Organization declared El Cartucho one of the most dangerous streets in the world. See Robledo Gómez and Rodríguez Santana, *Emergencia del sujeto excluido*, 173.

42. This quotation is from an interview that appears in Segura, *Conversaciones con Bogotá, 1945–2005*, 174.

43. Juan Forero, "Explosions Rattle Colombian Capital during Inaugural," *New York Times*, August 8, 2002. In light of the threats made by FARC before the inauguration, there were forty thousand armed soldiers, two hundred sharpshooters, and

a flotilla of aircraft patrolling a two-hundred-mile security zone radiating outward from the presidential palace on Inauguration Day.

44. "The Fight for the Cities," *Economist*, October 26, 2002.

45. Gilma Jiménez, "El fin de una vergüenza," *Semana*, December 21, 2003.

46. Villaveces, Londoño, and Colón, *Bogotá León de Oro 1990–2006*.

47. Rivas Gamboa, "In-quietud y doble-voz," 63.

48. On the one hand, the demolition of El Cartucho resembled what Andrew Lakoff and Stephen Collier call "sovereign state security," or the "practices oriented to the defense of territorial sovereignty against foreign enemies using military means." See Lakoff, "From Population to Vital System," 36. In response to the threat of insurgency, epitomized by the Inauguration Day missile, intensified force was used to physically remove one of the most infamous sites of disorder from the capital city. Its problem was the one Foucault associates with Machiavelli: the safety (*sûreté*) of the territory and of the sovereign who rules over it. See *Security, Territory, Population*, 65. The Caja's resettlement program, on the other hand, shifted to a form of what Lakoff and Collier define as "population security" or the "protection of the national population against regularly occurring internal threats, such as illness, industrial accident, or infirmity." No longer was the safety of the sovereign and his territory the primary concern, but rather, in Foucault's terms, "the security (*sécurité*) of the population and, consequently, of those who govern it."

49. See Durkheim, *Suicide* and *The Division of Labor in Society*; Simmel, "The Stranger."

50. See Park, Burgess, and McKenzie, *The City*; Wirth, "Urbanism as a Way of Life."

51. Lefebvre, *The Production of Space* and *Critique of Everyday Life*.

52. These concepts are elaborated in Harvey, *The New Imperialism* and "The Right to the City."

53. See also Smith, *The New Urban Frontier*. Others have elaborated on how "accumulation by dispossession" is an ongoing process central to capitalist expansion. See Elyachar, *Markets of Dispossession*; Hart, "Denaturalizing Dispossession"; Zhang, *In Search of Paradise*.

54. Harvey, "The Right to the City," 34.

55. For a more nuanced analysis of speculation on land markets in the informal settlements of the global South, see Desai and Loftus, "Speculating on Slums."

56. Harvey, "The Right to the City," 30. See also Lefebvre, *The Urban Revolution*. For a related approach under the rubric of "planetary urbanization," see Brenner, "Theses on Urbanization"; Brenner and Schmid, "The 'Urban Age' in Question."

57. For work on Baltimore and Paris, see Harvey, *Spaces of Hope* and *Paris, Capital of Modernity*. For commentary on urban transformations in Mumbai, see Harvey, "The Right to the City." For a critique of Harvey's account of housing politics in that city, see Anand and Rademacher, "Housing in the Urban Age."

58. For a counterargument about the case of slum demolition in Mumbai, see Weinstein, *The Durable Slum*.

59. In Rio de Janeiro, Harvey envisions a future that, from his perspective, is as inevitable as it is objectionable: "I wager that within fifteen years, if present trends continue, all those hillsides in Rio now occupied by favelas will be covered by high-rise condominiums with fabulous views over the idyllic bay, while the erstwhile favela dwellers will have been filtered off into some remote periphery." See Harvey, "The Right to the City," 36–37.

60. See Marx, *Capital*, 363–64.

61. Marx, "On the Jewish Question," 45. Like the feudal serfs Marx saw as being "emancipated" from their dependence on the soil, this population of low-wage workers is "liberated" from another constraint born of the relationship between humans and nature—the risk of floods, landslides, and earthquakes.

62. In 2006, the Caja was authorized to double the amount offered for relocation subsidies from twenty-five to fifty *salarios mínimos legales*, or from 10,925,000 pesos (US$5,462) to 21,850,000 pesos (US$10,925). This is for Vivienda Tipo 1, which contains thirty square meters of floor space and the option to expand.

63. Although this paradigm has been tightly connected to the work of Michel Foucault, the specific ways it has been applied within urban studies and related fields is what I take issue with here.

64. For discussions of this particular tendency among some geographers, anthropologists, and others, see Ferguson, "The Uses of Neoliberalism," 170–71; Brenner, Peck, and Theodore, "Variegated Neoliberalization."

65. Foucault, "Governmentality," in *Security, Territory, Population*.

66. See Ferguson, "The Uses of Neoliberalism."

67. For examples of work on the political economy of violence in Colombia, see Gill, "War and Peace in Colombia"; Hylton, *Evil Hour in Colombia*.

68. Discussions of the "postneoliberal" moment in Latin America can be found in Escobar, *Territories of Difference*; Leiva, *Latin American Neostructuralism*; Coronil, "The Future in Question."

69. Roy, "The 21st-Century Metropolis," 820. See also Robinson, *Ordinary Cities*.

70. Roy urges that the "distinctive experiences of the cities of the global South can generate productive and provocative theoretical frameworks for *all* cities." See "The 21st-Century Metropolis," 820.

71. Based on the analysis of contemporary forms of displacement in urban India, D. Asher Ghertner makes a related argument about the extension of the concept of "gentrification" throughout cities of the global South. I agree with his suggestion that "accumulation by dispossession" has more analytical purchase and that it, too, must be subjected to the same empirical scrutiny. See "India's Urban Revolution."

72. Mbembe and Nuttall, "Introduction: Afropolis," 25.

73. I use the term "urbanism" in a particular way throughout the book. In contrast to those who understand it as the habits, behaviors, and attitudes of city dwellers, such as Wirth, I use the term to refer to shared bodies of knowledge about cities and urbanization and their application in concrete situations. In other words,

"urbanism" refers to what groups of like-minded professional urbanists (planners, policymakers, consultants, bureaucrats, technical experts, designers, architects, and so on) think, say, and do. See Lefebvre, *The Urban Revolution*. However, I disagree with the derogatory connotation Lefebvre gives the term.

74. See Ferguson, "The Uses of Neoliberalism" and "Toward a Left Art of Government."

75. Ferguson, "The Uses of Neoliberalism," 173.

76. Ibid., 182. See also Collier, "The Spatial Forms and Social Norms of 'Actually Existing Neoliberalism,'" 2. For recent attempts by geographers to track the mobility and migration of neoliberal discourses and techniques across geographical as well as professional boundaries, see Peck, "Geographies of Policy," and Brenner, Peck, and Theodore, "Variegated Neoliberalization." Peck advocates an approach that is "attentive to the *constitutive* sociospatial context of policy-making activities, and to the hybrid mutations of policy techniques and practices across dynamized institutional landscapes" ("Geographies of Policy," 2).

77. Ferguson, "The Uses of Neoliberalism," 181. A related issue pertains to the field of urban political ecology. Scholars have challenged conventional urban poverty research and policy that ignore the ecology of the city as well as approaches to urban environmental problems that overlook their social, economic, and political dimensions. See Davis, *Planet of Slums*; Auyero and Swistun, *Flammable*; Swyngedouw, "Power, Nature and the City"; Hardoy and Pandiella, "Urban Poverty and Vulnerability to Climate Change in Latin America." These challenges coalesce in the rise of "urban environmental justice" as an important research and activist agenda linking social and environmental struggles in cities of the global North and South. See Martínez Alier, *The Environmentalism of the Poor*; Sze, *Noxious New York*; Bullard, *Unequal Protection*; Dorceta E. Taylor, *The Environment and the People in American Cities, 1600–1900s*; Baviskar, "Between Violence and Desire"; Sze, *Noxious New York*. This agenda intersects with dominant paradigms of urban theory in its identification of injustice, its critique of state negligence, its demands for the protection of vulnerable populations, and its calls for political action organized around various kinds of rights. Since the logic of environmental justice is already central to regimes of urban governance in Bogotá, we must examine what happens when governments do, in fact, set out to ameliorate what Auyero and Swistun call the "environmental suffering" of the urban poor.

78. As Foucault succinctly put it, such state-phobic positions have become pro forma for some voices on the Left and for neoliberalism itself: "All those who share in the great state phobia should know that they are following the direction of the wind and that in fact, for years and years, an effective reduction of the state has been on the way." See *The Birth of Biopolitics*, 191.

79. For a related formulation pertaining to rather different themes, see Choy, *Ecologies of Comparison*.

80. Elizabeth Povinelli suggests that this is what is needed to "close the gap between the instability and potentiality of local modes of security and the seeming

stability and regulatory nature of late liberal securitization." See "Defining Security in Late Liberalism."

81. My efforts to historicize risk were guided by studies tracking the emergence of political problems, governmental techniques, and scientific objects at particular moments. Especially noteworthy examples include Foucault, *Discipline and Punish*; Timothy Mitchell, *Rule of Experts*; Hacking, *The Emergence of Probability*.

82. This methodological approach takes inspiration from Actor-Network Theory. See Latour, *Reassembling the Social*; Law and Hassard, *Actor Network Theory and After*.

83. This approach follows anthropologists studying biosecurity, such as Collier, Lakoff, and Rabinow, "Biosecurity."

84. My approach combined an anthropological attention to the social and cultural construction of place, influenced by Gupta and Ferguson, *Anthropological Locations* and "Culture, Power, Place"; Hansen, *Wages of Violence*; Zhang, *Strangers in the City*; Ebron, *Performing Africa*. My emphasis was specifically on the techno-political rendering of space as knowable, productive, and governable, following the likes of Scott, *Seeing like a State*; Timothy Mitchell, *Rule of Experts*; Barry, "Technological Zones."

85. Here I followed a fairly standard approach in Science and Technology Studies. See Latour, *Science in Action* and *Aramis, or, The Love of Technology*.

86. Throughout the book I refer to "risk management" as the best translation of what in Bogotá is called *gestión del riesgo*.

87. I refer to what Ann Stoler calls the historical "blunting" enacted by some postcolonial scholarship. She remarks: "Rubrics such as 'colonial legacy' offer little help. They fail to capture the evasive space of imperial formations past and present as well as the perceptions and practices by which people are forced to reckon with features of those formations in which they remain vividly and imperceptibly bound." See "Imperial Debris," 192–93. See also Frederick Cooper, "Decolonizing Situations," 64.

88. For cautionary comments on the study of violence, see Caldeira, *City of Walls*; Escobar, "Las violencias a través de otras miradas."

1. Apocalypse Foretold

1. Sistema Informativo del Gobierno, Presidencia de la República de Colombia, recording of Santos's addresses to Armero, November 2010, http://wsp .presidencia.gov.co/Videos/2010/Diciembre/Paginas/Index.aspx (accessed February 8, 2013). I'm translating *damnificado* as "victim" here for analytical reasons despite the important semantic and political differences between *damnificados* and *víctimas*.

2. Mojica Patiño and José Alberto, "Iglesia busca testimonios que permitan santificación de Omaira," *El Tiempo*, November 30, 2010.

3. Ibid.

4. Attending to historical specificity and focusing on these tragic events will have implications for how we understand the politics of life amid widespread epochal proclamations. "Today's predominant mode of politics is post-political bio-politics," affirms Slavoj Žižek ("Censorship Today"). "Today politics knows no value . . . other than life," echoes Agamben (*Homo Sacer*, 10). "No other politics is conceivable other than a politics of life," declares Roberto Esposito (*Bíos*, 15). In explaining this phenomenon, scholars often cite a variety of large-scale sociological, political, and economic forces, each of which is relevant and none of which is sufficient—neoliberalism, securitization, globalization, etc. However, we ought to resist the temptation to lump them together in a baggy characterization of the global situation of the twenty-first century, and then look for their local effects in places like Colombia. Instead, this chapter will examine precisely how life has entered politics—not as a resource to be improved or managed, but rather as a precarious possession permanently in danger of being harmed or taken away—and is then governed in anticipation of a range of potentially catastrophic and eminently uncertain futures. For a related attempt, see Sánchez, "Alcances y límites de los conceptos biopolítica y biopoder en Michel Foucault."

5. This chapter draws on press archives, political discourse, journalistic accounts, ethnographic fieldwork, and cultural productions by artists and writers. This choice of sources reflects the fact that "events" are constituted by heterogeneous discursive practices that crosscut the political and cultural domains of society.

6. In recent years, ethnographic work has begun to reveal the processes through which *past* occurrences become constituted retroactively as "events." See Das, *Critical Events*; Fortun, *Advocacy after Bhopal*; Malkki, "News and Culture"; McLean, *The Event and Its Terrors*; Petryna, *Life Exposed*. Ethnographers have also developed tools with which to analyze the technical and political frames that determine how *future* events—such as accidents, attacks, or outbreaks—are defined, measured, and managed. See Collier, "Enacting Catastrophe"; Lakoff, "The Generic Biothreat"; Masco, *The Nuclear Borderlands* and "Bad Weather"; Samimian-Darash, "A Pre-event Configuration for Biological Threats." My analysis draws on both approaches to account for the complex temporality of events.

7. Koselleck, *Futures Past*. For a related argument in relation to pandemic preparedness in the United States, see Caduff, "Pandemic Prophecy, or How to Have Faith in Reason."

8. Events such as these can be analyzed not as isolated occurrences at single moments but, rather paradoxically, through that which precedes and follows them in chronological time. Thinking with Gilles Deleuze's philosophy of the event, this approach makes it possible to highlight how actual events emerge out of existing potentialities, how historical significance is subsequently attributed to them, and how they come to shape conditions of future possibility. See Deleuze, *The Logic of Sense* and *The Fold*; Colwell, "Deleuze and Foucault"; Patton, "The World Seen from Within." Of particular importance is the distinction Deleuze makes between "pure" or "virtual" events, on the one hand, and "actual" events on the other. His concept

of the event is based on his separation of historical time (*Chronos*), the linear scale according to which specific events are serially ordered, from the time of the event (*Aion*), which exceeds any determination of precise temporal boundaries and exists outside the chronology of past-present-future. See Deleuze, *The Logic of Sense*, 77; Colwell, "Deleuze and Foucault"; Badiou, "The Event in Deleuze," 38. These distinctions prevent us from taking an event at face value, in the sense of something that arises out of a past that produced it and then leads to a future in which its effects are realized. We might ask, instead, how particular events have been actualized through the description, expression, or attribution of sense to something that has happened. This is not simply the re-presentation of the past, but rather the process through which the virtual event becomes an actual event. And since virtual events can be actualized in multiple ways, and actual events can produce changes in the realm of the virtual, thereby influencing how future events will be actualized, events are fundamentally open to re-actualization.

9. On the political opening created by this historical conjuncture, see Ramírez Gomez and Cardona, "El sistema nacional para la prevención y atención de desastres en Colombia," 267. For an exemplary discussion of how a series of seemingly disparate events—terrorism, natural disasters, and epidemics—can be brought into the framework of "security threats," see Lakoff, "Preparing for the Next Emergency." In this essay, Lakoff analyzes the logic through which a range of potential threats to collective life are taken up as political problems. For how governmental technologies of calculating and responding to natural disaster risk shift to the problem of terrorist threat, see Collier, "Enacting Catastrophe."

10. Eduardo García Martínez, "Pacto incancelable con la esperanza tiene Colombia," *El Tiempo*, November 21, 1985.

11. For the editorial, see Guillermo Cano, "Libreta de apuntes," *El Espectador*, November 17, 1985.

12. Guillermo Pérez, "Coraje para hacer frente a enemigos de la democracia," *El Tiempo*, November 19, 1985.

13. Claudia, "When Will We Learn that It Is Better to Prevent than Lament?!," *El Tiempo*, November 16, 1985.

14. Daniel Samper Pizano, "Apocalipsis anunciado," *El Tiempo*, November 18, 1985.

15. Ibid.

16. Gloria Moanack, "Colombia, region de alto riesgo sísmico," *El Tiempo*, November 14, 1985.

17. Ibid.

18. Ibid.

19. For a discussion of the *crisis de "gubernabilidad"* that ensued after the coincidence of the Armero tragedy and the attack on the Palace of Justice, see Ramírez Gomez and Cardona, "El sistema nacional para la prevención y atención de desastres en Colombia," 267.

20. See the documentary produced by the periodical *El País* twenty-five years after the disaster: http://www.elpais.com.co/paisonline/especiales/popasite/.

21. Germán Santamaría, "Popayán: Como un Jerusalén destruida," *El Tiempo*, April 1, 1983.

22. Ibid.

23. "Popayán surgirá de sus escobros B.B.," *El Tiempo*, April 1, 1983.

24. Ibid.

25. Ibid.

26. Congreso de Colombia, Ley 11, 1983.

27. The fund would remain inactive until 1989. Ibid.; Ramírez Gomez and Cardona, "El sistema nacional para la prevención y atención de desastres en Colombia," 271.

28. Guillermo Goelkel C., "Poder de destrucción de 28,000 toneladas de dinamita," *El Tiempo*, April 1, 1983. Newspapers informed the public that the tremor that hit the city contained the destructive power of twenty-eight thousand tons of dynamite.

29. "Gran cruzada de ayuda a Popayán," *El Tiempo*, April 1, 1983, and "Llanto, dolor, muerte y destrucción," *El Tiempo*, April 3, 1983. So, too, was the international community, whose aid and support "began to flow just hours after the catastrophe."

30. "Popayán entierra a los muertos y comienza su reconstrucción," *El Tiempo*, April 2, 1985.

31. "Picture Power: Tragedy of Omayra Sanchez," *BBC News*, September 30, 2005, http://news.bbc.co.uk/2/hi/4231020.stm.

32. For my purposes, the ethical questions raised by his decision to communicate the powerlessness and suffering of the victims of the tragedy rather than assist in the rescue efforts cannot be answered. Rather, I see them as central to the national and international mediation process through which Omayra's life and death took on such cultural significance.

33. Germán Santamaría, "Juan Pablo II besará la tierra de la muerte," *El Tiempo*, July 6, 1986.

34. Ibid.

35. Santa, *Adiós, Omayra*, 13.

36. Ibid., 161.

37. Germán Santamaría, "La tragedia anunciada," *El Tiempo*, November 24, 1985.

38. "Picture Power: Tragedy of Omayra Sanchez," *BBC News*, September 30, 2005, http://news.bbc.co.uk/2/hi/4231020.stm.

39. The Chilean novelist Isabel Allende also wrote a short story, "And of Clay Are We Created," based on the events surrounding the eruption of the Nevado del Ruiz and the death of Omayra Sánchez (who was renamed "Azucena" in Allende's rendition).

40. In *The Hermeneutics of the Subject*, Foucault clarifies: "In the type of analysis I have been trying to advance for some time you can see that power relations, governmentality, the government of the self and of others, and the relationship of self to self constitute a chain, a thread, and I think it is around these notions that we should be able to connect together the question of politics and the question of eth-

ics." See Foucault, *The Hermeneutics of the Subject*, 252. See also "On the Genealogy of Ethics" and "Technologies of the Self."

41. "Picture Power: Tragedy of Omayra Sanchez," *BBC News*, September 30, 2005.

42. Inés, Sandoval, and Roa, *Armero*, cited in Viana Castro, *Armero, su verdadera historia*, 374.

43. Santa, *Adiós, Omayra*, 15.

44. Ibid., 13.

45. Ibid., 157.

46. Ibid., 161.

47. Villaveces Izquierdo, "Seguridad," 375.

48. This relates to Foucault's questions about biopower: "How can a power such as this kill, if it is true that its basic function is to improve life, to prolong its duration, to improve its chances, to avoid accidents, and to compensate for its failings? . . . Given that this power's objective is essentially to make live, how can it let die?" See Foucault, *"Society Must Be Defended,"* 254.

49. Sources consulted here were Castro Caycedo, *El Palacio sin máscara*; Echeverry and Hanssen, *Holocausto en el silencio*; Jimeno, *Noche de lobos*; Carrigan, *The Palace of Justice*.

50. Castro Caycedo, *El Palacio sin máscara*, 11.

51. Cited in ibid., 28.

52. Cited in Echeverry and Hanssen, *Holocausto en el silencio*, 46.

53. Cited in Castro Caycedo, *El Palacio sin máscara*, 86.

54. Cited in ibid., 239.

55. The Truth Commission reports that over one thousand troops were deployed in the battle against thirty-five guerrilla combatants and were ordered to "shoot anything that moves." Ibid.

56. Cited in ibid., 71–72.

57. Cited in ibid., 39–40.

58. Ibid., 39.

59. Colombian TV news station Noticias Uno released a video in August 2007 of magistrate Carlos Horacio Urán being rescued alive from the Palace of Justice.

60. Echeverry and Hanssen, *Holocausto en el silencio*, 35.

61. Castro Caycedo, *El Palacio sin máscara*, 124.

62. Ibid., 120.

63. Birkhofer, "Trace Memories," 50.

64. Salcedo et al., *Doris Salcedo*, 14.

65. Salcedo, "Traces of Memory."

66. Salcedo's *Noviembre 6 y 7* (2002) can be viewed on the website of London's White Cube gallery: http://whitecube.com/artists/doris_salcedo.

67. Salcedo, "An Act of Memory."

68. Ibid.

69. Ibid.

70. Ibid.

71. Ibid. As Salcedo put it in her initial proposal for the Palace of Justice installation: "One could say that art is impotent when confronting absolute power. Yet it is precisely in this impotency and uselessness that poetry resides. It is through art that one regains the humanity that has been desecrated. . . . In this context, art becomes the continuation of life."

2. On Shaky Ground

1. Morales, "Reasentamiento de población ubicada en zonas de alto riesgo no mitigable por remoción en masa en Bogotá."

2. Ciudad Bolívar represents 27 percent of the land area of the city. It is home to six hundred thousand people, 53 percent of whom are in Estrato 1 and 40 percent of whom are in Estrato 2. Ciudad Bolívar is also the locality with the highest number of people with "unsatisfied basic needs" (*necesidades básicas insatisfechas*). See Camara de Comercio de Bogotá, *Perfil económico y empresarial*; Poveda Gómez, "Reasentamiento de hogares por alto riesgo no mitigable."

3. Caja de la Vivienda Popular, *Informe de gestión 2004–2006*.

4. Discussions of the dynamics mentioned here can be found in Mejía Pavony, *Los años del cambio*; Palacios, *Between Legitimacy and Violence*.

5. Davis, *Planet of Slums*, 121.

6. Davis claims: "A hazardous, health-threatening location is the geographical definition of the typical squatters settlement." Ibid., 121–22.

7. Smith, *Uneven Development*.

8. Hodson and Marvin, "'Urban Ecological Security.'"

9. Lakoff and Klinenberg, "Of Risk and Pork." The literature on risk governance is too extensive to cover comprehensively here, but I analyze it in greater depth in Zeiderman, "On Shaky Ground," 1574–76. For key works, see Castel, "From Dangerousness to Risk"; Ewald, "Insurance and Risk"; Defert, "'Popular Life' and Insurance Technology"; Rose, "Governing 'Advanced' Liberal Democracies"; Osborne, "Security and Vitality"; O'Malley, "Risk and Responsibility." Another rich source of analysis is the journal *Economy and Society*, especially vol. 29, no. 4, on "configurations of risk." See also Baker and Simon, *Embracing Risk*; Ericson and Doyle, *Risk and Morality*.

10. Ramírez Gomez and Cardona, "El sistema nacional para la prevención y atención de desastres en Colombia," 256.

11. Ibid., 264.

12. Ibid., 265.

13. DNPAD, *Plan nacional para la prevención y atención de desastres*, 21.

14. Interview notes, August 19, 2009.

15. Ramírez Gomez and Cardona, "El sistema nacional para la prevención y atención de desastres en Colombia," 271.

16. Concejo de Bogotá, Acuerdo 11, 1987, http://www.alcaldiabogota.gov.co/sisjur /normas/Norma1.jsp?i=509.

17. However, this law was made official in 1990 during the administration of President Cesar Gaviria, at which time the National Office of Emergency Response was transferred to the Ministry of Government and given the name National Directorate for Disaster Prevention and Response (DNPAD). See Congreso de Colombia, Ley 46, 1988, http://www.sigpad.gov.co/sigpad/archivos/documentos/DPAD/Ley_46_de_1988.doc.

18. Congreso de Colombia, "Ponencia para primer debate al proyecto de ley número 124 Senado de 1987, 279 Cámara de 1987," 1988.

19. Congreso de Colombia, Ley 46, 1988, http://www.sigpad.gov.co/sigpad /archivos/documentos/DPAD/Ley_46_de_1988.doc.

20. Scientific authority for studying and mapping risks of geological and volcanic nature was assigned to what was then called the National Institute of Geological Study and Mining; risks of hydrologic and meteorological nature were charged to the Institute of Hydrology, Meteorology, and Land Adequacy; and the authority for the cartography and aerial photography corresponding to risk was assigned to the Agustín Codazzi Geographical Institute. See Presidente de la República de Colombia, Decreto 919, May 1, 1989, https://www.cancilleria.gov.co/sites/default/files /Normograma/docs/decreto_0919_1989.htm.

21. Ramírez Gomez and Cardona, "El sistema nacional para la prevención y atención de desastres en Colombia," 271–72.

22. Presidente de la República de Colombia, Decreto 919, Article 72, May 1, 1989, https://www.cancilleria.gov.co/sites/default/files/Normograma/docs/decreto_0919 _1989.htm.

23. Congreso de Colombia, Ley 9, 1989, http://webidu.idu.gov.co:9090/pmb /opac_css/index.php?lvl=categ_see&id=8608; Pecha Quimbay, *Historia institucional de la Caja de la Vivienda Popular*, 86.

24. Presidente de la República de Colombia, Decreto 1547, June 21, 1984, http:// www.icbf.gov.co/cargues/avance/docs/decreto_1547_1984.htm.

25. Presidente de la República de Colombia, Decreto 919, May 1, 1989, https://www .cancilleria.gov.co/sites/default/files/Normograma/docs/decreto_0919_1989.htm.

26. Congreso de Colombia, Ley 46, 1988, http://www.sigpad.gov.co/sigpad /archivos/documentos/DPAD/Ley_46_de_1988.doc.

27. Alcalde Mayor del Distrito Especial de Bogotá, Decreto 306, March 25, 1975, http://www.alcaldiabogota.gov.co/sisjur/normas/Norma1.jsp?i=3462.

28. Alcalde Mayor del Distrito Especial de Bogotá, Decreto 1388, December 30, 1976, http://www.alcaldiabogota.gov.co/sisjur/normas/Norma1.jsp?i=12868.

29. Congreso de Colombia, Ley 9, 1979, http://www.secretariasenado.gov.co /senado/basedoc/ley_0009_1979.html.

30. Ibid., Article 498. See also Presidente de la República de Colombia, Decreto 919, Article 72, May 1, 1989, https://www.cancilleria.gov.co/sites/default/files /Normograma/docs/decreto_0919_1989.htm.

31. UN General Assembly, "Resolution 42/236: International Decade for Natural Disaster Reduction," December 22, 1989, http://www.un.org/documents/ga/res/44 /a44r236.htm.

32. GFDRR, *Disaster Risk Management Programs for Priority Countries*, 224, 29.

33. Concejo de Bogotá, Acuerdo 11, 1987, http://www.alcaldiabogota.gov.co/sisjur/normas/Norma1.jsp?i=509.

34. Congreso de Colombia, Ley 9, 1989, http://webidu.idu.gov.co:9090/pmb/opac_css/index.php?lvl=categ_see&id=8608. See also Pecha Quimbay, *Historia institucional de la Caja de la Vivienda Popular*, 86.

35. Alcalde Mayor de Santa Fe de Bogotá DC, Decreto 657, October 25, 1994, http://www.alcaldiabogota.gov.co/sisjur/normas/Norma1.jsp?i=1654.

36. Ingeocim, *Zonificación de riesgo por inestabilidad del terreno*.

37. Martin and Ceballos, *Bogotá*, 222.

38. Rivas Gamboa, *Gorgeous Monster*, 157, 180–81.

39. Ibid., 180–81.

40. High threat was characterized by "hillsides exhibiting processes of active or inactive instability and/or intensive erosion," where the probability of landslide was above 44 percent in a ten-year period. Medium threat referred to "hillsides without evidence of current instability, with erosion processes of medium or high intensity," with a probability of landslide between 12 and 44 percent over the same period of time. And low threat corresponded to "low sloping hillsides, high sloping hillsides on rock, rectilinear hillsides, or flat zones in consolidated urban areas," with a probability of under 12 percent of landslide.

41. According to interviews conducted with government officials knowledgeable about risk management, however, "vulnerability" in these studies was predominantly based on physical and not social factors. See DPAE, *Concepto técnico N° 3280*; Ingeocim, *Zonificación de riesgo por inestabilidad del terreno*.

42. DPAE, *Concepto técnico N° 3280*.

43. These maps were at the scale of 1:10,000. In 1997, maps were issued for seismic and technological risk and in 2002 for forest fires in the Cerros Orientales.

44. See DPAE, *Instrumentos para la gestión del riesgo en Bogotá*.

45. For an exemplary analysis of risk data, see Ericson and Doyle, *Uncertain Business*.

46. Pecha Quimbay, *Historia institucional de la Caja de la Vivienda Popular*, 100.

47. Ibid., 101.

48. DPAE, *Anexo 4*.

49. DPAE, *Instrumentos para la gestión del riesgo en Bogotá*.

50. DPAE, *Plan de acción para la mitigación de riesgos y rehabilitación*.

51. Ibid.

52. Eligibility and entitlement are fraught issues, since the right to resettle is circumscribed and delimited on a number of levels. As I emphasize in chapters 3 and 4, accessing resettlement benefits is much more complicated than simply living within the boundaries of a zone of high risk.

53. This resembles what Asher Ghertner calls an "aesthetic mode of governing," whereby "if a development project looks 'world-class,' then it is most often declared planned; if a settlement looks polluting, it is sanctioned as unplanned and illegal."

See D. Asher Ghertner, "Rule by Aesthetics: World-Class City Making in Delhi," 280.

54. According to Mike Hodson and Simon Marvin, the rise of "urban ecological security" represents "a paradigm challenge to our conventional understanding of contemporary urbanism." See Hodson and Marvin, *World Cities and Climate Change*, 131.

3. Genealogies of Endangerment

1. Discussions of sensibilización among Caja officials resonate with Jacques Rancière's emphasis on the "sensible" as the domain in which politics and aesthetics combine to produce boundaries that govern the social world. See Rancière, *The Politics of Aesthetics*.

2. The official category of "beneficiary" (*beneficiario*) used by the resettlement program connotes one who holds an insurance policy, inherits a will, or receives the benefits of welfare policies.

3. Rose, *Powers of Freedom*, 74.

4. For an argument against the use of the term "slum" by one of the leading experts on urban planning and governance in Bogotá, see Gilbert, "The Return of the Slum."

5. Foucault, *The Birth of Biopolitics*, 2.

6. Rose, "The Death of the Social?"

7. Ahumada, *El modelo neoliberal y su impacto en la sociedad colombiana*; Hylton, *Evil Hour in Colombia*.

8. Pecha Quimbay, *Historia institucional de la Caja de la Vivienda Popular*, 17–19.

9. Noguera, *Medicina y política*, 69.

10. Pecha Quimbay, *Historia institucional de la Caja de la Vivienda Popular*, 33–35.

11. Lakoff, "Preparing for the Next Emergency," 271.

12. Secretaría Distrital de Hábitat, *Marco de política y metodología de reasentamientos de población localizada*.

13. Alcaldía Mayor de Bogotá, *Plan de desarrollo económico, social, ambiental y de obras públicas*, 19–22; Moreno Rojas, "Seguridad integral en la Bogotá Positiva."

14. Alcaldía Mayor de Bogotá, *Plan de desarrollo económico, social, ambiental y de obras públicas*, 19–22.

15. Locke, *Two Treatises of Government and A Letter concerning Toleration*, 111.

16. Ibid.

17. Congreso de Colombia, Ley 9, 1989, http://webidu.idu.gov.co:9090/pmb/opac_css/index.php?lvl=categ_see&id=8608.

18. Foucault, *"Society Must Be Defended,"* 241.

19. Macpherson, *The Political Theory of Possessive Individualism*, 221.

20. Ibid., 226–27.

21. Herzog, *Defining Nations*, 1–2.

22. Ibid., 8.

23. Anderson, *Imagined Communities*, 48.

24. Chambers, *From Subjects to Citizens*, 3; Walker, *Smoldering Ashes*, 3; Arrom, "Popular Politics in Mexico City."

25. Sabato, "On Political Citizenship in Nineteenth-Century Latin America," 1292.

26. Ibid., 1306.

27. Rojas, "Securing the State and Developing Social Insecurities," 232.

28. LeGrand, "Labor Acquisition and Social Conflict on the Colombian Frontier, 1850–1936"; Rausch, *The Llanos Frontier in Colombian History, 1830–1930*.

29. Cuéllar Sarmiento, "Entre la hacienda y la sociedad civil"; Tognato and Cuéllar Sarmiento, "Military 'Shipwrecks.'"

30. LeGrand, "Labor Acquisition and Social Conflict on the Colombian Frontier, 1850–1936," 36 n. 24. Some tenants paid rent for a small plot of land on which they could raise their own crops in exchange for providing labor in the landlord's fields; others were sharecroppers who were allowed to work the land in return for a share of the crop produced on it; and still others were allowed to clear and improve a parcel of land on the periphery of the hacienda for their own use provided they returned it to the landlord within a period of two or three years.

31. For the relationship between patronage and urbanization in Latin America, see Paley, *Marketing Democracy*; Castells, *The City and the Grassroots*. For "pirate" urbanization in Bogotá, see Mohan, *Understanding the Developing Metropolis*; Doebele, "The Private Market and Low Income Urbanization"; Blanco, "Discourses of Land Allocation and Natural Property Rights."

32. Rausch, "Church-State Relations on the Colombian Frontier," 59–60.

33. Abel, *Política, iglesia y partidos en Colombia, 1886–1953*.

34. Ibid.

35. Uribe, "Dismembering and Expelling"; Vega, "Desplazamiento forzado."

36. *El Tiempo*, April 4, 2009.

37. Foucault, *Security, Territory, Population*, 10–11.

38. For a related argument that develops the concept of "disjunctive democracy" as a way to understand similar phenomena in Brazil, see Caldeira and Holston, "Democracy and Violence in Brazil."

4. Living Dangerously

1. "Una familia, sepultada por el lodo en Bogotá," *El Tiempo*, May 7, 2006.

2. *Vivienda digna* (or decent housing) is a right guaranteed by Article 51 of the 1991 Constitution.

3. Chatterjee, *The Politics of the Governed*, 38. Holston cautions that discriminations and inequalities often arise not because some groups are excluded from the category of "citizen" but because it is a differentiated category to begin with

(e.g., formal vs. substantive citizenship). See Holston, "Spaces of Insurgent Citizenship," 168.

4. Chatterjee, *The Politics of the Governed*, 38.

5. Ibid.

6. Ibid., 74.

7. For an argument against the concept of "political society" on the grounds that it adopts a folk category as an analytic category, see Holston, foreword to *Urbanizing Citizenship*.

8. Although the Constitution grants everyone the right to decent housing, according to the Supreme Court this right is not justiciable; it is unreasonable to expect the state to guarantee housing to all 40 million Colombians.

9. This argument has been made persuasively by Goldstein, "Toward a Critical Anthropology of Security."

10. Key arguments along these lines can be found in the work of Ramírez, "Maintaining Democracy in Colombia through Political Exclusion, States of Exception, Counterinsurgency, and Dirty War"; Rojas, "Securing the State and Developing Social Insecurities"; Tate, *Counting the Dead.*

11. Goldstein maintains that neoliberalism is an essential frame for understanding the politics and ethics of security in Latin America. See Goldstein, "Toward a Critical Anthropology of Security," 489; see also Jean Comaroff and John L. Comaroff, *Law and Disorder in the Postcolony.*

12. A number of scholars have scrutinized the rhetoric of "post-neoliberalism" in Latin America while drawing attention to the challenges posed to neoliberalism in countries like Bolivia, Ecuador, and Venezuela. See Leiva, *Latin American Neostructuralism*; Postero, "The Struggle to Create a Radical Democracy in Bolivia."

13. Coronil, "The Future in Question," 234.

14. Holston and Appadurai, "Cities and Citizenship," 2.

15. See for example Harvey, *Paris, Capital of Modernity*; Lefebvre, *The Urban Revolution.*

16. Rojas argues that the ultimate goal was the creation of a *civilización mestiza,* or "mixed-race civilization." See Rojas, *Civilization and Violence.* For an in-depth engagement with the inclusionary and exclusionary dynamics of citizenship in nineteenth-century Colombia, see McGraw, *The Work of Recognition.*

17. Sarmiento, *Life in the Argentine Republic in the Days of the Tyrants.*

18. Castells, *The City and the Grassroots*; Holston, *Insurgent Citizenship.* For the period (1930s) in which legal recognition and rights were extended to workers and peasants in Colombia, see Roldan, *Blood and Fire*, 16–17.

19. I draw a distinction between liberalism and development despite their overlap in Europe and the Americas. "Social rights" established in twentieth-century Europe entitled citizens to developmental goods, such as housing, health care, and education. Moreover, there were civilizational imperatives attached to liberal citizenship in Europe. See Marshall, *Class, Citizenship, and Social Development.*

20. For the Colombian case, see Rojas, "Securing the State and Developing Social Insecurities"; Ramírez, "Maintaining Democracy in Colombia through Political Exclusion, States of Exception, Counterinsurgency, and Dirty War." For a comparative perspective from Bolivia, see Goldstein, "Human Rights as Culprit, Human Rights as Victim."

21. CODHES, *Gota a gota*, 42. Precise figures on internal displacement in Colombia are difficult to attain. CODHES (ibid.) estimates that between 1985 and 2006 about 666,590 displaced persons arrived in the Bogotá metropolitan area. This estimate, they clarify, is conservative, and the actual number is probably closer to 1 million.

22. *El Tiempo*, May 20, 2009.

23. CODHES, *Gota a gota*, 51.

24. Naranjo Giraldo, "El desplazamiento forzado en Colombia."

25. Until 2011, the Presidential Agency for Social Action and International Cooperation, Subdirectorate for Attention to the Displaced Population, determined the process one must follow to become legally recognized by the Colombian government as a desplazado. The Law of Victims and Land Restitution passed in that year transformed the way the Colombian state governs the problem of displacement. The public agency given responsibility for the internally displaced population was the Administrative Department for Social Prosperity, Attention to Victims Unit.

26. Povinelli, "The State of Shame"; Charles Taylor, *Multiculturalism*.

27. Hale, "Cultural Politics of Identity in Latin America"; Postero, *Now We Are Citizens*.

28. Restrepo, "Ethnicization of Blackness in Colombia"; Jackson, "Rights to Indigenous Culture in Colombia"; Paschel, "The Right to Difference."

29. Fassin and Pandolfi, *Contemporary States of Emergency*; Feldman and Ticktin, *In the Name of Humanity*.

30. Malkki, "Speechless Emissaries," 377.

31. Fassin and Rechtman, *The Empire of Trauma*.

32. Petryna, *Life Exposed*.

33. Rose, *The Politics of Life Itself*, 24–25. See also Rose and Novak, "Biological Citizenship." This resonates with what Fassin calls "biolegitimacy," which, he argues, "has become a generalized mode of governing." See Fassin, "Another Politics of Life Is Possible," 50–51.

34. This analysis is supported by the parallel distinction Lakoff makes between two regimes of global health: humanitarian biomedicine and global health security. See Lakoff, "Two Regimes of Global Health."

35. For the case of refugees seeking asylum, see Good, "'Undoubtedly an Expert'?"

36. This account and the one that follows in the next section are based on both ethnographic research and media analysis. My intent is to show how certain framings are produced in public and political discourse, and then to examine how these framings inform governmental strategies and interventions. Secondary

sources consulted were the Bogotá daily newspapers *El Tiempo* and *El Espectador*, the weekly news magazine *Semana*, and the news broadcasters *Caracol* and *Noticias rcn* from July 2008 to September 2009. Due to difficulty accessing the participants of the demonstrations and the authorities involved, many direct quotations are taken from these sources.

37. "Se desbordó megajornada para miles de desplazados," *El Tiempo*, July 31, 2008.

38. Alejandra Rodríguez, "Desplazados duermen en el Parque de la 93 hasta que les ayuden," *El Espectador*, July 31, 2008.

39. "Desplazados desistieron de bloquear Parque de la 93 tras promesa de Samuel Moreno," *El Tiempo*, July 31, 2008.

40. "Desplazados bloquearon la Carrera 11 con Calle 93 en el norte de Bogotá," *El Tiempo*, July 31, 2008.

41. "Desplazados desistieron de bloquear Parque de la 93 tras promesa de Samuel Moreno," *El Tiempo*, July 31, 2008.

42. "Edil Antonio Navia no agitó el bloqueo de desplazados," *El Tiempo*, September 3, 2008.

43. Hansen and Verkaaik, "Urban Charisma," 9.

44. This analysis would not have been possible without the ethnographic intuition and intellectual engagement of Paula Durán. This argument also draws inspiration from Thomas Osborne's injunction to analyze biopolitics as a relation between the *vital* and the *political* spheres. See Osborne, "Security and Vitality."

45. "Drama de desplazados en Parque de la 93," *El Tiempo*, August 1, 2008.

46. Alejandra Rodríguez, "Desplazados duermen en el Parque de la 93 hasta que les ayuden," *El Espectador*, July 31, 2008.

47. "'Aviones' ofrecen ayudar a desplazados," *Semana*, November 9, 2008.

48. Ibid.

49. "Siete personas fueron detenidas en toma de desplazados al parque de la 93, en el norte de Bogotá," *El Tiempo*, September 8, 2008.

50. "Los desplazados del parque, toma II," *El Espectador*, September 8, 2008.

51. Felipe Caro, "Su propio viacrucis viven 850 desplazados en la Plaza de Bolívar y el Parque Tercer Milenio," *El Tiempo*, April 10, 2009.

52. "Así vivió un grupo de desplazados el primer día en los 'alojamientos' luego de dejar Tercer Milenio," *El Tiempo*, May 27, 2009.

53. Ibid.

54. Ibid.

55. "Desplazados que siguen en el parque del Tercer Milenio denuncian que los amenazan para seguir allí," *El Tiempo*, July 9, 2009.

56. "Gobierno pide a los desplazados del Parque Tercer Milenio no usar los niños para protestar," *El Tiempo*, July 14, 2009.

57. "Bogotá lidera contagios por nueva gripa," *El Tiempo*, July 16, 2009.

58. Ibid.

59. "Secretaría de Salud de Bogotá pide al ICBF proteger a niños desplazados del parque Tercer Milenio," *El Tiempo*, July 13, 2009.

60. "En cuarentena parque Tercer Milenio," *Noticias RCN*, July 15, 2009.

61. "Secretaría de Salud inicia intervención del Parque Tercer Milenio," *Caracol Radio*, July 23, 2009.

62. David Acosta, "Cordón sanitario en parque Tercer Milenio hace sentir prisioneros a los desplazados que viven allí," *El Tiempo*, July 19, 2009.

63. "Declaran alerta sanitaria en Parque Tercer Milenio y anuncian retiro de los menores de edad," *El Tiempo*, July 22, 2009, and "Parque Tercer Milenio, en emergencia," *El Tiempo*, July 24, 2009.

64. "Cerca de 130 casos sospechosos de influenza tipo A en el parque del Tercer Milenio," *Caracol Radio*, July 23, 2009.

65. "Emergencia sanitaria en el Tercer Milenio," *El Tiempo*, July 24, 2009.

66. "Declaran alerta sanitaria en Parque Tercer Milenio y anuncian retiro de los menores de edad," *El Tiempo*, July 22, 2009.

67. Ibid.

68. "Evacuarán del parque Tercer Milenio a desplazados con gripa," *Caracol Radio*, July 23, 2009.

69. "Bomba de tiempo," *Semana*, July 25, 2009.

70. "Emergencia sanitaria en el Parque Tercer Milenio decretó la Alcaldía de Bogotá," *El Tiempo*, July 22, 2009, and Carlos Guevara and John Marcos Torres, "Cinco días tendrán los desplazados para desalojar el parque Tercer Milenio, ordena el Distrito," *El Tiempo*, July 22, 2009.

71. "Emergencia sanitaria en el Parque Tercer Milenio decretó la Alcaldía de Bogotá," *El Tiempo*, July 23, 2009.

72. "Parque Tercer Milenio necesita medidas urgentes," *Semana*, July 23, 2009.

73. "Fin al drama del Tercer Milenio: Los desplazados saldrán este domingo," *El Tiempo*, July 31, 2009.

74. "Desplazados abandonaron Tercer Milenio pero prometieron regresar si Gobierno no les cumple," *El Tiempo*, August 3, 2009.

75. The original phrase was *un proceso de vías de hecho,* which, in the Colombian legal system, refers to a judicial decision that contradicts the constitution or the law. "Abuse of discretion," or a judge's ruling that fails to consider established precedent or evidence, may be the closest translation available in English. In Colombia, however, the limit on discretion applies to all public servants and obligates them not to interpret legal statues in a way that challenges the rule of law. Secretary López was responding to criticisms that, by neglecting the responsibility to deal with the demonstration as an illegal occupation of public space, the government had normalized illegality. Instead, she invoked the public health emergency to justify a suspension of the rule of law. I am grateful here for the help of Meghan Morris.

76. "Alcaldes pagan tiquete a desplazados para que viajen a Bogotá, denuncia Secretaria de Gobierno," *El Tiempo*, July 30, 2009.

77. "Distrito pide responsabilidad de alcaldes: No permitirán más tomas de desplazados," *El Tiempo*, August 1, 2009.

78. This differs from much of what we have come to know from other studies of contemporary biopolitics.

79. Foucault, *The History of Sexuality*, 145. Broadly understood as a political rationality that takes the life of the population as its object, "biopolitics" has become widely studied and theorized throughout the social sciences and humanities. This recent engagement with the politics of life has been based, again, primarily on selected works of Foucault and their elaboration by political theorists such as Agamben, *Homo Sacer*; Hardt and Negri, *Multitude*; Esposito, *Bíos*. Not coincidentally, when Foucault discusses the concepts of "biopower" and "biopolitics" in 1976, it is in the context of twentieth-century fascism and state racism. In the politicization of biological life, he argues, we find clear expression of the singular form of power defining the modern era. The key texts for this strain of critical thought are "Part Five: Right of Death and Power over Life" from Foucault's *The History of Sexuality* and the final March 17 lecture from *"Society Must Be Defended."*

80. For a discussion of "make live" interventions for populations whose labor is "surplus" to the requirements of capital accumulation, see Li, "To Make Live or Let Die?"

81. A number of authors have pointed to the increasing centrality of "life" to governmental intervention, capital accumulation, and social mobilization around the world. See for example Rose, *The Politics of Life Itself*; Melinda Cooper, *Life as Surplus*; Escobar, *Territories of Difference*. Meanwhile, others have pointed to the frequency with which political struggle, from Cairo to New York, is now waged in and through the territory of the city. See Don Mitchell, *The Right to the City*; Harvey, *Rebel Cities*; Merrifield, *The New Urban Question*. Yet the connection between these emergent global phenomena has not been fully explored. Studies have shown how the politics of life reconfigures political institutions through domains as diverse as ecology, technology, and medicine, yet we understand little about how they function in urban contexts and how they affect the way cities are planned, built, governed, and inhabited.

82. Collier and Lakoff draw a distinction between biopolitical security, which seeks to protect the life of the population from regularly occurring events, and sovereign state security, which aims to defend the national territory against internal and external enemies. See Collier and Lakoff, "Distributed Preparedness." Occasionally Foucault seems to suggest their necessary interrelation: that the "formidable power of death" on which sovereignty is based is the "counterpart of a power that exerts a positive influence on life," or biopower. See Foucault, *The History of Sexuality*, 137. Following Agamben, many have understood this to mean that the sovereign power to take life is the "hidden foundation" lurking within all biopolitical formations. "Make live" and "make die," however, are not the transhistorical mutual constituents of power. As Paul Rabinow and Nikolas Rose insist, the power to command under threat of death is by no means "the guarantee or underpinning

principle of all forms of biopower in contemporary liberal societies." See Rabinow and Rose, "Biopower Today," 201.

83. Rojas, "Securing the State and Developing Social Insecurities," 241.

84. Agamben generalizes Foucault's early formulation by arguing that sovereign power is simply biopolitics *writ large*, and the proliferating studies relying on his work have reproduced this totalizing view by identifying the manifestation of "bare life" and the "state of exception" in innumerable variations. As Jean Comaroff points out, this reading of biopolitics has proven especially provocative and compelling in the aftermath of 9/11, when "crisis and exception have become routine." She cautions that the mode of argumentation at work tends to border on metaphysics and thus often reduces modern politics to a limited set of archetypes and metaphors that grossly oversimplify historical circumstances. See Jean Comaroff, "Beyond Bare Life," 207.

85. Donna V. Jones, *The Racial Discourses of Life Philosophy*.

86. Hardt and Negri, *Multitude*, 146.

87. Deleuze, *Foucault*, 77. Deleuze extends Foucault's comments as follows: "When power becomes bio-power, resistance becomes the power of life, a vital power that cannot be confined within species, environment or the paths of a particular diagram. Is not the force that comes from outside a certain idea of Life, a certain vitalism, in which Foucault's thought culminates? Is not life this capacity to resist force?"

88. Dussel, *Twenty Theses on Politics*, 83–87. See also Escobar, *Territories of Difference*.

89. For a summary of the modernity/coloniality/decoloniality paradigm of Latin American critical theory, see Escobar, "Worlds and Knowledges Otherwise."

5. Securing the Future

1. Corbridge et al., *Seeing the State*.

2. In a recent example, Vincanne Adams, Michelle Murphy, and Adele Clarke argue that one of the "defining qualities of our current moment is its peculiar management of time, or what might be called a politics of temporality." The peculiarity of the episteme in which we now live, they claim, is that *regimes of anticipation* increasingly define how we "think about, feel and address our contemporary problems." In their view, "anticipation is intensifying into a hegemonic formation" that is motivating speculative logics of capital accumulation, spreading through our institutions of government, and becoming an affective state that orients behavior on an individual and on a collective level. See Adams, Murphy, and Clarke, "Anticipation," 246. The sweeping phenomenon these scholars describe resonates throughout other works of social theory, where there is a heightened awareness of the future, of the proliferation of ways of acting on and reacting to it, and of the political conditions produced by a persistent view toward what has yet to come. See for example Massumi, "National Enterprise Emergency" and "Perception Attack"; Melinda Cooper,

"Pre-empting Emergence" and "Turbulent Worlds"; Randy Martin, *An Empire of Indifference*.

3. Rosenberg and Harding, "Introduction: Histories of the Future," 14. Critical urbanists are similarly predisposed to predictable diagnoses of temporal politics. For example, planning theorist Oren Yiftachel's concept of "urban apartheid" confines what he calls the "gray spaces" of urban informality to a state of "permanent temporariness." See Yiftachel, "Theoretical Notes on 'Gray Cities,'" 90. The localities, populations, and activities contained within these spaces are "concurrently tolerated and condemned, perpetually waiting 'to be corrected.'" In their ethnography of environmental suffering in urban Argentina, sociologist Javier Auyero and anthropologist Déborah Swistun also reveal how residents of a toxically contaminated shantytown are "condemned to live in a time oriented *to and by* others." See Auyero and Swistun, *Flammable*, 129. As residents anticipate better information, conclusive medical tests, alternative housing, and favorable legal settlements—none of which ever materialize—they wait. Waiting, Auyero and Swistun conclude, is a common way in which people experience submission to domination, and this relationship between power and temporality holds for "all powerless groups living in territories of urban relegation." See Auyero, "Patients of the State." Likewise, the geographer Katharyne Mitchell argues that temporal logics of security preordain certain bodies and populations in the city to inevitable futures of failure, dispossession, and death. Katharyne Mitchell, "Pre-Black Futures."

4. Koselleck, *Futures Past*, 2; cf. Koselleck, *The Practice of Conceptual History*.

5. Among the urban poor in northern Jakarta, AbdouMaliq Simone finds people "reading the anticipated maneuvers of stronger actors and forces and assessing where there might be a useful opportunity to become an obstacle or facilitator for the aspirations of others" (*City Life from Jakarta to Dakar*, 96). These anticipatory practices hinge on the recognition that dominant logics of capital accumulation and political rule are always fractured and inconclusive—they are "full of potential holes capable of providing, albeit always temporarily, shelter and maneuverability" (98). But in Simone's view, the politics of anticipation is "not just a form of resistance or simply a politics from below." It cuts both ways, as he puts it, since it is also by "continuously positioning themselves for alternative futures" that members of the urban poor are conditioned to believe that political change or economic development will eventually materialize, and this limits their options and reduces their leverage. Anticipatory politics constitutes a future-oriented "game of transactions" that brings differently positioned urban actors into contact and results in benefits and constraints for them all (101). It is both a resource and a danger—a "two-edged sword," as Simone puts it—and yet only under such compromised conditions do "the marginal and disenfranchised have some kind of opportunity to remake the city" (112–13). Since the city is "not hinged, not anchored" to any single trajectory, Simone urges us to remember that "by definition [it] goes toward many different futures at once" (115). See also Weszkalnys, "Anticipating Oil."

6. Abram and Weszkalnys, "Introduction: Anthropologies of Planning."

7. Friedmann, *Planning in the Public Domain*, 38.

8. Connell, "Planning and Its Orientation to the Future," 87.

9. Following Luhmann, Connell sees planning and risk as "modern" concepts that emerge at the same historical moment and reinforce one another: "Planning is making decisions on future decisions; risk is the consequence of such decisions." Connell also cites risk as ascendant in "post-modern society" where collective, determinate futures are on the decline. See ibid., 92.

10. Simone, *City Life from Jakarta to Dakar*.

11. This rarely transpires, however, since the use of force would be politically dangerous for mayoral administrations that claim to be in solidarity with the urban poor.

12. In English, the subjunctive is less common (words like "might," "should," and "could" are used instead). It is often indistinguishable from the ordinary indicative mood, since its form in most contexts is identical.

13. Verbs frequently conjoined with the subjunctive are *esperar*, which means "to wait," "to expect," or "to hope," and *querer*, "to want."

14. Foucault, *The Birth of Biopolitics*, 65–66.

15. Davis, *Planet of Slums*.

16. Bayat, *Life as Politics*.

17. Williams, *The Country and the City*.

18. Benjamin, "Theses on the Philosophy of History," 257–58.

19. Stoler, "Imperial Debris."

20. Boym, "Ruins of the Avant-Garde," 58.

21. Stoler, "Imperial Debris," 202; Hell and Schönle, *Ruins of Modernity*.

22. Scott, *Seeing like a State*; Ferguson, *Expectations of Modernity*.

23. Boym, "Ruins of the Avant-Garde," 59. See also Presner, "Hegel's Philosophy of World History via Sebald's Imaginary of Ruins."

24. Lomnitz, "Editor's Letter," 225.

25. Ibid.

26. Harvey, "Neoliberalism as Creative Destruction"; Klein, *The Shock Doctrine*; Hardt and Negri, *Empire*.

27. Appadurai, "The Capacity to Aspire."

28. Blanco, "Discourses of Land Allocation and Natural Property Rights."

29. Castells, *The City and the Grassroots*; Holston, *Insurgent Citizenship*.

30. Here I build on the work of anthropologist Robert Samet, who has studied the cultural and political significance of denuncias in Venezuela, and in Latin American history more generally. Samet, "The Victim's Voice."

31. This section draws on both ethnographic research and media analysis. Secondary sources consulted were the Bogotá daily newspaper *El Tiempo*, the weekly news magazine *Semana*, and the news broadcaster *Noticias RCN* from December 2010 to February 2012.

32. "Gobierno anunció Estado de Emergencia por víctimas del invierno," *El Tiempo*, December 7, 2010.

33. "Invierno: Las inundaciones no dan tregua," *Semana*, September 6, 2011.

34. "Bajo el agua," *Semana*, December 10, 2011; César García, "Wild Weather Hits Latin America," *Associated Press*, January 6, 2012.

35. FOPAE, "Bogotá."

36. "En alerta máxima por el río Bogotá," *El Tiempo*, December 5, 2011.

37. Ibid.

38. "Autorizan inundaciones controladas en baldíos del norte y sur de Bogotá," *Semana*, December 7, 2011; "Bogotá ahorró ayer 120.000 metros cúbicos de agua," *El Tiempo*, December 8, 2011.

39. "Bogotá busca bomba de extracción petrolera para disminuir grandes inundaciones," *Semana*, December 9, 2011.

40. "Autorizan inundaciones controladas en baldíos del norte y sur de Bogotá," *Semana*, December 7, 2011.

41. "Damnificados subieron a 45.196 en tres días," *El Tiempo*, December 9, 2011.

42. "Inundaciones: Gobierno entregará ayuda económica a damnificados en Bogotá," *Semana*, December 9, 2011.

43. Ibid.; "Ayuda para damnificados de Bosa será entregada la próxima semana," *El Tiempo*, December 10, 2011.

44. "En Bosa hay 5 mil damnificados a causa de las fuertes lluvias," *El Tiempo*, December 8, 2011; "Damnificados subieron a 45.196 en tres días," *El Tiempo*, December 9, 2011.

45. "Bogotá: Así se entregan las ayudas en Bosa y Kennedy," *Semana*, December 13, 2011.

46. "Víctimas de invierno en Bosa y Kennedy viven drama para recibir ayudas," *El Tiempo*, December 13, 2011.

47. "Damnificados subieron a 45.196 en tres días," *El Tiempo*, December 9, 2011.

48. "Después del diluvio," *Semana*, January 7, 2012.

49. "Cerca de 2.000 damnificados deja inundación en Bosa," *El Tiempo*, December 7, 2011; "Emergencia en Bogotá," *Semana*, December 7, 2011.

50. "Después del diluvio," *Semana*, January 7, 2012.

51. Yolanda Reyes, "No es la 'maldita niña,'" *El Tiempo*, December 12, 2011.

52. "La alcaldesa respondió a las denuncias por la entrega de ayudas," *El Tiempo*, December 14, 2011.

53. Ernesto Cortés, "Alcalde, ¿y del invierno . . . ?," *El Tiempo*, December 11, 2011.

54. "Al invierno, se suma drama para recibir ayudas," *El Tiempo*, December 13, 2011.

55. "Antonio Navarro Wolff asumió como secretario de Gobierno de Bogotá," *El Tiempo*, January 2, 2012; "Con modelo hidráulico buscan evitar nuevas inundaciones en Bogotá," *Semana*, January 17, 2012.

56. "Inundación en Bosa había sido denunciada desde hace tres meses," RCN *Noticias*, December 9, 2011.

Conclusion: Millennial Cities

1. Bogotá's achievements have been documented and discussed in Gilbert, "Good Urban Governance."

2. For the case of the "Bogotá model," see Berney, "Pedagogical Urbanism," 28. The broader phenomenon of "mobile urbanism" has become a central theme in urban studies. See Roy, "Urbanisms, Worlding Practices and the Theory of Planning"; Roy and Ong, *Worlding Cities*; McCann and Ward, *Mobile Urbanism*.

3. See the Tenth International Architecture Exhibition: Official Awards, Fondazione La Biennale di Venezia, 2006, http://www.labiennale.org/en/architecture/history/10.html?back=true.

4. GFDRR, "Disaster Risk Management Programs for Priority Countries," 224.

5. Ibid., 229.

6. "Bogotá's Rise and Fall: Can Enrique Peñalosa Restore a Tarnished Municipal Model?," *The Economist*, March 10, 2011. The article states: "The bright-red articulated buses of Bogotá's TransMilenio . . . were once the symbol of a city that had been transformed from chaos and corruption in the 1980s into a model of enlightened management admired and imitated across Latin America."

7. Berney, "Pedagogical Urbanism," 28.

8. For a discussion of the shifting frames of reference for the circulation of urban policy and planning models, see Roy, "Urbanisms, Worlding Practices and the Theory of Planning," 10.

9. The Washington, DC, Metro slogan is cited in Rosenberg and Harding, "Introduction: Histories of the Future." In 2015, Peñalosa was reelected as mayor of Bogotá and was proposing the development of elevated metro lines to supplement the existing BRT system.

10. For studies that do take up such questions, see Gilbert, "Good Urban Governance" and "Urban Governance in the South."

11. For arguments along these lines, see Roy, "Urban Informality," 156. See also Berney, "Pedagogical Urbanism."

12. This analytical position is discussed by Luhmann, *Observations on Modernity*. It is elaborated in Rabinow, *Marking Time*, 64–66.

13. For paradigmatic work on "global" and "world" cities, see Sassen, *Cities in a World Economy* and *The Global City*; Peter J. Taylor, *World City Network*; Castells, *The Rise of the Network Society*. The notion of "big but not powerful" adequately sums up the twin characteristics most often associated with the relatively new category of the "megacity": their massive demographic and spatial dimensions combined with their relative powerlessness (if not structural irrelevance) within the primary circuits of production and exchange of the global economy. See Massey, "Cities in the World," 115; cited in Robinson, "Global and World Cities," 540.

14. See Global Urban Observatory, cited in Koolhaas et al., *Mutations*, 6.

15. See, for example, a map published by *National Geographic* magazine in 2002 as part of a special feature on "megacities" (Zwingle, "Cities"). This map helps the

viewer visualize, thanks to clever graphic design, the magnitude of recent demographic projections. But this vision of the future is jarring, not only for its dramatic depiction of explosive population growth, but also in that it upends the most familiar of cartographic representations. It positions the viewer below the equator, below the Tropic of Capricorn even, and looking upward—that is, it offers Northern eyes a view from the South. The perspective it provides stands in direct opposition to the familiar Mercator projection, which famously exaggerated the size of temperate land areas relative to the tropics. Whereas with the Mercator projection, Europe grew to twice its true size relative to countries near the equator and the African continent shrunk tenfold to the size of Greenland, in *National Geographic*'s future-oriented image of the world, it is the cities of the global South that loom large. For an analysis of the epistemological influence of the Mercator projection, see Snyder, *Flattening the Earth*, 48.

16. Dasgupta, "The Sudden Stardom of the Third-World City."

17. Davis, *Planet of Slums*, 19.

18. Neuwirth, *Shadow Cities*.

19. Davis, *Planet of Slums*, 19.

20. For an analysis of these interrelated positions, see Gandy, "Learning from Lagos," 38–40.

21. Anjaria, "On Street Life and Urban Disasters."

22. Kaplan, "The Coming Anarchy," 46.

23. Ibid., my emphasis.

24. Montavalli et al., "Cities of the Future," 29.

25. Power, "The Magic Mountain," 57.

26. Packer, "The Megacity," 62–63.

27. Koolhaas et al., *Mutations*, 653, cited in Ferguson, "Formalities of Poverty," 75.

28. In a related example, in late February 2007, when a significant drop in the Shanghai stock market caused a global stock slide, commentators expressed shock at the spatiotemporal dimensions of the event, which reversed the presumed relationship between the New York Stock Exchange and Chinese financial markets. "It's not supposed to work this way," remarked a stunned financial analyst interviewed by the BBC.

29. Jean Comaroff and John L. Comaroff, *Theory from the South*.

30. As Timothy Mitchell puts it: "Accounts of the modern world that introduce a topsy-turvy view . . . typically reestablish the order of modernity by removing irregularities . . . and repositioning them within the West's uniform and singular history." See Timothy Mitchell, "The Stage of Modernity," 7.

31. Ferguson, *Global Shadows: Africa in the Neoliberal World Order*, 192.

32. Here, Nuttall and Mbembe are responding to a critique by geographer Michael Watts of an earlier article of theirs on Johannesburg. See Nuttall and Mbembe, "A Blasé Attitude," 194. See also Watts, "Baudelaire over Berea, Simmel over Sandton?"; Mbembe and Nuttall, "Writing the World from an African Metropolis."

33. Nuttall and Mbembe, "A Blasé Attitude," 194.

34. Timothy Mitchell, "The Stage of Modernity," 12.

35. The megacity is definitely not seen as a vision of the future by those for whom it is the present. As Ferguson argues, referring to the claim that we are in a "postdevelopment era," the "loss of credulity toward narratives of social and economic development has occurred not universally, but in specific ways and in specific places." See Ferguson, *Global Shadows*, 182–83.

36. This point has been made repeatedly by the likes of King, *Urbanism, Colonialism, and the World-Economy*; Harvey, *Spaces of Global Capitalism*.

37. In anthropology, Johannes Fabian powerfully revealed the implications of placing the "other" in a time not contemporary with that of the West. See Fabian, *Time and the Other*.

38. Grosfoguel, "Developmentalism, Modernity, and Dependency Theory in Latin America," 360.

39. To see Lagos as the terminal condition of the cities of the First World, for Matthew Gandy, "is to occlude the fact that every extremity of Lagos's deterioration over the past quarter century has been linked, in inverse proportion, to the capital accumulated in Chicago, London or Los Angeles." See Gandy, "Learning from Lagos," 42.

40. As Ferguson argues: "Once modernity ceases to be understood as a telos, the question of rank is de-developmentalized, and the stark differentiations of the global social system sit raw and naked, no longer softened by the promises of the 'not yet.'" See Ferguson, *Global Shadows*, 186.

41. Ibid., 183.

42. See the political theorist Wendy Brown's recent work, *Walled States, Waning Sovereignty*.

43. For globalist aspirations, see Tsing, *Friction*, 55–80. For provincial assumptions, see Chakrabarty, *Provincializing Europe*. As Nuttall and Mbembe point out, "Outsiders speak from places and within paradigms that carry their own baggage. One result may be a failure to see when one's own rules might not apply or when political, ideological, and hermeneutic certainty is not guaranteed." See Nuttall and Mbembe, "A Blasé Attitude," 193.

44. Mignolo's idea of the "locus of enunciation" is part of his larger critique of modernity/coloniality. Referring to philosopher Edmundo O'Gorman's thesis on the "universalism of Western culture," he argues: "Occidentalism . . . has two interrelated dimensions: First, it served to locate the geo-historical space of Western culture. But, less obviously, it also fixed the privileged locus of enunciation. It is from the West that the rest of the world is described, conceptualized, and ranked: that is, modernity is the self-description of Europe's role in history rather than an ontological historical process." See Mignolo, *The Idea of Latin America*, 35.

45. For "urban entrepreneurialism," see Harvey, "From Managerialism to Entrepreneurialism."

46. See Robinson, "Global and World Cities," 547.

47. See Rose, *Powers of Freedom*; Osborne and Rose, "Governing Cities"; Dean, *Governmentality*.

48. See Rose, "Governing 'Advanced' Liberal Democracies."

49. See for example O'Malley, "Risk and Responsibility" and *Risk, Uncertainty and Government*.

50. This history is noted in Mejía, "Involuntary Resettlement of Urban Population." In 2006, following years of aid and advice, the World Bank approved another loan of US$80 million to the city of Bogotá designated to disaster risk management. The bank's influence has not been limited to the city of Bogotá: in 2005, it was supporting forty-five similar resettlement programs in cities across Latin America. See Correa and Villegas, "El Banco Mundial y el Reasentamiento de Población en América Latina."

51. Escobar, *Encountering Development*.

52. United Nations General Assembly, "Resolution 42/236: International Decade for Natural Disaster Reduction."

53. For further discussion of key moments and positions in this debate, see Wamsler, "Mainstreaming Risk Reduction in Urban Planning and Housing"; Christoplos, Mitchell, and Liljelund, "Re-framing Risk."

54. There have also been related attempts by "disaster people" to connect the two schools of thought (disaster and development) by focusing on a common denominator, such as "vulnerability."

55. The UNDP report frames the linkage between disasters and development in the following way: "Natural disaster risk is intimately connected to processes of human development. Disasters put development at risk. At the same time, the development choices made by individuals, communities and nations can generate new disaster risk. But this need not be the case. Human development can also contribute to a serious reduction in disaster risk." UNDP, *Reducing Disaster Risk*, 2. See also DFID, *Disaster Risk Reduction*.

56. UNISDR, *Global Assessment Report on Disaster Risk Reduction*, 11.

57. World Bank, *Global Monitoring Report 2009*, xi.

58. See Wamsler, "Mainstreaming Risk Reduction in Urban Planning and Housing"; Bull-Kamanga et al., "From Everyday Hazards to Disasters." As development and disaster specialist Mark Pelling puts it: "Urbanisation looks set to be one of the most forceful drivers for and contexts of social change that will prefigure disaster risk in the medium to long term." See Pelling, "Disaster Risk and Development Planning," vii.

59. In this volume published by the World Bank, based on a conference held in 2002, the authors lay out the problem: "Vulnerability to disaster impacts is one of the most underestimated issues in urban development. By 2050, the world population is expected to grow by 3 billion people. Most of this growth will take place in developing countries—and within these countries, in cities and towns—more than doubling urban populations. Large numbers of people will be concentrated in megacities and on fragile lands, making reduction of vulnerability to disasters in metropolitan areas a critical challenge facing development." A primary journal for professionals and academics working at the intersection of development,

environmental management, and urban planning, *Environment and Urbanization*, has published a series of essays on risk and cities in the past decade, including a 2007 special issue on the topic: Huq et al., "Editorial: Reducing Risks to Cities from Disasters and Climate Change."

60. For a discussion of the "crisis" frame in which cities of the global South have conventionally been understood, see Roy, "Urban Informality," 147.

61. This relates to what Hodson and Marvin call the new paradigm of "urban ecological security." See Hodson and Marvin, "'Urban Ecological Security.'" Another key point of reference is Graham, *Cities under Siege*.

62. This would be to ignore the fact that places are situated within a set of relationships that extend far beyond their boundaries. See Massey, "Double Articulation."

63. "Place-in-the-world" is the term Ferguson uses to characterize Africa's standing within the wider categorical system he calls the "global order." See Ferguson, *Global Shadows*, 5–6.

64. See arguments along these lines in Lakoff, "Preparing for the Next Emergency"; Rose, *Powers of Freedom*.

65. As Roy argues: "This is not simply an issue of the inappropriateness of Euro-American ideas for Third World cities. Planning practices are constantly borrowed and replicated across borders. To attempt to stem this tide is rather useless and indeed under some circumstances can mark a turn to isolationism." See Roy, "Urban Informality," 147. While commensurability per se is not objectionable, we still must wonder what gives us confidence that the particular experience of a place like Bogotá offers a guide for other cities elsewhere.

66. Robinson and Simone both elaborate on the notion of "city-ness." See Robinson, *Ordinary Cities*; Simone, *City Life from Jakarta to Dakar*. Robinson argues that popular and scholarly thinking about cities of the global South "needs to decolonize its imagination about city-ness . . . if it is to sustain its relevance to the key urban challenges of the twenty-first century." Robinson, "Global and World Cities," 546.

67. Timothy Mitchell, "The Stage of Modernity," 7.

68. Simone, "People as Infrastructure," 408. Alternative urban imaginaries emerge from a number of different sources outside formal policy and planning circles, such as from the work of artists like the photographer Dionisio González, who accomplishes such a task by piecing together images of shantytowns and modern architecture to create representations of urban landscapes that challenge a number of the assumptions discussed above (see www.ft-contemporary.com).

69. Benjamin, *The Arcades Project*, N2,5.

Coda

1. In theory, the POT designates areas in which the city can expand, identifies zones to be protected, dictates the relationship between the city and the surrounding region, controls the use of land by different sectors, and establishes guidelines for public transportation, parks, utilities, schools, and hospitals.

2. Eduardo Behrentz, "Concejo debe hundir el POT," *El Tiempo*, May 28, 2013.

3. During his entire term, Petro was embroiled in legal and political battles with the far Right. He argued that the charges against him reflected the bankruptcy of Colombia's democracy and the fact that the Right wished to sabotage postconflict political reconciliation. In fact, some observers saw attempts by the conservative political establishment to ban him from politics as a way of derailing the peace negotiations with the FARC. He faced numerous attempts to oust him from office, and the efficacy of the programs he sought to implement were severely hindered as a result.

4. "Petro ordenó reubicar 12 mil familias que viven en zonas de riesgo," *El Tiempo*, June 17, 2013.

5. Key protagonists of this argument are Rancière, *Hatred of Democracy*; Žižek, "The Lesson of Rancière."

6. For commentary on the implications of this designation for the discipline of history, see Chakrabarty, "The Climate of History." For early arguments in favor of the "Anthropocene," see Crutzen and Stoermer, "The 'Anthropocene.'"

7. See Beck, "Climate for Change, or How to Create a Green Modernity?"; Badiou, "Live Badiou—Interview with Alain Badiou, Paris, December 2007"; Žižek, "Censorship Today."

8. "Disagreement is allowed, but only with respect to the choice of technologies, the mix of organizational fixes, the detail of the managerial adjustments, and the urgency of their timing and implementation, not with respect to the socio-political framing of present and future natures." See Swyngedouw, "The Non-political Politics of Climate Change," 6.

9. Swyngedouw, "Apocalypse Forever?," 228–29.

BIBLIOGRAPHY

Abel, Christopher. *Política, iglesia y partidos en Colombia, 1886–1953*. Bogotá: FAES, Universidad Nacional de Colombia, 1987.

Abram, Simone, and Gisa Weszkalnys. "Introduction: Anthropologies of Planning— Temporality, Imagination, and Ethnography." *Focaal—Journal of Global and Historical Anthropology* 61 (2011): 3–18.

Adams, Vincanne, Michelle Murphy, and Adele E. Clarke. "Anticipation: Technoscience, Life, Affect, Temporality." *Subjectivity* 28 (2009): 246–65.

Agamben, Giorgio. *Homo Sacer: Sovereign Power and Bare Life*. Stanford, CA: Stanford University Press, 1998.

Ahumada, Consuelo. *El modelo neoliberal y su impacto en la sociedad colombiana*. Bogotá: El Ancora Editores, 1996.

Alcaldía Mayor de Bogotá. *Plan de desarrollo económico, social, ambiental y de obras públicas, Bogotá, Colombia, 2008–2012*. Bogotá, 2008.

Althusser, Louis, and Étienne Balibar. *Reading Capital*. New York: Verso, 2009 [1968].

Anand, Nikhil, and Anne Rademacher. "Housing in the Urban Age: Inequality and Aspiration in Mumbai." *Antipode* 43, no. 5 (2011): 1748–72.

Anderson, Benedict. *Imagined Communities: Reflections on the Origin and Spread of Nationalism*. New York: Verso, 1991.

Anjaria, Jonathan Shapiro. "On Street Life and Urban Disasters: Lessons from a 'Third World' City." In *What Is a City? Rethinking the Urban after Hurricane Katrina*, edited by Phil Steinberg and Rob Shields, 186–202. Athens: University of Georgia Press, 2008.

Appadurai, Arjun. "The Capacity to Aspire: Culture and the Terms of Recognition." In *Culture and Public Action*, edited by Vijayendra Rao and Michael Walton, 59–84. Stanford, CA: Stanford University Press, 2004.

Arias, Enrique Desmond, and Daniel M. Goldstein, eds. *Violent Democracies in Latin America*. Durham, NC: Duke University Press, 2010.

Arrom, Silvia Marina. "Popular Politics in Mexico City: The Parián Riot, 1828." In *Riots in the Cities: Popular Politics and the Urban Poor in Latin America, 1765–1910*, edited by Silvia Marina Arrom and Servando Ortoll, 71–96. Wilmington, DE: Scholarly Resources, 1996.

Auyero, Javier. "The Hyper-Shantytown: Neo-liberal Violence(s) in the Argentine Slum." *Ethnography* 1, no. 1 (2000): 93–116.

———. "Patients of the State: An Ethnographic Account of Poor People's Waiting." *Latin American Research Review* 46, no. 1 (2011): 5–29.

Auyero, Javier, and Débora Alejandra Swistun. *Flammable: Environmental Suffering in an Argentine Shantytown*. New York: Oxford University Press, 2009.

Badiou, Alain. "The Event in Deleuze." *Parrhesia* 2 (2007): 37–44.

———. "Live Badiou—Interview with Alain Badiou, Paris, December 2007." In *Alain Badiou: Live Theory*, edited by Oliver Feltham, 136–40. London: Continuum, 2008.

Baker, Tom, and Jonathan Simon. *Embracing Risk: The Changing Culture of Insurance and Responsibility*. Chicago: University of Chicago Press, 2002.

Balibar, Étienne. "On the Basic Concepts of Historical Materialism." In *Reading Capital*, edited by Louis Althusser and Étienne Balibar, 223–345. New York: Verso, 2009 [1968].

Barry, Andrew. "Technological Zones." *European Journal of Social Theory* 9, no. 2 (2006): 239–53.

Barry, Andrew, Thomas Osborne, and Nikolas Rose, eds. *Foucault and Political Reason: Liberalism, Neo-liberalism, and Rationalities of Government*. London: UCL Press, 1996.

Bauman, Zygmunt. *Liquid Times: Living in an Age of Uncertainty*. Cambridge: Polity, 2006.

Baviskar, Amita. "Between Violence and Desire: Space, Power, and Identity in the Making of Metropolitan Delhi." *International Social Science Journal* 55, no. 1 (2003): 89–98.

Bayat, Asef. *Life as Politics: How Ordinary People Change the Middle East*. Stanford, CA: Stanford University Press, 2010.

Bear, Laura. "Doubt, Conflict, Mediation: The Anthropology of Modern Time." *Journal of the Royal Anthropological Institute* 20, no. s1 (2014): 3–30.

Beck, Ulrich. "Climate for Change, or How to Create a Green Modernity?" *Theory, Culture and Society* 27, nos. 2–3 (2010): 254–66.

———. *Risk Society: Towards a New Modernity*. Newbury Park, CA: Sage, 1992.

———. *World at Risk*. Cambridge: Polity, 2009.

Benjamin, Walter. *The Arcades Project*. Cambridge, MA: Belknap Press of Harvard University Press, 2002.

———. "Critique of Violence." In *Reflections: Essays, Aphorisms, Autobiographical Writing*, edited by Peter Demetz, 277–300. New York: Schocken, 1986 [1955].

———. "Theses on the Philosophy of History." In *Illuminations*, 253–64. New York: Schocken, 1968 [1950].

Berman, Marshall. "Falling Towers: City Life after Urbicide." In *Geography and Identity*, edited by Dennis Crowe, 172–92. Washington, DC: Maisonneuve, 1996.

Berney, Rachel. "Pedagogical Urbanism: Creating Citizen Space in Bogota, Colombia." *Planning Theory* 10, no. 1 (2012): 16–34.

Birkhofer, Denise. "Trace Memories: Clothing as Metaphor in the Work of Doris Salcedo." *Anamesa: An Interdisciplinary Journal* 6, no. 1 (2008): 49–66.

Blanco, Andres G. "Discourses of Land Allocation and Natural Property Rights: Land Entrepreneurialism and Informal Settlements in Bogotá, Colombia." *Planning Theory* 10, no. 1 (2011): 1–24.

Boym, Svetlana. "Ruins of the Avant-Garde: From Tatlin's Tower to Paper Architecture." In *Ruins of Modernity*, edited by Julia Hell and Andreas Schönle, 58–85. Durham, NC: Duke University Press, 2010.

Brenner, Neil. "Theses on Urbanization." *Public Culture* 25, no. 1 (2013): 85–114.

Brenner, Neil, Jamie Peck, and Nik Theodore. "Variegated Neoliberalization: Geographies, Modalities, Pathways." *Global Networks* 10, no. 2 (2010): 182–222.

Brenner, Neil, and Christian Schmid. "The 'Urban Age' in Question." *International Journal of Urban and Regional Research* 38, no. 3 (2014): 731–55.

Brown, Wendy. *Walled States, Waning Sovereignty*. New York: Zone Books, 2010.

Bull-Kamanga, L., K. Diagne, A. Lavell, E. Leon, F. Lerise, H. MacGregor, A. Maskrey, et al. "From Everyday Hazards to Disasters: The Accumulation of Risk in Urban Areas." *Environment and Urbanization* 15, no. 1 (2003): 193–204.

Bullard, Robert D. *Unequal Protection: Environmental Justice and Communities of Color*. San Francisco: Sierra Club Books, 1994.

Burchell, Graham, Colin Gordon, and Peter Miller, eds. *The Foucault Effect: Studies in Governmentality*. Chicago: University of Chicago Press, 1991.

Caduff, Carlo. "Pandemic Prophecy, or How to Have Faith in Reason." *Current Anthropology* 55, no. 3 (2014): 296–315.

Caja de la Vivienda Popular. *Informe de gestión 2004–2006*. Bogotá: Alcaldía Mayor de Bogotá, 2006.

Caldeira, Teresa P. R. *City of Walls: Crime, Segregation, and Citizenship in São Paulo*. Berkeley: University of California Press, 2000.

Caldeira, Teresa P. R., and James Holston. "Democracy and Violence in Brazil." *Comparative Studies in Society and History* 41, no. 4 (1999): 691–729.

Calvino, Italo. *Invisible Cities*. Translated by William Weaver. New York: Harcourt, 1974.

Camara de Comercio de Bogotá. *Perfil económico y empresarial: Localidad Ciudad Bolívar*. Bogotá: Camara de Comercio de Bogotá, 2007.

Cardoso, Fernando Henrique, and Enzo Faletto. *Dependency and Development in Latin America*. Berkeley: University of California Press, 1979.

Carrigan, Ana. *The Palace of Justice: A Colombian Tragedy*. New York: Four Walls Eight Windows, 1993.

Castel, Robert. "From Dangerousness to Risk." In *The Foucault Effect: Studies in Governmentality*, edited by Graham Burchell, Colin Gordon, and Peter Miller, 281–98. Chicago: University of Chicago Press, 1991.

Castells, Manuel. *The City and the Grassroots: A Cross-cultural Theory of Urban Social Movements*. Berkeley: University of California Press, 1983.

———. *The Rise of the Network Society*. Cambridge: Blackwell, 1996.

Castro Caycedo, Germán. *El Palacio sin máscara*. Bogotá: Editorial Planeta Colombiana, 2008.

Chakrabarty, Dipesh. "The Climate of History: Four Theses." *Critical Inquiry* 35 (2009): 197–222.

———. *Provincializing Europe: Postcolonial Thought and Historical Difference*. Princeton, NJ: Princeton University Press, 2000.

Chambers, Sarah C. *From Subjects to Citizens: Honor, Gender, and Politics in Arequipa, Peru, 1780–1854*. University Park: Pennsylvania State University Press, 1999.

Chatterjee, Partha. *The Politics of the Governed: Popular Politics in Most of the World*. New York: Columbia University Press, 2004.

Choy, Tim. *Ecologies of Comparison: An Ethnography of Endangerment in Hong Kong*. Durham, NC: Duke University Press, 2011.

Christoplos, Ian, John Mitchell, and Anna Liljelund. "Re-framing Risk: The Changing Context of Disaster Mitigation and Preparedness." *Disasters* 25, no. 3 (2001): 185–98.

CODHES. *Gota a gota: Desplazamiento forzado en Bogotá y Soacha*. Bogotá: Consultoría para los Derechos Humanos y el Desplazamiento, 2007.

Collier, Stephen J. "Enacting Catastrophe: Preparedness, Insurance, Budgetary Rationalization." *Economy and Society* 37, no. 2 (2008): 224–50.

———. "The Spatial Forms and Social Norms of 'Actually Existing Neoliberalism': Toward a Substantive Analytics." *International Affairs Working Paper 2005–04* (2005).

———. "Topologies of Power: Foucault's Analysis of Political Government beyond 'Governmentality.'" *Theory, Culture and Society* 26, no. 6: 78–108.

Collier, Stephen J., and Andrew Lakoff. "Distributed Preparedness: The Spatial Logic of Domestic Security in the United States." *Environment and Planning D* 26, no. 1 (2008): 7–28.

Collier, Stephen J., Andrew Lakoff, and Paul Rabinow. "Biosecurity: Towards an Anthropology of the Contemporary." *Anthropology Today* 20, no. 5 (2004): 3–7.

Colwell, C. "Deleuze and Foucault: Series, Event, Genealogy." *Theory and Event* 1, no. 2 (1997).

Comaroff, Jean. "Beyond Bare Life: AIDS, (Bio)Politics, and the Neolibeal Order." *Public Culture* 19, no. 1 (2007): 197–219.

Comaroff, Jean, and John L. Comaroff. *Law and Disorder in the Postcolony*. Chicago: University of Chicago Press, 2006.

———. *Theory from the South: or, How Euro-America Is Evolving toward Africa*. Boulder: Paradigm, 2012.

Connell, David J. "Planning and Its Orientation to the Future." *International Planning Studies* 14, no. 1 (2009): 85–98.

Cooper, Frederick. "Decolonizing Situations: The Rise, Fall, and Rise of Colonial Studies, 1951–2001." *French Politics, Culture and Society* 20, no. 2 (2002): 47–76.

Cooper, Melinda. *Life as Surplus: Biotechnology and Capitalism in the Neoliberal Era.* Seattle: University of Washington Press, 2008.

———. "Pre-empting Emergence: The Biological Turn in the War on Terror." *Theory, Culture and Society* 23, no. 4 (2006): 113–35.

———. "Turbulent Worlds: Financial Markets and Environmental Crisis." *Theory, Culture and Society* 27, no. 2–3 (2010): 167–90.

Corbridge, Stuart, Glyn Williams, Manoj Srivastava, and René Véron. *Seeing the State: Governance and Governmentality in India.* New York: Cambridge University Press, 2005.

Coronil, Fernando. "The Future in Question: History and Utopia in Latin America (1989–2010)." In *Business as Usual: The Roots of the Global Financial Meltdown,* edited by Craig Calhoun and Georgi Derluguian, 231–92. New York: New York University Press, 2011.

Correa, Elena, and Jorge Villegas. "El Banco Mundial y el reasentamiento de población en América Latina: Tendencias y retos." In *El foro técnico sobre reasentamiento de población en América Latina y el Caribe.* Bogotá: World Bank, Inter-American Development Bank, 2005.

Crutzen, Paul J., and Eugene F. Stoermer. "The 'Anthropocene.'" *Global Change Newsletter* (2000): 17–18.

Cuéllar Sarmiento, Sebastián. "Entre la hacienda y la sociedad civil: Lógicas culturales de la guerra en Colombia." MA thesis, Universidad Nacional de Colombia, 2009.

Das, Veena. *Critical Events: An Anthropological Perspective on Contemporary India.* New York: Oxford University Press, 1996.

Dasgupta, Rana. "The Sudden Stardom of the Third-World City." *New Statesman,* March 27, 2006.

Davis, Mike. *Planet of Slums.* New York: Verso, 2006.

Dean, Mitchell. *Governmentality: Power and Rule in Modern Society.* Thousand Oaks, CA: Sage, 1999.

Defert, Daniel. "'Popular Life' and Insurance Technology." In *The Foucault Effect: Studies in Governmentality,* edited by Graham Burchell, Colin Gordon, and Peter Miller, 211–33. Chicago: University of Chicago Press, 1991.

Deleuze, Gilles. *The Fold: Leibniz and the Baroque.* Minneapolis: University of Minnesota Press, 1993.

———. *Foucault.* New York: Continuum, 2006.

———. *The Logic of Sense.* New York: Columbia University Press, 1990.

Denyer Willis, Graham. *The Killing Consensus: Police, Organized Crime, and the Regulation of Life and Death in Urban Brazil.* Berkeley: University of California Press, 2015.

Derrida, Jacques. "Force of Law: The 'Mystical Foundation of Authority.'" In *Acts of Religion,* edited by Gil Anidjar, 230–98. New York: Routledge, 2002.

Desai, Vandana, and Alex Loftus. "Speculating on Slums: Infrastructural Fixes in Informal Housing in the Global South." *Antipode* 45, no. 4 (2012): 789–808.

DFID. *Disaster Risk Reduction: A Development Concern*. London: Department for International Development, 2004.

DNPAD. *Plan nacional para la prevención y atención de desastres*. Bogotá: Ministro del Interior, Dirección Nacional para la Prevención y Atención de Desastres, 1998.

Doebele, William A. "The Private Market and Low Income Urbanization: The 'Pirate' Subdivisions of Bogota." *American Journal of Comparative Law* 25, no. 3 (1977): 531–64.

Donovan, Michael G. "Informal Cities and the Contestation of Public Space: The Case of Bogotá's Street Vendors, 1988–2003." *Urban Studies* 45, no. 1 (2008): 29–51.

Douglas, Mary. *Purity and Danger: An Analysis of Concepts of Pollution and Taboo*. New York: Praeger, 1966.

———. *Risk and Blame: Essays in Cultural Theory*. New York: Routledge, 1992.

Douglas, Mary, and Aaron B. Wildavsky. *Risk and Culture: An Essay on the Selection of Technical and Environmental Dangers*. Berkeley: University of California Press, 1982.

DPAE. *Anexo 4: Amenaza por fenómenos de remoción en masa*. Bogotá: Dirección de Prevención y Atención de Emergencias, Secretaría de Gobierno, Alcaldía Mayor de Bogotá, DC, 2007.

———. *Concepto técnico N° 3280*. Bogotá: Dirección de Prevención y Atención de Emergencias, Área de Análisis de Riesgos, Secretaría de Gobierno, Alcadia Mayor de Santa Fe de Bogotá, 1999.

———. *Instrumentos para la gestión del riesgo en Bogotá*. Bogotá: Dirección de Prevención y Atención de Emergencias, Secretaría de Gobierno, Alcaldía Mayor de Bogotá, DC, n.d.

———. *Plan de acción para la mitigación de riesgos y rehabilitación en el sector Altos de la Estancia, localidad de Ciudad Bolívar*. Bogotá: Dirección de Prevención y Atención de Emergencias, Secretaría de Gobierno, Alcaldía Mayor de Bogotá, DC, 2006.

Durkheim, Émile. *The Division of Labor in Society*. Translated by W. D. Halls. New York: Free Press, 1984 [1933].

———. *Suicide: A Study in Sociology*. New York: Free Press, 1997 [1897].

Dussel, Enrique. *Twenty Theses on Politics*. Durham, NC: Duke University Press, 2008.

Ebron, Paulla A. *Performing Africa*. Princeton, NJ: Princeton University Press, 2002.

Echeverry, Adriana, and Ana María Hanssen. *Holocausto en el silencio: Veinte años en busca de la verdad*. Bogotá: Editorial Planeta Colombiana SA, 2007.

Elyachar, Julia. *Markets of Dispossession: NGOs, Economic Development, and the State in Cairo*. Durham, NC: Duke University Press, 2005.

Ericson, Richard V., and Aaron Doyle. *Risk and Morality*. Toronto: University of Toronto Press, 2003.

————. *Uncertain Business: Risk, Insurance and the Limits of Knowledge.* Toronto: University of Toronto Press, 2004.

Escobar, Arturo. *Encountering Development: The Making and Unmaking of the Third World.* Princeton, NJ: Princeton University Press, 1995.

————. "Las violencias a través de otras miradas: Comentarios de Arturo Escobar." *Journal of Latin American Anthropology* 7, no. 1 (2002): 310–15.

————. *Territories of Difference: Place, Movements, Life, Redes.* Durham, NC: Duke University Press, 2008.

————. "Worlds and Knowledges Otherwise: The Latin American Modernity/Coloniality Research Program." *Cultural Studies* 21, no. 2–3 (2007): 179–210.

Esposito, Roberto. *Bíos: Biopolitics and Philosophy.* Minneapolis: University of Minnesota Press, 2008.

Ewald, François. "Insurance and Risk." In *The Foucault Effect: Studies in Governmentality*, edited by Graham Burchell, Colin Gordon, and Peter Miller, 197–210. Chicago: University of Chicago Press, 1991.

————. *L'État providence.* Paris: B. Grasset, 1987.

Fabian, Johannes. *Time and the Other: How Anthropology Makes Its Object.* New York: Columbia University Press, 2002.

Fassin, Didier. "Another Politics of Life Is Possible." *Theory, Culture and Society* 26, no. 5 (2009): 44–60.

Fassin, Didier, and Mariella Pandolfi. *Contemporary States of Emergency: The Politics of Military and Humanitarian Interventions.* New York: Zone Books, 2010.

Fassin, Didier, and Richard Rechtman. *The Empire of Trauma: An Inquiry into the Condition of Victimhood.* Princeton, NJ: Princeton University Press, 2009.

Feldman, Ilana, and Miriam Ticktin. *In the Name of Humanity: The Government of Threat and Care.* Durham, NC: Duke University Press, 2010.

Ferguson, James. *Expectations of Modernity: Myths and Meanings of Urban Life on the Zambian Copperbelt.* Berkeley: University of California Press, 1999.

————. "Formalities of Poverty: Thinking about Social Assistance in Neoliberal South Africa." *African Studies Review* 50, no. 2 (2007): 71–86.

————. *Global Shadows: Africa in the Neoliberal World Order.* Durham, NC: Duke University Press, 2006.

————. "Toward a Left Art of Government: From 'Foucauldian Critique' to Foucauldian Politics." *History of the Human Sciences* 24, no. 4 (2011): 61–68.

————. "The Uses of Neoliberalism." *Antipode* 41, no. S1 (2010): 166–84.

FOPAE. *Bogotá: Una vez más, cero muertos, cero heridos.* Bogotá: Fondo de Prevención y Atención de Emergencias, Secretaría de Gobierno, Alcaldía Mayor de Bogotá, DC, n.d.

Fortun, Kim. *Advocacy after Bhopal: Environmentalism, Disaster, New Global Orders.* Chicago: University of Chicago Press, 2001.

Foucault, Michel. *The Birth of Biopolitics: Lectures at the Collège de France, 1978–79.* Translated by Graham Burchell; edited by Michel Senellart. New York: Palgrave Macmillan, 2008.

———. *Discipline and Punish: The Birth of the Prison*. New York: Pantheon, 1977.

———. "Governmentality." In *The Foucault Effect: Studies in Governmentality*, edited by Graham Burchell, Colin Gordon, and Peter Miller, 87–104. Chicago: University of Chicago Press, 1991.

———. *The Hermeneutics of the Subject: Lectures at the Collège de France, 1981–82*. Edited by Frédéric Gros, François Ewald, and Alessandro Fontana. New York: Palgrave Macmillan, 2005.

———. *The History of Sexuality, Volume 1: An Introduction*. Translated by Robert Hurley. New York: Vintage Books, 1990 [1976].

———. "On the Genealogy of Ethics: An Overview of a Work in Progress." In *The Foucault Reader*, edited by Paul Rabinow, 340–72. New York: Pantheon, 1984.

———. *Security, Territory, Population: Lectures at the Collège de France, 1977–78*. Translated by Graham Burchell; edited by Michael Senellart. New York: Palgrave Macmillan, 2007.

———. *"Society Must Be Defended": Lectures at the Collège de France, 1975–1976*. Translated by David Macey; edited by Mauro Bertani and Alessandro Fontana. New York: Picador, 2003.

———. "Technologies of the Self." In *The Essential Foucault*, edited by Paul Rabinow and Nikolas Rose, 145–69. New York: New Press, 2003.

Frank, Andre Gunder. *Capitalism and Underdevelopment in Latin America: Historical Studies of Chile and Brazil*. New York: Monthly Review Press, 1969.

Friedmann, John. *Planning in the Public Domain: From Knowledge to Action*. Princeton, NJ: Princeton University Press, 1987.

Gandy, Matthew. "Learning from Lagos." *New Left Review*, no. 33 (2005): 37–52.

Geertz, Clifford. *The Interpretation of Cultures*. New York: Basic Books, 1973.

Geschiere, Peter. *The Modernity of Witchcraft: Politics and the Occult in Postcolonial Africa*. Charlottesville: University Press of Virginia, 1997.

GFDRR. *Disaster Risk Management Programs for Priority Countries*. Washington, DC: World Bank, Global Facility for Disaster Reduction and Recovery, International Strategy for Disaster Reduction, 2009.

Ghertner, D. Asher. "India's Urban Revolution: Geographies of Displacement beyond Gentrification." *Environment and Planning A* 46, no. 7 (2014): 1554–71.

———. "Rule by Aesthetics: World-Class City Making in Delhi." In *Worlding Cities: Asian Experiments and the Art of Being Global*, edited by Ananya Roy and Aihwa Ong, 279–306. Malden, MA: Wiley-Blackwell, 2011.

Giddens, Anthony. *The Consequences of Modernity*. Stanford, CA: Stanford University Press, 1990.

———. "Risk and Responsibility." *Modern Law Review* 62, no. 1 (1999): 1–10.

Gilbert, Alan. "Good Urban Governance: Evidence from a Model City?" *Bulletin of Latin American Research* 25, no. 3 (2006): 392–419.

———. "The Return of the Slum: Does Language Matter?" *International Journal of Urban and Regional Research* 31, no. 4 (2007): 697–713.

———. "Urban Governance in the South: How Did Bogota Lose Its Shine?" *Urban Studies* 52, no. 4 (2015): 665–84.

Gill, Lesley. "War and Peace in Colombia." *Social Analysis* 52, no. 2 (2008): 131–50.

Goldstein, Daniel M. "Human Rights as Culprit, Human Rights as Victim: Rights and Security in the State of Exception." In *The Practice of Human Rights: Tracking Law between the Global and the Local,* edited by Mark Goodale and Sally Engle Merry, 49–77. Cambridge: Cambridge University Press, 2007.

———. *Outlawed: Between Security and Rights in a Bolivian City.* Durham, NC: Duke University Press, 2012.

———. "Toward a Critical Anthropology of Security." *Current Anthropology* 51, no. 4 (2010): 487–517.

Good, Anthony. "'Undoubtedly an Expert'? Anthropologists in British Asylum Courts." *Journal of the Royal Anthropological Institute* 10, no. 1 (2004): 113–33.

Graham, Stephen. *Cities under Siege: The New Military Urbanism.* London: Verso, 2010.

Grosfoguel, Ramón. "Developmentalism, Modernity, and Dependency Theory in Latin America." *Nepantla: Views from South* 1, no. 2 (2000): 347–74.

Gupta, Akhil, and James Ferguson. *Anthropological Locations: Boundaries and Grounds of a Field Science.* Berkeley: University of California Press, 1997.

———. "Culture, Power, Place: Ethnography at the End of an Era." In *Culture, Power, Place: Explorations in Critical Anthropology,* edited by Akhil Gupta and James Ferguson, 1–29. Durham, NC: Duke University Press, 1997.

Hacking, Ian. *The Emergence of Probability: A Philosophical Study of Early Ideas about Probability, Induction and Statistical Inference.* 2nd ed. New York: Cambridge University Press, 2006.

Hale, Charles R. "Cultural Politics of Identity in Latin America." *Annual Review of Anthropology* 26 (1997): 567–90.

Hansen, Thomas Blom. *Wages of Violence: Naming and Identity in Postcolonial Bombay.* Princeton, NJ: Princeton University Press, 2001.

Hansen, Thomas Blom, and Oskar Verkaaik. "Urban Charisma: On Everyday Mythologies in the City." *Critique of Anthropology* 29, no. 1 (2009): 5–26.

Hardoy, Jorgelina, and Gustavo Pandiella. "Urban Poverty and Vulnerability to Climate Change in Latin America." *Environment and Urbanization* 21, no. 1 (2009): 203–24.

Hardt, Michael, and Antonio Negri. *Empire.* Cambridge, MA: Harvard University Press, 2001.

———. *Multitude: War and Democracy in the Age of Empire.* New York: Penguin Press, 2004.

Hart, Gillian. "Denaturalizing Dispossession: Critical Ethnography in the Age of Resurgent Imperialism." *Antipode* 38, no. 5 (2006): 977–1004.

Harvey, David. "From Managerialism to Entrepreneurialism: The Transformation in Urban Governance in Late Capitalism." *Geografiska Annaler* 71, no. 1 (1989): 3–17.

——. "Neoliberalism as Creative Destruction." *Annals of the American Academy of Political and Social Science* 610, no. 1 (2007): 21–44.

——. *The New Imperialism.* New York: Oxford University Press, 2003.

——. *Paris, Capital of Modernity.* New York: Routledge, 2003.

——. *Rebel Cities: From the Right to the City to the Urban Revolution.* New York: Verso, 2012.

——. "The Right to the City." *New Left Review* 53 (2008): 23–40.

——. *Spaces of Global Capitalism: Towards a Theory of Uneven Geographical Development.* New York: Verso, 2006.

——. *Spaces of Hope.* Berkeley: University of California Press, 2000.

Healey, Mark A. *The Ruins of the New Argentina: Peronism and the Remaking of San Juan after the 1944 Earthquake.* Durham, NC: Duke University Press, 2011.

Hell, Julia, and Andreas Schönle, eds. *Ruins of Modernity.* Durham, NC: Duke University Press, 2010.

Herzog, Tamar. *Defining Nations: Immigrants and Citizens in Early Modern Spain and Spanish America.* New Haven, CT: Yale University Press, 2003.

Hodson, Mike, and Simon Marvin. "'Urban Ecological Security': A New Urban Paradigm?" *International Journal of Urban and Regional Research* 33, no. 1 (2009): 193–215.

——. *World Cities and Climate Change: Producing Urban Ecological Security.* New York: Open University Press / McGraw Hill Education, 2010.

Holston, James. Foreword to *Urbanizing Citizenship: Contested Spaces in Indian Cities*, edited by Renu Desai and Romola Sanyal, ix–xii. New Delhi: Sage Publications India, 2011.

——. *Insurgent Citizenship: Disjunctions of Democracy and Modernity in Brazil.* Princeton, NJ: Princeton University Press, 2008.

——. "Spaces of Insurgent Citizenship." In *Cities and Citizenship*, edited by James Holston, 155–76. Durham, NC: Duke University Press, 1999.

Holston, James, and Arjun Appadurai. "Cities and Citizenship." In *Cities and Citizenship*, edited by James Holston, 1–18. Durham, NC: Duke University Press, 1999.

Huq, Saleemul, Sari Kovats, Hannah Reid, and David Satterthwaite. "Editorial: Reducing Risks to Cities from Disasters and Climate Change." *Environment and Urbanization* 19, no. 1 (2007): 3–15.

Hylton, Forrest. *Evil Hour in Colombia.* New York: Verso, 2006.

Inés, Carmen, Francisco Parra Sandoval, and Nelsy Gined Roa. *Armero: Diez Años de Ausencia.* Ibagué, Colombia: Fondo Resurgir-FES, 1995.

Ingeocim. *Zonificación de riesgo por inestabilidad del terreno para diferentes localidades en la ciudad de Santa Fe de Bogotá D.C.* Bogotá: Fondo de Prevención y Atención de Emergencias de Santa Fe de Bogotá, Unidad de Prevención y Atención de Emergencias de Santa Fe de Bogotá, 1998.

Jackson, Jean E. "Rights to Indigenous Culture in Colombia." In *The Practice of Human Rights: Tracking Law between the Global and the Local*, edited by Mark

Goodale and Sally Engle Merry, 204–41. Cambridge: Cambridge University Press, 2007.

Jimeno, Ramón. *Noche de lobos: Una investigación sobre los hechos del 6 y 7 de noviembre de 1985 en el Palacio de Justicia*. 2nd ed. Bogotá: Ediciones Folio, 2005.

Jones, Donna V. *The Racial Discourses of Life Philosophy: Negritude, Vitalism, and Modernity*. New York: Columbia University Press, 2010.

Jones, Gareth A., and Dennis Rodgers. "Gangs, Guns, and the City: Urban Policy in Dangerous Places." In *The City in Urban Poverty*, edited by Charlotte Lemanski and Colin Marx, 205–26. London: Palgrave-Macmillan, 2015.

——., eds. *Youth Violence in Latin America: Gangs and Juvenile Justice in Perspective*. New York: Palgrave Macmillan, 2009.

Joseph, Gilbert M., and Mark D. Szuchman, eds. *I Saw a City Invincible: Urban Portraits of Latin America*. Wilmington, DE: SR Books, 1996.

Kagan, Richard L., and Fernando Marías. *Urban Images of the Hispanic World, 1493–1793*. New Haven, CT: Yale University Press, 2000.

Kaplan, Robert. "The Coming Anarchy: How Scarcity, Crime, Overpopulation, Tribalism, and Disease Are Rapidly Destroying the Social Fabric of Our Planet." *Atlantic Monthly*, February 1994, 44–76.

King, Anthony D. *Urbanism, Colonialism, and the World-Economy: Cultural and Spatial Foundations of the World Urban System*. New York: Routledge, 1990.

Klein, Naomi. *The Shock Doctrine: The Rise of Disaster Capitalism*. New York: Metropolitan Books / Henry Holt, 2007.

Koolhaas, Rem, Stefano Boeri, Sanford Kwinter, Nadia Tazi, and Hans-Ulrich Obrist. *Mutations*. Barcelona: ACTAR, 2001.

Koselleck, Reinhart. *Futures Past: On the Semantics of Historical Time*. New York: Columbia University Press, 2004.

——. *The Practice of Conceptual History: Timing History, Spacing Concepts*. Stanford, CA: Stanford University Press, 2002.

Lakoff, Andrew. "From Population to Vital System: National Security and the Changing Object of Public Health." In *Biosecurity Interventions: Global Health and Security in Question*, edited by Andrew Lakoff and Stephen J. Collier, 33–60. New York: Columbia University Press, 2008.

——. "The Generic Biothreat, Or, How We Became Unprepared." *Cultural Anthropology* 23, no. 3 (2008): 399–428.

——. "Preparing for the Next Emergency." *Public Culture* 19, no. 2 (2007): 247–71.

——. "Two Regimes of Global Health." *Humanity: An International Journal of Human Rights, Humanitarianism, and Development* 1, no. 1 (2010): 59–79.

Lakoff, Andrew, and Eric Klinenberg. "Of Risk and Pork: Urban Security and the Politics of Objectivity." *Theory and Society* 39, no. 5 (2010): 503–25.

Latour, Bruno. *Aramis, or, The Love of Technology*. Cambridge, MA: Harvard University Press, 1996.

——. *Reassembling the Social: An Introduction to Actor-Network-Theory*. New York: Oxford University Press, 2005.

———. *Science in Action: How to Follow Scientists and Engineers through Society.* Cambridge, MA: Harvard University Press, 1987.

Law, John, and John Hassard. *Actor Network Theory and After.* Malden, MA: Blackwell, 1999.

Lefebvre, Henri. *Critique of Everyday Life.* New York: Verso, 1991.

———. *The Production of Space.* Cambridge: Blackwell, 1991 [1974].

———. *The Urban Revolution.* Minneapolis: University of Minnesota Press, 2003 [1970].

LeGrand, Catherine. "Labor Acquisition and Social Conflict on the Colombian Frontier, 1850–1936." *Journal of Latin American Studies* 16, no. 1 (1984): 27–49.

Leiva, Fernando Ignacio. *Latin American Neostructuralism: The Contradictions of Post-neoliberal Development.* Minneapolis: University of Minnesota Press, 2008.

Li, Tania Murray. "To Make Live or Let Die? Rural Dispossession and the Protection of Surplus Populations." *Antipode* 41, no. s1 (2010): 66–93.

Llano, María Clara. "Plaza de Bolívar: La manzana de la discordia." In *Pobladores urbanos,* edited by Julián Arturo, 211–35. Bogotá: Instituto Colombiano de Antropología, Cocultura, Tercer Mundo Editores, 1994.

Llorente, María Victoria, and Ángela Rivas. "La caída del crimen en Bogotá: Una década de políticas de seguridad ciudadana." In *Seguridad ciudadana: Experiencia y desafíos,* edited by Lucía Dammert, 311–41. Valparaíso: Municipalidad de Valparaíso, 2004.

Locke, John. *Two Treatises of Government and A Letter concerning Toleration.* Edited by Ian Shapiro. New Haven, CT: Yale University Press, 2003 [1689].

Lomnitz, Claudio. "Editor's Letter." *Public Culture* 19, no. 2 (2007): 225–26.

Luhmann, Niklas. *Observations on Modernity.* Stanford, CA: Stanford University Press, 1998.

Macpherson, C. B. *The Political Theory of Possessive Individualism: Hobbes to Locke.* Oxford: Clarendon, 1962.

Maldonado-Torres, Nelson. *Against War: Views from the Underside of Modernity.* Durham, NC: Duke University Press, 2008.

Malkki, Liisa. "News and Culture: Transitory Phenomena and the Fieldwork Tradition." In *Anthropological Locations: Boundaries and Grounds of a Field Science,* edited by Akhil Gupta and James Ferguson, 86–101. Berkeley: University of California Press, 1996.

———. "Speechless Emissaries: Refugees, Humanitarianism, and Dehistoricization." *Cultural Anthropology* 11, no. 3 (1996): 377–404.

Mamdani, Mahmood. *Citizen and Subject: Contemporary Africa and the Legacy of Late Colonialism.* Princeton, NJ: Princeton University Press, 1996.

Marshall, T. H. *Class, Citizenship, and Social Development.* Westport, CT: Greenwood, 1973.

Martin, Gerard, and Miguel Ceballos. *Bogotá: Anatomia de una transformación, 1995–2003.* Bogotá: Editorial Pontificia Universidad Javeriana, 2004.

Martin, Randy. *An Empire of Indifference: American War and the Financial Logic of Risk Management.* Durham, NC: Duke University Press, 2007.

Martínez Alier, Juan. *The Environmentalism of the Poor: A Study of Ecological Conflicts and Valuation.* New York: Oxford University Press, 2005.

Marx, Karl. *Capital.* Edited by David McLellan. Oxford: Oxford University Press, 1999 [1867].

——. "On the Jewish Question." In *The Marx-Engels Reader,* edited by Robert C. Tucker, 26–52. New York: Norton, 1978 [1844].

Masco, Joseph. "Bad Weather: On Planetary Crisis." *Social Studies of Science* 40, no. 1 (2010): 7–40.

——. *The Nuclear Borderlands: the Manhattan Project in post-Cold War New Mexico.* Princeton, NJ: Princeton University Press, 2006.

——. *The Theater of Operations: National Security Affect from the Cold War to the War on Terror.* Durham, NC: Duke University Press, 2014.

Massey, Doreen. "Cities in the World." In *City Worlds,* edited by Doreen Massey, John Allen, and Steve Pile, 99–156. London: Routledge, 1999.

——. "Double Articulation: A Place in the World." In *Displacements: Cultural Identities in Question,* edited by Angelika Bammer, 110–21. Bloomington: Indiana University Press, 1994.

Massumi, Brian. "National Enterprise Emergency: Steps toward an Ecology of Powers." *Theory Culture and Society* 26, no. 6 (2009): 153–85.

——. "Perception Attack: Brief on War Time." *Theory and Event* 13, no. 3 (2010).

Mbembe, Achille, and Sarah Nuttall. "Introduction: Afropolis." In *Johannesburg: The Elusive Metropolis,* edited by Sarah Nuttall and Achille Mbembe, 1–33. Durham, NC: Duke University Press, 2008.

——. "Writing the World from an African Metropolis." *Public Culture* 16, no. 3 (2004): 347–72.

McCann, Eugene, and Kevin Ward. *Mobile Urbanism: Cities and Policymaking in the Global Age.* Minneapolis: University of Minnesota Press, 2011.

McGraw, Jason. *The Work of Recognition: Caribbean Colombia and the Postemancipation Struggle for Citizenship.* Chapel Hill: University of North Carolina Press, 2014.

McLean, Stuart. *The Event and Its Terrors: Ireland, Famine, Modernity.* Stanford, CA: Stanford University Press, 2004.

Meade, Teresa A. *"Civilizing" Rio: Reform and Resistance in a Brazilian City, 1889–1930.* University Park: Pennsylvania State University Press, 1997.

Meillassoux, Claude. "From Reproduction to Production: A Marxist Approach to Economic Anthropology." *Economy and Society* 1, no. 1 (1974): 93–105.

Mejía, María Clara. "Involuntary Resettlement of Urban Population: Experiences in World Bank–Financed Development Projects in Latin America." Washington: World Bank, 1996.

Mejía Pavony, Germán Rodrigo. *Los años del cambio: Historia urbana de Bogotá, 1820–1910.* Bogotá: CEJA, 2000.

Merrifield, Andy. *The New Urban Question*. London: Pluto, 2014.

Mignolo, Walter. *The Idea of Latin America*. Malden, MA: Blackwell, 2005.

———. "Introduction: Coloniality of Power and De-colonial Thinking." *Cultural Studies* 21, no. 2–3 (2007): 155–67.

———. *Local Histories / Global Designs: Coloniality, Subaltern Knowledges, and Border Thinking*. Princeton, NJ: Princeton University Press, 2000.

Mitchell, Don. *The Right to the City: Social Justice and the Fight for Public Space*. New York: Guilford, 2003.

Mitchell, Katharyne. "Pre-black Futures." *Antipode* 41, no. S1 (2009): 239–61.

Mitchell, Timothy. *Colonising Egypt*. Berkeley: University of California Press, 1991.

———. *Rule of Experts: Egypt, Techno-Politics, Modernity*. Berkeley: University of California Press, 2002.

———. "The Stage of Modernity." In *Questions of Modernity*, edited by Timothy Mitchell, 1–34. Minneapolis: University of Minnesota Press, 2000.

Mohan, Rakesh. *Understanding the Developing Metropolis: Lessons from the City Study of Bogotá and Cali, Colombia*. New York: Published for the World Bank by Oxford University Press, 1994.

Montavalli, Jim, Divya Abhat, Shauna Dineen, Tamsyn Jones, Rebecca Sanborn, and Kate Slomkowski. "Cities of the Future: Today's 'Mega-cities' Are Overcrowded and Environmentally Stressed." *E: The Environmental Magazine*, September/October 2005, 26–36.

Montezuma, Ricardo. "The Transformation of Bogotá, Colombia, 1995–2000: Investing in Citizenship and Urban Mobility." *Global Urban Development Magazine* 1, no. 1 (2005).

Moore, Donald S. *Suffering for Territory: Race, Place, and Power in Zimbabwe*. Durham, NC: Duke University Press, 2005.

Moore, Sally Falk. *Social Facts and Fabrications: "Customary" Law on Kilimanjaro, 1880–1980*. New York: Cambridge University Press, 1986.

Morales, Leonardo. "Reasentamiento de población ubicada en zonas de alto riesgo no mitigable por remoción en masa en Bogotá." In *El Banco Mundial y el reasentamiento de población en América Latina: Tendencias y retos*. Bogotá: World Bank, Interamerican Development Bank, 2005.

Moreno Rojas, Samuel. "Seguridad integral en la Bogotá Positiva." In *¡Bogotá preparada!* Bogotá: Informe especial de *El Espectador*, Dirección de Prevención y Atención de Emergencias (DPAE), Alcaldía Mayor de Bogtotá, 2008.

Naranjo Giraldo, Gloria. "El desplazamiento forzado en Colombia: Reinvención de la identidad e implicaciones en las culturas locales y nacionales." *Scripta Nova, Revista Electrónica de Geografía y Ciencias Sociales* 94, no. 1 (2001).

Neuwirth, Robert. *Shadow Cities: A Billion Squatters, a New Urban World*. New York: Routledge, 2005.

Niño Murcia, Soledad. *Territorios del miedo en Santafé de Bogotá: Imaginarios de los ciudadanos*. Santafé de Bogotá: Instituto Colombiano de Antropología, Observatorio de Cultura Urbana, TM Editores, 1998.

Noguera, Carlos E. *Medicina y política: Discurso médico y prácticas higiénicas durante la primera mitad del siglo XX en Colombia*. Medellín: Fondo Editorial Universidad EAFIT, 2003.

Nuttall, Sarah, and Achille Mbembe. "A Blasé Attitude: A Response to Michael Watts." *Public Culture* 17, no. 1 (2005): 193–202.

O'Malley, Pat. "Risk and Responsibility." In *Foucault and Political Reason: Liberalism, Neo-liberalism, and Rationalities of Government*, edited by Andrew Barry, Thomas Osborne, and Nikolas S. Rose, 189–207. London: UCL Press, 1996.

———. *Risk, Uncertainty and Government*. Portland: GlassHouse, 2004.

O'Neill, Kevin Lewis. "Left Behind: Security, Salvation, and the Subject of Prevention." *Cultural Anthropology* 28, no. 2 (2013): 204–26.

O'Neill, Kevin Lewis, and Kedron Thomas, eds. *Securing the City: Neoliberalism, Space, and Insecurity in Postwar Guatemala*. Durham, NC: Duke University Press, 2011.

Osborne, Thomas. "Security and Vitality: Drains, Liberalism and Power in the Nineteenth Century." In *Foucault and Political Reason: Liberalism, Neo-liberalism, and Rationalities of Government*, edited by Andrew Barry, Thomas Osborne, and Nikolas Rose, 99–121. Chicago: University of Chicago Press, 1996.

Osborne, Thomas, and Nikolas Rose. "Governing Cities: Notes on the Spatialisation of Virtue." *Environment and Planning D: Society and Space* 17, no. 6 (1999): 737–60.

Packer, George. "The Megacity: Decoding the Chaos of Lagos." *New Yorker*, November 13, 2006, 62–75.

Palacios, Marco. *Between Legitimacy and Violence: A History of Colombia, 1875–2002*. Durham, NC: Duke University Press, 2006.

Paley, Julia. *Marketing Democracy: Power and Social Movements in Post-dictatorship Chile*. Berkeley: University of California Press, 2001.

Park, Robert Ezra, Ernest Watson Burgess, and Roderick Duncan McKenzie. *The City*. Chicago: University of Chicago Press, 1967.

Paschel, Tianna S. "The Right to Difference: Explaining Colombia's Shift from Color-Blindness to the Law of Black Communities." *American Journal of Sociology* 116, no. 3 (2010): 729–69.

Patton, Paul. "The World Seen from Within: Deleuze and the Philosophy of Events." *Theory and Event* 1, no. 1 (1997).

Pecha Quimbay, Patricia. *Historia institucional de la Caja de la Vivienda Popular*. Bogotá: Alcaldía Mayor de Bogotá, DC, Secretaría General, Archivo de Bogotá, 2008.

Peck, Jamie. "Geographies of Policy: From Transfer-Diffusion to Mobility-Mutation." *Progress in Human Geography* 35, no. 6 (2011): 773–97.

Pelling, Mark. "Disaster Risk and Development Planning: The Case for Integration." *International Development Planning Review* 25, no. 4 (2003): i–ix.

Petryna, Adriana. *Life Exposed: Biological Citizens after Chernobyl*. Princeton, NJ: Princeton University Press, 2002.

Postero, Nancy. *Now We Are Citizens: Indigenous Politics in Postmulticultural Bolivia.* Stanford, CA: Stanford University Press, 2007.

———. "The Struggle to Create a Radical Democracy in Bolivia." *Latin American Research Review* 45 (2010): 59–78.

Poveda Gómez, Narzha. *Reasentamiento de hogares por alto riesgo no mitigable en el marco del plan de rehabilitación y reconstrucción y desarrollo sostenible post evento de Nueva Esperanza.* Bogotá: World Bank, Fondo Global de Reducción de Desastres y Reconstrucción, 2008.

Povinelli, Elizabeth A. "Defining Security in Late Liberalism: A Comment on Pedersen and Holbraad." In *Times of Security: Ethnographies of Fear, Protest and the Future,* edited by Martin Holbraad and Morten Axel Pedersen, 28–32. London: Routledge, 2013.

———. "The State of Shame: Australian Multiculturalism and the Crisis of Indigenous Citizenship." *Critical Inquiry* 24, no. 2 (1998): 575–610.

Power, Matthew. "The Magic Mountain: Trickle-Down Economics in a Philippine Garbage Dump." *Harper's,* December 2006, 57–68.

Presner, Todd Samuel. "Hegel's Philosophy of World History via Sebald's Imaginary of Ruins: A Contrapuntal Critique of the 'New Space' of Modernity." In *Ruins of Modernity,* edited by Julia Hell and Andreas Schönle, 193–211. Durham, NC: Duke University Press, 2010.

Rabinow, Paul. *French Modern: Norms and Forms of the Social Environment.* Cambridge, MA: MIT Press, 1989.

———. *Marking Time: On the Anthropology of the Contemporary.* Princeton, NJ: Princeton University Press, 2008.

Rabinow, Paul, and Nikolas Rose. "Biopower Today." *BioSocieties* 1, no. 2 (2006): 195–217.

Ramirez, Fernando, Francis Ghesquiere, and Carlos Costa. *Un modelo para la planificación de la gestión del riesgo de desastres en grandes ciudades.* Panama City: United Nations International Strategy for Disaster Risk Reduction (UNISDR), Plataforma Temática de Riesgo Urbano, 2009.

Ramírez, María Clemencia. "Maintaining Democracy in Colombia through Political Exclusion, States of Exception, Counterinsurgency, and Dirty War." In *Violent Democracies in Latin America,* edited by Enrique Desmond Arias and Daniel M. Goldstein, 129–65. Durham, NC: Duke University Press, 2010.

Ramírez Gomez, Fernando, and Omar Darío Cardona. "El sistema nacional para la prevención y atención de desastres en Colombia." In *Estado, sociedad y gestión de los desastres en América Latina: En busca del paradigma perdido,* edited by Allan Lavell and Eduardo Franco, 255–307. Lima: La RED, FLACSO, ITDG-Perú, 1996.

Rancière, Jacques. *Hatred of Democracy.* London: Verso, 2009.

———. *The Politics of Aesthetics: The Distribution of the Sensible.* New York: Continuum, 2004.

Rausch, Jane M. "Church-State Relations on the Colombian Frontier: The National Intendancy of Meta, 1909–1930." *The Americas* 49, no. 1 (1992): 49–68.

———. *The Llanos Frontier in Colombian History, 1830–1930.* Albuquerque: University of New Mexico Press, 1993.

Restrepo, Eduardo. "Ethnicization of Blackness in Colombia: Toward De-racializing Theoretical and Political Imagination." *Cultural Studies* 18, no. 5 (2004): 698–715.

Rivas Gamboa, Ángela. *Gorgeous Monster: The Arts of Governing and Managing Violence in Contemporary Bogotá.* Saarbrücken: VDM Verlag Dr. Müller, 2007.

———. "In-quietud y doble-voz: Una mirada etnográfica sobre prácticas de gobierno y tecnologías de seguridad en Bogotá." *Universitas Humanística* 57 (2004): 60–69.

Robinson, Jennifer. "Global and World Cities: A View from Off the Map." *International Journal of Urban and Regional Research* 26, no. 3 (2002): 531–54.

———. *Ordinary Cities: Between Modernity and Development.* New York: Routledge, 2006.

Robledo Gómez, Ángela María, and Patricia Rodríguez Santana. *Emergencia del sujeto excluido: Aproximacíon genealógica a la no-ciudad en Bogotá.* Bogotá: Editorial Pontificia Universidad Javeriana, 2008.

Rodgers, Dennis. "'Disembedding' the City: Crime, Insecurity and Spatial Organization in Managua, Nicaragua." *Environment and Urbanization* 16, no. 2 (2004): 113–24.

Rofel, Lisa. *Other Modernities: Gendered Yearnings in China after Socialism.* Berkeley: University of California Press, 1999.

Rojas, Cristina. *Civilization and Violence: Regimes of Representation in Nineteenth-Century Colombia.* Minneapolis: University of Minnesota Press, 2002.

———. "Securing the State and Developing Social Insecurities: The Securitisation of Citizenship in Contemporary Colombia." *Third World Quarterly* 30, no. 1 (2009): 227–45.

Roldan, Mary. *Blood and Fire: La Violencia in Antioquia, Colombia, 1946–1953.* Durham, NC: Duke University Press, 2002.

Rose, Nikolas. "The Death of the Social? Re-figuring the Territory of Government." *Economy and Society* 25, no. 3 (1996): 327–56.

———. "Governing 'Advanced' Liberal Democracies." In *Foucault and Political Reason: Liberalism, Neo-liberalism, and Rationalities of Government,* edited by Andrew Barry, Thomas Osborne, and Nikolas S. Rose, 37–64. London: UCL Press, 1996.

———. *The Politics of Life Itself: Biomedicine, Power, and Subjectivity in the Twenty-First Century.* Princeton, NJ: Princeton University Press, 2007.

———. *Powers of Freedom: Reframing Political Thought.* New York: Cambridge University Press, 1999.

Rose, Nikolas, and Carlos Novak. "Biological Citizenship." In *Global Assemblages: Technology, Politics, and Ethics as Anthropological Problems,* edited by Aihwa Ong and Stephen J. Collier, 439–63. Malden, MA: Blackwell, 2005.

Rosenberg, Daniel, and Susan Harding. "Introduction: Histories of the Future." In *Histories of the Future,* edited by Daniel Rosenberg and Susan Harding, 3–18. Durham, NC: Duke University Press, 2005.

Roy, Ananya. "The 21st-Century Metropolis: New Geographies of Theory." *Regional Studies* 43, no. 6 (2008): 819–30.

——. "Urban Informality: Toward an Epistemology of Planning." *Journal of the American Planning Association* 71, no. 2 (2005): 147–58.

——. "Urbanisms, Worlding Practices and the Theory of Planning." *Planning Theory* 10, no. 1 (2012): 6–15.

Roy, Ananya, and Aihwa Ong, eds. *Worlding Cities: Asian Experiments and the Art of Being Global*. Malden, MA: Wiley-Blackwell, 2011.

Sabato, Hilda. "On Political Citizenship in Nineteenth-Century Latin America." *American Historical Review* 106, no. 4 (2001): 1290–315.

Salcedo, Doris. "An Act of Memory: Proposal for a Project for the Palace of Justice, Bogotá, 2002." In *Shibboleth*, edited by Doris Salcedo and Mieke Bal, 82–83. London: Tate, 2007.

——. "Traces of Memory: Art and Remembrance in Colombia." *ReVista: Harvard Review of Latin America* (Spring 2003).

Salcedo, Doris, Carlos Basualdo, Nancy Princenthal, and Andreas Huyssen. *Doris Salcedo*. London: Phaidon, 2000.

Samet, Robert. "The Photographer's Body: Populism, Polarization, and the Uses of Victimhood in Venezuela." *American Ethnologist* 40 (2013): 525–39.

——. "The Victim's Voice: Crime Journalism and Practices of Denunciation in Caracas, Venezuela." Annual Meeting of the Law and Society Association, San Francisco, May 30–June 6, 2011.

Samimian-Darash, Limor. "A Pre-event Configuration for Biological Threats: Preparedness and the Constitution of Biosecurity Events." *American Ethnologist* 36, no. 3 (2009): 478–91.

Sánchez, Rubén A. "Alcances y límites de los conceptos biopolítica y biopoder en Michel Foucault." In *Biopolítica y formas de vida*, edited by Rubén A. Sánchez, 17–43. Bogotá: Pontificia Universidad Javeriana, 2007.

Santa, Eduardo. *Adiós, Omayra: La catástrofe de Armero*. Bogotá: Alfaguara, 1988.

Sarmiento, Domingo Faustino. *Life in the Argentine Republic in the Days of the Tyrants; or, Civilization and Barbarism*. New York: Collier, 1961 [1868].

Sassen, Saskia. *Cities in a World Economy*. Thousand Oaks, CA: Pine Forge, 1994.

——. *The Global City: New York, London, Tokyo*. Princeton, NJ: Princeton University Press, 2001.

Schmitt, Carl. *Political Theology: Four Chapters on the Concept of Sovereignty*. Chicago: University of Chicago Press, 2005 [1922].

Schwartz, Stuart B. "Cities of Empire: Mexico and Bahia in the Sixteenth Century." *Journal of Inter-American Studies* 11 (1969): 616–37.

Scott, James C. *Seeing like a State: How Certain Schemes to Improve the Human Condition Have Failed*. New Haven, CT: Yale University Press, 1998.

Secretaría Distrital de Hábitat. *Marco de política y metodología de reasentamientos de población localizada en zonas de alto riesgo no mitigable, e inundación y obras públicas*. Bogotá: Alcaldía Mayor de Bogotá DC, 2007.

Segura, Martha, ed. *Conversaciones con Bogotá, 1945–2005*. Bogotá: Sello Editorial Lonja de Propiedad Raíz de Bogotá, 2005.

Silva Téllez, Armando. *Bogotá imaginada*. Bogotá: Convenio Andrés Bello, Universidad Nacional de Colombia, Taurus, 2003.

Simmel, Georg. "The Stranger." Translated by Kurt H. Wolff. In *The Sociology of Georg Simmel*, edited by Kurt H. Wolff, 402–8. New York: Free Press, 1950 [1908].

Simone, AbdouMaliq. *City Life from Jakarta to Dakar: Movements at the Crossroads*. New York: Routledge, 2010.

———. "People as Infrastructure: Intersecting Fragments in Johannesburg." *Public Culture* 16, no. 3 (2004): 407–29.

Smith, Neil. *The New Urban Frontier: Gentrification and the Revanchist City*. New York: Routledge, 1996.

———. *Uneven Development: Nature, Capital, and the Production of Space*. 3rd ed. Athens: University of Georgia Press, 2008.

Snyder, John Parr. *Flattening the Earth: Two Thousand Years of Map Projections*. Chicago: University of Chicago Press, 1993.

Socolow, Susan Migden. Introduction to *Cities and Society in Colonial Latin America*, edited by Louisa Schell Hoberman and Susan Migden Socolow, 3–18. Albuquerque: University of New Mexico Press, 1986.

Stoler, Ann Laura. "Imperial Debris: Reflections on Ruins and Ruination." *Cultural Anthropology* 23, no. 2 (2008): 191–219.

———. *Race and the Education of Desire: Foucault's History of Sexuality and the Colonial Order of Things*. Durham, NC: Duke University Press, 1995.

Swyngedouw, Erik. "Apocalypse Forever? Post-political Populism and the Spectre of Climate Change." *Theory, Culture and Society* 27, no. 2–3 (2010): 213–32.

———. "The Non-political Politics of Climate Change." *ACME: An International E-Journal for Critical Geographies* 12, no. 1 (2013): 1–8.

———. "Power, Nature and the City: The Conquest of Water and the Political Ecology of Urbanization in Guayaquil, Ecuador: 1880–1980." *Environment and Planning A* 29, no. 2 (1997): 311–32.

Sze, Julie. *Noxious New York: The Racial Politics of Urban Health and Environmental Justice*. Cambridge, MA: MIT Press, 2007.

Tate, Winifred. *Counting the Dead: The Culture and Politics of Human Rights Activism in Colombia*. Berkeley: University of California Press, 2007.

Taussig, Michael. *The Devil and Commodity Fetishism in South America*. Chapel Hill: University of North Carolina Press, 1980.

———. *Shamanism, Colonialism, and the Wild Man: A Study in Terror and Healing*. Chicago: University of Chicago Press, 1987.

Taylor, Charles. *Multiculturalism: Examining the Politics of Recognition*. Princeton, NJ: Princeton University Press, 1994.

Taylor, Dorceta E. *The Environment and the People in American Cities, 1600–1900s: Disorder, Inequality, and Social Change*. Durham, NC: Duke University Press, 2009.

Taylor, Peter J. *World City Network: A Global Urban Analysis*. New York: Routledge, 2004.

Tognato, Carlo, and Sebastián Cuéllar Sarmiento. "Military 'Shipwrecks': Legitimizing War in a Fragmented Civil Sphere." Mimeo, Department of Sociology, National University of Colombia, Bogotá (2009).

Tomaselli, Wesley. "Colombia's New Export: War and Security Know-How." *Ozy.com*, June 14, 2014, http://www.usatoday.com/story/news/world/2014/06/14/ozy-exporting-fighting-skills/10440719/.

Tsing, Anna Lowenhaupt. *Friction: An Ethnography of Global Connection*. Princeton, NJ: Princeton University Press, 2005.

UNDP. *Reducing Disaster Risk: A Challenge for Development*. Geneva: UN Development Programme, 2004.

UNISDR. *Global Assessment Report on Disaster Risk Reduction*. Geneva: UN International Strategy for Disaster Risk Reduction, 2009.

Uribe, María Victoria. "Dismembering and Expelling: Semantics of Political Terror in Colombia." *Public Culture* 16, no. 1 (2004): 79–96.

Valverde, Mariana. "'Despotism' and Ethical Liberal Governance." *Economy and Society* 25, no. 3 (1996): 357–72.

Vega, Felipe. "Desplazamiento forzado: Biopolítica de la invisibilidad." *Theologica Xaveriana* 149 (2004): 119–34.

Viana Castro, Hugo. *Armero, su verdadera historia*. 2nd ed. Bogotá: Viana Ediciones, 2005.

Villaveces, Jeffrey, Ximena Londoño, and Luis Carlos Colón, eds. *Bogotá León de Oro 1990–2006: El renacer de una ciudad*. Bogotá: Alcaldía Mayor de Bogotá, Instituto Distrital de Cultura, 2006.

Villaveces Izquierdo, Santiago. "Seguridad." In *Palabras para desarmar: Una mirada crítica al vocabulario del reconocimiento cultural*, edited by Margarita Rosa Serje de la Ossa, María Cristina Suaza Vargas, and Roberto Pineda Camacho, 373–77. Bogotá: Ministerio de Cultura, Instituto Colombiano de Antropología e Historia, 2002.

Von Schnitzler, Antina. "Citizenship Prepaid: Water, Calculability, and Techno-Politics in South Africa." *Journal of Southern African Studies* 34, no. 4 (2008): 899–917.

Walker, Charles. *Shaky Colonialism: The 1746 Earthquake-Tsunami in Lima, Peru, and Its Long Aftermath*. Durham, NC: Duke University Press, 2008.

———. *Smoldering Ashes: Cuzco and the Creation of Republican Peru, 1780–1840*. Durham, NC: Duke University Press, 1999.

Wallerstein, Immanuel. *The Modern World-System*. New York: Academic Press, 1974.

Wamsler, Christine. "Mainstreaming Risk Reduction in Urban Planning and Housing: A Challenge for International Aid Organisations." *Disasters* 30, no. 2 (2006): 151–77.

Watts, Michael. "Baudelaire over Berea, Simmel over Sandton?" *Public Culture* 17, no. 1 (2005): 181–92.

Weinstein, Liza. *The Durable Slum: Dharavi and the Right to Stay Put in Globalizing Mumbai*. Minneapolis: University of Minnesota Press, 2014.

Weszkalnys, Gisa. "Anticipating Oil: The Temporal Politics of a Disaster Yet to Come." *Sociological Review* 62 (2014): 211–35.

Williams, Raymond. *The Country and the City*. New York: Oxford University Press, 1973.

———. *Marxism and Literature*. Oxford: Oxford University Press, 1977.

Wirth, Louis. "Urbanism as a Way of Life." In *Classic Essays on the Culture of Cities*, edited by Richard Sennett, 143–64. New York: Appleton-Century Crofts, 1969 [1938].

World Bank. *Global Monitoring Report 2009: A Development Emergency*. Washington: World Bank, 2009.

Yiftachel, Oren. "Theoretical Notes on 'Gray Cities': The Coming of Urban Apartheid?" *Planning Theory* 8, no. 1 (2009): 88–100.

Zeiderman, Austin. "On Shaky Ground: The Making of Risk in Bogotá." *Environment and Planning A* 44, no. 7 (2012): 1570–88.

Zhang, Li. *In Search of Paradise: Middle-Class Living in a Chinese Metropolis*. Ithaca, NY: Cornell University Press, 2010.

———. *Strangers in the City: Reconfigurations of Space, Power, and Social Networks within China's Floating Population*. Stanford, CA: Stanford University Press, 2001.

Žižek, Slavoj. "Censorship Today: Violence, or Ecology as a New Opium for the Masses." Lecture at the Jack Tilton Gallery, New York, November 26, 2007.

———. "The Lesson of Rancière." In *The Politics of Aesthetics*, edited by Jacques Rancière, 69–79. London: Continuum, 2011.

———. *Living in the End Times*. New York: Verso, 2010.

Zwingle, Erla. "Cities: Challenges for Humanity." *National Geographic*, November 2002, http://ngm.nationalgeographic.com/ngm/0211/feature3/.

INDEX

Note: Items in boldface indicate a table; items in italics indicate a figure; n indicates an endnote

accidents: attempt to control risk of (Bogotá), 75, 95–96; as future events, 222n6; household and domestic, 59, 95–96, 100; industrial, 74, 218n48; response mechanisms (Colombia), 68, 71

accountability: democratic transparency and, 212; government, 42, 46, 54, 113; household, 96; neoliberal vs. populist policies of, 108; state under *denuncias prospectivas*, 180–81, 184, 188–90; willful personal risk, 113

accumulation: capital, 17–19, 172, 192, 200, 235nn80–81, 236–37n2, 237n5; by dispossession, 17–18, 21, 22, 218n53, 219n71; expense of others, 113, 242n39; Lockean rationality, 113; primitive, 17

Afro-Colombians (*afrodescendente*): Jairo, 142–45, 148, 156; stereotypes and assumptions, 144–45, 157–58

Agamben, Giorgio, 214–15n14, 222n4, 235n79, 235–36n82, 236n84

Angelus Novus, 175

Anjaria, Jonathan Shapiro, 198

Anthropocene, 32, 211, 212, 245n6

anticipation: anticipatory urbanism, 161–65, 170, 176, 180–85, 189–90, 191–92;

in "at risk" populations, 163, 166, 172–76; *denuncias prospectivas*, 180–81, 188–90, 192; and endangered city (concept of), 27, 30, 205; of future harm as a basis for governance, 1, 5, 27, 50, 60, 205, 222n4; government control and, 192; government failure in, 180–85, 189–90; government responsibility for, 42, 50, 54, 180–81; November 1985 tragedies, 42, 46, 58, 60; politics of temporality, 176–77, 190, 191–92, 236–37n2; productive force, 31, 38, 132, 170–72, 191–92, 237n3, 237n5; resource and danger, 172–75, 191–92; risk management, 37, 60; socioeconomic improvement and, 172–76, 191; state-subject interactions, 189–90; subjunctive state, 170–72, 191; threats underlying "voluntary" resettlement, 170, 191; uncertainty and insecurity, 5. *See also* foresight; future; possibility

Appadurai, Arjun, 177

architects: Caja staff, 16, 64, 76, 106, 117, 173; city and its future as a concern for, 199, 215–16n25, 219–20n73, 244n68; risk and security, 164–65, 191

Armero: forewarnings, 38, 39–41; influence on security policies, 34, 37–39, 42, 52, 223n19; Nevado del Ruiz volcano, 38, 42, 49, 68, 70; November 1985 disaster, 38, 43, 52, 72; Palace of Justice tragedy, compared to, 46, 52, 55–56; pilgrimage site, 33–35, 47–48; Popayán earthquake, compared to, 46; Pope John Paul II, 47–48; Omayra Sánchez, 46–49, 52, 55–56

assassinations: commonplace events in late twentieth-century Bogotá, 9, 39–40, 73, 217n34; Pablo Escobar, 217n34; Jorge Eliécer Gaitán, 13, 67

"at risk" population: Bogotá, 16, 18, 28, 64, 164; category of entitlement, 146, 156, 157–58, 162, 171, 178, 190; Ciudad Bolívar, 106; formal legal status, 131–32; *sensibilización* of, 103–6, 115–16, 229n1; target of government intervention, 23, 29–30, **109**, 143–44; Third Millennium Park *desplazados*, 156; visibility to government, 60, 91, 110, 114–15, 131–34, 136–38, 145; vulnerability to death, 110, 114–15, 133–34, 136–38, 141, 144–46; vulnerability to threat, 82, 143. *See also* risk management; threat

avalanches, 47, 71, 131. *See also* landslides; mudslides

Barco, Virgilio, 10, 69

barrio: *barrios populares modelos*, 108; Bogotá, 75; Chapinero Alto, 107; definition in Colombia, 108; El Cartucho, 13–16, 217n41, 218n48; El Recreo, 183, 188; other terms for, 107; San Rafael, 77; Sierra Morena, 132; slum vs., 107. *See also* neighborhoods; slums

Beck, Ulrich, 2

beneficiaries of resettlement: Afro-Colombian and indigenous, 143–44; assimilation and education, 103–6, 115–17, 118–21; Caja workers and, 118–21; co-responsibility with Caja, 104, 165–70; eligibility requirements, 77, 86–88, 140–43, 162, 229n2; self-initiative, 63–64, 117, 124–25, 132–33, 165–66, 172–75; subsidies for, 19, 210

Benjamin, Walter, 175–76, 207, 214–15n14

Betancur, Belisario, 9, 38–39, 43–45, 52–55, 68–69

Bien-Aimé, Minister Paul Antoine (Haiti), 6–7

biopower/biopolitics: Agamben, 236n84; Deleuze and Dussel, 158–59, 236n87; *desplazados*, 149, 150; Foucault, 113, 157, 214n9, 225n48, 235n79, 235n82; frameworks for *el vivo* and *los vulnerables*, 148; juridical rights vs., 157; "make live," 113, 225n48, 235n80, 235–36n82; politics of risk and security, 214n9, 233n44; protection of life, 113, 222n4; sovereign state security vs., 235–36n82; vulnerability and victimhood, 145. *See also* life; politics

Bogotá: Acueducto (water utility), 128, 187, 188; Bogotá model, 194–96, 240n2; Ciudad Bolívar, 16, 23–24, 63–66, 103–6, 119, 161, 226n2; *denuncia* process, 143; environmental guards, 139, 178–80; Fund for Emergency Prevention and Response, 181–85; global city, 20; high seismic risk areas, 64, 74, 228n43; homicides in, 217n40; honors bestowed on, 194, 206, 240n3; map of risk, 63–65, 69, 73–74, 76, 88; master plan for, 74, 209, 244n1; Ninety-third Street Park, 146, 152; General Rodolfo Palomino (police chief), 149–50; population growth in, 64; Procuraduría, 143; Third Millennium Park, 14, 15, 150–56; TransMilenio, 167, 195, 240n6; Unified Information System of Violence and Delinquency, 73; Héctor Zambrano (secretary of health), 152, 154; zones of high risk, 6, 16, 63–65, 73–77, 109–12, 161–62, 172–75

Bogotá, mayors of: Luis Eduardo ("Lucho") Garzón (2004–7), 25, 105, 106; Clara López (secretary and interim mayor, 2011–12), 147, 152, 155, 156, 182–83, 185, 234n75; Antanas Mockus (1995–96, 2001–3), 12–14, 73–75, 115; Samuel Moreno (2008–11), 25, 105, 147, 149, 154–55, 217n36; Enrique Peñalosa (1998–2002, 2016–), 12–13, 75, 105, 184, 195–96, 240n6,

240n9; Gustavo Petro (2012–15), 209–11, 245n3

Bogotá, neighborhoods: Bosa, 182, 183, 184–85, 188–90; El Cartucho barrio, 13–16, 217n41, 218n48; El Valle, 83; Kennedy, 182, 183, 185; Nueva Esperanza, 82–88; San Rafael barrio, 77

Bogotá River, 182, 184, 185, 186, 190

Boym, Svetlana, 176

Caja (Caja de la Vivienda Popular): architects, 16, 64, 76, 106, 117, 173; Bogotá's urban periphery, 16, 161; *corresponsabilidad*, 104; disaster response functions, 86; DPAE collaboration, 75, 76, 86, 106, 132; educational role, 23, 103–6, 115–17; engineers, 16, 106, 117; field office, 23, 63, 65, 103–6, 117, 142–43, 161–62; infrastructure improvement, 110; interactions with beneficiaries, 31, 102, 118–21, 128–29, 137; interactions with residents, 87–89, 161, 162; lawyers, 63, 117, 127; map of risk, 64, 69, 73–77, 78, 228n43; mission, 22–23, 28–29, 63, 105–6, 108–10, 218n48; oversight of resettlement program, 22, 63, 110–11, 114, 165–67, 170, 219n62; protection of vulnerable lives, 110–11, 117, 142–43, 162, 210–11; public housing, 108, 110; reconciliation of social welfare and risk management, 110–14, 117–18, 124, 129, 161–63; relationship with "invaders" of evacuated zones of high risk, 101–2; relationships with residents of zones of high risk, 16, 63–64, 115–22, 124–27, 142–44, 172–75; rental assistance, 88; resettlement program, 210–11; right to housing, 113–14; "risk," 106–8, 110–11; *sensibilización* process, 103–6, 115–16, 229n1; social workers, 88–89, 103–11, 124–26, 162–64, 175, 191; staff, 16, 25–26, 28, 63, 105, 106, 162–63; technical and social teams, 106; zones of high risk, 64–65, 77, 132, 172–75

calculations of risk: for Bogotá, 64, 73, 74, 76, 90, 107, 111; for Colombia, 42, 68–69;

Foucault, 3; and government intervention, 3, 117, 128–29, 176–77; potential harm, 31, 223n9; predicting risk, 2–3; resettlement program, 107, 111, 117, 143–44, 162; social interaction and probabilistic, 81, 88, 90; technical diagnosis, 76; threats beyond statistical, 98–100; tool of urban governance, 67, 70, 74, 228n40; total loss index, 74

Cali, 73

campesinos (rural peasants), 115–17

capitalism, 17–18, 21, 24, 158, 200, 214n12

catastrophe. *See* disaster

Catholic Church, 43, 65, 120, 121, 125, 129

Caycedo, Germán Castro, 53, 54, 225n49

Chatterjee, Partha, 133–34

Chernobyl, 146

children: *desplazado* demands for assistance, 140, 146–50, 151–55, 162; exposure to danger and government concern, 93–96; focus of *el ya*, 163; household dangers, 95; incentive to demonstrate familial vulnerability, 131–33, 140; *los vulnerables,* 143, 147–48, 152, 157–58; *sensibilización*, 103

cities: Africa, 198, 199, 200, 201; Bogotá model, 194–96, 203, 206–7; calculations of probabilities and risk as tools of urban governance, 67, 70; capitalism and transformation of, 17–18; Chicago, 18, 21, 197, 242n39; citizenship and urban poor, 133, 157, 172, 192, 235n81; city-ness, 206, 244n66; Colombia, 9–10, 27, 38, 42, 70, 73; colonial Spanish America, 135–36; dispossession and displacement in, 20, 21, 219n71; exploitative relationships with hinterlands, 4–5, 200; future as point of orientation in governance of, 1–2, 20, 90, 164; global, 21, 197, 202, 240n13, 244n66; global North, 2, 17–18, 21, 197, 200; global South, 2, 5, 21–22, 197–202, 219n70, 240n13, 244n60; Harvey on development of, 17–18; hierarchical spaces, 135–36, 157, 201, 237n3; Johannesburg, 195, 197, 200, 241n32; Lagos, 198–99, 200, 201, 241n20, 242n39; Latin American, 2, 5–6, 135–36, 157, 243n50; Lima, 107, 200; lived cities (*continued*)

realities of, 21–22, 90–91, 201–2, 219n73, 220n77; London, 4, 21, 196, 197, 201, 204, 242n39; managing risk and security, 5, 30, 193–94, 203–7, 215n20; Manila, 199; Marxist assumptions, 135; migrations from rural areas to, 17; Mumbai, 18, 197, 204, 218nn57–58; Nairobi, 197; New York City, 4, 18, 21, 196, 197, 200, 203; Paris, 4, 18, 21, 196, 197, 200, 218n57; pinnacles of human achievement, 4–5, 135, 215–16n25; Rio de Janeiro, 18, 107, 197, 203, 219n59; risk and security in governance of, 66–67, 70, 90–91, 194–95; squatter settlements, 90, 123, 135, 177–78, 198, 237n3; transportation systems, 195–96; urban populations, 91, 133, 196–97, 198, 243–44n59; urban theory, 2–5, 17–18, 21–22, 193–202, 205–7, 244nn65–66; welfare state, 20–21; Western cities and modernization, 2, 196, 197; zones of high risk, 72–76, 90–91, 107. *See also* megacities; urbanism

citizenship: culture of Mayor Mockus, 14, 115; government obligations to protect life, 22, 49, 112, 132–34, 232n33; gradations of entitlement, 114, 144, 157–58, 230–31n3, 231n16; liberal concepts of, 19, 115, 129, 136, 158, 231n19; Locke on eligibility for, 113, 157; molding populations into citizens, 18, 115–17, 231n7, 231n18; obligations of, 18, 34, 51, 98–100, 115–16, 205; poor urban dwellers, 27, 131, 133–34, 158; resettlement program and, 29, 31, 115–17, 161; right to housing, 110, 113, 202–3; risk and security, 30, 60, 213n1; Spanish colonial concepts in Colombia, 114–15, 128–29, 135–36, 231n16; subordination of rights to risk and security, 134, 136, 147, 150–51, 205, 231n19; *vecindad*, 114; vigilance against danger, 98–100, 152; visibility and "life at risk," 10, 60, 132–34, 143, 145–46, 156; vulnerability, 31, 91, 114, 141, 157–58, 178. *See also* entitlement; rights

city-ness, 206, 244n66

ciudadanos (urban citizens), 115–17

Ciudad Bolívar: Bogotá's risk management program, 63–65, 104–5; Caja field office, 23, 63, 103–4, 106, 119, 161; physical environment, 65–66, *174*; poverty in, 16, 226n2; squatting, 23–24; temporary rental housing for beneficiaries, 132; zones of high risk, 64–65, 104, 124, 131

civilization: "barbarism" and, 5, 135, 215–16n25; city as epitome of, 135, 136, 198, 215–16n25; "will to civilization" as rejection of colonial past, 135, 231n16, 231n19

climate change, 181, 184, 203–4, 209–12, 213n1, 220n77

collective life: anticipation, 236–37n2; citizen watchdog, 100; health, 71; identity, 134, 135, 144, 145, 150, 212; memory, 47, 49; mobilization and action, 149–50, 187–90; risk management and insecurity, 1, 3, 27, 42, 103, 223n9, 238n9; social collectivity, 31, 111, 115, 129. *See also* life

Collier, Stephen, 3, 218n48, 221n83, 222n6, 223n9, 235–36n82

Colombia: active combat zones, 140; Armenia, 6–7, 216n30; cities, 9–10, 27, 38, 42, 73; constitution (1991), 10, 55, 108, 110–13, 134, 231n8, 234n75; economic recession, 11; El Refugio, 7; emergency response, 67–68; internal displacement, 11, 12, 136, 232n21; legal rights of *desplazados*, 146–47, 149, 150; mapping of natural risks, 70, 227n20, 228n43; model for disaster risk management, 7, 67, 194–95; national army, 10, 11, 38, 52–58, 65, 68–69; National Disaster Fund, 46, 71; National Office of Emergency Response, 69, 70, 72; National Plan for Disaster Prevention and Response, 68; Polo Democrático Alternativo, 12, 105; protector vs. provider, 37, 136, 178; Socorro Nacional de la Cruz Roja, 67–68; Truth Commission and Palace of Justice tragedy, 53–56, 225n55

Colombia, presidents of: Virgilio Barco (1986–90), 10, 69; Belisario Betancur (1982–86), 9, 38–39, 43–45, 52–55, 68–69; César Gaviria (1990–94), 10, 227n17;

Álvaro Uribe (2002–10), 11–12, 14–15, 121, 122–23, 136, 216–17n32

colonialism: Catholic Church, 125; coexistence of colonial and modern institutions, 4–5, 29, 215nn18–19, 221n87, 236n89, 242n44; decolonial politics of oppressed, 158–59; hacienda system, 121–23, 129; Latin American cities, 5, 135, 200–201; postcolonial enfranchisement, 114–15

Comaroff, Jean, 199, 231n11, 236n84

Comaroff, John, 199, 231n11

Connell, David, 165, 238n9

constitution: 1991 constitution, 10, 108; "abuse of discretion" rulings, 234n75; right to decent housing, 104–5, 110, 112–13, 131, 134, 230n2, 231n8; right to life, 112, 155; transfer of responsibilities from state to subject, 108; Truth Commission, 55. *See also* rights

Coronil, Fernando, 6, 134, 219n68

Cortés, Ernesto, 185

crime: drug-related, 7, 9–13, 53, 67, 83–85, 209; everyday exposure in zones of high risk, 83–85, 104, 142; protection rackets, 83–85, 142–43; robberies, 83–85, 88, 95, 104, 162; suspected informants as targets, 85–86; theft, 13, 123, 162. *See also* violence

crisis. *See* disaster

Cuéllar Sarmiento, Sebastián, 122

Cundinamarca, 182, 185

danger. *See* threat

Dasgupta, Rana, 197

Davis, Mike, 66, 172, 197–98, 220n77, 226n6

death: death threats, 84, 127, 142–43; intense rainfall, 33, 70, 181; Nevado del Ruiz eruption, 48, 58; Palace of Justice massacre, 52, 55–59; paramilitary death squads, 10; Popayán earthquake, 43; population displacement, 137, 140; Omayra Sánchez, 33–34, 35–37, 46–52, 224n39; sovereign power, 235–36n82; violence (Bogotá, 1983–92), 217n40; in zones of high risk, 84–86, 132, 210

Deleuze, Gilles, 158, 222–23n8, 236n87

democracy: autonomy and citizenship, 114–15, 128–29, 135; coexistence with nondemocratic traditions, 129; democratic republics, 114–15; democratic security, 11, 26, 121, 136; democratic values, 212; effect of violence, 158; liberal democracy, 129, 133, 135, 136, 157; subordination to security, 10, 136, 157–58

demonstrations and protests: Armero, 41; Bosa and Kennedy, 183, 184, 187–88

demonstrations and protests, by *desplazados*: 1999, 147; April 2009, 150–56; in areas symbolic of wealth and comfort, 147; July 2008, 146–49; media coverage, 147, 148–49, 151, 151–52, 153, 155, 232–33n6; nonviolent, 146–47, 149, 150–56, 234n75; objectives, 146–47, 149, 150, 151; observers' interpretations, 147–48, 149–50, 151–52; occupation of Red Cross office, 147; September 2008, 149–50

denuncias prospectivas (prospective denunciations), 180–81, 188–90, 192

desplazados (internally displaced persons): Afro-Colombian and indigenous, 144; Assistance to Displaced Persons Day, 146; Bogotá's failure to assist, 20, 136; Colombia's failure to assist, 141, 146–47, 232n25; dispossession, 18; *invasiones*, 82–83, 107, 138–39, 143; legal entitlements, 146–47, 149, 150; legal status of, 141, 144–45, 175, 232n25; *los vulnerables*, 148, 149–52, 157; media portrayals of, 147–49, 151–56; newly arrived in Bogotá, 140–42, 177–80; occupation of urban periphery, 18, 75, 82, 137; occupation of evacuated zones of high risk, 137–39, 177–78; opportunists, 139; pirate urbanizers, 65, 123, 177–78, 230n31; rights asserted by, 148–49, 150; rural violence and economic decline, 11; self-built settlements, 11, 18; statistics, 18, 137, 155, 232n21. *See also* demonstrations and protests, by *desplazados*; displacement; poor development and modernization: in Bogotá, 73–75, 112, 163–65, 172, 180, 194–96, 205; Cali's Program for Development, Security, and Peace, 73; city, 4, 21, 135–36, 196–97, 200; close planning and disaster, 203, 243n58; de-development, 201, 205, 206; disasters as threats to, 198, 203, 204, 243n55, 243–44n59; integration of disaster planning with, 70, 72, 165, 203, 243n54, 243n58; integration of risk and security with, 60, 68, 72, 170, 176–77, 191, 195; in Latin America, 108–9, 129, 135–36; megacities, 196–201, 205–6, 228–29n53, 242n35; neoliberal influences, 111, 136, 202–3; risk and security concerns, 31, 60, 136, 196, 202, 204–5, 206–7, 210–12, 231n19; temporal assumptions, 5, 21, 178, 193–94, 198–204, 215n19, 237n5; underdevelopment, 200–201; USAID, 68; Western models, 135, 180, 193, 195–201, 204, 242n40

disaster: Armenia earthquake, 6–7, 216n30; Armero, 33, 41–42, 47–50, 68, 71; Bosa and Kennedy floods, 182–83; cities, 176, 198–99, 204, 243–44nn58–9; develop-ment, 203; economic and financial crises, 17, 67, 204, 241n28; emergency preparedness and civil defense, 67–68, 69; global fears and insecurities, 1, 198; Haiti earthquake, 6, 216n29; individual behavior during, 33, 47, 50; International Decade for Natural Disaster Reduction, 72, 203, 227n31; landslides in Bogotá, 77; legal definition, 71; links between man-made and natural, 213n1; management, 68–69, 74; National Disaster Fund, 46, 71; nongovernmental organizations, 67–68; November 1985 tragedies, 39, 42–43, 51–52, 59–60, 61, 68, 223n19; Palace of Justice tragedy, 52–56, 68; political ca-tastrophe, 58–59; politics of (Argentina), 215–16n25; Popayán earthquake, 43–46, 68, 223n20, 224n29; rainfall-induced, 70, 86–87, 127–28, 181; recovery, 216n30; reduction, 72, 203, 216n30; relief, 67;

religious significance, 43, 46, 126, 128; shift from emergency response to risk management, 68–71; social and political instability, 68, 69; Socorro Nacional de la Cruz Roja, 67–68; symbolism and Omayra Sánchez, 47–51, 52, 55–56; threat for poor, 66, 86–87, 103–4, 131–32, 163, 170, 185; volcanic eruption, 71

disaster risk: anticipation, 5, 37, 170–72, 191–92, 205, 222n4, 236–37n2; calcula-tions and predictions, 7, 42, 64, 67, 69–70, 74, 223n9; Colombia as global model for preparedness and management, 7, 67, 194–95; development and, 203–4, 243n58, 243nn54–55; DPAE and Caja management of evacuations and resettle-ment, 75–78, 86–87, 210–11; exposure of poor, 66, 86–87, 103–4, 131–32, 163, 170, 185; Fund for Emergency Prevention and Response (Bogotá), 69, 72–73, 181; globalization of management policy, 72; global South, 72, 203; governmental failures in management, 38–39, 41–42, 49, 58–60, 69, 184–85, 188–90; governmen-tal responsibility, 37, 39, 42, 68, 145–46; international influences on Colom-bia's policies, 69, 72, 195, 243n50; legal definition of risk, 71–72; management in Bogotá, 6, 16, 30, 76–77, 181, 194–95, 210–12; management in Colombia, 33–34, 37, 68–70, 191, 194–95; mapping, 64, 69, 70–71, 73; National Office of Emergency Response, 69, 70; National Plan for Disaster Prevention and Response, 68; National System for Disaster Prevention and Response, 70, 227n17; opportunity and, 176–77, 180, 190, 191–92; policy changes, 68–71; public, 93–104; security threats, 223n9; Socorro Nacional de la Cruz Roja, 69; zones of high risk, 64, 69, 70–71, 72–77, 86–87, 170, 216n28. *See also* risk management

discrimination and racial bias: accusa-tions of opportunism, 143–45, 148, 152, 157; Afro-Colombians, 142, 144–45, 148,

157–58; *costeños*, 148; endowment of citizenship, 114–15, 144–45; indigenous people, 114, 145–46, 158, 232n28; inequality, 111, 230–31n3; stereotyping, 148; *vivo*, 148, 157

displacement: "accumulation by dispossession," 17–18, 21–22, 219n71; mass migrations and rural populations, 17, 137, 149, 155, 232n21, 232n25; natural disasters, 7, 33, 77, 128, 181, 183; urban risk and security policies, 16, 137, 139–41; violence and economic recession, 11–12, 18, 136, 151. *See also desplazados*

dispossession: "accumulation by," 17–19, 22, 218n53, 219n71; creative destruction, 17, 21–22, 238n26; entitlement, 112–13; government power, 20, 22, 159, 237n3; Locke, 112–13; resettlement programs, 18–19, 22, 24; socioeconomic implications, 144, 158–59; urbanization, 21

Directorate for Emergency Prevention and Response (DPAE): Caja collaboration, 75, 76, 86, 106, 132; calculations of risk, 75–77, 88, 142–43; emergency response function, 86; map of risk oversight, 63–65, 69, 73–74, 76–77, 81, 88; monitoring activities, 76–82; on-site visits to zones of high risk, 76–82, 87, 138–41; technical responsibilities, 75, 76, 78; zones of high risk designations, 76, 86–87, 132, 142

drug trafficking and narcoterrorism, 7, 9–13, 53, 67, 83–85, 209

Durkheim, Émile, 17, 218n49

Dussel, Enrique, 158–59

earthquakes: antiseismic regulations (Popayán), 46; Armenia, 6, 216n30; high seismic risk areas (Bogotá) 64, 74, 228n43, (Colombia) 42, 216–17n32; Popayán, 43–46, 60, 68–69, 224n29; seismic preparedness, 96–98; seismic-resistant housing, 7

education: citizenship, 104–5; *convivencia*, 121; *desplazados*, 146–47; development and modernization, 135–36, 203, 231n19;

residents of zones of high risk, 172; risk awareness, 93–100, 103–4, 204; Omayra Sánchez, 61; *sensibilización*, 103–6, 229n1; subordinate to preservation of life, 202, 205, 206–7

ELN (National Liberation Army), 11, 24

emergency: declarations of, 86, 181, 182; Fund for Emergency Prevention and Response, 69, 72–73, 181–82; health and pandemic, 156; hotlines, 98; National Directorate for Disaster Preparedness, 96–98, 182, 185, 216n29; National Directorate for Disaster Prevention and Response, 227n17; National Office of Emergency Response, 69, 73, 227n17; preventable, 185, 189; religious significance, 42, 128; response, 67, 69, 71, 128, 190, 216n29, 227n17; rule of law during, 234n75

endangered city: Bogotá, 32, 38, 107–8, 161, 193, 205–6; global concern, 30, 91, 202, 204–6, 211; governmental intervention, 66, 82; personhood and citizenship, 51, 60, 66, 102–3, 134, 145, 191; product of Colombia's history, 27, 29, 60–61; risk management, 128–29, 164, 170; vulnerability and risk, 51, 66, 82, 91, 145–46, 156

endangerment: capacity to extend beyond danger or violence, 27, 30, 31, 88, 131; concept of, 131, 213n1; ethnography of, 26–27; power to shape policies and planning, 72, 93, 102; rights, 162. *See also* security; violence

engineers, 16, 76, 106, 117, 142, 164, 191

entitlement: citizenship, 105, 112, 114; *desplazados*, 146–47, 149, 150; exercise by previously excluded socioeconomic groups, 22, 114, 124, 131–37, 141, 143, 170–71; fraudulent petitions, 145, 149, 187; "life at risk," 110, 124, 137, 143, 146, 157, 176; means of becoming visible to state, 132–33, 134, 136–37, 140, 145, 146, 191; product of vulnerability, 74, 113, 114, 142, 144, 162; racial bias and, 143–45; resettlement beneficiaries, 18–19, 77, 101–2, 112–13, 123,

entitlement (*continued*)
170, 228n52; right to protection of life,
11–12, 110, 134, 136, 162, 231n19. *See also*
citizenship; rights
environmental threats. *See* avalanches;
floods; landslides; mudslides; rains;
volcanoes and volcanic eruptions
Escobar, Pablo, 53, 217n34
Espectador, El: *desplazados* demonstrations, 148–49, 232–33n36; November 1985
tragedies, 39, 40. *See also* media
ethics: Colombian traditions, 102, 121, 129,
193; Fournier's coverage of Omayra Sánchez, 47, 50, 224n32; Salcedo and political
violence, 56–57; Omayra Sánchez, 50, 51;
of security, 231
events: accidents as future, 222n6; calculations of probabilities, 42, 67, 74, 222n6,
223n9; crisis of government, 34, 37,
39, 42, 52, 223n19; Deleuze, 222–23n8;
extreme weather, 33, 70, 127–28, 181,
210–11; foresight, 38–42, 46, 59–60,
187–91, 204–5, 223n9; framing of, 39, 52–
53, 59, 146–56, 201, 222nn5–6, 232–33n36;
global interconnections, 6–7, 197, 203–4,
232n34, 240n13, 241n28; informational
secrecy and censorship, 53–57; interconnections of natural and manmade,
44–45, 68–69, 213n1; juxtaposed as indicators of broader problems, 30, 37–39,
42–43, 46–47, 52–53; legacies, 27, 29, 30,
37–39, 42, 56–59; political attitudes and
actions, 1, 37–39, 42, 59, 70–71, 204–5,
222n4; power of fear, 27, 131–32; risk of
ignoring historic precedents, 42, 46,
68; virtual, 222–23n8. *See also* history;
specific events; *types of events*
eviction: *desplazados*, 139–41; neighborhood
population density, 19; resettlement, 16,
17; in zones of high risk, 78, 79
exclusion: Afro-Colombians and indigenous people, 144, 145, 232n28; challenges to, 135; development policies, 212;
national policies, 201, 231n10; "right to
city," 112; socioeconomic, 28, 136, 157, 172,

230–31n3; in Spanish colonial times, 114,
136, 231n16, 232n20. *See also* inclusion

FARC (Revolutionary Armed Forces of Colombia), 9, 11–12, 14–15, 24, 37, 217–18n43,
245n3
Fassin, Didier, 146, 232n33
fear: enduring influence, 27; environments
and cultures of, 27, 83–88; insecurity, 15,
132; sociopolitical influence, 6, 15, 95, 195,
197, 201
Ferguson, James: developmental time, 176,
200, 201, 242n35, 242n40; global order
and status of cities and countries within
it, 244n63; neoliberal governmentality,
219n64; progressive arts of government,
25, 220n77
floods: in Bosa and Kennedy, 182–90; Caja
assistance, 142, 144, 145, 162; calculations
of threat, 70, 74; damage, 33, 128, 181,
183–84; designating a zone of high risk, 6,
74–75, 100, 216n28; *denuncias prospectivas*, 184, 189–90; disproportionate
exposure of poor to, 66, 168, 181, 186, 190;
DPAE, 75; foresight as a governmental
responsibility, 41, 171, 182, 184–90; legal
recognition under disaster laws, 71; mapping of threat, 75; resettlement program,
16, 63, 110; risk management program, 75,
88, 90, 182; seasonal, 69; susceptibility in
Ciudad Bolívar, 66
flu, 108, 152–55
FOPAE (Fund for Emergency Prevention
and Response), 181–85
foresight, 34, 38–39, 42, 46, 49, 53, 59.
See also anticipation
Foucault, Michel: biopolitics, 113, 157–58,
222n4, 225n48, 235n79, 235–36n82,
236n87; governmentality, 20, 50, 107–8,
224–25n40; historical coexistence of modalities of power, 3–4, 214n11, 222–23n8;
liberalism, 214n7; risk, 3–4, 129, 214n6,
214n9, 218n48, 221n81; state phobia,
220n78
Fournier, Frank, 47, 49, 50, 224n32

Friedmann, John, 165

future: anticipating degeneration of global cities, 5, 31–32, 176–77, 197–201, 203–7, 237n3, 240–41n15; anticipation, action and reaction, 236–37n2; anticipation, forecasts of global crises and catastrophes, 5, 203–4, 212; Bogotá model, 194–96; consensus as attempt to constrain, 212, 245n8; creative destruction, 17–18, 219n59; "crisis of modern futurity," 5; "culture of citizenship," 14; Deleuze and influence of historical events, 222–23n8; demanding protection and assistance, 61, 146, 157, 177–78, 180, 222n4; *denuncias prospectivas*, 180–81, 188–90; divine providence, 46, 126–27, 191; ecology/security vs. development/modernization, 180, 191, 197, 202, 204–7; of evacuated zones of high risk, 20, 139, 179–80; governance in anticipation of harm, 1–2, 37–39, 42, 67; governance in anticipation of threat, 30, 63, 73–74, 76, 124, 164, 180–81; governance in anticipation of uncertainty, 2, 5, 67, 69, 71, 171; government intervention, 90, 93–101; historic events as influence on governance, 9–10, 38–39, 42, 45–46, 68, 70, 185; individual decision-making, 3, 98–103, 117–18, 173, 180, 214n4, 238n9; influence on present, 3, 163–65, 188–90, 222nn6–7, 236–37n2; Paul Klee and visual parable in *Angelus Novus*, 175–76; perception as "better," 2, 4–5, 31, 162–63, 166, 171–77; perception of time as a linear movement, 2, 4–5, 165, 200–201, 222–23n8; political interactions between subjects and authorities, 31, 134, 161, 162–63, 171–72, 191, 237n5; predictive or probabilistic calculations of harm, 3, 67, 128–29, 162; range of possibilities, 171, 176–77, 191, 212; risk management, 73–76, 103, 107, **109**, 111, 172, 191; risk management as a neutral approach to governance, 12–13, 63–64; Ann Stoler and ruins, 176–77; uncertainty, 32, 126, 134; uncertainty in global cities, 90, 163–64,

242n35; uncertainty in Latin American cities, 5–6; urban theories, 163–65, 176–77, 192, 193, 194–201, 203–7; voluntary embrace of risk, 177–78, 179–80. *See also* anticipation

Gaitán, Jorge Eliécer, 13, 67

Garzón, Luis Eduardo ("Lucho"), 25, 105, 106

Gaviria, César, 10, 227n17

gentrification, 17, 19, 219n71

geological threats. *See* avalanches; landslides; mudslides; volcanoes and volcanic eruptions

Giddens, Anthony, 2–3, 214n4

godfathers and godmothers. *See padrinos and madrinas*

governance: Bogotá model, 15, 22–23, 194–96, 220n77, 240n1; environmental justice and, 220n77; "good," 23, 90, 194, 202; liberal, 2, 3, 102, 194, 214n10, 214–15n14; postpolitical or consensus, 211–12; religion and, 214–15n14; urban, 15, 194–95, 220n76, 229n4, 240n1; violence, endangerment, risk, and security, 2, 23, 30, 32, 90, 102, 193–94, 202, 226n9; welfare, progressive-oriented, 20–21, 202

governmental intervention. *See* intervention

governmentality, 17, 20–22, 25, 214n11, 224–25n40

Graham, Stephen, 215n20, 244n61

Grosfoguel, Ramón, 201, 215n19

guerrillas: conflicts with army, 9, 11, 14; conflicts with paramilitaries, 11; displacement of peasants, 65, 151, 175; leftist funding through kidnappings, 10; M-19, 9–10, 37–38, 52–56, 68, 209, 225n55; mid- and late twentieth century, 15, 37, 45; recruiting grounds in Bogotá, 15; rightist fears and antagonisms, 14, 15; violence in peripheral neighborhoods, 24

H1N1 (*gripa porcina* or swine flu) epidemic, 152–56

hacienda system, 65, 121–24, 129, 230n30

Haiti, 6–7, 216–17nn29–32
Hansen, Thomas Blom, 148
Harding, Susan, 5, 163, 237n3, 240n9
Hardt, Michael, 158, 235n79
Harvey, David, 17–18, 218n52, 218n57, 219n59, 242n45
health: Bogotá, **109**, 135, 174; *desplazado* demonstrators, 152, 154, 156, 234n75; healthcare as a right, 154–55; humanitarian biomedicine vs. global health security, 232n32; occupational policies, 71; risk and security, 202–3, 205–7, 231n19; squatter settlements, 226n6; unhealthy living conditions, 70. *See also* flu
history: capitalism and global cities, 18, 21–22, 200; citizenship in Spanish America, 114–15, 144–48, 152, 157–59; collective memory, 34–35, 47–49, 50, 55–57; cultural significance of historic locations, 43–45, 215n18; Foucault and coexistence of modalities of power, 3–4, 214n11, 235n79, 235–36n82; hacienda system and modern social relationships, 121–23; historical referents and lingering influences, 42, 89, 121–23, 129–30, 146, 221n87, 222–23nn8–9; historical specificity, 25, 29, 129–30, 184, 221n87, 222n4; Latin American cities, 2, 202, 215n20, 243n50; linear, temporal movement, 2, 102, 129, 165, 196–201, 214n12, 215n19; lived reality vs. theory, 21, 25, 27, 29, 163–64; model of urban development in West, 4, 21–22, 195–97, 200, 241n30, 242n44; natural disasters in Colombia, 33, 42, 46, 52, 181; overlap of natural and human, 32, 211–12, 213n1, 223n9, 245n6; patterns of urban development, 21–22, 135, 178, 193, 195–202; risk and security in twentieth-century Bogotá, 23–27, 30, 64–66, 146, 193, 196, 202–3; risk and security in twentieth-century Colombia, 23–26, 129; risk of ignoring, 184–85, 238n9; ruins, 175–77; technical calculations and predictions, 42, 46, 66–67, 74, 184; temporality, possibility, and, 163–65, 175–77, 237nn3–5, 238n9;

violence and security, 9, 30, 59, 205, 215n20, 221n81; violence in Colombia, 56, 57. *See also* events; temporality
homelessness, 13, 87, 110, 178
housing: Afro-Colombians and indigenous people, 144; Caja, 22–23, 63, 108–14, 134, 202–3; constitutional right, 16, 230n2, 231n8; deregulation, 108; *desplazado* demonstrations, 146–47, 150, 155–56; *inquilinatos* and *desplazados*, 65; *invasiones*, 23–24, 82, 107, 109–10, 137–43, 179; market in Bogotá, 19, 177–79, 184; pirate urbanizers, 178; policy, 108–11, 123, 184, 210–11; public housing in Bogotá, 108–9; relocations of residents of zones of high risk, 6, 111–13, 165–66; rental and resettlement beneficiaries, 88, 170; rights, 11, 104, 110, 112–14, 131; rights to housing vs. right to life, 203, 205, 206–7, 231n19; security and risk logics, 139–42, 162, 177–78; seismic-resistant public, 7; self-built, 11, 18, 64–65, 75–78, 82, 123, 173–74; shortage in Bogotá, 65–66, 75; social or public, 11, 19, 22–23, 108–9, 116, 165–69, 184–86; socioeconomic strata in Bogotá, 110–11; subsidies for relocation beneficiaries, 16, 64, 77, 106, 117, 141, 173
housing developments: Alta Vista de Sidel, 83; Arborizadora Alta, 119, 120; Ciudadela Porvenir, 166–69; Metrovivienda, 184; planning failures, 184–85, 190; Quintas de Santa Ana, 169; relocation points for resettlement beneficiaries, 7, 16, 28, 83, 128, 166–69, 174–75; Towers of Progress, 127, 174
humanitarian aid, 67, 145–47, 156, 181, 183, 190, 232n34

inclusion, social: citizenship, 133; crime, 12. *See also* exclusion
inclusion, socioeconomic, 133, 145, 157, 171, 178, 231n16
indigenous Colombians (*indígenas*), 114, 145–46, 158, 232n28
inequality, 65–66, 111, 230–31n3

informants (*sapos*), 85–86
infrastructure: activist-led squatting on properties, 137; to attract foreign investment, 205; billable public benefit, 19; Bogotá's investments in, 12; Caja, 109–10; construction and resettlement beneficiary prepayments, 168–69; DPAE investigations in zones of high risk, 76, 80–81; electrical service, 19, 116, 168, 178; financial impact of resettlement, 19; garbage service, 168; guidelines in Bogotá, 244n1; payments by residents for services not received in zones of high risk, 19, 173; roads and highways, 77; sewage, 168, 182, 185; TransMilenio bus system, 167, 195, 240n6; utilities thefts, 80–81; water service and maintenance, 19, 80, 183, 187, 188; in zones of high risk, 74, 77–78, 167; zones of high risk as sources for construction materials, 65
Ingeocim, 73–75, 228n36
insecurity: in Bogotá, 13, 15, 73, 93–100; in cities, 2, 5, 6, 194; criminal opportunism, 83, 142; epidemiological problem, 73; global, 1, 5, 194, 203; influence on security policies, 27, 67, 175, 193; poverty, inequality, crime, and violence, 6, 13, 83, 87–88, 140–41; temporal overlap of methods for confronting collective insecurity, 3; *vacuna* rackets, 83, 142; in zones of high risk, 75, 117–18, 171
internal displacement. *See desplazados*; displacement
intervention: calculations of vulnerability, 3, 73–74, 81, 101–2; divine, 46, 51, 87, 126–27, 132–33, 174–75; framings of governmental, 211, 232–33n36; governmental, in response to nonhuman vs. human threats, 68, 74, 82, 141–42, 156; governmental parameters and targets for, 93–100, 108–11, 129, 133, 145–46; poor urban populations as targets of government control, 108–11, 133, 135–36, 235n80; public health, 135; reorientation of housing policies, 22–23, 108–10, 211; security

and risk, 81, 88–90, 101–2, 124, 136–37, 145–46, 235n81; zones of high risk, 30–31, 66, 73–74, 162, 211. *See also* protection; recognition; threat
invasiones (invasions), 23–24, 82, 107, 109–10, 137–43, 179. *See also* squatting

Jiménez, Ricardo, 146, 149–50

Kaplan, Robert, 198
kinship, 31, 102, 118–21, 128–29, 137
Klee, Paul, 175
Koselleck, Reinhart, 38, 164, 222n7

Lakoff, Andrew, 111, 218n48, 221n83, 222n6, 223n9, 232n34, 235–36n82
land: access for poor, 137, 173, 177–78, 226n2; capital accumulation and gentrification, 17–18, 19; damaged and geologically unstable, 65–66, 227n20; deregulation of urban markets, 108; dispossession from poor, 17–19, 170; evacuation and reforestation in Bogotá, 20, 77, 179–80; hacienda system, 112, 122, 123, 230n30; illegal reoccupation, 137–41, 178; *invasiones*, 82–83, 107–10, 123, 137, 137–42, 177, 179; Marx and dispossession, 18–19; peasant displacement, 65, 232n25; pirate urbanization, 123, 178, 230n31; prices in Bogotá and environs, 82–83, 169; speculation, 19, 218n55; squatting, 23–24, 135, 137, 177; titles, 75, 104, 110, 113, 123–24, 127, 173; urban use and planning, 75, 182, 185, 244n1
landslides: Caja, 104, 110, 124, 127, 132, 143–45, 162; calculations of threat, 70, 74, 81, 216n28; damage caused by, 33, 77, 124, 128, 131–32, 181; disaster laws, 71; disproportionate exposure of poor, 66, 165, 170–71, 178, 190; DPAE on-site monitoring, 76–82; human contributions to, 65, 81, 82; mapping, 74, 76, 228n40; *remoción en masa*, 77, 81, 226n1; resettlement program, 16, 63, 70–71, 110, 124, 165, 210–11; risk management program, 75, 83, 88,

landslides (*continued*)

90, 95, 104, 181; zones of high risk, 6, 70, 74–75, 100, 172–73. *See also* avalanches; mudslides

Latin America: assertion of rights by urban residents, 133, 145, 158–59; cities as symbols of civilization, 5, 135–36, 215n23; civil defense agencies, 68; *denuncia*, 180–81, 238n30; development and modernization patterns, 201, 215n19, 242n38, 242n44; economic recession, 11; emergency response to disasters, 67; inequality and social hierarchy, 134–36, 157–58, 230n25, 232n27; influence of Spanish colonialism, 5–6, 114–15, 135, 236n89; informal urban settlements and land squatting, 90, 123, 178, 230n31; insecurity and urban environments, 2, 6, 216n27, 243n50; neoliberalism, 21, 134, 219n68, 220n77, 231nn11–12

Lefebvre, Henri, 17–18

liberalism: assumptions of reason and logic, 112–13, 118, 128–29; biopower, 235–36n82; coexistence of liberal and illiberal institutions, 4, 31, 102–3, 128–30, 135, 214n10, 214–15n14; freedom vs. state intervention, 3, 102–3, 116–18, 120, 133; historic coexistence with other forms of power, 3–4, 128–30, 231n19; liberal democracy, 10, 116, 129–30, 135, 136, 157, 214n9; liberal governance, 2–3, 102, 194, 214n10, 214–15n14, 220n80; liberal governmentality, 3–4, 171, 211, 220–21n80; Lockean, 112–13; modernity and, 3–4, 128–29, 202, 231n19; risk, security, and, 2–4, 10, 102–3, 128–30, 134–36, 157–58, 194

life: anticipation of threat and government responsibility, 53, 59–60; biopower and biopolitical imperatives, 113, 157–59, 222n4, 225n48, 232n33, 235–36nn79–84, 236n87; Caja, 63, 110–11, 117–18, 143–44; democratic participation, 158–59; *denuncia* process and death threats, 84, 127, 140, 142–43; dependence of hacienda *peón* on *patrón*, 122; endangerment, 27,

30, 72, 88, 93–101, 131–32, 213n11; everyday imperiled and disrupted, 17, 27, 30, 32, 84, 88, 131, 191; individual responsibility to protect, 95–100, 142–43; "life at risk," 20, 110, 114, 132–38, 141, 143–46, 156–58; lives to be protected vs. those that threaten, 46–47, 51–52, 55, 158; Locke, property, and, 112–13; Gabriel García Márquez, 1; political concern, 42, 190–91, 223n9, 235–36nn79–82; political disagreement over definition and worthiness of an individual, 26, 46–47, 51–52, 60–61, 144–45; power of state to "make live," 113, 225n48, 235n80, 235–36n82; probable statistical risk and defining zones of high risk, 74–75; protection in Bogotá, 13–14, 16, 20, 93–100, 112, 210–11; right to, 37, 49, 94–95, 112, 134, 193, and ideas of democracy and security, 11–12, 158–59, vs. other freedoms and entitlements, 11–12, 134, 150; risk and urban governance, 26, 30, 38, 90; risk management in Bogotá, 26, 29, 72–74, 82, 86, 90, 110; risk management in Colombia, 67–72, 82, 112, 195; security interpreted through right to, 12, 39, 67, 215n20; state's obligation to protect, 18, 30, 50, 52–53, 113, 146; technical concerns, 27, 222n6; threats to, 39, 67–69, 155, 177, 181, 190; urban, 5–6, 38, 82, 90, 115–17, 135–36, 237n5; value of, 60, 102, 157, 222n4; vulnerability and recognition as a life to be protected, 31, 60, 143, 145–46, 172, 180, 193. *See also* biopower and biopolitics; collective life

Locke, John, 112–13

Lomnitz, Claudio, 176–77

López, Clara, 147, 152, 155, 156, 182–83, 185, 234n75

M-19 guerrillas: attempts to establish peace with, 9, 53; Palace of Justice siege, 9–10, 37, 38, 52–56, 68, 225n55

Macpherson, C. B., 113

madrinas. See padrinos and *madrinas*

map of risk, 64, 69, 73–77, 88, 228n43

Marx, Karl, 17–19, 135, 214n12, 219n61
Mbeme, Achille, 22, 200, 241n32, 242n43
Medellín, 12, 53, 107, 181, 217n34
media: 2009 rainstorm, 127–28; Caracol television, 187, 232–33n36; demolition of El Cartucho neighborhood, 15; *desplazado* demonstrations, 147–49, 151–54, 232–33n36; flooding in Bosa and Kennedy, 184–85, 187–88, 190; Haitian earthquake, 6, 216n29; news broadcasts, 232–33n36, 238n31; Noticias Uno television, 189, 225n59, 232–33n36, 238n31; Palace of Justice tragedy, 39, 54–56, 225n59; Popayán earthquake, 43–46; radio, 43, 54; Omayra Sánchez, 46–50, 56; television, 50, 54, 225n59; tourism campaign, 7–9. *See also El Espectador*; *Semana*; *El Tiempo*
megacities: evolutionary assumptions, 21, 199–202, 242n35; global cities vs., 201–2, 240n13; harbingers of an ominous urban future, 196–99, 203–4, 243–44n59; *National Geographic* map, 240–41n15; sites of future population explosions, 196–98, 237n3. *See also* cities
Mercator projection, 240–41n15
mestizos, 135, 144, 148, 231n16
Mignolo, Walter, 4, 202, 242n44
migration. *See desplazados*; displacement
militias, 10, 15, 24
Mitchell, Timothy, 200, 206, 215n18, 221n81, 221n84, 241n30
modernity: assumption of a "better" future, 4–5, 31, 174–76, 193–94, 199–200, 214–15n14, 215n19; Walter Benjamin, 175–76; catastrophes and crises, 1; city as embodiment, 4–5, 21, 135–36, 176–80, 193–98, 205–6; coloniality and, 4–5, 236n89, 242n44; "hybrid," 128–30; liberal, 3–4, 128–29, 202; megacity and, 193–201, 206, 218n57, 241n30, 242n40; risk, 2–5, 102, 128, 180, 193–94, 214n4; Western, 4, 21, 129, 197–98, 202, 241n30, 242n44
modernization. *See* development and modernization

Moreno, Samuel, 25, 105, 147, 149, 154–55, 217n36
mudslides: Armero, 33, 38–43, 47; Ciudad Bolívar, 131–32. *See also* avalanches; landslides
multiculturalism, 5, 10, 145, 146

Negri, Antonio, 158, 235n79
neighborhoods: coexistence practices, 120; criminal and paramilitary activities, 13–14, 84–86; DPAE representatives, 81; El Cartucho, 13–16, 217n41, 218n48; emergency management, 86, 182–83; epidemics, 108; evacuations, 170; government intervention, **109**, 110; high-risk, 13–16, 63–66, 83–88, 127, 142–44, 217n41, 226n2; hygiene, 108–9; informants, 85–86; infrastructure, 74, 76, 80–81, 110, 182; intersection of risk and poverty, 74; mitigation works to protect, 77; model, 108–9; monitoring by Caja, 64, 76–82, 109–10; neighborhood improvement programs, 75, 110; Nueva Esperanza, 82–88; overlap of natural and manmade risks, 73–74, 88, 182; pirate urbanization, 65, 123, 178, 230n31; political bases for settlement, 123; risk maps, 27, 74, 76, 88, 228n43; risk of natural disasters, 64, 77, 86, 184, 188; risk of violence and crime, 73; statistical calculations for risk, 74, 76; threat of poor, 15. *See also* barrio; slums; zones of high risk
neoliberalism: critiques of, 20–21; influence on globalization of Colombian markets, 10; neoliberal governmentality, 20, 23, 25, 104, 220n76; postneoliberal era, 134, 219n68, 231n12; prudentialism, 162, 202, 205; risk and security policies, 4, 21, 102, 134, 231n11; urban displacement, 17; urban transformations, 20, 21; welfare projects, 25, 104–5, 111, 220n77; welfare state behaviors, 136, 202, 220n78
Neuwirth, Robert, 198
Nevado del Ruiz volcano (Tolima), 38, 42, 49, 68, 70

Nueva Esperanza, 82–83, 85–86, 88

Nuttall, Sarah, 22, 200, 241n32, 242n43

opportunism: *el vivo* and *los vulnerables*, 143, 148, 152, 157; impersonation of disaster victims, 183–84; *invasores* and *desplazados*, 139; racial bias, 143–46, 148, 157; resettlement and the wealthy, 170

padrinos (godfathers) and *madrinas* (god-mothers), 118–22, 124–25, 166

Palace of Justice tragedy: President Betan-cur, 39, 52, 54; censorship and secrecy, 52, 53, 55, 56; disappearance of live victims, 56, 225n59; failure of governmental foresight, 39, 41–42, 52–53, 223n19; invis-ibility of victims, 55–56; known actions of Colombian armed forces, 52, 55; known events of siege, 38, 52; massacre, 52, 53, 58, 225n49; media coverage, 42, 54–56, 225n59; military coup, 53, 54–55, 56; Daniel Samper Pizano, 39, 41–42; politi-cal context, 9–10, 53–54; Doris Salcedo, 56–59, 225n65, 226n70; significance to risk management policies, 39, 52–53; Truth Commission, 53, 55; victims, 52, 55–56; works commemorating and me-morializing, 53, 56, 59

paramilitaries (*autodefensas*): blurring distinctions with other armed groups, 10; conflicts with guerrillas, 11; criminal tactics to control neighborhoods, 84–86, 143; persecution of activists and radical sympathizers, 75; protection racketeering and *vacuna*, 83–86, 142; rightist affilia-tions, 10, 209–10; socioeconomic and po-litical powers, 10; terror campaigns and massacres of peasants, 11, 65, 175; violence in peripheral neighborhoods, 24, 83–85, 142–43, 156

paternalism: Caja's *padrino*-beneficiary rela-tionships, 118, 120–21, 129; hacienda sys-tem and *patrón-peón* relationships, 121–24; patronage, 31, 102, 121–23, 128, 230n31; Uribe presidential regime, 121, 122–23

patronage, 31, 102, 122–23, 128–29, 230–31

Peñalosa, Enrique, 12–13, 75, 105, 184, 195–96, 240n6, 240n9

Petro, Gustavo, 209–11, 245n3

Petryna, Adriana, 146, 222n6

pirate urbanization (*urbanización pirata*), 65, 123, 178, 230n31

Pizano, Daniel Samper, 38, 39–42

police: conflicts with paramilitary groups, 10; emergency evacuations, 86; final evacuations of zones of high risk, 16, 113, 170; *invasión* evictions, 23, 139–41, 179; neighborhood crime, 85; Palace of Justice tragedy, 54; quarantine cordons, 152–53; responses to public demonstrations, 149, 155

political rationalities, 60, 66–67, 108–10, 132, 158–59, 205, 214n10; biopolitics, 132, 189–90, 235n79; collective life, 235n79; liberalism, 171, 214n10; rationalities of rule, 102–3, 122, 171, 191, 202; risk and security, 3–4, 9, 38–39, 46–47, 67, **109**, 136, 142, 158, 190, 202, 206, 212; shifts in, 108–10, 136, 205; welfare and develop-ment, 25, 60, 108–10, 136

politics: activists, 24–25, 53, 56, 58–59, 75, 158, 220n77; anticipatory urban, 163–64, 170, 176–77, 180–81, 189, 191–92; center-left and moderate parties, 10, 11, 12, 25, 26, 105, 209; collective life, 42; demo-cratic, 158; democratic security policies of Uribe, 11, 26, 121, 136; increased militarization and liberalization during 1990s, 11; leftist and guerrillas, 9, 10, 14; leftist and urban periphery, 24, 25, 26, 105, 144, 209; of life, 133–34, 145, 158–59, 222n4, 232n33, 235n79, 235n81; of life vs. of rights, 133–34; moderates vs. rightist extremism, 11; Patriotic Union, 9; of recognition, 145; rightist paramilitary tactics, 10, 14; of rights, 60, 134, 158; right-wing hegemony, 10, 12, 26, 245n3; of security and risk, 26–27, 29, 30, 34, 60, 118; state-phobic positions, 220n78; of time or temporality, 163–64; urban political ecology, 220n77; vulnerability, 142, 190. *See also* biopower and biopolitics; political rationalities; power; recognition

poor: anticipatory politics, 172–77, 237n5; assistance from political activists, 23–25, 137; Bogotá mayors as advocates and protectors, 11, 12–13, 75–76, 105–6, 210–11, 238n11; Caja, 16, 103–12, 115–16, 162, 170, 202–3; Ciudad Bolívar, 16, 63–66; *desplazados*, 137–42, 177; disaster risk management program, 16, 20, 25–26, 31; disproportionate exposure to threats, 66–67, 90–91, 106–8, 131; financial incentives for relocating, 19; *invasiones* by, 23–24, 82, 101–2, 107, 109–10, 137–42, 179; land dispossession, 17–18, 19; "life at risk," 28, 106–8, 110–13, 156–59, 185, 190; Lockean perceptions of, 113; neoliberal principles of risk and security, 110–12, 191–92; neoliberal vs. progressive attitudes, 20–21, 25, 104, 108; resettlement program, 16, 102, 131, 172–75; right to housing, 113–14, 134; settlement in southern periphery, 23–24, 65, 123; sociopolitical threat, 14–15; targets of governmental intervention and control, 133, 135–36; urban piracy, 123; vulnerability and rights, 10, 31, 60, 113–14, 124, 131–34, 191–92; vulnerability to environmental problems, 185, 190, 220n77. *See also desplazados*; poverty; zones of high risk

Popayán, 43–46, 60, 68–69, 224n29

possibility: conditions of, 38, 196, 222–23n8; danger and threat, 38, 55; hope and promise, 166; logic for preemptive destruction, 15, 55; shaping and circumscribing of, 26, 38, 164, 177–78, 191–92, 196, 222–23n8; subjunctive state, 170–72, 191. *See also* anticipation

poverty: alleviation, 109–10, 111, 203, 205, 206–7; aspirations to escape from, 163, 172–77; in Colombia, 12; crime and violence, 6, 90, 107; *el ya*, 163; inequality and, 111, 230–31n3; megacities, 198–99; toxic

environments, 220n77; urban spaces and zones of high risk, 107. *See also* poor

power: accumulation and displacement, 17–18; balances of, 215–16n25; church-based political, 125–26; coexistence of different modalities, 3–4, 200, 214n11, 215n19; decentralization of government, 108; denounced and resisted, 20–21; *denuncias prospectivas*, 180–81, 188–90; empowerment of powerless individuals, 3, 26, 172; exposure, definition, and denunciation, 26; genealogies of, 102, 118, 121, 129; hierarchy-based, 120–22, 124; kinship-based, 118–20; opportunism of *vivo*, 148; powerlessness, 170, 224n32, 237n3, 240n13; of rational, liberal citizen, 128–29; risk, 9, 143–46, 170–71, 220n77; security, 129; spiritual, 61, 126, 127, 174; state and intervention, 100, 145–46; state failure to protect life, 42, 59–61; state or sovereign, 18, 51–52, 94–100, 102–3, 118, 135, 235–36n82; state responsibility to protect life, 94–95, 129, 134, 158–59, 224–25n40; of state to circumscribe, 26; of state to kill with impunity, 51–52; temporal aspect, 163–64, 214n11, 215nn18–19, 237n3; victimhood, 145–46; of violence, 29, 59, 94–95. *See also* politics

preparedness: in Bogotá, 6, 182, 185, 216n29; in Colombia, 7; emergency response systems, 67–68; government responsibility, 42, 46; natural disaster, 59, 100–101; pandemic, 222n7; urban, 204, 205

prevention: accountability for, 96, 98, 184; Directorate for Emergency Prevention and Response, 75–82; Fund for Emergency Prevention and Response, 69, 72–73, 181–82; government failures, 39, 41–42, 52–54, 59, 184–85, 187, 190; government intervention, 154, 156; government responsibility, 33–34, 42, 71–72; household accidents, 95–96; individual responsibility, 98–100, 152; National Office of Emergency Response, 69, 70, 227n17; National Plan for Disaster prevention (*continued*)

Prevention and Response, 68, 69; National System for Disaster Prevention and Response, 70; Office of Emergency Prevention and Response, 73; social and political instability, 68; violence prevention strategies, 73–74; zones of high risk, 73–74. *See also* protection

property: demolition in zones of high risk, 173–74, 178–79; DPAE inspections, 76, 78–82, 132; FOPAE inspections, 183; hacienda system, 122–24; invasions, 23–24, 82–83, 107–10, 123, 137–42, 177, 179; landowner vs. property owner, 113; legalization of ownership, 19; Locke and, 112–13; Marx and, 19, 135; one's body as, 112; pirate urbanization, 65, 123, 178, 230n31; private, 112; proof of ownership and resettlement, 104, 112, 124; resettlement program, 18–19, 131–32, 143, 173, 176; right to vs. right to life, 94–95; risk designation and map of risk, 64, 74; squatting, 135, 137, 177; taxes, 116; titles, 75, 104, 113; total loss index, 74; values and real estate market in Bogotá, 19, 65, 106; zones of high risk, 72–76, 124, 131–32

protection: of Afro-Colombian and indigenous people, 144, 146; assumption of risk, 177–78; biomedical vulnerability, 150, 152–56; Caja, 16, 26, 118–19, 202–3; citizenship, 10, 29, 114–15, 132–33, 138–43, 157; city center, 13, 218n48; climate change, 211; collective actions, 146–47, 149–56, 180–81, 188–90; compared to other rights and entitlements, 11–12, 37, 136, 185; *denuncias prospectivas*, 180–81, 188–90; divine providence, 46, 87, 132–33, 174–75; environmental hazard, 18, 88, 91, 112, 128, 131, 177; evacuated zones of high risk, 20, 77, 178–80; government and, 12, 37, 94–95, 157, 190; hacienda *patrón*, 121–24; inequality and privilege, 144, 146, 158; lives "at risk" vs. violence, 29–30, 88; mitigation, 77; private militias vs. guerrillas, 10; resettlement program, 63, 66, 86,

110–13, 202–3; right vs. left, 26; risk and state protection policies, 39, 59, 60, 66; risk management, 67–72, 112–14; Omayra Sánchez and state's obligation to protect vulnerable lives, 34, 46–47, 49, 51–52, 61; security logics, 12, 39; self-, 28, 85, 95–102, 103–5, 142–43; *sensibilización*, 103–5; social protection, 12; state constitutional obligation, 18, 22, 30, 112, 155; state failure, 49, 52–53, 55, 171, 184; state responsibility, 52–53, 67–69, 94–101, 141–42, 144–45, 156, 218n48; urban security, 204; *vacuna* rackets in zones of high risk, 83–85, 142; verification and identification, 144–46; vulnerability to nonhuman threat, 150, 156, 157; vulnerable individuals and government, 31, 88, 113, 132–34, 136–37, 171, 188–92; vulnerable populations, 12, 16, 31, 74–75, 93–95, 193; zones of high risk, 73–76, 83–88, 137, 142–43. *See also* intervention; prevention; risk management; threat

protests. *See* demonstrations and protests

prudentialism, 162, 202, 205

Rabinow, Paul, 235–36n82, 240n12

rains: in Colombia, 33, 70, 127–28, 181–82; flooding in urban periphery, 127–28, 182–83, 185, 187–88; mudslides in urban periphery, 86, 127–28, 131; Nueva Esperanza residents, 84, 87; regularity in Bogotá, 210–11

rationality: calculative, risk-oriented, 3, 5, 9–10, 38–39, 42, 117, 128–29; citizen, 23, 104, 112, 202; endowment of rights, 113, 128–29; irrationality and irrational behavior, 112–13; Lockean, 112–13; neoliberalism, 104; rational prognosis vs. religious prophecy, 38; reason, 112; subjunctive state, 170–72. *See also* political rationalities

Rechtman, Richard, 146

recognition: authentication, 146; Colombian peasants and workers during 1930s, 231n18; *denuncias prospectivas*, 180–81,

188–90, 192; exploitation and pirate urbanizers, 178; governmental, 146, 162, 171, 178, 180, 188–92; identification, 146; indigeneity, 146; internally displaced person, 144–45, 232n25; medical threat, 150, 156; resettlement program, 22, 105, 145; *sensibilización*, 103–6, 115–16, 229n1; sociopolitical, 110, 133–34, 141–44, 156; victimhood and governmental assistance, 145–46, 156; visibility and "life at risk," 60, 110, 114, 124, 131–34, 145, 158, 162; vulnerability to nonhuman threat, 136, 138, 141–43, 145, 150, 156. *See also* intervention; politics

Red Cross, 67, 69, 147

religion: divine providence, 46, 87, 126–27, 132–33, 174–75, 191; everyday experience, 6, 31, 102–3, 168; political authority, 125, 128–29; prophecy vs. rational prognosis, 38; religious symbolism and Popayán earthquake, 43–46, 60; worldly vs. otherworldly symbolisms, 61

resettlement: beneficiary status, 77, 88, 101–4, 110, 112–14, 137–38, 229n2; Caja and oversight, 22–23, 63–65, 106, 110–12, 162, 165–66, 210–11; Caja and re-education of beneficiaries, 23, 103–5, 115–16, 118–20, 162–63; Caja and site visits to zones of high risk, 63, 88–89, 119; Caja staff, 23–26, 106–8, 118–21, 124–25, 143–44, 162–63; changes in program, 19, 25–26, 105–6, 113, 210–11, 218n48; construction quality in zones of high risk, 79–80, 81, 172–74, 180; *co-responsabilidad*, 104; dispossession, 18–19; DPAE role in facilitating, 27–28, 75, 76, 106, 117–18; DPAE staff, 76, 79–81; DPAE visits to zones of high risk, 76–82; efforts by residents of zones of high risk, 22, 81, 124, 162, 172–75, 180; environmental guards, 139, 178–80; environmental threat, 26, 65–66, 77–78, 80–83, 86, 88, 110; evacuations of zones of high risk, 16, 86, 113, 170; human threats in zones of high risk, 83, 88, 228n52; *invasiones* and illegal occupations, 19, 101–2, 113,

117–18, 123, 137–41, 143; map of risk, 64, 76, 77, 81–82, 88, 124; reforestation of evacuated zones of high risk, 20, 139, 178–80; risk, security, and protection of life, 26, 64–65, 75, 81–82, 110–14, 134, 141–42; self-directed process, 16, 63–64, 104, 117, 127–28, 131, 165; shortcomings of program, 23, 106, 111–12, 184–85; skepticism and distrust among residents in zones of high risk, 19, 79, 87–89, 162, 170; social housing, 16, 19, 165–69, 174; socioeconomic problems of poor, 73–75, 82, 88, 104–12, 210–11; statistics, 11–12, 75; subsidies for, 16; transfer of property ownership, 18–19, 82–83, 127, 165–66, 173; transformative process, 23; utility companies, 19; voluntary program, 23, 103, 113, 117–18, 168–71, 243n50; zones of high risk, 65–67, 72–77, 107, 109, 117–18, 131

responsibility: autonomy and decision-making capacity, 128–29; Caja and ethics lessons for beneficiaries, 23, 119–21, 161; civic, 12, 14, 115 *condescender*, 119–21; hacienda-based *patrón* and *peón*, 122–24; neoliberal perception of, 23, 104, 111, 118; resettlement beneficiaries, 171; self and family, 94–102, 202; self-management, 120; *sensibilización*, 103–6, 115–16, 229n1; state and anticipating potential threats, 46, 49–50, 53, 59–60, 70; state and right to life, 30, 34, 37, 51, 112, 132; state and social welfare, 20, 112, 202–3, 205; state and subject, 22, 64, 104–5, 117–18; transfer from state to subject, 20, 108, 111

Reyes Echandía, Supreme Court President Alfonso, 54

Reyes, Yolanda, 184–85

rights: of Afro-Colombians and indigenous populations, 145, 232n28; to city, 112, 136–37, 141, 150, 178, 218n52; collective actions of rights-bearers, 133, 134, 150; constitution (1991), 10, 112; *desplazado* demonstrations, 150, 154–55; *desplazado* status, 141; in early modern Spain and Spanish America, 114, 122, 135–36, rights (*continued*)

231n18; education of beneficiaries, 118,
161; government and right to life, 94–95,
113–14, 133, 137–38, 143, 157, 220n77;
hacienda *patrón*, 122; to housing, 18–19,
104, 110–14, 131, 134, 230n2, 231n8; human
rights violations, 12; liberal democratic
ideas, 129, 136; Locke and endowment
of, 113–14; Personería de Bogotá mission, 138–39; to private property, 112–13;
resettlement beneficiaries and right
to housing, 19, 63–64, 86–88, 142–45,
165–66, 172–75; resettlement program,
22, 28, 31, 60, 114, 132–33, 137; right to life,
11–12, 77, 113, 117–18, 131, 133–34, 141, 150,
157–58, 205, 228n52, 235–36nn79–84; risk
and security, 60, 112, 134, 136, 157; social,
231n19; tenuous, ambiguous status of
poor urban dwellers, 133. *See also* citizenship; Constitution; entitlement

risk: economic and social liberalization, 202;
governance, 3, 717; political rationalities of danger, 3–4; total loss index, 74,
228n41; urban life, 30; voluntary embrace
of, 177–78, 179–80

risk management: Caja, 63, 76, 102, 103,
109–11, 114; Ciudad Bolívar, 63–65;
climate change, 210–11; development
and, 203–5; disaster program, 16; divine
providence, 126–28; DPAE responsibility,
28, 76, 105, 132; dynamic nature of risks,
64, 76–77, 90–91, 203; emergency response vs., 69; emphasis on security, 26;
flexible nature, 12; FOPAE, 181, 216–17n32,
243n50; Fund for Emergency Prevention
and Response, 181–85; global concerns,
72, 90, 202, 203–5; human vs. nonhuman
threats, 82; international cooperation,
6–7, 67, 72, 155–56, 202, 243n50; kinship,
culture, and tradition, 102–3, 123–24,
126–29; map of risk, 63–65, 69, 73–74,
76, 88; national security vs., 69; natural
domain of government, 37; participation
by those being protected, 90, 102, 132, 143,
172–75, 180; policies and goals in Bogotá,

27–28, 63–65, 75–76, 90, 106, 109–12,
194–95; policies and goals in Colombia, 64, 67–70, 75, 82, 110–12, 191, 194;
preparedness and warning systems in
Bogotá, 182, 194–95, 216–17n32; progressive, pro-poor, 25, 106, **109**; protection of
life and anticipation of threat, 60; *sensibilización*, 103–6, 115–16, 229n1; SNPAD,
70; social elements, 30–31, 90, *140*, 143,
158, 191, 228n41; technical expertise, 28.
See also "at risk" population; disaster risk;
protection; security; threat; vulnerability;
zones of high risk

Rivas, Ángela, 15

Robinson, Jennifer, 202, 244n66

Rojas, Cristina, 121, 135, 158, 231n16

Rosenberg, Daniel, 5, 163, 237n3, 240n9

Rose, Nikolas, 108, 146, 214n9, 232n33,
235–36nn81–82

Roy, Ananya, 21, 219n70, 240n2, 240n8,
244n60, 244n65

ruins, 176–77

Salcedo, Doris, 56–59, 225n65, 226n70

Samper Pizano, Daniel, 38, 39, 41–42

Sánchez, Omayra: Armero, 46–47; Frank
Fournier's documentation, 47, 49, 50,
224n32; global news coverage, 47–48, 49,
50, 52, 56, 224n31; inspiration for multiple
works, 48–49, 224n39; national symbol,
33–34, 47, 49, 50, 51; pilgrimages to and
offerings at grave of, 34–35, 36, 47–48,
61; religious significance of, 35–37, 61;
Eduardo Santa's novelization, 49, 50–51;
symbol of a life worth saving, 50–51; symbol of Colombia's failure in catastrophe,
49–50, 55, 56, 61

Santa, Eduardo, 49, 50–51

Santamaría, Germán, 35, 49

Santos, President Juan Manuel, 12, 13, 33–34,
181, 183–84, 186–87, 221n1

Scott, James, 176, 221n84

security: Bogotá model, 194–96, 203, 206;
civil defense agencies, 68; Colombia's
long-term concerns with risk, 6–13,

45, 68–69, 134, 217–18n43; Colombian policies, 10, 37, 60–61, 108, 129, 136–37, 231nn10–11; "comprehensive security," 217n36; definitions of, 26, 214nn9–11, 220–21n80, 223n9, 229n54, 244n61; "democratic," 11, 26, 121, 136; democratic rights vs., 10, 11–12, 60–61, 136, 158; *denuncias prospectivas*, 180–81, 188–90, 192; Foucault, 214n6, 214n9, 214n11, 218n48; global, 27, 90, 129, 134, 214n9; individual responsibility, 98–105, 163, 170, 202; paramilitary vigilantism, 10; probabilities of threat and risk, 67, 69; resettlement program, 23–26, 128–29, 171–72, 202–3, 218n48; right to life, 60, 134, 150, 157–59, 235–36n82, 237n3; right to protection, 31, 136–37, 142; risk management, 30–31, 67, 76, 128–30, 143–44, 202; *sensibilización*, 103–5; sovereign state, 218n48, 235–36n82; state intervention, 3, 66–67, 129, 146, 152–56, 232n34; state responsibility, 37–41, 60, 180–81, 188–90; threats to, 15, 45, 51–52, 68, 147, 158; tool for protection and assistance, 11–13, 16, 22, 31, 108–9, 136, 210–12; tragedies of 1985 and Colombia's policy, 34, 38–39, 56; urban, 5–6, 26–27, 30, 32, 67, 134–36, 164–65, 177, 193, 201–7, 216n27; President Uribe's management of, 13–15, 136, 218n48; *vacuna* rackets in zones of high-risk, 83, 84, 85, 142; violence, 29–30, 73–74, 134, 213n2, 215n20; vulnerability, 142, 143, 144–45, 152–58, 177–78; zones of high risk, 16, 73–76, 90–91, 128, 164. *See also* endangerment; risk management; threat

seismic activity. *See* earthquakes

self-built settlements: Bogotá's mountainous periphery, 11, 64; Caja, 29, 161, 211; *desplazado* populations, 18, 100, 136, 175; houses in, 77–78, 82, 173–74; infrastructures in, 80–81; population growth in, 11, 18, 64–65; violence and crime, 16; vulnerability to environmental hazards, 75; zones of high risk, 11, 64–65, 164, 202, 210. *See also* zones of high risk

Semana: demolition of El Cartucho, 15; *desplazado* demonstrations, 149, 155, 232–33n36; flooding in Bosa and Kennedy, 183. *See also* media

sensibilización, 103–6, 115–16, 229n1

Simmel, Georg, 17, 218n49

Simone, AbdouMaliq, 164, 170, 206, 237n5, 244n66, 244n68

slums: Caja, upgrading and eradication, 109–10; illegal occupations, 23–24, 82, 107, 109–10, 137–39, 179; "planet of slums," 179, 196–200, 220n77; profit-motivated, 18, 218–19nn55–59; right to decent housing, 105, 110, 112, 131, 230n2; security-motivated, 16; socioeconomic factors, 65–66; use of term, 107, 229n4; zones of high risk, 107. *See also* barrio; neighborhoods; zones of high risk

SNPAD (National System for Disaster Prevention and Response), 70–71

Soacha, Colombia, 16, 141, 169

social workers: education, 103–6, 163; facilitating, 16, 103, 106, 116–18, 175; management of resettlement program, 102, 162–64, 166, 191; on-site visits, 88–89, 161; relationships with resettlement beneficiaries, 118–22, 124–26, 143, 166; "risk," 106–11, 162, 191

Spain: colonial concept of city, 5, 135, 200–201; concepts of citizenship and entitlement, colonial and modern, 114–15, 119–20, 125; hacienda system, 122–23; Televisión Española, *48*, 54

squatting: by demonstrators and protesters, 151; by *desplazado* households, 177; global megacities, 135, 198, 226n6; invasions, 23–24, 82, 107, 109–10, 137–39, 179; pirate urbanization, 123. *See also invasiones*

Stoler, Ann, 176, 221n87

subjunctive state, 170–72, 191

subsidies: buying power of housing relocation, 106, 169, 210, 219n62; changes in terms for housing in Bogotá, 106; displaced persons, 146–47, 155–56; eligibility for housing relocation, 101–2, 131, 137, 139,

subsidies (*continued*)
141, 143, 177; evidence of endangerment,
162; expiration dates and pressure on
beneficiaries, 117–18, 168, 170; flood victims in Bosa and Kennedy, 183, 186–87;
property demolition requirements, 173;
resettlement beneficiaries, 16, 18–19, 26,
64, 77, 111, 210; terms and expectations,
117, 123, 142, 162, 165–66
swine flu (H1N1 or *gripa porcina*), 152–56
Swyngedouw, Erik, 212, 220n77, 245n8

taxes and tax relief, 116, 173, 183
temporality: anticipation and politics of,
236–37nn2–3; in calculations of risk
probabilities, 76, 170–71; *denuncias
prospectivas*, 189–90; endangerment and
danger vs. violence, 29–30; framings of
future, 31, 162–64, 170–71, 176–77, 191, 206,
236–37nn2–3; and geographic locations,
4–5, 193–94, 198–200, 241n28; history as
a progressive, linear movement, 2–4, 29,
164, 199–201, 214n12, 222n6, 222–23n8;
modernization, 3, 31, 193–94, 198–200;
multiple framings of events, 60, 191–92,
206, 214n12, 222n6, 222–23n8; past and
government policies of intervention, 146,
161, 164; past, preparedness, and emergency response, 146; power relations and,
163–64, 192. *See also* history
terrorism: calculations and predictions,
223n9; Colombia's actions to end within
its borders, 55, 59–60, 110, 223n9; Colombia and global "War on Terror," 11, 12,
15; narcoterrorism, 11, 67; paramilitary
groups against peasants, 11, 175; urban
security, 204
threat: authentication of vulnerability, 110,
114, 124, 132, 134, 141–43, 146; in Bogotá,
93–100, 102, 127, 158, 162–63; Bogotá's
management and preparedness, 6,
16, 74–77, 88–90, 193, 212; calculative
predictions, 68, 69, 76, 90, 100, 162;
city vs. countryside, 175, 177–78; to collective life, 27, 42, 152, 185, 190, 218n48;

convergence of, 82–88, 137, 141–42, 143;
danger, 2–3, 27, 31, 37, 71, 93–96, 98;
denuncia process and death threats, 84,
127, 140, 142–43; *denuncias prospectivas*,
180–81, 188–90; displaced persons, 137,
140, 175, 177–78, 226n6; endangerment
and, 3–4, 213n1; environmental, 6, 16,
71; failures in government foresight,
37–41, 43–53, 58–60, 182–90, 217–18n43;
future-oriented governance, 10, 37–41,
191; global increase in magnitude and
frequency, 1, 72, 196–99, 200–201,
243–44n59; history, 3–5; to life, 12, 37,
59–60; national security, 68–69; natural
or environmental, 69–70, 76, 137–38,
177–78, 212, 228n40; nonhuman vs.
human, 16, 60, 68–69, 74, 82, 156; political
debates, 26–27, 61, 191–92, 223n9, 237n5;
public awareness campaigns, 93–100,
103–4; risk and, 3; risk management,
68–71, 82, 88–90, 158; security, 15–16, 68,
147, 218n48; self-protection, 93–100, 102,
162–63; *sensibilización*, 103–6; state responsibility to protect vulnerable groups,
31, 34, 134, 136, 137; technical approaches,
27, 69, 76, 79, 90–91; transition from "life
at risk" to entitled citizen, 31, 157, 162,
170–71, 174–75, 177–78, 190–92; unseen,
95–100; urban governance and, 30, 74,
193–94, 204–6, 215n20. *See also* "at risk"
population; intervention; protection; risk
management; security; vulnerability
Tiempo, El: 2009 rainstorm, 128; Armero
eruption, 39–42; *desplazados* demonstrations, 147, 151, 232–33n36; flooding
in Bosa and Kennedy, 182, 184–85, 188;
Haitian earthquake aftereffects, 216n29;
Popayán earthquake, 43, 45, 224nn28–9;
resettlement program, 210; risk management, 216–17n32; Omayra Sánchez, 49,
224n37. *See also* media
Tognato, Carlo, 122
Tolima Department, 37, 61, 151
tourism, 7, 204–5
TransMilenio, 167, 195, 240n6

Union of South American Nations, 216–17n32

United Nations: International Decade for Natural Disaster Reduction, 72, 203, 227n31, 243n52; International Strategy for Disaster Reduction, 72; links between development and disasters, 203, 243n55; praise of Bogotá, 194, 216–17n32; praise of El Refugio, 6–7, 216n30; United Nations Development Programme assistance, 69, 72; United Nations High Commissioner for Refugees mediation of Third Millennium Park demonstration, 155–56; World Health Organization, 217n41

United States, 11, 49, 201, 222n7

urbanism: anticipatory, 163–64, 170, 176–77, 180–81, 189, 191–92; definitions of, 219–20n73, 229n54, 240n8; futuristic orientation, 165; global, 195–96, 204; mobile, 240n2; models, 194–96, 198, 202, 205–6; neoliberal, 22–25; nonlinear, coeval developments, 165, 194; probabilistic calculations of urban events, 66–67; progressive, pro-poor, 26; and ruins, 5, 31. See also cities

urbanization: creative destruction and accumulation by dispossession, 17–21; pirate, 65, 123, 178, 230n31

urban periphery: Bogotá's mayors, 13, 75–76, 106, 143, 210–11; Caja, 16, 25, 28–29, 64–65, 108–9, 123, 161; citizenship, 29, 31, 60, 133–34; desplazados, 18, 136, 139; disaster management, 16, 64; families living at risk, 16, 22, 24, 25, 64–65, 88; invasiones, 24, 137–42; life-threatening nonhuman dangers, 113, 114, 134, 157, 180, 184–86, 190; physical environment, 64–66, 82, 186; population, 64; poverty, 60, 64–66; reforestation in evacuated zones of high risk, 20, 139; resettlement from zones of high risk, 23, 106, 162, 164, 170, 210–11; self-built settlements, 11, 18, 64, 82; social housing, 169–71, 184–85, 190; socioeconomic improvement, 135, 136–37, 162, 172–75, 180, 191; survival as a

daily concern, 88, 127, 142; urban piracy, 178; violence, 24, 82–88, 127, 142–45; zones of high risk, 75–76, 111–12, 113, 137, 143–44, 193

urban planners, 1, 15, 165, 194

urban planning, 20, 72, 229n4, 243n53, 243–44n59

urban renewal, 13–14, 15, 16, 109–10, 150

urban theory, 2, 16–25, 66, 135, 193–94, 205–7, 220n77

Uribe, Álvaro, 11–12, 14–15, 121, 122–23, 136, 216–17n32

vacuna ("vaccination" or protection fee), 83–85, 142–43

Venice Biennale, 194, 206, 240n3

Verkaaik, Oskar, 148

victimhood, 31, 51, 58, 61, 144–46, 157–58, 180–81

victim syndrome, 33, 221n1

violence: assassinations, 9, 39–40, 73, 217n34; assaults, 9, 162; death threats, 127, 142–43; disappearances, 56, 59; drug-related, 7, 9–13, 53, 67, 83–85, 209; far-reaching influences of, 27, 29–30, 57–58, 136; homicides, 9, 73, 85, 95, 142–43, 217n40; kidnapping, 9, 10, 54, 95, 104; paramilitary in zones of high risk, 83–85, 90, 142–43, 156; political, 56–58; riots and revolts, 13, 67; in twentieth-century Bogotá, 13–15, 38–39, 85, 217n40; in twentieth-century Colombia, 9, 21, 29, 67, 71, 134, 136. See also crime; endangerment

visibility. See recognition

vivos and vulnerables, 143, 148, 152, 157–58

volcanoes and volcanic eruptions: Armero, 9, 33, 37–43, 49, 224n39; Colombia, 71, 216–17n32, 227n20; Galeras, 70; Nevado del Ruiz, 38, 41–42, 47, 49, 54, 59, 68, 70

vulnerability: Colombia's failure to protect vulnerable populations, 34, 49, 61; desplazados, 11, 138–39, 144, 152–53; disaster and development, 243nn54–55, 243–44nn58–59; governmental gradations, 113–14, 132–33, 141–43, 145, 147–53, 155–59,

vulnerability (*continued*)
162; governmental intervention, 93–94,
100, 104, **109**, 113–14, 152–53, 193; government obligations, 12, 28, 31, 34, 60, 70–71,
73–74; potential threat and "life at risk,"
146, 152–56, 157, 171, 189–90, 191–92; recognition of citizenship, 10, 28–29, 110, 114,
134, 136, 157–58; resettlement program,
22, 63, 66–67, 102, 110, 162, 171–72; threats,
12, 16, 90–91, 143–45, 211, 220n77, 228n41;
victimhood, 31, 51, 58, 61, 144–46, 157–58,
180–81; in zones of high risk, 6, 16, 74–75,
100, 181–82. *See also* threat

welfare: Caja, 22–23; democratic, 20–21;
discrediting and displacement, 60, 108,
111, 129, 136, 202; neoliberalism vs., 21,
104, 111, 202; post–World War II Western
cities, 20–21; risk and security vs., 111–12,
136, 202–3, 205
women: activists, 23–24, 186–88; assistance,
protection, and housing, 63–64, 131,
139–42, 165–66; in Bogotá's government,
147, 152, 155, 156, 182–83, 185, 234n75;
Caja employees, 23–24, 64, 104–5, 113–14,
118–19, 127, 162–63; *denuncias prospectivas*, 188–90; depictions as irrational
and gullible beings, 148; DPAE employees,
77–82, 138–41; heads of households, 114,
124, 131; journalists, 184–85; *los vulnerables*, 148, 152, 157–58
World Bank: disaster risk management
funding, 72, 194, 195; Global Facility

for Disaster Reduction and Recovery,
72; loans and Bogotá, 23, 202, 203,
243n50; visions of global future, 203–4,
243–44n59; on vulnerability of global
megacities, 243–44n59

zones of high risk (*zonas dealto riesgo*):
boundaries, 64, 76, 77, 81; Caja, 16, 23,
63, 75, 110–11, 132, 161–62; calculative
predictions, 64, 74, 76, 81; conversion,
20; crime and violence, 16, 64–65, 82,
88–90, 107, 111–12, 162; dismantling of
vacated housing, 172–75; DPAE, 75,
76–82, 78, 132, 164; emergency preparedness, 182, 185; environmental
guards, 178–80; government imperative to protect lives, 63, 102, 109–12,
134, 202–3, 210; Ingeocim study, 74–75;
landslides, earthquakes, and floods as
risk factors, 6, 70, 74–76, 100, 172–73;
map of risk, 63–65, 69, 73–74, 76, 88;
neighborhoods designated as, 16, 27–28,
216n28; origins, 64–66; physical environments, *78, 80, 101, 138, 174*; population, 16, 65; poverty, 65, 66, 107–8, 111;
relocation program, 63, 65, 70–71, 88,
112–13, 161; reoccupation, 100–102,
137–38, 178; residents, 18–19, 88, 111, 117,
131–34, 165–66, 170; total loss index, 74;
urban piracy, 178; vulnerability to natural disasters, 6, 11, 64–65, 216n28. *See
also* neighborhoods; poor; risk management; self-built settlements; slums